T0314972

The Essential Hirschman

The Essential Hirschman

Albert O. Hirschman

EDITED AND WITH AN INTRODUCTION BY JEREMY ADELMAN
AFTERWORD BY EMMA ROTHSCHILD
& AMARTYA SEN

PRINCETON UNIVERSITY PRESS
Princeton and Oxford

Contents

CONTENTS

Introduction

Jeremy Adelman

SIZE MATTERED TO ALBERT O. HIRSCHMAN. If big is supposed to be better—large dams, tall buildings, wide avenues, loud music, big theories, and grand schemes to solve the world's problems—Hirschman was a dissenter. One of the twentieth century's most original social scientists, he found beauty in the diminuitive, gained insight from the little. While writing a complicated book about the World Bank in 1966, he confided to his sister Ursula that he felt at odds with those who sought big theories to explain everything. "I very much like the expression that Machiavelli used in one of his letters for his own constructions," he confessed. These were "castelluzzi [little castles, as easy for reality to destroy as for a fecund imagination to construct]—that is probably what Eugenio called a piccole idee and the only thing I can really do." Piccole idees, small ideas . . . lesser thoughts that yield great insights, close-up shots that give way to a new panorama, these were touchstones of Hirschman's intellectual style.[1]

The lens to focus on the seemingly unimportant came from Hirschman's brother-in-law, Eugenio Colorni, but Hirschman made the style all his own; it also made him truly unique. The preference for lesser scales did not reflect a lack of ambition. Far from it. Hirschman had a project that transcended the norms of professionalized American social science and defied easy categorization. His was a quest to reveal how acts of intellectual imagination might unlock sweeping possibilities. By finding seams in even the most impregnable structures, one might create openings and prospective alternatives. These were tasks for the intellectual. Oftentimes this meant challenging elaborate certainties, from the doomsdayish or futile sort to the euphoric conviction that one could

---

[1] Albert O. Hirschman to Ursula Hirschmann, 23/3/66, Personal Papers of Albert O. Hirschman, in possession of Katia Salomon.

change everything at once—given "the necessary conditions." These words were staples of the social science diet; few words were more responsible for leading scholars to chasing their tails. Those with whom Hirschman sparred included preachers of Communist orthodoxies in the 1930s or liberal "Big Push" economic planners in the 1960s, to the reactionary apostles of the 1980s. Instead of wielding grand models of society or history, Hirschman preferred modesty—which cycled him back to lower-case, unconventional, approaches. Among Hirschman's targets were the establishment gurus of "balanced growth" for the Third World, the belief that economists could conjure development by simultaneously moving an entire economy's complex parts in lock step. Hirschman took the contrasting view. He opted for a more partial, unbalanced, approach, which favored strategic focus over comprehensive breadth. He summarized his view thus: "To look at unbalanced growth means . . . to look at the dynamics of the development process *in the small*. But perhaps it is high time that we do just that."[2]

Scale was not just about observational preferences or scientific method. It comes across in Hirschman's narrative style as well. Hirschman was more than an original thinker; he was also a master essayist. Nowadays, the heavy monograph or the technical, peer-reviewed article predominate in the world of scholarship. Hirschman wrote his share of those, but where his originality shone through was as the author of essays— small, sometimes miniature, literary masterpieces. This volume presents a selection of sixteen essays from a lifework of action and observation, advocacy and reflection, the work of a man who respected and used the analytical tools of the social sciences but felt resolutely unconstrained by their boundaries—and yet who managed to compress his wide-ranging insights into the tightly bound format of the essay.

Hirschman's essays constitute an art form, how he could use words so economically to say so much. It is not just the breadth of his analysis that readers see at work; it is also Hirschman's commitment to the idea that how we behave (the domain of the psychologist) is connected to the

---

[2] "The Economics of Development Planning," Institute on ICA Development Programming, 5/15/59, Strategy Papers. Archives of Albert O. Hirschman, Seeley Mudd Library, Princeton University (hereafter AOHP). This would later appear as the preface to the 1961 paperback edition.

experience of the marketplace (the economist's territory), which affects civic and political life (the habitus of the political scientist or sociologist). Moreover, the concepts we use in turn have histories. Hirschman's prose is ever full of reminders that some basic insights came from a day and age in which the human scientist was free of the modern academy's disciplines— which is why he had such an affection for reading, rereading, and citing the classics. The experience of reading Hirschman is frequently to feel poised before a whole tradition of humanistic thought. As the twentieth century unfolded, fewer and fewer intellectuals were able to summon its breadth; our social sciences became increasingly carved into walled provinces called "disciplines." Crossing them now often seems forced or heavy handed—which is one reason why Hirschman's ability to move across the frontiers of knowledge appear so effortless, almost natural. Another reason is because he was simply a gifted writer, and indeed imagined the social sciences as a branch of literature. For the nostalgic among us, Hirschman's prose is a reminder of an earlier age, one that has arguably passed. The essays in this volume bear witness to a propensity to cross from psychology to history, from economics to political sciences, and back again—all the while weaving in the works of great literature. It is rare to find a writer in our times so at ease with the modern tools of the social scientist and yet so concerned with the complexity of the human condition that he or she can bring to life the frictions and tensions that come from looking at our world at the junctions of political, economic, and emotional life.

If there were a pantheon for great essayists, Hirschman would stand as one of its finest practitioners. This is because he was a modern alchemist, able to transform the mundane into the marvelous. Few could mix the sharpness of an economist's precision with the elegance of a literary imagination. And even fewer could mix them in just the right proportions—which is precisely what the essay form demands. After all, it has to be short. And none had access to the breadth of linguistic commonplaces and traditions that gave him his range. Hirschman's affection for, and command of, languages—his native German, French, Spanish, Italian, Portuguese, and English—gave him a repertoire that made him a most uncommon of writers. In an age in which our academic disciplines require ever-greater specialization, redoubled by monolinguality, it is rare to find a scholar who can affect how we think about inequality by writing about traffic, or slip in a quote from Flaubert's correspondences to reveal something surprising about taxes.

The essay is more than just a shortened argument that, blown up, becomes a book. It is a form unto itself. Its brevity is an opportunity for an author to pull the veil back on the personal nature of a viewpoint, for the reader to know that there is a viewpoint at all, thereby providing a bridge between practical knowledge and theoretical analysis. In many of Hirschman's essays, readers are urged to follow a passage from Rousseau alongside him. Increasingly, Hirschman himself became the subject of his own essays. Some might see this as an elegant form of narcissism. But there was more to the practice of making the first-person singular a subject; the essay, to Hirschman, was a way of collapsing the distance between author and reader, inviting the reader to trace, close up, the mental working of an author at work, thereby conjoining writerly and readerly experiences.

Over a lifetime, Hirschman was to write great books. This volume brings together a selection of his great essays into the form of a book. But it is more than a sum of parts. The range alone is astonishing. We find that his subjects include how to think about industrialization in Latin America, the imagining of reform as more than repair, the relationship between imagination and leadership, some of the most astute observations about routine thinking about the marketplace, and reflections on how our arguments affect democratic life. Economics, sociology, political theory, intellectual history—these subfields of the social sciences are found here woven together as a compendium. And throughout we find humor, unforgettable metaphors, brilliant analysis, and the elegance of style that gave Hirschman such a singular voice, at once playful and curious, yet provocative and committed.

Given the breadth of the oeuvre, what can be "essential" about Hirschman? The very act of selecting for this volume threatens to impose boundaries he deliberately sought to cross. And yet, while Hirschman had a style, he was never removed from history. Indeed, he thought of his concepts and ideas as deeply embedded in the history that made them, not universal abstractions that stand outside time or above the human condition. As Hirschman joked to Clifford Geertz in 1976, too many of their colleagues fell prey to the "Law No. 1 of the Social Sciences": "Whenever a phenomenon in the social world is fully explained, it ceases to operate."[3] In the spirit

---

[3] "Conversation with Clifford Geertz and Albert Hirschman on 'The Hungry, Crowded, Competitive World.'" Box 10, f. 3, AOHP.

of locating Hirschman in the world, this volume organizes his essays into three sections. Roughly—very roughly—they reflect a sequence of his preoccupations. From the 1950s through the 1960s, he was concerned with development in what was then called the Third World, especially Latin America, and engaged in fierce debates about the nature of economic growth, the role of expertise, and the importance of imagining possible futures beyond the circular snares of poverty traps and backwardness. The selections here represent key essays that intervened in those debates, and which have enduring relevance as we think in our day about the prospects for change and fundamental reform in an increasingly unequal world. In the 1970s he turned his gaze on markets, concerned about how the rise of a "neoconservative" brand of market mentality imposed only one way to think about personal interests and collective welfare. What Hirschman argued for was a broader repertoire and more complex thinking, appreciating as he did the vital functions of the market, and therefore urging us to take them more seriously than as simple signaling devices for the allocation of scarce resources. Finally, in the 1980s, reflecting his engagements with democracy in Latin America, the possibilities of a post–Cold War Germany, and increasing concern that Anglo-Americans were locking themselves into intransigent ways of talking about policy, he wrote a series of breathtaking essays about discourse, rhetoric, and public life. Here too there is an obvious enduring quality to the insights and arguments, as the squeeze of globalization and polarizing language of its defenders and critics leave citizens feeling increasingly stuck in a quagmire, yet yearning for alternatives.

The Essential Hirschman allows a reader to think about changes and continuities in intellectual style as well as political concerns, the biography of an imagination. His imagination and his skills as an essayist have a history inscribed in the way he lived the twentieth century. Indeed, his life can be seen as a parable of the horrors and hopes of the twentieth century, and by living in it, he sought to change it even in the darkest of times; he learned to theorize from experience, to conceptualize from observation. How he developed this knack was the result of an early exposure to the father of the essay, Michel de Montaigne. And his encounter with Montaigne had everything to do with how a committed socialist grappled with the destruction of the cosmopolitan world in which he was raised.

Born in Berlin in 1915, Hirschman fled in early 1933 with the rise of Hitler and the tragic death of his father. That year marked the end of a long dream for Jews like the Hirschmanns (the name would change when Albert moved to the United States), who staked their faith in the Enlightenment and the trade-off that came with assimilation, civic and political membership. One might say that the end of adolescence closed the door on a boy's dream, incarnate in the spirit of tolerance, experimentation, and reform that we associate with the Weimar Republic. But it was not so. A love of Goethe and a dedication to fight for and understand the cosmopolitan values of his deceased republic accompanied Hirschman through his life.

The flight from Berlin was the first of many; intolerance hounded him from country to country. Someone more vulnerable to embitterment might have considered this trademark of life in the modern age a sign of decline from the exalted ideas of the Enlightenment. Hannah Arendt's name comes to mind, as do so many other Mitteleuropa exiles thrown into the world to transform its artistic and intellectual landscape, to spread, understandably, a shadow of doubt and pessimism over the modern condition.

But Hirschman was not one of them. Indeed, a hallmark of his politics—and his intellectual genius—was to see that what appears as immutable, stubborn, and impervious to change could be a source of options. With a little imagination, some lateral thinking and daring, alternatives were almost always there. "Aren't we interested in what is (barely) possible, rather than what is probable?" he asked himself privately in his diary. Instead of obsessing over certainty and prediction—which reminded him of Flaubert's injunction against *la rage de vouloir conclure* as sure to lead us to dead ends and foreclosed outcomes— should we, maybe, be more humble and more hopeful? His credo planted a flag against creeping disenchantment with reform, development, and modernization by introducing the world to a figure he called "the possibilist" in a famous essay written not long after a trip to Argentina in 1970 and included in this volume. The ethical compass for the possibilist was a notion of freedom defined, as Hirschman put it, as "the right to a non-projected future," the liberty to explore fates that were not predicted by iron laws of social science.

The elements of Hirschman's thinking were gathered from a life of living and acting in the world. Though he had a precocious intellect from the time he was a boy, it was from the combination of his *vita contemplativa* and *vita activa* that he assembled a worldview. The flight from Berlin took him to Paris, where he joined the swelling numbers of refugees—Russian Mensheviks, Italian socialists, German communists. In Paris, and later at the London School of Economics and the University of Trieste, he learned economics—although, perhaps, taught himself economics is more correct. Either way, from the start he concocted a unique blend from reading classics like Adam Smith and Karl Marx, French debates about balance of payments, and Italian concerns about industrial production. It was against the backdrop of the Depression and the concern with the causes and solutions to mass unemployment and the spread of economic autarky and imperialism that he made his first forays into the discipline. There is a sense that he was, from the start, uncompelled by orthodoxies of all sorts. While in London, Keynes published his monumental *General Theory*. Keynes's detractors, Lionel Robbins and Friedrich Hayek, were towering figures at the London School of Economics. And yet Hirschman could not get too excited about rival grand theoretical claims. His quarry lay elsewhere: how to fathom the underlying roots of Europe's economic turmoil, concerns that would lead him eventually to the instabilities and disequilibrium of the development process more generally.

More than the plight of an exile or the economics of the Great Depression shaped him. So too did the political crisis that metastasized across Europe. Paris had replaced Berlin as the pivot of Hirschman's life; he moved in and out of the city from England, Spain, and Italy. It was there that a second political and intellectual education began, one that removed him from her German idealist roots. The French capital was a hub of intrigue for a continental diaspora, Russians, Italians, Germans, Spaniards, eventually Austrians and Czechs. Hirschman soon found himself moving away from the German Left, with which he had affiliated, to drift into an Italian circle much less concerned with getting the ideological diagnosis "correct" than with changing history through action. Especially under the spell of Eugenio Colorni, whose philosophical and political heterodoxy was a model, Hirschman became much more eclectic in his reading. A family connection was involved. Colorni had courted and married Hirschman's sister, Ursula, and became the single most important intellectual influence on Hirschman's cognitive style. The relationship, leavened by shared reading and long conversation, deepened when Hirschman moved to Trieste, where Colorni and Ursula had moved a year earlier, after a brief and bitter experience fighting on the Republican side during the Spanish Civil War.

Colorni came from an Italian variant of the same European cosmo-politanism. An assimilated Jew, he was a member of a movement that tried to combine the freedom-loving spirit of liberalism with the justice-seeking impulse of socialism, not unlike Hirschman himself. This eclectic democratic tradition is perhaps best represented by the late Norberto Bobbio, with whom one might pair Hirschman as archetypes of a different, more open scholarly style; neither lost sight of the normative and political features of intellectual activity; both were essayists. It was Colorni who impressed Montaigne and the beauty of the essay genre upon Hirschman. It was Colorni who pointed out that the freedom of the essay was a kind of analogue to a more open way of thinking about politics. They would spend many hours together, in Paris and Trieste, and especially in the Colorni family retreat at Forte di Marmi on the Tuscan coastline, crossing the borders of the human sciences together.

As of Trieste, Hirschman and Montaigne would not be parted; not so Hirschman and Colorni, who was gunned down by fascist thugs in the streets of Rome.

One important feature of Montaigne informed Hirschman's spirit: that one's insights were equally drawn from the well of a lived experience. Unlike Montaigne, Hirschman had a lived experience made of border crossings, of exits that were closely tied to his political loyalties; he became what we might now call a cosmopolitan—though Hirschman would probably wince at the label. Living in Europe, especially as an active socialist, implied in some basic way committing to the struggle against fascism. No sooner did Generalissimo Franco rebel against the Republican government in Madrid than Italians in Paris began to organize the first volunteers—and Hirschman was among them. Within weeks of the outbreak of the Spanish Civil War in July 1936, he was in Barcelona. There he stayed, fought, and was wounded on the Aragonese front; when the Communist Party sought to assert control over militia-men, anarchists, and motley progressives, Hirschman, appalled by the same intransigence he'd seen in the waning days of the Weimar Republic, left for Italy to participate in a new front of the continent-wide struggle. Mussolini's 1938 anti-Semitic decrees cut short the sojourn in Italy, though not before Hirschman got his PhD from the University of Trieste. Once again, a flight to Paris.

War sent so many people ricocheting around the world. What was unique about Hirschman's mobility was that it was tied to being a professional volunteer in other peoples' armies, not as a mercenary but as a loyalist to a cause. For one of the great theorists of human responses to organizational decline, inscribed in his pioneering work *Exit, Voice and Loyalty* (1970; dedicated to Colorni), the shifting engagements and departures had a long personal history. When it came to tyranny, there was no question where his loyalties lay. After 1939 he joined two more armies—the French and then the American—to fight fascism. In both cases, he did so as a foreigner. And yet the life of a soldier meant submitting to the numbing rules and bureaucracy of mass organization. More to his liking was the collaboration with the American journalist, Varian Fry, in an operation in Marseilles that rescued hundreds of refugees from Europe, including Marc Chagall, Max Ernst, André Breton, and Hannah Arendt. Here was a stealthy form of struggle that appealed much more to Hirschman's temperament—that is, until Vichy police chased him across the Pyrenees.

It is easy to forget that there was a time in which the life of the mind was not so severed from engagement in the world. For much of Hirschman's life, the making of an intellectual did not always imply the making of an academic. Indeed, by the time he got his first real position as an economist, Hirschman was not working for a university at all, but for the Federal Reserve Board in Washington on the Marshall Plan and European reconstruction. Moreover, he was no longer a single man. After fleeing Europe, he made his way to Berkeley, California. There, he met his wife, Sarah Chapiro, the daughter of Russian émigrés who raised her in Paris before, sensing the dawn of war, they migrated to the United States. Albert and Sarah would have two daughters and make the US capital their home. That is, until the reactionary paranoia of the McCarthyite purging of the American civil service drove him once more to cross borders in search of safer settings—and if possible, adventure. In 1952 he moved to Colombia with his wife and two daughters.

Thus began Hirschman's Latin Americanization and with it his reinvention. Some basic traits of his style were by then becoming clear. He was no orthodox thinker. He defied categorization. And when times were bleak, it was all the more important to think differently about the source of the problem and potential remedies. But it was the encounter with the challenges of capitalist development and democracy in Latin America that brought his imagination into relief. In Colombia he worked not in an ivory tower but as a consultant, helping to tackle everyday problems of investment in irrigation schemes and housing projects. From his years working and observing in the field came the publications that would remake his career—and catapult him, at middle age, into the citadels of American higher education, to Yale, Columbia, Harvard, and finally to the Institute for Advanced Study in Princeton.

Encounters in Latin America fueled a quarter century of groundbreaking work, from *Strategy of Economic Development* (1958) and *Journeys Toward Progress* (1963), to his overlooked but brilliant essay *Getting Ahead Collectively* (1983). Charting Hirschman's work is like tracing the enchantments and disenchantments of how we think about development as voiced by the planners, World Bankers, engineers, and grassroots activists, practitioners of the art of making progress. It was up to the economist, he felt, to "sing the epic" of the labors of those who worked in the fields of development. Not surprisingly, among the aphorisms he enjoyed most was Camus's likening of the struggle for social change as "a long confrontation between man and a situation." This was always a more appealing approach than the mindless overconfidence in the solvability of all problems or its twin, the fatalism that nothing can be changed willfully at all.

There is a motif worth noting in Hirschman's narrative style: the delicate equilibrium between impassioned observation and critical involvement. Here was knowledge aimed at changing understandings of the world. The readerly experience of a Hirschman book or essay was intended to be one that destabilized the common sensical and the orthodox. Whether he was dealing with the gurus of balanced growth in the 1960s or the Milton Friedmanite zealots of the 1980s, Hirschman's purpose was to challenge closed certainties—pointing out, as he does in an essay included in this volume, that searching for the right paradigm can often get in the way of basic understanding. This was an affliction not just of writers on the Right but equally a feature of those on the Left. It is often forgotten that in his famous book exposing the wordplay of what we now call "neo-liberal" apostles in *Rhetoric of Reaction* (1991), one chapter was devoted to progressive forms of intransigence. The essay that gave rise to that influential book, published in the *Atlantic Monthly*, is also included here.

What made Hirschman so original was that he emerged from the margins of the university and so was never truly of the university. This freed him to cross boundaries with great abandon. But faculty meetings and the rituals of academic life bored him to tears.

And yet it was for intellectuals that he above all wrote, and it was in his essays that one hears this voice most clearly. One might say that intellectuals were both the subjects and audience of his work. In discovering that a major factor in development was the way in which intellectuals imagined the possibilities for progress, Hirschman insisted that how we understand the world affects how we might change it; intellectuals have a critical role in the business of creating fields of meaning. In the 1960s he urged Latin American thinkers to get over their trenchant pessimism. He did the same for American social thought in the 1980s. In between, he would write a luminescent essay about the history of thinking about capitalism, *The Passions and the Interests: Political Arguments for Capitalism before Its Triumph* (1977) precisely to show that the experience of the marketplace was affected by the words and quarrels invented and conducted by writers, with enormous consequences for policies. This was followed by a remarkable series of essays on rival views of the market (the best of which are also included here) that insisted that there were alternative ways of thinking about economics and politics, ways that were more humane, more creative—and ultimately more liberating than the schema produced by the calloused defenders and critics of capitalism.

As he put it in the last line of *The Passions and the Interests*, it may be in the history of ideas that we can find clues to raise the level of the debate. Few left more clues behind him for precisely this purpose than Hirschman. It would be hard to imagine a better time to elevate the debate than now. The essays in this volume, indeed this whole volume, are dedicated to this purpose.

The Essential Hirschman

POLITICAL ECONOMICS
AND POSSIBILISM

The United Nations dubbed the 1960s the "development decade." As those ten years drew to a close, however, there was more skepticism, more doubt, and more pessimism about the prospects for social change in the Third World. In that context, Albert O. Hirschman gathered together a collection of his essays on development and, to defy the tenor of the times, called it *A Bias for Hope: Essays on Development in Latin America*. In fact, the essays were much more than about either Latin America or about development. His introduction in particular, "Political Economics and Possibilism," was not just aimed at doomsayers, but also to those who presumed that economic and political forces were separable. Instead, he pointed to the importance of the interplay between the two: not just economic theories of politics, nor simply political dimensions of economic phenomena, but interactions between two fields that opened up spaces for alternatives. He urged more flexibility and realism and less reliance on general laws to explain social phenomena. Freedom and creativity—in short, "a passion for the possible"—were his watchwords.

—*Jeremy Adelman*

IN REFLECTING ON THE ESSAYS brought together in this volume I noted two principal common characteristics. In the first place, I frequently encounter and stress the political dimensions of economic phenomena just as I like to think in terms of development sequences in which economic and political forces interact. This focus seems to come almost naturally to me in connection with any problem I happen to be attacking and the first part of this introductory essay is an attempt at identifying the central concepts that underlie this "decentralized" activity of building bridges between economics and politics.

Another pervasive characteristic of the writings here assembled is a preoccupation with processes of social change. Understanding social change is obviously not something that can "come naturally" to anyone; one can only grope for it. Consequently the second part of this essay inquires into the nature of my own gropings.[1] It is necessarily more speculative—and, mercifully, much shorter—than the first part.

Economics and Politics

If demand generated its own supply in the social sciences as it is supposed to do in the marketplace, there would exist by now a number of intellectually satisfying and empirically tested models of the social system based on the intimate interactions and interdependence of economic and political factors. In fact, of course, nothing of the sort is anywhere in sight. Economists continue to identify scientific progress with the elimination of "exogenous" forces from their constructs, while political scientists are similarly most at ease when they have explained political events by appealing to purely political categories.[2] Where the linkage between political and economic forces is too obvious to be disregarded, both categories of scholars have held to the most primitive linkage models in which typically a phenomenon belonging to the "foreign" discipline is introduced as some sort of prerequisite—and can then promptly be forgotten as purely "domestic" or endogenous forces take over. Insofar as economists are concerned, this practice goes back to Adam Smith's dictum that "little else is requisite to carry a state to the highest degree of opulence from the lowest barbarism, but peace, easy taxes, and a tolerable administration of justice." Political scientists, from Montesquieu and Rousseau to Hayek and Holt-Turner, have similarly looked for some unique and permanent economic characteristic—a certain level and distribution of welfare, or a certain organization of economic life—which makes the emergence of some type of political organization possible, probable, or even inevitable. Once again, no allowance is made in such theories for any continuing interplay between economic and political factors.

2

How is it possible to overcome the parochial pride of economists and political scientists in the autonomy of their respective disciplines and to go beyond the primitivism of the briefly noted efforts at linking them? Rather than issue another clarion call for an integrated social science, I find it more useful to survey the building blocks that have already been assembled, however inadequate they may be for the construction of an imposing or systematic structure. As just noted, I have frequently turned up some mini-building-blocks of the sort, and a classification and evaluation of these finds may be helpful in bringing a more systematic search underway. The following survey will therefore be largely intro- and retrospective, but I shall make an effort both to note contributions of other writers and to introduce some new points.

Economic Theories of Politics

A first distinction that is not always clearly made is that between economic theories of politics and theories of political economics (or, better perhaps, theories of economics-cum-politics). The former term has come into use to designate the increasingly numerous and important contributions to political science that have been made, mostly by economists, through the application to political phenomena of modes of reasoning and analytical tools originally developed within economics. The logic of allocation of scarce resources among competing ends, of input-output relationships, and of decision making under uncertainty, to name just a few, should obviously be able to elucidate a great many areas of social and political life other than the strictly economic ones for which that logic was originally devised. Some of the better known efforts of this kind are the *Economic Theory of Democracy* by Anthony Downs and *The Logic of Collective Action* by Mancur Olson.[3] An example in the present book is the note on the "stability of neutralism" (chap. 9) where I use the apparatus in indifference and transformation curves to explain the behavior of an underdeveloped country that can choose between two aid givers and wishes both to receive aid and to maintain its independence.

Two general points can be made about these writings. First, while they may throw much new light on politics, they do not normally deal, nor do they set out to deal, with the interaction between politics and economics.[4] Secondly, there are serious pitfalls in any transfer of analytical tools and modes of reasoning developed within one discipline to another. As the economist, swollen with pride over the comparative rigor of his discipline, sets out to bring the light to his heathen colleagues in the other social sciences, he is likely to overlook some crucial distinguishing feature of the newly invaded terrain which makes his concepts and apparatus rather less applicable and illuminating than he is wont to think. As I argue for imported ideologies, the distance between reality and intellectual schema is here likely to be both wider and more difficult to detect than was the case as long as the scheme stayed "at home."[5]

For example, Downs's assumption that parties are uniquely motivated to maximize votes is several notches more unrealistic than the one that entrepreneurs are profit maximizers; the resulting theory is therefore likely to be contradicted by the facts with special vehemence, as I have recently shown.[6]

In the case of my own study on neutralism, I became aware that the ease with which the apparatus of indifference and transformation curves could be transferred from the realm of economics to those of international relations and aid giving was deceptive: in the process, the independence of the indifference map from the production-possibility schedule, so important for the determinateness and normative significance of equilibrium, was largely lost.

The theory of public goods supplies a third example of the care that must be taken when economic concepts are transferred to the realm of politics. It is particularly striking and instructive, and I shall deal with it at somewhat greater length. One of the principal points made by the theory is that the true demand for public goods cannot be ascertained in the market or even by survey methods[7]: since the availability of public goods to an individual consumer is by definition not depleted through consumption on the part of others, each consumer is likely to understate his true preference for the public good as he hopes that others will be willing to pay for all of the supply he wishes to secure; in this manner he would get a "free ride." The free rider problem has thus become a principal focus of the theory and its existence provides the basic justification for the provision of public goods by the government (and for financing through taxes).

This is all very acute and pertinent with respect to the supply of a wide variety of public services under modern conditions. Yet, if taken in the widest possible context, public goods include not only police protection, parks, and similar amenities, but public policies that are felt as right and perhaps even gratifying by large groups of citizens. Such policies could even be considered as specially pure public goods since they can be enjoyed by all citizens at the same time, whereas the capacity of parks, police protection, and the like is necessarily limited so that at some point of mass use, their consumption becomes "rival," as is always the case for private goods. Now the "production" of these public policies often requires an effort of advocacy, lobbying, and agitation on the part of the citizens, and here the free rider problem raises its head again: in normal times, with many other needs and interests claiming his time and energy, the average citizen will tend to "let George do it" even though he may be mildly or even strongly interested in the outcome. But the times, like the weather, are seldom wholly normal; on quite a few occasions, lately, they have been abnormal and "a-changin'," and astoundingly large numbers of citizens, far from attempting to get a free ride, have been taking to the streets, to the nation's capital, or to other places where they expect to exert some influence for change. In this connection, it is interesting to note that while economists keep on worrying about the free rider problem, political scientists have become increasingly concerned about the "participation explosion." The latter phenomenon is clearly the obverse of the former: in many cases the individual citizen will insist on being present in a march or demonstration, on participating in a letter-writing campaign, and perhaps even on contributing to an election campaign, although his marginal contribution to the "production" of the public policy he desires to bring about may be close to zero (if not negative at times). To justify his participation in this case, he will perhaps exaggerate to himself the likely importance of his contribution; vis-à-vis others, he may well overstate his "true" preference for the public good in question and will certainly not understate it as he is supposed to according to the theory.

Why would he act in so strange a way? Because he senses his participation not as a cost, but as a benefit, because participation in a movement to bring about a desirable public policy is (and, unfortunately, may be for a long time) the next best thing to actually having that policy. The sudden, historically so decisive outbursts of popular energies must be explained by precisely this change in sign, by the turning of what is normally sensed as a cost that is to be shirked into a benefit, a rewarding experience, and a "happiness of pursuit" in which one simply must share. The possibility of this mutation is fundamental for the understanding of political change and leadership; for achieving change often requires such a mutation and a leader is he who knows how to effect it. Yet the concept of costs turning into benefits is difficult to grasp for the economist trying to reason about "the logic of collective action" by applying tools essentially grounded in the analysis of the market economy.[8] To find someone who knew all about these matters one must go back to Rousseau, who wrote, in *The Social Contract* (bk. 3, chap. 15): "In a truly free country, the citizens . . . far from paying to be exempted from their duties, would pay for the privilege of being allowed to fulfill these duties themselves."[9]

One might suggest, then, that economists setting out to elucidate political problems by wielding nothing but their own tools are likely to stumble. Fortunately, their very stumbles can turn out to be illuminating.

Political Dimensions of Economic Phenomena

In proceeding now from economic theories of politics to political economy (or political economics, or politics-cum-economics) proper, I shall stay away, for the time being, from any semblance of a general theory; rather I shall bring together numerous partial observations with the intent of learning something about the nature and structure of the interrelationship between economics and politics.

The observations I wish to relate here can be characterized as political dimensions (or side effects) of economic phenomena. That such dimensions and side effects exist is of course no great discovery. The trouble is that the search for them has been undertaken primarily by sociologists or political scientists who have naturally focused on the most obvious, large-scale features of the economic landscape, such as economic wealth, growth, industrialization, inflation, mass unemployment, and so on. The effects of such economic macrofeatures or -events on politics are either evident and hence uninteresting, or are so complex and depend on so many other variables as to be unpredictable and inconclusive. It is for example not a very fascinating discovery that private wealth can often be translated into political power and vice versa; or that a government's public support will ordinarily be eroded by accelerated inflation or mass unemployment. On the other hand, the effect of economic growth and industrialization on, say, political stability in an underdeveloped country is quite unfathomable in the absence of detailed information about economic, social, and political conditions.

Speculation about connections between economics and politics becomes much more profitable when one focuses not on the roughest outline, but on the finer features of the economic landscape. This can of course best be done by the economist who knows about them; the trouble is that his professional interests do not ordinarily lie in this direction. At the same time, the political scientist who has the motivation to look for such connections lacks the familiarity with economic concepts and relationships that is required. Hence the field is happily left to a few mavericks like myself.

My first discovery of the "finer" kind I am talking about was made almost thirty years ago when I was examining the ways in which a country can acquire political influence through its foreign trade. It occurred to me that there is a straightforward connection between the old established economic concept of the gain from trade which country B achieves by trading with A and the influence which A can exert in B as long as the trade is foreign and is therefore subject to interruption or termination at A's will. The entire theory of the gain from trade and of its distribution became therefore relevant for an understanding of the influence and power relationships that arise out of trade.[10]

A very similar exploration of the political implications of an old established economic concept is undertaken in my most recent book. There it is shown that the famous "consumer surplus" measures not only the consumer's gain from being able to buy a product at competitive market prices, rather than at prices set by a discriminating monopolist, but also the consumer's readiness to react strongly through either "exit" or "voice" should the quality of the product deteriorate. To the extent that voice is chosen, the size of the consumer surplus can be directly related to political action which consumers are liable to engage in to resist and fight deterioration.

Or let us turn to the economic theory of customs unions. For over twenty years now, the analysis of the static economic effects of such unions has been based on the distinction, first suggested by Jacob Viner, between trade creation and trade diversion. It was shown that the trade-creating effects of a customs union had to outweigh the trade-diverting ones for the union to make a positive contribution to the efficient use of world resources. The distinction between trade creation and trade diversion is certainly not one of the more difficult ones in economics. Nevertheless, I have yet to see a political analysis of customs unions which

7

would take advantage of the considerable value of that distinction for an appraisal of the political forces favoring or opposing a union. As a first approximation, it could be said that the political chances of the formation of a union are the exact obverse of its economic effects: the larger the trade-creating effects, that is, the greater the need to reallocate resources in the wake of tariff abolition, the greater will be the resistance to the union among the producer interests of the potential participating countries. On the other hand, trade-diverting effects imply that producers of the member countries will be able to snatch business from their competitors in nonmember countries: the trade-diverting effects will therefore be highly popular with them and will provide a needed cement of interest group advocacy for the union. In the appraisal of the political appeal and feasibility of customs unions, trade creation and trade diversion thus turn out to be extremely useful categories; but the signs which they must be given there are opposite to the ones they carry in the economist's analysis of the welfare effects of customs unions.

Other dichotomies which have long been used by economists can be similarly made to yield considerable food for political thought and analysis. Attempts in this direction are made in chapter 11 with the distinction between portfolio and direct investment and in chapter 10 with that between project and program aid.[11] In the latter respect, it is pointed out that a form of aid giving such as program aid which seemed far more rational to the economist than project aid carried severe political side effects and liabilities. These are now widely recognized, but escaped detection, not only at the time when program aid was first proposed, but for a considerable period thereafter.[12]

Hidden political implications thus exist for some theoretical economic concepts, such as gain from trade and consumer surplus, and for categories originally devised for analyzing, from the economic point of view, such institutions as customs unions, international investment, or foreign aid. Further examples can be drawn from economic history. Here again it normally takes an economist or an economic historian to do the job of uncovering the political implications.[13] For the latter arise out of the characteristic detail of economic events. This is the case, for example, for the pattern of industrialization among twentieth-century latecomers: the early stages of their industrialization are largely concerned with the production of finished consumer goods on the basis of imported machinery and intermediate goods; also, during a prolonged period, this production takes place entirely for the domestic market, to substitute previously imported commodities, with no thought of exporting. In chapter 3 it is shown that such observations on the specific differential nature of industrialization can explain much about the frequently noted lack of political assertiveness and power of the industrial bourgeoisie in the developing countries, particularly in Latin America.

When one focuses on primary production and its history in these countries, purely technical economic characteristics also turn out to be politically relevant. The wide fluctuations of coffee prices are a good example. These fluctuations have long been explained by the large number of producers, by the five-year interval between planting and full bearing of the coffee tree which means that even a strong response of producers to price changes has little immediate effect on supply, and by the tendency of the tree to yield a bumper crop at irregular intervals. But these very economic and botanical characteristics also account for the tendency of coffee growers to join together as a powerful interest group which will exert pressures on the state to undertake price support schemes in times of distress. In response to these pressures, the state can then be led to assume responsibilities with respect to the formulation and direction of national economic policy at a relatively early stage.

The low price elasticity of short-run supply characteristic of coffee has interesting further consequences for public policy making. Once the coffee-growing country becomes ripe for industrialization, that characteristic makes it possible for the state to finance the needed infrastructure and to subsidize the nascent industries by a policy of squeezing the coffee sector by direct or indirect taxation. Such a policy would be far less successful if the to-be-squeezed primary product had a higher price elasticity of short-run supply, as is for example the case for cattle or wheat. In that case the policy might soon "kill the goose that lays the golden eggs," a phrase that has often been used to describe the ill-fated attempts of Perón to push industrialization in postwar Argentina at the expense of the agricultural sector. With respect to coffee, however, there appears the possibility of a truly dialectical sequence: first, the special production and market characteristics of coffee make for the formation of a strong pressure group of coffee growers which pushes the state into assuming responsibilities for interference with market forces. As a result, the state becomes aware of its capabilities and duties as the maker of national economic policy for development. At a later stage of growth, such a policy will require that income be redistributed away from the coffee growers and toward other sectors which need to be nurtured. And this redistribution can then be carried out with success because of the very characteristics of coffee that originally made for the vigorous and successful pressures of the coffee planters on the state.

It was necessary to show at some length the way in which political forces and relationships grow right out of specific economic situations and characteristics. For through the variety of instances surveyed, I hope to have established a double proposition. On the one hand, it appears that the number of connections between economics and politics is limited only by the ability of social scientists to detect them. On the other hand, it seems quite unlikely that there exists somewhere a master key which would bring into view the usually hidden political dimensions of economic relationships or characteristics in some more or less automatic or systematic manner. Each time, it seems to be a matter of a specific ad hoc discovery; at the same time, he who makes such a discovery increases his chances of making yet another one. For what is required is a certain turn of mind, the desire to speculate and to search in a certain direction, rather than the application of any infallible and objective technique. At most, our examples point to some practical hints or heuristic devices which might help the researcher to "catch" these elusive connections. One such device is the notion of "blessing in disguise" (or mixed blessing, i.e. curse in disguise) with which I have long been taken.[14] Frequently (but by no means unfailingly) it appears that the political dimensions takes the sign opposite to the one that attaches to the economic concept or characteristic. For example, the "gain from trade" measures also the opportunity for domination. In the same vein, the sluggish response of coffee supply to price changes and, in general, a deficient "ability to transform" which would normally be considered unfortunate characteristics by economists, turn out to be advantageous for the development of the coffee-producing country's political (and industrial) capabilities. This sort of compensatory relationship is now familiar to everyone because of the manifold noxious side effects of technical progress that have come into view. But situations in which the political side effects of economic events do not at all exhibit this contrapuntal character certainly cannot be ruled out—what has been said about late industrialization is a case in point. Here we have rather an example of a cumulative sequence à la Myrdal where an intrinsically none-too-favorable economic event—delayed industrialization—has further adverse political consequences. The notion of cumulative disequilibrium can indeed serve as another heuristic device. But there are good reasons to think that the connections between economics and politics which result from the use of this device are comparatively easy to find; therefore they are apt to be less interesting and have probably been overemphasized in what there exists of political economics today.[15]

In view of the large number of political implications of economic concepts which the politically inclined economist can uncover, I have little doubt that a similarly long list could be manufactured by the political scientist who would focus, to start with, on some political characteristic or event and would then draw attention to its economic side effects. Unfortunately, the inclination to explore such lines of causation seems to be just as weak among political scientists as it is unusual for economists to be interested in the reverse nexus. As an amateur political scientist, I shall give just one example of the potential fruitfulness of political economy speculations that would have their starting point in politics rather than in economics. One important political characteristic of some Third World societies, particularly in Africa and Asia, is the number and seriousness of cleavages along linguistic, religious, and racial-tribal lines. In comparison to Nigeria or Pakistan, countries like Colombia or even Brazil (not to speak of modern England or France) look remarkably unitary and homogeneous. Besides its many consequences for politics, the existence of such cleavages has profound implications for the appropriate strategy of economic development. For example, in countries affected by such cleavages the tolerance for income inequalities arising in the wake of development is likely to be much smaller than it is in more unitary countries. Hence, in the former, a capitalist strategy will be particularly hazardous, and may well either be abortive or lead the country straight into civil war. This is a vast topic which can only be touched upon here; it serves, however, to point up the important contribution that political scientists could make to the body of knowledge we are looking for.

Interaction between Economics and Politics

The line of inquiry outlined in the preceding section has intrinsic value since it permits political factors to permeate economic analysis and vice versa; it can also furnish important elements for a systematic economics-cum-politics. Without the prior accumulation of a large number of such elements, any call for a more integrated social science is bound to be futile. We even came close to describing a particular form of mutual interaction between economic and political forces in discussing the political consequences of high fluctuations in coffee prices. I probably derive special pleasure from the almost chance encounters with politics of the last section in much the same way in which I prefer the sudden, unexpected view of the main piazza one comes upon in a medieval city to the elaborate panoramic layout of later periods more given to "rational, comprehensive planning." Nevertheless, I shall now make a brief attempt to examine head-on the possible outline of general models in which economic and political forces would both be treated as endogenous variables.

Long acquired habits of thought interpose enormous obstacles to such an enterprise. The idea of a self-regulating economic system (erected on the basis of some political prerequisite such as law and order, but otherwise perfectly self-sustained) has retained a considerable grip on the economist's imagination; it has in fact been bolstered in recent years by the confection of similarly self-regulating equilibrium growth models. In such constructs, political factors and forces are wholly absent; if they play any role at all it is that of spoilers. Examples of the latter situation come easily to mind. The imposition of a price ceiling in the wake of political pressures feeding on temporary shortages and price rises makes the shortages more serious and protracted than they would be otherwise. Nationalist agitation leads to the imposition of a tariff, and a loss of welfare is the regrettable result. Lately it has been argued that the loss may not be regrettable, that the willingness to bear the loss may be explained and perhaps justified by a "taste" for economic nationalism; but since it is understood that such a taste is exceedingly odd and unenlightened this condescending "empathy" hardly changes the substance of the more old-fashioned—and more forthright—argument. The view of political factors as spoilers is bolstered by the many tales of how "controls beget more controls," how a simple political interference with economic forces will eventually make the whole system bog down in a maze of official regulations, corruption, and "perverse incentives." Clearly the construction of a model of interaction of economic and political forces will not come easily to those who have been brought up to believe that the admission of politically motivated actors into the economic arena amounts to a pact with the devil.

But economists are not alone in casting political forces in the role of spoilers. The inconclusive discussion on the relation between economic growth and political stability is instructive in this regard. The conjecture that economic growth would lead to the lowering of political tensions and to greater cohesiveness has been increasingly disputed by those who hold that growth tends to have destabilizing political effects. On the basis of the latter view it is then of some (but hardly overwhelming) interest to construct an economics-cum-politics replica of the economic demographer's "low-level-equilibrium trap": first there is economic growth, then this growth leads to adverse political developments which in turn cause economic decline so that economy and society revert to the low level from which they started out.

Such models in which economic growth either dispels or generates political storm clouds are really quite primitive. It is odd that they should have been taken so seriously and tested so doggedly when all the while a much superior construct was available: the Marxian concept of the historical process which rests on a far more realistic, if more complex, interaction between economic and political factors. If one replaces—and this does not do undue violence to Marx's thought—his "productive forces" and "relations of production" by economic and political factors, respectively, the representation of this process is somewhat as follows: at any one historical stage, the economy functions within a given political and institutional framework; on the basis of and owing to this framework, economic forces left to themselves can achieve some forward movement, but beyond a certain point further development becomes more difficult and eventually is held back by the unchanging political framework which from a spur to progress turns into a "fetter"; at that point, political-institutional change is not only necessary to permit further advances, but is also highly likely to occur, because economic development will have generated some powerful social group with a vital stake in the needed changes.

For the economist, this vision has actually a pleasantly familiar look. It reminds him of one of the basic paradigms of his own science, namely the law of diminishing returns. It is strange that the close resemblance of this law to the Marxian concept of historical change should have been overlooked. Generations of economists have been taught that the output of any productive process will increase at a decreasing rate if the quantity of one cooperating factor of production is kept constant while that of the others is increased. Marx essentially affirmed the same relationship: the fixed factor of production causing decreasing returns was for him any given political and institutional order. In Marx's thought, this order is not subject to small incremental changes and improvements. Hence, the need for revolutionary change.

I was not aware how close I was to this generalized Marxian model of interaction between economic and political forces when I wrote in *The Strategy of Economic Development* that "nonmarket (i.e. political) forces are not necessarily less automatic than market forces"[16] and showed repeatedly how such forces are likely to arise when market mechanisms by themselves would cause shortages of social overhead capital, or would lead to regional imbalances or to other types of disequilibria which required—and were likely to entrain—the intervention of political action. Why did I fail to make the connection between one of my principal theses and Marxism? Largely, I think, because I rediscovered the possible alternation of economic and political forces in propelling societies forward in the context of processes that take place on a small scale as compared to the huge canvas on which Marx painted. But much of the fruitfulness of the Marxian scheme may well lie in applying it to slices of reality rather smaller than was intended by the master.

In any event, this is what I have been doing. An example is a description of import-substituting industrialization: in combination with import controls, the existence of an overvalued exchange rate is shown to be at first a considerable help in getting the process underway in a certain political environment, but it eventually turns into a hindrance to further industrial development because it holds back both the expansion of capital goods manufacture and the achievement of a substantial volume of industrial exports. I also identify interest groups and political forces that are likely to advocate ever more powerfully the needed institutional changes.

A number of points can be made about such transpositions of the Marxian scheme to smaller-scale processes of economic-political development. In the first place, the political and institutional changes that are needed in any one of these sequences are less likely to be revolutionary than in those that interested Marx. Clearly, passing from a highly overvalued exchange rate to a slightly undervalued one is less likely to require a revolution than the transition from the capitalist to the socialist mode of production. Nevertheless, even such comparatively minor changes in institutional structure require discontinuous decisions which are often difficult and replete with political struggles and risks.

Another way in which the Marxian scheme can be usefully varied is by examining more closely the nature of political change that is supposed to resolve "contradictions" which have arisen in the preceding phase. Marx thought here in terms of revolutions that sweep away all of the institutions of whatever ancien régime needs to be done away with, and that then set up sociopolitical conditions ideal for the vigorous and unhampered unfolding of the "productive forces" during a prolonged period until such time as a new batch of contradictions emerges. Most of the time, historical reality is, of course, far less neat: sociopolitical change entrained by the contradictions is often partial, grudging, and with a lot of unfinished business left behind, so that the need for further change makes itself felt once again in fairly short order. The frequently fragmentary character of political-institutional change thus explains why the Marxian scheme is found to be so surprisingly useful on a far smaller historical scale than that for which it was conceived. This reasoning also suggests that the amplitude, length, and frequency of the interaction cycles will vary considerably over time and from country to country. One element in this variation could be the freedom different countries have to undertake large-scale political change. Untrammeled in this respect, the hegemonic powers will often go in for all-inclusive, apocalyptic, and cathartic crises that will be widely spaced in time, thereby conforming rather closely to the Marxian vision. Dependent countries, on the other hand, are kept from having their revolutions or their civil wars by some hegemonic power standing watch over them, always ready to dispatch armies or economic advisers commissioned to forestall a real crisis;[17] they must therefore introduce political change in a more stealthy and imperfect fashion[18] and are likely to exhibit more numerous interaction cycles that will revolve rapidly, so that the "next" required measure of public policy is never very far away. This is one reason why many observers of the reality of the dependent countries have found it so utterly indispensable to think systematically about the interaction of economics and politics.

A real advantage of visualizing growth processes in the manner previously outlined lies in the greater flexibility and realism with which it becomes possible to appraise economic policies and developments. No longer will one condemn any policy that is not immediately directed toward establishing the ideal tax or exchange rate system, or the most advanced agrarian reform legislation. Rather, the observer and policy maker will think in terms of sequences in the course of which a forward step in one direction will induce others, perhaps after a period of "decreasing returns" and political-action-inducing disequilibria. It is not just a matter of "[moving] the economy wherever it can be moved";[19] on the contrary, while there will be less need for trenchant statements about uniquely correct policies and absolute priorities, the policy maker will often have to engage in difficult speculations about what I called "efficient sequences" in the *Strategy of Economic Development*: from among the various directions in which it is possible to move, he will have to form a judgment about the one that is most likely to achieve eventually certain objectives which are not within the direct reach of policy making. It is perhaps of interest to note here that the "pure economist" who refuses ever to think in terms of certain second-best policies which, via consequential political changes, could lead indirectly to the achievement of a desired objective, has a counterpart in the revolutionary who asks for the needed political changes right away, as an absolute prerequisite to any forward movement: neither seems ever to think in terms of economics-cum-politics (or politics-post-economics) sequences.

The most difficult and critical problem in thinking about such sequences is an appraisal of the likelihood that the needed political changes will actually take place once the phase of decreasing returns to economic forces acting alone has set in or, in Marxian terms, once the productive forces have entered into sharp contradiction with the relations of production. Reflecting on the role of the bourgeoisie in the French Revolution, Marx thought he had solved the problem, insofar as the societies he analyzed were concerned, by identifying the industrial proletariat as the force that would have both the will and the power to make the socialist revolution. While in this respect his vision has turned out to be faulty, the kind of search he engaged in remains an essential part of the enterprise I am advocating here for smaller-scale sequences. There was never an intention on my part to assert that any sort of imbalance would be automatically corrected. Nor is it a question of the right size of the imbalance. The Toynbeean notion of a proper response arising directly from the challenge (provided only it is of the right size) is entirely foreign to my thinking.[20] Whenever I noted the phenomenon of economic forces alone leading to an imbalance or otherwise tension-laden or unsatisfactory state of affairs which needs to be corrected by political action, I have tried to locate specific "agents of change" which, much like Marx's industrial proletariat, would have the motivation and power to bring about that action.

Here is one example of this type of concrete search: after describing the economic forces which could make for increasing interregional disequilibrium in the course of a country's economic development, I pointed out that political counterforces might arise from the fact that "the poorer sections of the country, where careers in industry and trade are not promising, often produce, for that very reason, a majority of the country's successful politicians and thereby acquire influential spokesmen in the councils of government."[21] Similarly, in the treatment of import-substituting industrialization (chap. 3) I engage in a determined search for forces that might counteract the tendency of industrialization to bog down after the "easiest" import substitution opportunities in the last stages of production have become exhausted.

It is nevertheless tempting to inquire whether there are any general reasons to expect political actions to be forthcoming in the situations that have been described. A very general model could be derived from the observation that many actors in a society can choose, at any one point of time, to engage either in economic or in political action. It has often been noted that an industrialist, for example, has the option of spending most of his time and energy either on improving the efficiency of his production and sales organization or on lobbying in the nation's capital for special tariff protection or other legislation favoring his firm and industry. Disregarding the adverse value judgment that attaches in this example to political action, we may bring this sort of option into contact with the tendency of economic growth to run into decreasing returns when it proceeds within an unchanging institutional framework. Surely, the decreasing returns will somehow impress themselves on the consciousness of the individual economic-political actors. Once they notice that the marginal productivity of economic action is diminishing in comparison to the prospective marginal productivity of political action, there will be a tendency on their part to substitute political for economic action. Hence, it is likely that an effort to carry out the needed political changes will actually be undertaken.

This very general reasoning by no means dispenses the social scientist from engaging in a detailed search for specific "agents" or "carriers" of change. But it is useful in permitting him to get away from one feature of the Marxian system which is still very much on the—conscious or unconscious—mind of numerous contemporary writers: the obsessive search for the vanguard or spearhead of the revolution, for the one or at least the principal class or homogeneous group that can be counted on to overthrow the existing order or to effect needed changes. The model just sketched makes it quite plausible that the "decreasing returns" phenomenon will impress itself on the consciousness of a wide variety of groups and individuals; if political change comes, then, it may well result from the combined efforts of many parties rather than from the exertions of a single group. I believe that thinking about the likelihood and strategy of currently needed social and political change, in the United States and elsewhere, would considerably gain in realism if it could free itself of the notion that such change is impossible without the discovery of a single, homogeneous vanguard group.[22]

Misperception and Interaction

In the preceding treatment the emergence of "contradictions" or of "decreasing returns" has retained rather an aprioristic character. The notion has been made plausible to the economist by equating any given political framework with the existence of a factor of production in fixed supply, but I will admit that the analogy need not be wholly compelling.

Is it possible to provide a more solid foundation for the assertion that "economic forces acting alone" need to be relayed at periodic intervals by political-institutional changes? Perhaps there is really no need for an elaborate justification of this point, for it is overwhelmingly unlikely that any institutions devised by human minds will be able to accommodate indefinitely and efficiently any new economic and technological change that happens to come along. The specific reasons for which existing sociopolitical institutions are inadequate in dealing with newly arising economic forces are likely to be vastly different from one case to another, but the emergence of some such inadequacy would appear to be a remarkably safe bet. I shall nevertheless attempt to go a little farther and conclude this part of the introductory essay by pointing to one particular (and perhaps particularly interesting) class of economic-political sequences.

In market economies, the intervention of government through taxes, subsidies, and direct provision of goods and services has ordinarily been justified for cases of "market failure," the most typical of which is the presence of monopoly or of external economies and diseconomies. Government action in the economic field is thus conceived as a corrective and complement of private action. The picture that emerges from this way of looking at things is that, little by little, all the areas in which the market tends to fail will be ferreted out, and the best possible mix of market and nonmarket decision making will be approached and permanently established.

This "asymptotic" conception of the state's role is unsatisfactory because it leaves unexplained the continuous seesaw action between market and nonmarket forces which has in fact been taking place in all market economies. One way of accounting for the seesaw may be found in the notion that economic decision makers are frequently subject to misperceptions of newly emerging opportunities. Along such lines I have argued that opportunities in underdeveloped regions tend to be seriously underrated by private investors at some stage of their country's development; similarly, at some other stage, the need for continued reliance on capital from abroad will be overrated. In both cases, perception lags behind reality: the economy of the underdeveloped region and the capacity to raise industrial capital domestically have grown, but institutional inertia and past habit make it hard to take advantage of these changes or even to notice them. Decisive acts of public policy—such as the establishment of exceptional incentives for the underdeveloped region or a restrictive policy toward foreign investment—may then be necessary to acquaint economic operators with an emerging reality which they stubbornly ignore. In the case of the underdeveloped region, such acts are essentially designed to "change ingrained attitudes, both of self-deprecation within the region and of prejudices against it, its people, and resources in the rest of the country."[23]

When public policy measures are motivated by this need to change perceptions, the possibility of an optimal, once-and-for-all corrective intervention disappears. Instead, there arises the perspective of a *sequence* of interactions between market and nonmarket forces. For policy measures correctly designed to change expectations and perceptions will no longer be optimal once they have accomplished the mission assigned to them. In the short run, policy measures will thus have to overshoot any long-run goal. To give an example: the incentives essentially needed if misperceiving entrepreneurs are to set up their first industrial ventures in an underdeveloped region are bound to be much stronger than those that need or should prevail once a broadly based industrial establishment has come into being and entrepreneurs have been thoroughly cured of their previous misperceptions. In contrast to market failures grounded in objectively existing externalities, the presence of misperceptions therefore creates the need for a series of properly spaced corrective moves, each one requiring of course its own constellation of political pressures, alliances, and other favorable circumstances.[24]

Moreover, the series is not necessarily convergent, for it is quite conceivable, and indeed likely, that new misperceptions arise at each successive stage. As a result, I am tempted to argue that the relentless search for permanently optimal policies and institutions which characterizes much of social science is often misdirected. In many situations, it may be possible to define optimality only with respect to the width and frequency of periodically needed reversals of policies and changes in institutions.

Let me again give an example from the area of international development policy. A discussion has long been raging about whether close contact by means of trade and capital flows with the advanced industrial countries is beneficial or harmful to the less developed countries. Some authors have been able to cite important static and dynamic, direct and indirect benefits that accrue to these countries from close contact. Others have shown that close contact had a number of exploitative, retarding, stunting, and corrupting effects on the underdeveloped countries and that spurts of development in the periphery have often been associated with periods of interruption of contact, such as world wars and depressions. To neither of these two warring parties has it apparently occurred that they may quite conceivably both be right. In order to maximize growth the developing countries could need an appropriate alternation of contact and insulation, of openness to the trade and capital of the developed countries, to be followed by a period of nationalism and withdrawnness. In the period of openness, crucial learning processes take place, but many are of the latent kind and remain unnoticed and misperceived. They come to fruition only once contact is interrupted or severely restricted: the previous misperceptions are then forcibly swept away. Thus both contact and insulation have essential roles to play, one after the other.

This conclusion upsets deeply rooted modes of thought. Everywhere, not only in relation to the international economic policy of the developing countries, social scientists are looking for optimal policies and states, and that generally means that they are looking for optimal combinations of desirable, but mutually antagonistic ingredients of such states. Thus we look for the correct combination not only of contact and insulation, but of central control and decentralized initiative, of moral and material incentives, of technical progress and social justice, and so on.

It is here suggested that we devote at least a portion of our time and efforts to understanding the possible usefulness of alternation and oscillation, as opposed to optimal combination.[25] In the first place, it is possible, as in the case of contact and insulation, that certain patterns of alternation would yield results superior to the best that could be obtained by stable combination. Secondly, the focus on alternation would permit one to acquire a feeling for the right amplitudes of the many swings that do occur anyway in the real world. Finally, attention to these patterns of alternation would yield a special bonus from the point of view of this essay: it would reveal a good many sequences in which economics and politics relay each other repeatedly as principal actors.

A Passion for the Possible

The intensive practice of economics-cum-politics is no doubt a principal characteristic of the essays here collected. At the same time, however, these essays are pervaded by certain common feelings, beliefs, hopes, and convictions, and by the desire to persuade and to proselytize which such emotions usually inspire. I would not be true to the purpose of this introduction as proclaimed in the preface, if I did not make at least a brief attempt to talk also about these matters.

Most social scientists conceive it as their exclusive task to discover and stress regularities, stable relationships, and uniform sequences. This is obviously an essential search, one in which no thinking person can refrain from participating. But in the social sciences there is a special room for the opposite type of endeavor: to underline the multiplicity and creative disorder of the human adventure, to bring out the uniqueness of a certain occurrence, and to perceive an entirely new way of turning a historical corner.

The coexistence as equals of the two types of activities just outlined is characteristic of the social sciences. In the natural sciences the unexplained phenomenon and alertness to it are also of the greatest importance, but only as a means to an end, as the beginning of a new search for an improved general theory which would subsume the odd fact, thus overcoming its recalcitrance and destroying it in its uniqueness.[26] In the social sciences, on the other hand, it is not at all clear which is means and which is end: true, most social scientists behave in this respect as if they were natural scientists; but they would be more surprised than the latter and, above all, considerably distraught if their search for general laws were crowned with total success. Quite possibly, then, all the successive theories and models in the social sciences, and the immense efforts that go into them, are motivated by the noble, if unconscious, desire to demonstrate the irreducibility of the social world to general laws! In no other way would it have been possible to affirm so conclusively the social world as the realm of freedom and creativity. But by now there surely is something to be said for pursuing this theme in a less roundabout fashion.

The importance of granting equal rights of citizenship in social science to the search for general laws and to the search for uniqueness appears particularly in the analysis of social change. One way of dealing with this phenomenon is to look for "laws of change" on the basis of our understanding of past historical sequences. But the possibility of encountering genuine novelty can never be ruled out—this is indeed one of the principal lessons of the past itself. And there is a special justification for the direct search for novelty, creativity, and uniqueness: without these attributes change, at least large-scale social change, may not be possible at all. For, in the first place, the powerful social forces opposed to change will be quite proficient at blocking off those paths of change that have already been trod.[27] Secondly, revolutionaries or radical reformers are unlikely to generate the extraordinary social energy they need to achieve change unless they are exhilaratingly conscious of writing an entirely new page of human history.

I have of course not been disinterested in claiming equal rights for an approach to the social world that would stress the unique rather than the general, the unexpected rather than the expected, and the possible rather than the probable. For the fundamental bent of my writings has been to widen the limits of what is or is perceived to be possible, be it at the cost of lowering our ability, real or imaginary, to discern the probable.

The nature of these persistent widening attempts—or of what I shall call my "possibilism"[28]—varies with the public I am addressing. In putting together the essays of this volume, I found that I have been playing to two quite different galleries. The essays of part II criticize policies of the rich and powerful countries toward the developing countries and advocate substantial changes in those policies. In making my proposals, I refuse, on the one hand, to be "realistic" and to limit myself to strictly incremental changes. At the same time, however, these proposals are not presented as being so revolutionary or so utopian that they have no chance whatever to be adopted in the absence of prior total political change. On the contrary, I feel an obligation to make them in concrete institutional detail thereby deliberately creating the optical illusion that they could possibly be adopted tomorrow by men of good will.

This "naive" disregard of sociopolitical realities and of vested interests is precisely rooted in my possibilism: I propose fundamental changes in institutions such as international aid and investment, but I am not willing to prejudge categorically the extent, much less the modality, of the wider social and political transformations that may or may not be a prerequisite for such proposals ever being adopted. The reason for this agnosticism is in this case the observation that the constraints on policy makers are far less binding in a number of conceivable historical constellations than at "normal" times. Moreover, one important condition for such constellations to yield real change is the prior availability and discussion (followed then, of course, by contemptuous dismissal) of "radical reform" ideas that can be readily picked up when times suddenly cease to be normal.

The essays of part III deal in large measure with ideologies and concepts characteristic of the literature on economic and political development and of the intellectual climate in the developing countries. Here I have found an exceptionally good hunting ground for exaggerated notions of absolute obstacles, imaginary dilemmas, and one-way sequences. The essence of the possibilist approach consists in figuring out avenues of escape from such straitjacketing constructs in any individual case that comes up. But to go about this task efficiently it is helpful to be equipped with a few conceptual tools. In the following I shall therefore describe in general terms how I have come to practice "possibilism," how I have found it possible to increase the number of ways in which the occurrence of change can be visualized.

One handy device is, once again, the notion of blessing (or curse) in disguise. By pointing to the ways in which many presumed "obstacles" to development have in some situations turned into an asset and a spur, one obviously casts doubt on any statements about this or that "obstacle" having to be eliminated if there is to be this or that desirable development.

But the notion of "blessing in disguise" is like a label for a certain class of sense data; it has little explanatory value. An intellectually more satisfying, though more specialized, foundation for possibilism was encountered in the theory of cognitive dissonance. A group of social psychologists has shown through this theory that changes in beliefs, attitudes, and eventually in personality can be entrained by certain actions instead of being a prerequisite to them. This idea is so congenial to my thinking that I pointed to one such "inverted" sequence even before I had become acquainted with Festinger et al.: in many situations, so I argued, the Protestant ethic is not the cause of entrepreneurial behavior, but rather arises as its consequence.[29]

Similar critiques of widely accepted ideas on the one-way nature of certain sequences can now be found elsewhere in the social sciences. Take the seemingly self-evident notion that a consensus on basic values and political procedures is a precondition for the establishment of a viable democratic system. According to a recent paper which appeals to historical evidence as well as to cognitive dissonance theory, the causation has often run the other way—democracy has come into being as a result of an accidental, but prolonged standoff between forces originally quite bent on crushing each other; and what basic consensus about political decision making is later found to prevail in these cases can be shown to have been the consequence of democracy, rather than its cause.[30]

The idea that beliefs, attitudes, and values can be refashioned and molded by more or less accidentally undertaken practice is put forward here only for the purpose of justifying the existence of alternatives to certain "orderly" sequences. There is no intention, at least on my part, to claim primacy for the inverted sequence over the orderly one. In fact, I recognize that the former can give rise to special problems and tensions in comparison to the latter. Moreover, I have lately come to criticize certain aspects of cognitive dissonance theory that in turn imply an excessive denial of human choice and freedom.[31] For the theory predicts that once a certain action is engaged in, beliefs will be changed to suit that action, whereupon renewed resort to the same type of action becomes more likely, leading to a further strengthening of the changed beliefs, and so forth, in a cumulative sequence. To show how it is possible to break out of such sequences is an important task of the possibilist, as will shortly be shown.

A third general foundation for possibilism is in the notion of unintended consequences of human action and in its relation to change. An episode from the recent history of Peru will serve to introduce this topic with which I shall deal at somewhat greater length.

The immediate cause of the military takeover of 1968 in that country was a public uproar over a proposed settlement of the long dispute over United States–owned petroleum interests. The expropriation of these interests by the strongly nationalistic military was a natural consequence of their seizure of power and served to justify it in the eyes of the nation. But then, in 1969, the military government struck out once again, this time at the powerful domestic "oligarchy," by expropriating the large coastal sugar plantations and in general by decreeing a far-reaching land reform. Yet, not long before, an Argentine sociologist had proved definitively, in a widely reprinted article, that the days of the progressive military coup in Latin America were gone forever! The military, he showed, had turned from being occasional, if unreliable, innovators into staunch and cruel defenders of the socioeconomic status quo.[32]

What went wrong with this prediction in Peru's case? In the discussion of the deeper-lying causes for the actions of the Peruvian colonels and generals, two explanations recur most frequently. First, in the fifties, it was decided that the technical instruction of upper echelon officers should be supplemented by training in citizenship; as a result, a center for high military studies (CAEM —Centro de Altos Estudios Militares) was established where Peruvian anthropologists and sociologists held teaching positions and exposed the officers to modern ideas and theories of social integration and development. Secondly, these officers had conducted an antiguerrilla campaign in the early and middle sixties, during which they had efficiently destroyed the guerrilla movement; that experience, it is generally reported, was so searing for them, that they became determined to change the basic conditions which imposed such tasks upon them.

Those who supply or routinely repeat the latter explanation do so generally without realizing what a sensational and paradoxical theory they are propounding. Because this miserable century has presented psychologists with unprecedented opportunities for studying human cruelty, torture and assorted atrocities, the psychological mechanism of progressive brutalization is now well known: a person may commit his first brutality more or less by accident or on command, but then, having committed it, has to justify it to himself and in this progressive fashion he becomes ever more committed to his inhumanity—the widespread existence of this sort of cumulative movement is, alas, well established.

In the Peruvian case, on the other hand, the experience of one's own brutality appears to have produced not greater brutalization, but the determination to change the state of the world which caused the brutality in the first place—an almost miraculous conversion appears to have taken place for once among the perpetrators of cruelty. The reason may lie in the previously noted combination of circumstances: officers who had been taught in the CAEM that it was their mission to forge a united Peru which could be a true fatherland for all of its sons, including the most miserable Indian, were suddenly placed in the position of napalming the villages of those very Indians and of killing them, as well as young poets and intellectuals from the cities who had taken seriously those very teachings. As a result, the tension between ideology and actual behavior as imposed by the environment was exceptionally wide and painful. On the other hand, the military had bred into them a high degree of confidence that the environment is subject to change at their hands. Jointly, then, that painful tension and that confidence may account for their reforming zeal, for their refusal to submit to the cumulative spiral of brutalization.

The story has several points. For example, it contains a nice instance of a blessing in disguise, a part that is played here by the thinness of the country's intellectual elite. This ordinarily much lamented characteristic of Peruvian (or Latin American) society meant that army officers, once they were to be taught sociology and political science, came (unintentionally, of course) under the influence of the very few social scientists and intellectuals whom Peru could muster and who were all strongly oriented toward fundamental changes in the status quo.

A more noteworthy lesson of the Peruvian story is that social scientists may have become overimpressed with the cumulative character of the processes they study. We are by now thoroughly conditioned to explain and anticipate cumulative spirals by Myrdal's process of circular causation, by Merton's self-fulfilling prophecy, and by some just noted aspects of cognitive dissonance theory, not to speak of more routine reinforcement and feedback processes. As a result, any change in the direction of a process—the turnaround or dialectical reversal or *Umschlagen*—takes us by surprise, except, perhaps, for the outbreak of revolution in its classic form.

It is ironic that Myrdal proposed his notion of circular causation in order to get away from the self-equilibrating models in economics and sociology and from their conservative, laissez faire implications. For, in a sense, he threw out the revolutionary baby with the conservative bathwater. According to his analysis, the cumulative processes of discrimination, deterioration, and underdevelopment, disastrous as they are, do not awaken by themselves any counterforces—the only exception is the intellectual who observes things from the outside and somberly predicts that they will get much worse unless some appropriate action is taken. The many insurgent and radical social scientists who have embraced this sort of model have thus fallen unwittingly into a profoundly undialectical and, what is worse, unperceptive and unimaginative way of thinking.

One important way of rekindling perception and imagination and of developing an alertness to dialectical, as opposed to purely cumulative, social processes is to pay attention to the unintended consequences of human actions. This is extraordinarily well illustrated by the Peruvian story. Here both the training in citizenship the military received (though not in the actual form it took at CAEM) and the suppression of the guerrillas in the Sierra were activities purposefully designed to ensure the maintenance of the status quo; but in combination they had unintended side effects which led to irreversible social change.

The concept of unintended consequences of human actions has of course a distinguished ancestry. Intimated by Vico and propounded as a paradox by Mandeville, it was developed systematically by Adam Smith and his contemporaries. But the concept was always cast in one particular mold: a set of rather unprepossessing activities, such as the pursuit by everyone of his own material gain, was shown to have edifying consequences because through their unintended side effects these activities would guarantee the overall functioning, stability, and rationality of the existing social system.

Perhaps it is because many of the later critics of this way of thinking were social reformers that its rich potential for understanding and expecting social change, rather than equilibrium, rationality and optimality, has not been actively exploited. The idea that change, particularly major social change, is something to be wrought by the undeviatingly purposeful actions of some change agents is certainly far more widespread than the view that change can also occur because of originally unintended side effects of human actions which might even have been expressly directed toward system maintenance.

The possibilist will not contend that the predominant view of change is wrong; but he will challenge its predominance by collecting evidence supporting the alternative point of view. The Peruvian story was one case in point, but since it is a personal interpretation of still unfolding events, I shall invoke some more authoritative examples.

In the first place, I can refer to two anthropologists who attempted, a few years ago, to give a comprehensive account of the "human revolution" and proposed as their principal theoretical construct the following principle which they called "Romer's rule," "after the paleontologist A. S. Romer who has applied it so effectively . . . in his own work":

> The initial survival value of a favorable innovation is conservative, in that it renders possible the maintenance of a traditional way of life in the face of changed circumstances.

The authors continue:

> Later on, of course, the innovation may allow the exploration of some ecological niche not available to the species before the change; but this is a consequence, not a cause.
>
> One of Romer's examples concerns the evolution of Devonian lungfishes into the earliest amphibians. The invasion of the land was feasible only with strong fins (which in due time became legs). But strong fins were not developed "in order to" invade the land. The climate of the epoch was tempestuous; the water level of the pools in which the lungfishes lived was subject to sudden recessions. There was thus selection for those strains of lungfishes which, when stranded by such a recession, had strong enough fins to get back to the water. Only much later did some of their descendants come to stay ashore most of the time.[33]

In other words, the lungfishes' attempt at system maintenance (the desire to get back to the water and thus to remain amphibians) leads here to system change. A similar view of change and innovation is put forward by an economist in a book on agrarian development under population pressure.[34] Initially, so the author shows, population growth in primitive agricultural communities leads merely to reduction of fallowing and consequently to lower output per man hour. But, at the same time, the intensification of agriculture may cause work habits to become more regular and more efficient, and larger numbers may lead to new forms of the division of labor. These secondary effects can then "set off a genuine process of economic growth."[35]

It should not be inferred from these two examples that change via unintended side effects is in any way restricted to "lower forms of life" such as animals or "primitive people." Efforts to maintain or restore a social organization or a way of life or a standard of living that is threatened or weakened have yielded unintended innovational change in modern societies just as among the lungfish. At the threshold of the modern age, the discovery of America originated in an effort at "system maintenance," in the search, that is, to keep up or restore maritime contact with India. Many technical inventions which then led to further important transformations of technology occurred as a result of sudden interruptions of normal trade flows due to war or blockade and the consequent need to maintain prior output levels through the production of substitutes. Industrialization in many countries, particularly among the twentieth-century latecomers, was similarly brought underway not so much by the will to industrialize as by the need to keep up the supply of consumer goods whose importation became suddenly impossible during the world wars and the Great Depression.

In short, history could be viewed as the process of men in general, and the ruling classes in particular, continually outsmarting themselves in their efforts to reproduce and maintain the existing order.

Change that occurs in such manner as a result of unintended side effects can be compared from several points of view to the kind of voluntaristic change that is brought about consciously by some change agent, be he a revolutionary or an agricultural extension officer. In the first place, the unintended change is often likely to be more revolutionary than change brought about by the most revolutionary of change agents, for the simple reason that the imagination of the change agent is severely limited by his immediate experience and historical precedent. More important, unintended change is of course far more difficult to detect and to block by the forces opposed to change; for that matter, these forces often participate unwittingly yet actively in bringing it about. On the other hand, unintended change may be less satisfying to those profiting from it than voluntaristic change, since it "falls into one's lap" without either advance planning or sustained struggle.

Actually these two types of change are little more than analytically useful distinctions; most of the time they will be found to be closely intertwined in the real world. For example, voluntaristic change will often take over after unintended change has done the spadework and created conditions in which the outline of previously hidden possibilities of change can begin to be perceived by an activist change agent. In other situations, such voluntarist activists may be futilely trying to make "the last revolution," as Regis Debray put it, but since they draw all the fire and monopolize the attention of the pro-status-quo forces, they make it even easier for the unintentional processes of change to come to fruition. Elements of both these combined situations are present in the Peruvian story.

Such, then, are some of the devices which the possibilist can use to sharpen the perception of available avenues toward change. There are probably quite a few others. For these devices cannot be expected to trace out by themselves new, hitherto undiscerned avenues; they are only meant to help defend the right to a nonprojected future as one of the truly inalienable rights of every person and nation; and to set the stage for conceptions of change to which the inventiveness of history and a "passion for the possible" are admitted as vital actors.

Notes

The author is grateful to the Rockefeller Foundation which, in the summer of 1970, offered the magnificent hospitality of the Villa Serbelloni at Bellagio for the writing of this introductory essay. Its first part was presented as the Harvard Lecture at Yale University in November 1970.

[Editor's note: In the notes that follow, all references to chapters or page numbers without mention of another source are directed toward the original volume in which this essay appeared.]

1. A related attempt is in the second half of chap. 16, below.

2. Note, for example, the success of Samuel Huntington's explanation of political development in terms of "institutionalization" in his *Political Order in Changing Societies* (New Haven: Yale University Press, 1968).

3. See also the collection of articles in Bruce M. Russett, ed., *Economic Theories of International Politics* (Chicago: Markham, 1968).

4. This body of writings should therefore not be grandly designated as the "new political economy" as is done in the otherwise very useful survey article by Bruno S. Frey, "Die Ökonomische Theorie der Potitik oder die neue Politische Ökonomie: Eine Übersicht," *Zeitschrift fur die gesamten-Staatswissenschaften* 126 (January 1970): 1–23.

5. See below, chap. 15, pp. 335–37.

6. See Albert O. Hirschman, *Exit, Voice, and Loyalty* (Cambridge, Mass.: Harvard University Press, 1970), chap. 6.

7. See Robert Dorfman, "General Equilibrium with Public Goods" in J. Margolis and H. Guitton, eds., *Public Economics* (New York: St. Martin's Press, 1969), pp. 270–72, and James M. Buchanan, *The Demand and Supply of Public Goods* (Chicago: Rand McNally, 1968).

8. See Mancur Olson, Jr., *The Logic of Collective Action* (Cambridge, Mass.: Harvard University Press, 1965). In this book, individual participation in collective action to obtain a public good is made to depend on the balancing of the private benefits to be expected from the good against the private costs of participation. At one point in the argument, Olson grants a role to "social pressures" and "social incentives" in the cost-benefit calculus: participation could occur because without it the individual would lose prestige, or the esteem and friendship of his peers (pp. 60–63). In other words, participation is always costly, but on occasion this cost is more than offset by the cost of nonparticipation. This view has much in common with the logic that shows how man always acts out of selfish motives.

In *Exit, Voice, and Loyalty,* I allowed myself to be imprisoned by the traditional notion that the use of voice is always costly. My case for the potential superiority of voice over exit would have been considerably strengthened had I realized that in certain situations the use of voice becomes acutely pleasurable and should therefore no longer be computed as a cost, but as a benefit.

9. One can also profitably go back to Pascal who was perhaps the first to note the distinction between private and public goods, in the following terms: "[Those] who have come closest to the truth have considered that the universal good which all men desire does not consist in any of the particular things which can only be possessed by a single individual . . . they have understood that the true good must be such that all can possess it at the same time, without diminution or envy" (*Pensées,* 425). As Pascal intimates here, God is the purest public good imaginable: my possession of Him does not detract in the slightest from that of anyone else. At no point can the possession of God ever become "rival" or "exclusive." Note that for this quintessential public good the free rider

problem is totally solved. The possibility of obtaining a free ride through the religious exertions of others is excluded by the personal relationship between the god-seeking individual and God. At the same time, striving for God is not sensed as a cost by the religious person particularly since there is no clear dividing line between striving and possessing, so that a free ride would not be desirable even if it were possible.

Yet, various carefully circumscribed free rides are perhaps present in the Christian religion through the concept of grace, the possibility of praying for others, and the sacrifice of Jesus. Indeed, Paul's Epistle to the Romans (5: 12–21) contrasts the free ride to salvation available to Christians through Jesus' death with the free ride to sinfulness forced on all men as a result of Adam's fall.

10. See my *National Power and the Structure of Foreign Trade* (Berkeley: University of California Press, 1945, rev. ed., 1969).

11. With respect to the implications of direct as opposed to portfolio investment, see also Hans O. Schmitt, "Integration and Conflict in the World Economy," *Journal of Common Market Studies* 8 (September 1969): 1–18.

12. For an early warning by a politically sophisticated economist, see Thomas C. Schelling, "American Aid and Economic Development: Some Critical Issues" in *International Stability and Progress*, American Assembly (Columbia University, 1957), p. 137.

13. The work of Barrington Moore, Jr., is an important exception to this norm. In his *Social Origins of Dictatorship and Democracy* (Boston: Beacon Press, 1966), he attributes a major role in the shaping of the political destinies of various nations to the "success or failure of the upper class in taking up commercial agriculture" (p. 459). But he does not stop with this comparatively grand dichotomy and elsewhere points out the vastly different political consequences deriving from land-intensive and linkage-rich sheep raising in England, from labor-intensive grain growing in Prussia, and from the linkage-poor wine trade in France. See his chap. 1 and pp. 45–50, 460–63.

14. See chap. 14 below, and the introduction to my *Journeys Toward Progress* (New York: Twentieth Century Fund, 1963).

15. See below, p. 33. The two heuristic devices just mentioned—the notion of blessing (or curse) in disguise and the concept of cumulative disequilibrium— do not by any means permit us to discover all the possible connections between economics and politics. A simple reason is that it is impossible, in many cases, to assign an unambiguous positive or negative sign to the sociopolitical implications of an economic event or characteristic. This point is stressed and

illustrated in my *Development Projects Observed* (Washington: Brookings Institution, 1967), pp.186–88.

16. New Haven: Yale University Press, 1958, p. 63.

17. The role economic advisers play in short-circuiting crises is illustrated in my *Journeys Toward Progress,* pp. 206–10.

18. See chap.15, pp. 333–35.

19. Chap. 2, p. 82.

20. See also chap. 14, pp. 318–19.

21. *Strategy,* p. 193.

22. The grip of the homogeneous vanguard-group concept is evident in the writings of otherwise highly diverse authors. Thus, Heilbroner in *The Limits of American Capitalism* (1966) and Galbraith in *The New Industrial State* (1967) look to the "scientific elites" or to the "Educational and Scientific Estate," respectively, for accomplishing the social changes they deem desirable, and New Left writers are focusing their search on youth or Blacks. See Massimo Teodori, ed., *The New Left: A Documentary History* (Indianapolis: Bobbs-Merrill, 1969), particularly the selections for chap. 16, "In Search of a Class Analysis."

23. Chap. 4 below, p. 154.

24. In the case just noted and in a number of others, the need for corrective public policy measures could be obviated by the timely arrival on the scene of creative Schumpeterian entrepreneurs, who are able to perceive the change in circumstances or the new opportunities that go unrecognized by their more routine-ridden and prejudiced contemporaries. My point here is precisely that in some key situations the likelihood of such a providential appearance is infinitesimal.

It should be obvious, incidentally, that misperception and underestimate of newly and gradually emerging opportunities and capabilities is no monopoly of private decision makers. Public authorities are, if anything, even more subject to the inertia that breeds misperception and that can be corrected and overcome only by incentives and ideologies which are excessive from any long-run point of view. The extremes of early laissez faire capitalism can perhaps be interpreted in this fashion.

25. While I have only now formulated this idea as a general principle, I have long "applied" it in a variety of contexts. See *Strategy,* pp. 173–75; *Exit, Voice, and Loyalty,* pp. 124–25; and this book, chap. 12, passim, chap. 15, pp. 340–41, and chap. 16, p. 349. A similar point of view is expressed by Erik Erikson who exalts the Hindu life cycle scheme which "allows for a succession of pointedly different life styles" over "the almost vindictive monotony of Judean-Christian

strictures by which we gain or forfeit salvation by the formation of one consistently virtuous character almost from the cradle to the very grave" (*Gandhi's Truth* [New York: W. W. Norton, 1969], p. 37).

26. I find that I am here doing an injustice to at least one natural scientist. In his recent book, Le Hasard et la nécessité (Paris, Seuil, 1970), pp. 160–61, the biologist Jacques Monod argues in favor of the "disagreeable idea" that the emergence of both life and man may have resulted from unique occurrences whose a priori probabilities were close to zero.

27. See also chap. 16 below, p. 358.

28. The meaning I am trying to bestow on this term has nothing in common with the watered-down environmental determinism for which it has stood among geographers.

29. *Strategy*, pp. 185–86. Somewhat earlier, Pascal had pointed out that religious feelings can be the consequence, rather than the cause, of devotional acts, such as kneeling (*Pensées*, 233, 250).

30. Dankwart Rustow, "Transitions to Democracy: Toward a Dynamic Model." *Comparative Politics* 2 (April 1970): 337–64. This idea also is a rediscovery: Machiavelli noted in a famous passage that the "perfection" of the Roman Republic and "all the laws that were made in favor of liberty" were due to the so often lamented "disunion between the Plebs and the Senate" (*Discorsi*, bk. 1, chaps. 2 and 4).

31. *Exit, Voice, and Loyalty*, pp. 92–96.

32. José Nun, "The Middle Class Military Coup," in Claudio Veliz, ed., *The Politics of Conformity in Latin America* (London: Oxford University Press, 1967), pp. 66–118.

33. Charles F. Hockett and Robert Ascher, "The Human Revolution," *Current Anthropology* 5 (June 1964): 137.

34. Esther Boserup, *The Conditions of Agricultural Growth* (Chicago: Aldine, 1965).

35. Ibid., p. 118.

UNDERDEVELOPMENT, OBSTACLES TO THE PERCEPTION OF CHANGE, AND LEADERSHIP

The summer of 1967 was a busy one for Hirschman. He had recently completed a study of World Bank development projects. A civil war had just erupted in Nigeria, one of the sites he'd visited for the Bank, and it haunted him. He also returned to Brazil, Chile, and Colombia, where he had lived for several years in the 1950s. Latin America was in the throes of great changes. Bolivian marines were hunting for Che Guevara; Argentina had recently seen its civilian government toppled; Chile and Colombia had embarked on major reform efforts in part to stem revolution. Hope and anguish filled the air. Latin American social scientists were characteristically pessimistic, some worrying that the reforms were doomed, others concluding that the only way out was full-blown revolution. They tended to agree that "structural causes"—entrenched obstacles that made all efforts to change self-defeating—lay at the heart of the problems. Hirschman came away from meetings with friends and colleagues determined not only to challenge their defeatism but to explain that many of these obstacles were ideological constructs. They obscured the real, "stealthy" change that was actually occurring and ignored the vital role of political and intellectual leadership.

—*Jeremy Adelman*

DURING A RECENT VISIT to a Latin American capital, I wished to resume contact with X, an economic historian who had returned there some time ago after spending several years in Europe. I had been invited for dinner by a sociologist whom I asked whether he knew X; he did indeed, quite well, but did not have X's telephone number; no doubt, however, he could find it by calling a common friend. Unfortunately the friend was not home. I asked whether there might be a chance that X would be listed in the telephone directory; this suggestion was shrugged off with the remark that the directory makes a point of listing only people who have either emigrated or died. After a while, the other dinner guests, an economist and his wife, appeared. They were asked about X's telephone number. The economist said that X must be both much in demand and hard to reach, as several people had inquired about how to get in touch with him within the past few days. The subject was dropped as hopeless, and everybody spent a pleasant evening.

Upon waking up the next morning in my hotel room, I noticed the telephone directory on the night table. I could not resist opening it to look for a listing under X's name. I found it immediately and dialed the number, still sure that it must be the one he owned five years ago before leaving for Europe. But the familiar voice answered my call from the other end of the line.

Special Obstacles to the Perception of Change in Underdeveloped Countries

It so happens that X is Claudio Véliz, at present the director of a new Institute of International Studies in Santiago and editor of the recent volume *Obstacles to Change in Latin America.*[1] In the course of our conversation, he asked me to give a talk at his Institute. Since the episode I had just lived through confirmed my longstanding suspicion that obstacles to change are intertwined in Latin America and in other less developed areas with considerable obstacles to the *perception* of change, I suggested that an exploration of these obstacles might be an interesting, if somewhat disrespectful, topic. The observations in this section are based on the talk that ensued and also owe much to the lively discussion it provoked.

To a considerable extent, the difficulties of perceiving change are universal. At all stages of development, men are loath to abandon the old clichés and stereotypes that have served them so well, for they make the world around them intelligible, comfortable, and meaningful—or, as in our episode, almost endearingly absurd. Historians and psychologists have documented the difficulties of perceiving what, on the basis of previous experience, is felt to be incongruous as well as the reluctance to absorb new information that conflicts with established beliefs or is otherwise unpleasant.[2] Here, however, I am not so much interested in the general phenomenon as in the possible existence of *special* or additional obstacles to the perception of change in countries where economic and social development has been laggard.

As a preliminary, a not quite terminological point must be briefly discussed. A distinction is often made between "real" and "apparent" or between "fundamental" and "superficial" changes: This device permits one to categorize as superficial a great number of changes that have, in effect, taken place and to assert in consequence that there has not yet been any real change. The decision to assert that *real* change has occurred is made to hinge on one or several tests. For example, it is often affirmed that there has been "no real change" *unless* the absolute distance which separates the per-capita income of the underdeveloped countries from that of the developed has been substantially narrowed or *unless* there has been the kind of radical and sudden redistribution of wealth and power which comes as the result of a socialist revolution. But to set up such demanding tests is in itself an indication of a special difficulty and reluctance to concede change except when it simply can no longer be denied. It is precisely our task to explain this reluctance and this difficulty.

Persistence of the "Little Tradition"

A first, still rather general obstacle to the perception of change derives from the persistence of traits which are related to what Robert Redfield has called the "little tradition." An example: I land at the Bogotá airport after a five-year absence, and the first thing I notice on leaving the plane is the characteristic manner in which several of my fellow passengers are folding handkerchiefs around their noses; having long known this to be a strange custom of the Bogotanos as they emerge from their homes, movie theaters, or bordellos into the dangerous open air, I immediately whisper to myself: "Nothing has changed here!"

Numerous traits of this kind are both harmless and perfectly compatible with the highest levels of economic and political development. Since they were first encountered at a time when the country was backward, however, they have taken on an aroma of backwardness, and the impression is created—by no means only among foreign visitors—that modernization requires a surrender of these traits.

Clearly the observer is in error when he decides that nothing has changed because a number of traits of the "little tradition" are still extant. But the error is not only pardonable, it is almost inevitable. When backwardness is pervasive, it is easy to overestimate by the interrelatedness of its components and correspondingly difficult to diagnose correctly which traits will and must be changed in the course of modernization and which ones may be—and perhaps should be—safely kept.[3]

The Bias in the Perception of Cumulative Change

Our next obstacle to the perception of change depends more critically on the division of the world into advanced and less developed countries and is, therefore, central to our argument. It arises because what leads to cumulative change in one country does not necessarily do so in another. In other words, the extent to which a given social event or innovation— industrialization, agrarian reform, the achievement of mass literacy, and so forth—involves a society in further important social and political changes varies considerably from country to country and from period to period. A fundamental transformation of the socio-political structure accompanied the coming of industry to England and France; for Germany, Russia, and Japan, the transformation was less radical or more delayed; and for the "late-late-comers" of Latin America, industrialization has ordinarily brought even less immediate and fundamental sociopolitical changes. Somehow the existing structures in these countries seem to be better at absorbing and accommodating the new industries and their promoters, technicians, and labor force than was the case in those societies where industry first raised its head.[4]

A similar development may be in the making *within* Latin America with respect to agrarian reform. Whereas the elimination of the *latifundio* in Mexico, Bolivia, and Cuba required nothing less than a revolution, a number of countries (Chile, Venezuela, Colombia, and perhaps even Peru) seem to be able to achieve substantial progress in land-tenure conditions without a concomitant or prior drastic change in the socio-political environment.

Marx said that when history repeats itself, it reproduces in the form of comedy what first appeared as tragedy. The preceding situations suggest a slight variant: It looks as though a given change or innovation appears for the first time with revolutionary, history-making force, but tends to be reported the next time in the "News-in-Brief" column. If we had put our finger on a historical law here, we would then have encountered a reason why fundamental change is less easy to come by in countries which introduce the "revolutionary" innovations of the advanced countries after a substantial time lag.

The matter is not settled so easily, however, for our historical law breaks down as soon as we consider some additional examples. While some innovations cause less cumulative change among the latecomers than they did among the pioneers, the opposite relationship can be shown to hold for others. Take, as a striking example, the transistor radio; its impact is far more revolutionary in countries where a large part of the population had previously been wholly out of touch with national and international events than in countries where, as a result of fairly universal literacy and electrification, the transistor radio is merely one additional medium for the transmission of information.

Another example is the truck (or bus), which has become an important medium of not only geographical, but *social* mobility in some African and Latin American countries. While social mobility had long been a feature of the societies which *invented* the truck, the possibility of achieving truck ownership opened up an important new avenue toward social improvement in more rigidly stratified societies. In a similar vein, I have related recently how the telephone led to the replacement of cash by credit operations in Ethiopia[5]; such a revolutionary role was obviously denied the telephone in North America and Europe, where credit instruments had been perfected for several centuries prior to Bell's invention.

Objectively, therefore, it is hardly possible to assert that cumulative change is more difficult to ignite in underdeveloped countries than in advanced ones. But subjectively the situation looks quite different, for observers in the less developed countries will expect a cumulative change to be connected with those processes which had a revolutionary function in the advanced countries. When these processes fail to perform in this way in their own countries, the observers will disappointedly conclude that "nothing ever changes here." Instances of the opposite relation—namely, that some innovations which were easily accommodated by the existing sociopolitical structure of the advanced countries will cause considerable ferment when transplanted to the less advanced—are not likely to occur to these observers since they always expect changes to take place in accordance with the patterns of the "leading" countries which they emulate and with which they attempt to catch up. This expectation, then, induces a bias in perception—that is, an emphasis on those processes which wrought considerable change in the advanced countries, but are easily domesticated when they are transplanted, while the opposite situations are ignored.

Styles of Change in Dependent and Leading Countries

The less-developed countries are usually *dependent* countries: They have considerably less freedom of movement than the leading or more nearly independent countries.[6] This situation is likely to have important consequences for the manner in which change is typically brought about in each kind of country, and it turns out that such differences in styles of change once again create special difficulties for the perception of change in the dependent countries.

In its extreme form, dependence of a formally independent underdeveloped country is revealed through military intervention of a leading power. But, operating as it does in an open international economic system, the dependent country is also subject to a whole range of intermediate pressures and potential threats: denial of international financing, domestic capital flight, diversion of purchases of goods for export and of tourist services to alternative suppliers, and so forth. Some of these potential threats are likely to become actual not only when the interests of a dominant foreign country are under direct attack, but even when a determined attempt is made to change the domestic social and economic structure. Often there is considerable uncertainty about the international repercussions of internal reform moves. Leading countries are subject neither to such threats nor to such uncertainties.

The consequence for the style of change of the two kinds of countries is obvious: The leading countries can afford to place all their cards on the table and to shout about their achievements in change from the rooftops. When, on the other hand, the desire for change comes to the fore in a dependent country, *and as long as dependent status is accepted as a datum and a constraint*, there will be an instinctive tendency to play it safe by introducing change in small doses so that each individual unit of change will either not be noticed at all or will remain below some "foreign repercussion threshold." The dependent country, thus, will endeavor to dissimulate change by making it as gradual and non-spectacular as possible. Brazil's well-known record of gradual and comparatively nonviolent transitions may be an example of this *stealthy* style of change, and Colombia supplies us once again with an illustrative story. A Polish mission recently visited Colombia and found out all at once about the many basic and not-so-basic economic activities which are at present in the hands of the government, the Central Bank, or other public bodies; not realizing that this state of affairs is the end result of a gradual process which had extended over a period of many years, the Poles are reported to have asked: "Excuse our ignorance, but in which year did you make The Revolution?"

The non-spectacular, stealthy style of change is a defense mechanism used by political leadership in the dependent countries, and in many ways it is admirably clever. Like any human institution, moreover, the style has a tendency to perpetuate itself even when the circumstances which have given rise to it no longer prevail. There is something to be said for turning necessity into virtue and for celebrating the style, as has often been done in Brazil, as a genuine invention and contribution to the art of history-making.

The trouble is that the style is too clever. It may fool the intervention-prone foreigner or the traditional domestic power-holder whose position it slowly erodes. But the general public and, even more, the intellectuals also fail frequently to recognize that change is being achieved. The reason is clear: Because of the overriding prestige of the dominant countries, change is widely equated with that particular "loud" *style* of change which these countries can so well afford; thus, change is denied to have occurred at all until and unless it takes the particular shape—violent revolution, civil war, and so forth—which is familiar to us from the history of change in the leading countries. A country that is not taking this particular road to change is considered by its own countrymen as too "lazy to make history" or as a country of "ambiguity and half tones."[7] Thus, once again, fascination with the patterns of change characteristic of the leading, dominant countries makes it difficult to perceive processes of change actively at work among latecoming and dependent countries.

The Special Misfit and Durability of Imported Ideologies

In addition to the biases in perception already described, observers in less-developed countries can be affected by a special difficulty in detecting changes in their own societies, regardless of any comparison with what happens or has happened elsewhere. A reason for this difficulty can be found in the image which these observers have of their own societies, in the lenses they use to look at them, or, for short, in their ideologies. It is probably a principal characteristic of less-developed, dependent countries that they *import* their ideologies, both those that are apologetic and those that are subversive of the status quo. There always exists a considerable distance between variegated and ever-changing reality, on the one hand, and the rigid mold of ideology, on the other. The distance and the misfit, however, are likely to be much more extensive when the ideology is imported than when it is homegrown. In the latter case, an important social change which is not accounted for by the prevailing ideology will soon be noted and the ideology will be criticized and either adapted to the new situation or exchanged for a new one. A good example is the Revisionist criticism of orthodox Marxism which appeared even during the lifetime of Engels as a result of certain developments in German society which were hard to fit into Marxist doctrine.

When the ideology is imported, on the other hand, the extent to which it fits the reality of the importing country is usually quite poor from the start. Given this initial disparity, additional changes in the country's social, economic, or political structure that contradict the ideology do not really worsen the fit *substantially* and are therefore ignored or else easily rationalized. The free-trade doctrine imported from England into Latin America in the nineteenth century and so poorly adapted to the needs of that continent was fully routed there only as a result of the two World Wars and the Depression.[8] The long life of the oft-refuted explanation of Latin American societies in terms of the dichotomy between oligarchy and mass may be another case in point. On the North American Left, the notion, imported by Marxist thought, that the white working class is the "natural ally" of the oppressed Negro masses also held sway for an extraordinarily long period, considering the overwhelming and cumulative evidence to the contrary.[9]

Thus, an ideology can draw strength from the very fact that it does so poorly at taking the basic features of socio-economic structure into account. Among ideologies, in other words, it is the least fit that have the greatest chance of survival! And as long as the misfit ideology survives, perception of change—and of reality in general—is held back.

To illustrate the point further, I must tell one last story: A man approaches another exclaiming: "Hello, Paul. It's good to see you after so many years, but you have changed so much! You used to be fat, now you are quite thin; you used to be tall, now you are rather short. What happened, Paul?" 'Paul' rather timidly replies: "But my name is not Paul." Whereupon the other retorts, quite pleased with his interpretation of reality: "You see how much you have changed! Even your name has changed!"

In sum, our search for obstacles to the perception of change specific to underdeveloped countries has been surprisingly successful. This success will give us pause and concern: When there are special difficulties in perceiving ongoing change, many opportunities for accelerating that change and taking advantage of newly arising openings for change will surely be missed. The obstacles to the *perception* of change thus turn into an important obstacle to *change itself.* The matter can also be put in the form of a vicious circle: To the extent that a country is underdeveloped, it will experience special difficulties in perceiving changes within its own society; hence, it will not notice resulting opportunities for even larger and more decisive changes. A country that fails to perceive these opportunities is likely to remain underdeveloped.

Perception of Change and Leadership: Charisma vs. Skill

Might it not be possible, one could ask, to break out of this vicious circle by the right kind of change-perceiving leadership? To link in this way the problem of perception of change to that of leadership may seem far-fetched; yet these problems are so difficult that roundabout approaches are worth trying. One useful indirect approach to the leadership problem would consist in first ascertaining, as I have just done, some *average* beliefs, attitudes, and perceptions that prevail not only in the community at large, but also among its elites. One could then inquire whether and how leaders are liable to deviate from these averages and try to define leadership in terms of such deviations.

The trouble with such a definition (but also its interest) is that deviations from average attitudes and perceptions can take several contrasting forms. In the first place, leadership may be achieved by those who hold to the average perceptions with an uncommon degree of "passionate intensity," who articulate them most forcefully, and who best reflect and express what is in everybody's heart and mind. Average *mis*perceptions, such as those we have reviewed, are of course also reflected and accentuated by this sort of leader, and his ability to empathize with them or his blindness to ongoing change may be an important part of his appeal. Robert Tucker observes elsewhere in this volume that *charismatic* leadership rests to a considerable extent on the leader's ability "to accentuate the sense of being in a desperate predicament,"[10] presumably regardless of whether this sense is justified by actual events.

Yet, accentuation, exaggeration, and forceful articulation of prevailing attitudes and perceptions cannot be the only basis for leadership. Another is surely the ability to overcome and transcend some of these attitudes. In our case, it is precisely the ability to perceive change when most of one's contemporaries are still unable to do so that would enable a leader to take advantage of new opportunities as soon as they arise; in this situation, a leader often appears to *create* such opportunities singlehandedly.

An illustration of this sort of leadership which is based on the perception rather than the denial of opportunity was recently supplied by Carlos Lleras Restrepo, whose masterful "reform-mongering" performance in initiating agrarian-reform legislation and then seeing it through the Colombian Congress I reported on a few years ago.[11] Elected President in 1966, but lacking the two-thirds majority in Parliament that is required for passing all legislation of any importance, he and his Administration seemed condemned to even more immobilism than had plagued earlier governments elected under the "National Front" arrangement in which Conservatives and Liberals shared the responsibilities and privileges of power. But in the first year of his Administration, Lleras had given so many tokens of a determination to push for socio-economic reforms that he was able to attract votes from the opposition which included a left-wing Liberal group that had split from the main Liberal Party in the late-fifties. Eventually, this group decided to rejoin the main party in August 1967, thereby enabling the Administration to muster the needed two-thirds majority. On commenting on these developments in a televised speech, Lleras exclaimed:

[There are those] who took pleasure in predicting difficulties, who were sure that we would never be able to resolve our problems. . . .

[They said that] because we did not have the two-thirds majority, the whole life of the country was threatened and that the future was somber. *As though there were not the art of politics! As though all situations were unchangeable! As though there were no possibilities of achieving agreements!* The truth is that all these predictions came to naught—in fact, even *before* the Liberal union was sealed and *before* the two-thirds majority was secure, several important laws had been passed.[12]

Here is a leader who excels at perceiving opportunities, takes great pleasure in his special powers of perception, acts successfully on what he perceives, and strengthens his claims to leadership as a result.

Through our indirect approach—ascertaining first some "average" attitudes and perceptions and then defining leadership in terms of deviations from the norm—we have, in fact, come upon two contrasting components of leadership: skill, on the one hand, and charisma, on the other. Skill requires a stronger-than-average ability to perceive change, while charisma is based in part on a stronger-than-average refusal to do so. The charisma and the skill requirements of leadership, thus, are often at loggerheads, and the most effective leaders are likely to be those who can somehow accommodate both. Lenin with his extraordinary powers to rouse people to action *and* the "infinite fertility of his tactical imagination"[13] is a particularly fascinating example.

But such an even blend of charisma and skill is most uncommon. Usually any one leader is likely to be better either at charisma or at skill, precisely because these two qualities are in part based on opposite deviations from the norm. Once in a while, one encounters a "division of labor" between leaders working in informal concert toward the same goal, as in the remarkable case of the charismatic Garibaldi and the skilled Cavour. Again, however, such an arrangement is not easy to come by.

Finally, the contradiction between the two ingredients of leadership may be attenuated because one ingredient, usually charisma, can be allowed to predominate in the first period of struggle and mobilization, while the skill requirements are more needed in the next stage, when the leader moves closer to or actually into power. That leadership often requires this successive display of contrasting characteristics by the same person is noted by several contributors to this volume.[14] It is indeed a fundamental point about the difficulty of securing continuity in effective leadership. As such, the point was unlikely to escape Machiavelli who made it while discussing the chances that violent seizure of power might change a corrupt republic for the better:

> The project to reform the state presupposes a generous and upright citizen. To become sovereign by force . . . presupposes, on the contrary, an ambitious and evil citizen. Hence it will be difficult to find a person who would wish to use reprehensible means to achieve a just end, or an evil man who will suddenly act like a fine citizen and make virtuous use of an ill-gotten authority.[15]

However the conflict between the skill and charisma requirements may be resolved, a minimum of skill will have to be forthcoming in almost any conceivable situation if leadership is to be at all successful. In recent theorizing on leadership, we probably have had an overemphasis on the charisma component—and in recent practice, we certainly have had an *overdose* of it and a corresponding underdose of skill, particularly in the Third World. Names of highly charismatic leaders who failed because they were short on skill come to mind only too readily.

What has been said applies to both revolutionary leaders and "reform-mongers." Both need a minimum of skill—or, in terms of our preceding analysis, both would do a better job if they trained themselves to overcome the obstacles to the perception of change and to recognize change when it happens. Only in this way can they do better for the communities which they pretend to lead than these communities would be expected to do if one were to predict their future on the basis of their average attitudes, perceptions, and misperceptions. This is the ultimate function and justification of the leader: to improve on the *average* prospects for advance of those whom he leads, to raise the expected value of their future.

References

1. Claudio Véliz, *Obstacles to Change in Latin America* (New York, 1965).
2. Some basic references from the psychological literature are Jerome S. Bruner and Leo Postman, "On the Perception of Incongruity: A Paradigm,"

Journal of Personality, Vol. 18 (1949), pp. 206–23; and Leo Festinger, *A Theory of Cognitive Dissonance* (Stanford, 1957). For a remarkable historical case study of blocks to perception in a highly developed country, see Roberta Wohlstetter, *Pearl Harbor: Warning and Decision* (Stanford, 1962).

3. See my article "Obstacles to Development: A Classification and a Quasi-Vanishing Act," *Economic Development and Cultural Change* (July, 1965). It can be argued that keeping some seemingly backward traits is essential if modernization is to be successful since one element of success is the maintenance of a separate identity on the part of the modernizing society.

4. "Latin American politics is something of a 'living museum' in which all the forms of political authority of the Western historic experience continue to exist and operate, interacting one with another in a pageant that seems to violate all the rules of sequence and change involved in our understanding of the growth of Western civilization." Charles W. Anderson, *Politics and Economic Change in Latin America* (Princeton, 1967), p. 104. See also my article, "The Political Economy of Import-Substituting Industrialization in Latin America," *Quarterly Journal of Economics,* Vol. 82 (February, 1968), pp. 1–32.

5. See my *Development Projects Observed* (Brookings, 1967), pp. 151–52.

6. The term "dependent," in lieu of underdeveloped, less-developed, and so forth, is beginning to have currency in Latin America. See, for example, Osvaldo Sunkel, "Politica nacional de desarrollo y dependencia externa," *Estudios Internacionales,* Vol. 1 (Santiago, Chile; April, 1967).

7. The first term is used by Antonio Callado in *Tempo di Arraes* (Rio de Janeiro, 1965), p. 16; the other by Fernando Pedreira in the *Correo da Manhã,* July 16, 1967.

8. See, for example, Nicia Vilela Luz, *A luta pela industrialização do Brasil* (São Paulo, 1961).

9. See Harold Cruse, *The Crisis of the Negro Intellectual* (New York, 1967), pp. 174–75, 262–63, and *passim.*

10. Robert C. Tucker, "The Theory of Charismatic Leadership," p. 751.

11. See my *Journeys Toward Progress* (New York, 1963), Chapter 2.

12. *El Tiempo* (Bogotá), September 14, 1967.

13. Tucker, "The Theory of Charismatic Leadership," p. 751.

14. "The talents of the founder of a state are different from those of the ruler of an established one." (Dankwart A. Rustow, "Ataturk as Founder of a State," p. 821.) "The qualities necessary for a charismatic . . . leader's coming to power are not those that he needs in order to stay in power or to protect

his work." (Stanley and Inge Hoffmann, "de Gaulle as Political Artist," p. 869.) I would add that, in many cases, the required switch from one set of qualities to another must take place not after the conquest of power, but at some point prior to it, when agitation and mobilization give place to negotiation with and partial winning over of the existing powerholders.

THE RISE AND DECLINE OF
DEVELOPMENT ECONOMICS

In 1979 Hirschman was invited to write an essay in honor of William Arthur Lewis. That same year, Lewis won the Nobel Prize in economics. Hirschman had sparred with Lewis in the 1960s: Lewis was a champion of more balanced growth; Hirschman favored disequilibrium. Lewis' winning the Nobel Prize meant—as Clifford Geertz, Hirschman's long-time friend, noted—that Hirschman would likely not. By then, Hirschman was growing more and more concerned that the field had grown stale. So he used the invitation to take stock of development economics, to show that it was mixed from the start. But the combination of a narrowing of the field (what he called "monoeconomics") and the insistence on the part of some (neo-Marxists) that economics in the periphery somehow earned it a different brand of social science sent the field off into a desert. In a sleight of hand, Hirschman affiliated Lewis with this trend. Now that the great hopes of development were largely dashed, the field had rallied around the opposite of what once motivated it; scholars replaced hope with futility. What Hirschman advocated was an approach premised on the idea that peoples of the Third World could chart their own futures, and did, despite the long-standing convictions of development economics that only outside forces and expertise could shake them from their lot.

—*Jeremy Adelman*

D EVELOPMENT ECONOMICS IS a comparatively young area of inquiry. It was born just about a generation ago, as a subdiscipline of economics, with a number of other social sciences looking on both skeptically and jealously from a distance. The forties and especially the fifties saw a remarkable outpouring of fundamental ideas and models which were to dominate the new field and to generate controversies that contributed much to its liveliness. In that eminently "exciting" era, development economics did much better than the object of its study, the economic development of the poorer regions of the world, located primarily in Asia, Latin America, and Africa. Lately it seems that at least this particular gap has been narrowing, not so much unfortunately because of a sudden spurt in economic development, but rather because the forward movement of our subdiscipline has notably slowed down. This is of course a subjective judgment. Articles and books are still being produced. But as an observer and longtime participant I cannot help feeling that the old liveliness is no longer there, that new ideas are ever harder to come by and that the field is not adequately reproducing itself.

When scientific activity is specifically directed at solving a pressing problem, one can immediately think of two reasons why, after a while, interest in this activity should flag. One is that the problem is in fact disappearing—either because of the scientific discoveries of the preceding phase or for other reasons. For example, the near demise of interest in business-cycle theory since the end of World War II was no doubt due to the remarkably shock-free growth experienced during that period by the advanced industrial countries, at least up to the mid-seventies. But this reason cannot possibly be invoked in the present case: The problems of poverty in the Third World are still very much with us.

The other obvious reason for the decline of scientific interest in a problem is the opposite experience, that is, the disappointing realization that a "solution" is by no means at hand and that little if any progress is being made. Again, this explanation does not sound right in our case, for in the last thirty years considerable advances have taken place in many erstwhile "underdeveloped" countries—even a balance sheet for the Third World as a whole is by no means discouraging.[1]

In sum, the conditions for healthy growth of development economics would seem to be remarkably favorable: the problem of world poverty is far from solved, but encouraging inroads on the problem have been and are being made. It is therefore something of a puzzle why development economics flourished so briefly.

In looking for an explanation, I find it helpful to take a look at the conditions under which our subdiscipline came into being. It can be shown, I believe, that this happened as a result of an a priori unlikely conjunction of distinct ideological currents. The conjunction proved to be extraordinarily productive, but also created problems for the future. First of all, because of its heterogeneous ideological makeup, the new science was shot through with tensions that would prove disruptive at the first opportunity. Secondly, because of the circumstances under which it arose, development economics became overloaded with unreasonable hopes and ambitions that soon had to be clipped back. Put very briefly and schematically, this is the tale I shall tell—plus a few stories and reflections on the side.

A Simple Classification of Development Theories

The development ideas that were put forward in the forties and fifties shared two basic ingredients in the area of economics. They also were based on one unspoken political assumption with which I will deal in the last section of this paper.

The two basic economic ingredients were what I shall call the rejection of the *monoeconomics claim* and the assertion of the *mutual-benefit claim*. By rejection of the monoeconomics claim I mean the view that underdeveloped countries as a group are set apart, through a number of specific economic characteristics common to them, from the advanced industrial countries and that traditional economic analysis, which has concentrated on the industrial countries, must therefore be recast in significant respects when dealing with underdeveloped countries. The mutual-benefit claim is the assertion that economic relations between these two groups of countries could be shaped in such a way as to yield gains for both. The two claims can be either asserted or rejected, and, as a result, four basic positions exist, as shown in the following table.

Types of development theories

Mutual-benefit claim:	Monoeconomics claim: Asserted	Rejected
Asserted	Orthodox economics	Development economics
Rejected	Marx?	Neo-Marxist theories

Even though there are of course positions that do not fit neatly just one of its cells, this simple table yields a surprisingly comprehensive typology for the major theories on development of the periphery. In the process, it makes us realize that there are two unified systems of thought, orthodox economics and neo-Marxism, and two other less consistent positions that are therefore likely to be unstable: Marx's scattered thoughts on development of "backward" and colonial areas, on the one hand, and modern development economics, on the other. I shall take up these four positions in turn, but shall give major attention to development economics and to its evolving relations with and harassment by—the two adjoining positions.

The orthodox position holds to the following two propositions: (a) economics consists of a number of simple, yet "powerful" theorems of universal validity: there is only one economics ("just as there is only one physics"); (b) one of these theorems is that, in a market economy, benefits flow to all participants, be they individuals or countries, from all voluntary acts of economic intercourse ("or else they would not engage in those acts"). In this manner, both the monoeconomics and the mutual-benefit claims are asserted.

The opposite position is that of the major neo-Marxist theories of development which hold: (a) exploitation or "unequal exchange" is the essential, permanent feature of the relations between the underdeveloped "periphery" and the capitalist "center"; (b) as a result of this long process of exploitation, the political-economic structure of the peripheral countries is very different from anything ever experienced by the center, and their development cannot possibly follow the same path—for example, it has been argued that they cannot have a successful industrialization experience under capitalist auspices. Here, both the mutual-benefit claim and the monoeconomics claim are rejected.

A cozy internal consistency, bent on simplifying (and oversimplifying) reality and therefore favorable to ideology formation, is immediately apparent in both the orthodox and the neo-Marxist positions. This is in contrast with the remaining two positions. It should be clear why I have placed Marx into the southwesterly cell (mutual-benefit claim rejected, monoeconomics claim asserted). Writing in *Capital* on primitive accumulation on the one hand, Marx describes the process of spoliation to which the periphery has been subject in the course of the early development of capitalism in the center. Thus he denies any claim of mutual benefit from trade between capitalist and "backward" countries. On the other hand, his well-known statement, "The industrially most developed country does nothing but hold up to those who follow it on the industrial ladder, the image of its own future," coupled with the way in which he viewed England's role in India as "objectively" progressive in opening the way to industrialization by railroad construction, suggests that he did not perceive the "laws of motion" of countries such as India as being substantially different from those of the industrially advanced ones. Marx's opinions on this latter topic are notoriously complex and subject to a range of interpretations, as is indicated by the question mark in the table. But to root *neo* Marxist thought firmly in the southeasterly cell took considerable labors (which involved, among other things, *uprooting* an important component of the thought of Marx). The story of these labors and revisions has been told elsewhere,[2] and my task here is to deal with the origin and dynamics of the other "hybrid" position: development economics.

It is easy to see that the conjunction of the two propositions—(a) certain special features of the economic structure of the underdeveloped countries make an important portion of orthodox analysis inapplicable and misleading, and (b) there is a possibility for relations between the developed and underdeveloped countries to be mutually beneficial and for the former to contribute to the development of the latter—was essential for our subdiscipline to arise where and when it did: namely, in the advanced industrial countries of the West, primarily in England and the United States, at the end of World War II. The first proposition is required for the creation of a separate theoretical structure, and the second was needed if Western economists were to take a strong interest in the matter—if the likelihood or at least the hope could be held out that their own countries could play a positive role in the development process, perhaps after certain achievable reforms in international economic relations. In the absence of this perception it would simply not have been possible to mobilize a large group of activist "problem solvers."

The Inapplicability of Orthodox Monoeconomics to Underdeveloped Areas

Once a genuinely new current of ideas is firmly established and is being busily developed by a large group of scholars and researchers, it becomes almost impossible to appreciate how difficult it was for the new to be born and to assert itself. Such difficulties are particularly formidable in economics with its dominant paradigm and analytical tradition—a well-known source of both strength and weakness for that social science. Accordingly, there is need for an explanation of the rise and at least temporary success of the heretical, though today familiar, claim that large portions of the conventional body of economic thought and policy advice are not applicable to the poorer countries—the more so as much of this intellectual movement arose in the very "Anglo-Saxon" environment which had long served as home for the orthodox tradition.

Elements of such an explanation are actually not far to seek. Development economics took advantage of the unprecedented discredit orthodox economics had fallen into as a result of the depression of the thirties and of the equally unprecedented success of an attack on orthodoxy from within the economics "establishment." I am talking of course about the Keynesian Revolution of the thirties, which became the "new economics" and almost a new orthodoxy in the forties and fifties. Keynes had firmly established the view that there were *two* kinds of economics: one—the orthodox or classical tradition—which applied, as he was wont to put it, to the "special case" in which the economy was fully employed; and a very different system of analytical propositions and of policy prescriptions (newly worked out by Keynes) that took over when there was substantial unemployment of human and material resources.[3] The Keynesian step from one to two economics was crucial: the ice of monoeconomics had been broken and the idea that there might be yet another economics had instant credibility—particularly among the then highly influential group of Keynesian economists, of course.

Among the various observations that were central to the new development economics and implicitly or explicitly made the case for treating the underdeveloped countries as a sui generis group of economies, two major ones stand out, that relating to rural underemployment and that stressing the late-coming syndrome in relation to industrialization.

1. Rural underemployment. The early writers on our subject may have looked for an even closer and more specific connection with the Keynesian system than was provided by the general proposition that different kinds of economies require different kinds of economics. Such a connection was achieved by the unanimous stress of the pioneering contributions—by Kurt Mandelbaum, Paul Rosenstein-Rodan and Ragnar Nurkse—on *underemployment* as a crucial characteristic of *under*development. The focus on rural *under*employment was sufficiently similar to the Keynesian concern with *un*employment to give the pioneers a highly prized sensation of affinity with the Keynesian system, yet it was also different enough to generate expectations of eventual independent development for our fledgling branch of economic knowledge.

The affinities were actually quite impressive. As is well known, the Keynesian system took unemployment far more seriously than had been done by traditional economics and had elaborated a theory of macroeconomic equilibrium with unemployment. Similarly, the early development economists wrote at length about the "vicious circle of poverty"—a state of low-level equilibrium—which can prevail under conditions of widespread rural underemployment. Moreover, the equilibrium characteristics of an advanced economy with urban unemployment and those of an underdeveloped economy with rural underemployment were both held to justify interventionist public policies hitherto strictly proscribed by orthodox economics. The Keynesians stressed the task of expansionary fiscal policy in combating unemployment. The early development economists went farther and advocated some form of public investment planning that would mobilize the underemployed for the purpose of industrialization, in accordance with a pattern of "balanced growth."

In these various ways, then, the claim of development economics to stand as a separate body of economic analysis and policy derived intellectual legitimacy and nurture from the prior success and parallel features of the Keynesian Revolution.

The focus on rural underemployment as the principal characteristic of underdevelopment found its fullest expression in the work of Arthur Lewis. In his powerful article "Economic Development with Unlimited Supplies of Labour" he managed—almost miraculously—to squeeze out of the simple proposition about underemployment a full set of "laws of motion" for the typical underdeveloped country, as well as a wide range of recommendations for domestic and international economic policy.

With the concept of rural underemployment serving as the crucial theoretical underpinning of the separateness of development economics, it is not surprising that it should have been chosen as a privileged target by the defenders of orthodoxy and monoeconomics.[4] For example, Theodore W. Schultz devoted a full chapter of his well-known book *Transforming Traditional Agriculture* (Yale, 1964) to an attempt at refuting what he called "The Doctrine of Agricultural Labor of Zero Value."[5] This suggests an interesting point about the scientific status of economics, and of social science in general. Whereas in the natural or medical sciences Nobel prizes are often shared by two persons who have collaborated in, or deserve joint credit for, a given scientific advance, in economics the prize is often split between one person who has developed a certain thesis and another who has labored mightily to prove it wrong.

At the outset of his celebrated article, Lewis had differentiated the underdeveloped economy from Keynesian economics by pointing out that in the Keynesian system there is underemployment of labor as well as of other factors of production, whereas in an underdevelopment situation only labor is redundant. In this respect, my own work can be viewed as an attempt to generalize the diagnosis of underemployment as the characteristic feature of underdevelopment. Underdeveloped countries did have hidden reserves, so I asserted, not only of labor, but of savings, entrepreneurship, and other resources. But to activate them, Keynesian remedies would be inadequate. What was needed were "pacing devices" and "pressure mechanisms"; whence my strategy of unbalanced growth.

My generalization of the underemployment argument may have somewhat undermined the claim of development economics to autonomy and separateness. As the work of Herbert Simon on "satisficing" and that of Harvey Leibenstein on "X-efficiency" were to show, the performance of the advanced economies also "depends not so much on finding optimal combinations for given resources as on calling forth and enlisting . . . resources and abilities that are hidden, scattered, or badly utilized"—that was the way I had put it in *The Strategy of Economic Development* for the less developed countries.[6] A feature I had presented as being specific to the situation of one group of economies was later found to prevail in others as well. Whereas such a finding makes for reunification of our science, what we have here is not a return of the prodigal son to an unchanging, ever-right and -righteous father. Rather, our understanding of the economic structures of the West will have been modified and enriched by the foray into other economies.

This kind of dialectical movement—first comes, upon looking at outside groups, the astonished finding of Otherness, and then follows the even more startling discovery that our own group is not all that different—has of course been characteristic of anthropological studies of "primitive" societies from their beginning and has in fact been one of their main attractions. In the field of development economics, something of this sort has also happened to the ideas put forward by Arthur Lewis. The dynamics of development with "unlimited" supplies of labor, which was supposed to be typical of less developed countries, have in fact prevailed in many "Northern" economies during the postwar period of rapid growth, owing in large part to massive immigration, temporary or permanent, spontaneous or organized, from the "South."[7] One of the more interesting analytical responses to this situation has been the dual labor market theory of Michael Piore and others. This theory is easily linked up with the Lewis model, even though that connection has not been made explicit as far as I know.

2. Late industrialization. I have suggested in the preceding pages that the concept of underemployment achieved its position as foundation stone for development economics because of its affinity to the Keynesian system and because of the desire of the early writers on our subject to place themselves, as it were, under the protection of a heterodoxy that had just recently achieved success. There was, moreover, something arcane about the concept, often also referred to as "disguised unemployment," that served to enhance the scientific aura and status of the new field.

Along with the mysteries, however, the common sense of development also suggested that some rethinking of traditional notions was required. It became clear during the depression of the thirties and even more during World War II that industrialization was going to hold an important place in any active development policy of many underdeveloped countries. These countries had long specialized—or had been made to specialize—in the production of staples for export to the advanced industrial countries which had supplied them in return with modern manufactures. To build up an industrial structure under these "late-coming" conditions was obviously a formidable task that led to the questioning of received doctrine according to which the industrial ventures appropriate to any country would be promptly acted upon by perceptive entrepreneurs and would attract the required finance as a result of the smooth working of capital markets. The long delay in industrialization, the lack of entrepreneurship for larger ventures, and the real or alleged presence of a host of other inhibiting factors made for the conviction that, in underdeveloped areas, industrialization required a deliberate, intensive, guided effort. Naming and characterizing this effort led to a competition of metaphors: big push (Paul Rosenstein-Rodan), takeoff (Walt W. Rostow), great spurt (Alexander Gerschenkron), minimum critical effort (Harvey Leibenstein), backward and forward linkages (Albert O. Hirschman). The discussion around these concepts drew on both theoretical arguments—new rationales were developed for protection, planning, and industrialization itself—and on the experience of European industrialization in the nineteenth century.

In the latter respect, the struggle between advocates and adversaries of monoeconomics was echoed in the debate between Rostow and Gerschenkron. Even though Rostow had coined what became the most popular metaphor (the "takeoff"), he had really taken a monoeconomics position. For he divided the development process into his famous five "stages" with identical content for all countries, no matter when they started out on the road to industrialization. Gerschenkron derided the notion "that the process of industrialization repeated itself from country to country lumbering through [Rostow's] pentametric rhythm"[8] and showed, to the contrary, how the industrialization of the late-coming European countries such as Germany and Russia differed in fundamental respects from the English industrial revolution, largely because of the intensity of the "catching-up" effort on the part of the latecomers. Even though it was limited to nineteenth-century Europe, Gerschenkron's work was of great importance for development economics by providing *historical* support for the case against monoeconomics. As industrialization actually proceeded in the periphery, it appeared that Third World industrialization around mid-twentieth century exhibited features rather different from those Gerschenkron had identified as characteristic for the European latecomers.[9] But for the historically oriented, Gerschenkron's work supplied the same kind of reassurance Keynesianism had given to the analytically minded: he showed once and for all that there can be more than one path to development, that countries setting out to become industrialized are likely to forge their own policies, sequences, and ideologies to that end.

Subsequent observations strengthened the conviction that industrialization in the less developed areas required novel approaches. For example, modern, capital-intensive industry was found to be less effective in absorbing the "unlimited supplies of labor" available in agriculture than had been the case in the course of earlier experiences of industrialization. Advances in industrialization were frequently accompanied by persistent inflationary and balance-of-payment pressures which raised questions about the adequacy of traditional remedies and led, in Latin America, to the "sociological" and "structuralist" theses on inflation, which, interestingly, have now gained some currency in the advanced countries, usually without due credit being given.[10] Also, the vigorous development of the transnational corporation in the postwar period raised entirely new "political economy" questions about the extent to which a country should attract, restrict, or control these purveyors of modern technology and products.

The Mutual-Benefit Assumption

The new (far from unified) body of doctrine and policy advice that was built up in this manner was closely connected, as noted earlier, with the proposition that the core industrial countries could make an important, even an essential, contribution to the development effort of the periphery through expanded trade, financial transfers, and technical assistance.

The need for large injections of financial aid fitted particularly well into those theories advocating a "big push." It was argued that such an effort could only be mounted with substantial help from the advanced countries, as the poor countries were unable to generate the needed savings from within. Here the underlying model was the new growth economics, which, in its simplest (Harrod-Domar) version, showed a country's growth rate to be determined by the propensity to save and the capital-output ratio. Growth economics had evolved independently from development economics, as a direct offshoot of the Keynesian system and its macroeconomic concepts. While devised primarily with the advanced industrial countries in mind, it found an early practical application in the planning exercises for developing countries that became common in the fifties. These exercises invariably contained projections for an expansion of trade and aid. Their underlying assumption was necessarily that such enlarged economic relations between rich and poor countries would be beneficial for both. Now this proposition fits nicely into orthodox monoeconomics, but it might have been expected to arouse some suspicion among development economists and to mix rather poorly with some of the other elements and assertions of the new subdiscipline. For example, so it could have been asked, why are the countries of the South in a state where, according to some, it takes a huge push to get them onto some growth path? Why are they so impoverished in spite of having long been drawn into the famous "network of world trade"[11] which was supposed to yield mutual benefits for all participants? Is it perhaps because, in the process, some countries have been *caught* in the net to be victimized by some imperialist spider? But such indelicate questions were hardly put in the halcyon days of the immediate postwar years, except perhaps in muted tones by a few faraway voices, such as Raúl Prebisch's. Of that more later.

Action-oriented thought seldom excels in consistency. Development economics is no exception to this rule; it was born from the marriage between the new insights about the sui generis economic problems of the underdeveloped countries and the overwhelming desire to achieve rapid progress in solving these problems with the instruments at hand, or thought to be within reach, such as large-scale foreign aid. A factor in "arranging" this marriage, in spite of the incompatibilities involved, was the success of the Marshall Plan in Western Europe. Here the task of postwar reconstruction was mastered with remarkable speed, thanks, so it appeared at least, to a combination of foreign aid with some economic planning and cooperation on the part of the aid recipients. It has often been pointed out that this European success story led to numerous failures in the Third World, that it lamentably blocked a realistic assessment of the task of development, in comparison with that of reconstruction.

But the matter can be seen in a different light. True, the success of the Marshall Plan deceived economists, policymakers, and enlightened opinion in the West into believing that infusion of capital helped along by the right kind of investment planning might be able to grind out growth and welfare all over the globe. But—and here is an application of what I have called the "Principle of the Hiding Hand"—on balance it may have been a good thing that we let ourselves be so deceived. Had the tough-ness of the development problem and the difficulties in the North-South relationship been correctly sized up from the outset, the considerable intellectual and political mobilization for the enterprise would surely not have occurred. In that case, and in spite of the various "development di-sasters" which we have experienced (and which will be discussed later in this essay), would we not be even farther away from an acceptable world than we are today?

In sum, one historical function of the rise of development economics was to inspire confidence in the manageability of the development enter-prise and thereby to help place it on the agenda of policymakers the world over. The assertion of the mutual-benefit claim served this purpose.

The Strange Alliance of Neo-Marxism and Monoeconomics against Development Economics

Predictably, when the path to development turned out to be far less smooth than had been thought, the hybrid nature of the new subdis-cipline resulted in its being subjected to two kinds of attacks. The neoclassical Right faulted it for having forsaken the true principles of monoeconomics and for having compounded, through its newfangled policy recommendations, the problem it set out to solve. For the neo-Marxists, on the other hand, development economics had not gone far enough in its analysis of the predicament of the poor countries: so seri-ous was their problem pronounced to be that nothing but total change in their socioeconomic structure and in their relations to the rich countries could make a difference; pending such change, so-called development policies only created new forms of exploitation and "dependency." The two fundamentalist critiques attacked development economics from op-posite directions and in totally different terms: but they could converge in their specific indictments—as they indeed did, particularly in the im-portant arena of industrialization. Because the adherents of neoclassical economics and those of various neo-Marxist schools of thought live in quite separate worlds, they were not even aware of acting in unison. In general, that strange de facto alliance has hardly been noted; but it plays an important role in the evolution of thinking on development and its story must be briefly told.

Doubts about the harmony of interests between the developed and underdeveloped countries arose at an early stage among some of the major contributors to the new subdiscipline. There was widespread acceptance of the view that the advanced industrial countries could henceforth contribute to the development of the less advanced, particularly through financial assistance, but questions were raised in various quarters about the equitable distribution of the gains from trade, both in the past and currently. In 1949, Raúl Prebisch and Hans Singer formulated (simultaneously and independently) their famous "thesis" on the secular tendency of the terms of trade to turn against countries exporting primary products and importing manufactures.[12] They attributed this alleged tendency to the power of trade unions in the advanced countries and to conditions of underemployment in the periphery. The argument was put forward to justify a sustained policy of industrialization. Arthur Lewis was led by his model in a rather similar direction: as long as "unlimited supplies of labor" in the subsistence sector depress the real wage throughout the economy, any gains from productivity increases in the export sector are likely to accrue to the importing countries; moreover, in a situation in which there is surplus labor at the ruling wage, prices give the wrong signals for resource allocation in general and for the international division of labor in particular; the result was a further argument for protection and industrialization.

Both the Prebisch-Singer and the Lewis arguments showed that without a judiciously interventionist state in the periphery, the cards were inevitably stacked in favor of the center. On the whole, it looked as though this was the result of some unkind fate rather than of deliberate maneuvers on the center's part. Critics from the Left later took Arthur Lewis to task for viewing unlimited supplies of labor as a datum, rather than as something that is systematically *produced* by the colonizers and capitalists.[13] Lewis was of course fully aware of such situations and specifically notes at one point that in Africa the imperial powers impoverished the subsistence economy "by taking away the people's land, or by demanding forced labour in the capitalist sector, or by imposing taxes to drive people to work for capitalist employers."[14] For Lewis these practices were simply not a crucial characteristic of the model—after all, a decline in infant mortality could have the same effect in augmenting labor supply as a head tax.

It appears nevertheless that the debate among development economists in the fifties included the canvassing of some antagonistic aspects
of the center-periphery relation. The theories just noted attempted to
show that the gain from trade might be unequally distributed (perhaps
even to the point where one group of countries would not gain at all) but
did not go so far as to claim that the relationship between two groups of
countries could actually be exploitative in the sense that trade and other
forms of economic intercourse would enrich one group at *the expense*
of another—an assertion that would be unthinkable within the assumptions of the classical theory of international trade. Yet, even this kind
of assertion was made at a relatively early stage of the debate. Gunnar
Myrdal invoked the principle of cumulative causation (which he had first
developed in his *American Dilemma*) in seeking to understand the reason for persistent and increasing income disparities *within* countries; but
the notion was easily extended to contacts between countries. Myrdal's
argument on the possibility of further impoverishment of the poor region (or country) was largely based on the likelihood of its losing skilled
people and other scarce factors, and also on the possible destruction of
its handicrafts and industries. Independently of Myrdal, I had developed
similar ideas: Myrdal's "backwash effect"—the factors making for increasing disparity—became "polarization effect" under my pen, whereas
his "spread effect"—the factors making for the spread of prosperity from
the rich to the poor regions—was named by me "trickling down effect."
(Optimal terminology is probably achieved by combining Myrdal's
"spread" with my "polarization" effects.) We both argued, though with
different emphases, that the possibility of the polarization effect being
stronger than the spread effect must be taken seriously, and thus went
counter not only to the theory of international trade, but to the broader
traditional belief, so eloquently expressed by John Stuart Mill,[15] that contact between dissimilar groups is always a source of all-around progress.
Anyone who had observed the development scene with some care could
not but have serious doubts about this view: in Latin America, for example, industrial progress was particularly vigorous during the World Wars
and the Great Depression when contacts with the industrial countries
were at a low ebb. To me, this meant no more than that *periods* of isolation may be beneficial and I saw some alternation of contact and isolation as creating optimal conditions for industrial development.[16] In any

event, both Myrdal and I looked at the polarization effects as forces that can be opposed and neutralized by public policies; and I tried to show that instead of invoking such policies as a deus ex machina (as I thought Myrdal did), it is possible to see them as arising out of, and in reaction to, the experience of polarization.

A strange thing happened once it had been pointed out that interaction between the rich and poor countries could in certain circumstances be in the nature of an antagonistic, zero-sum game: very soon it proved intellectually and politically attractive to assert that such was the essence of the relationship and that it held as an iron law through all phases of contacts between the capitalist center and the periphery. Just as earlier those brought up in the classical tradition of Smith and Ricardo were unable to conceive of a gain from trade that is not mutual, so did it become impossible for the new polarization enthusiasts to perceive anything but pauperization and degradation in each of the successive phases of the periphery's history.[17] This is the "development of underdevelopment" thesis, put forward by André Gunder Frank, and also espoused by some of the more extreme holders of the "dependency" doctrine. Given the historical moment at which these views arose, their first and primary assignment was to mercilessly castigate what had up to then been widely believed to hold the promise of economic emancipation for the underdeveloped countries: industrialization. We are now in the mid-sixties, at which time real difficulties and growing pains were experienced by industry in some leading Third World countries after a prolonged period of vigorous expansion. This situation was taken advantage of in order to characterize all of industrialization as a total failure on a number of (not always consistent) counts: it was "exhausted," "distorted," lacked integration, led to domination and exploitation by multinationals in alliance with a domestic "lumpen bourgeoisie," was excessively capital-intensive and therefore sabotaged employment, and fostered a more unequal distribution of income along with a new, more insidious, kind of dependency than ever before.

At just about the same time, the neoclassical economists or mono-economists—as they should be called in accordance with the terminology of this essay—were sharpening their own knives for an assault on development policies that had pushed industrialization for the domestic market. In contrast to the multiple indictment from the Left, the mono-economists concentrated on a single, simple, but to them capital, flaw of these policies: misallocation of resources. By itself this critique was highly predictable and might not have carried more weight than warnings against industrialization emanating from essentially the same camp ten, or twenty, or fifty years earlier. But the effectiveness of the critique was now greater for various reasons. First of all, as a result of the neo-Marxist writings just noted, some of the early advocates of industrialization had now themselves become its sharpest critics. Second, specific policies which in the early stage had been useful in promoting industrialization, though at the cost of inflationary and balance-of-payments pressures, did run into decreasing returns in the sixties: they achieved less industrialization at the cost of greater inflation and balance-of-payments problems than before. Third, the practice of deliberate industrialization had given rise to exaggeration and abuse in a number of countries, and it became easy to draw up a list of horrible examples that served to incriminate the whole effort. Fourth, a new set of policies emphasizing exports of manufactures from developing countries became attractive, because of the then rapid expansion of world trade, and the possibilities of success of such policies was demonstrated by countries like Taiwan and South Korea. Under these conditions, the neoclassical strictures became more persuasive than they had been for a long time.

The target of the complementary neo-Marxist and neoclassical writings was not just the new industrial establishment, which in fact survived the onslaught rather well; on the ideological plane, the intended victim was the new development economics, which had strongly advocated industrial development and was now charged with intellectual responsibility for whatever had gone wrong. The blows from Left and Right that fell upon the fledgling and far from unified subdiscipline left it, indeed, rather stunned: so much so that the most intrepid defense of what had been accomplished by the postwar industrialization efforts in the Third World came not from the old stalwarts, but from an English socialist in the tradition of Marx's original position on the problem of backward areas, the late Bill Warren.[18]

The Real Wounding of Development Economics

It would of course be silly—just as silly as the German proverb *Viel Feind, viel Ehr* (many enemies, much honor)—to hold that any doctrine or policy that is attacked simultaneously from both Left and Right is, for that very reason, supremely invested with truth and wisdom. I have already noted that the neoclassical critics made some valid points, just as the neo-Marxists raised a number of serious issues, particularly in the areas of excessive foreign control and of unequal income distribution. But normally such criticisms should have led to some reformulations and eventually to a strengthening of the structure of development economics. In fact, however, this was not to be the case. No new synthesis appeared. Several explanations can be offered. For one thing, development economics had been built up on the basis of a construct, the "typical underdeveloped country," which became increasingly unreal as development proceeded at very different rates and took very different shapes in the various countries of Latin America, Asia, and Africa. Lenin's law of uneven development, originally formulated with the major imperialist powers in mind, caught up with the Third World! It became clear, for example, that, for the purpose of the most elementary propositions of development strategy, countries with large populations differ substantially from the ever more numerous ministates of the Third World,[19] just as there turned out to be few problems in common between petroleum exporters and petroleum-importing developing countries. The concept of a unified body of analysis and policy recommendations for all underdeveloped countries, which contributed a great deal to the rise of the subdiscipline, became in a sense a victim of the very success of development and of its unevenness.

But there was a more weighty reason for the failure of development economics to recover decisively from the attacks it had been subjected to by its critics. It lies in the series of political disasters that struck a number of Third World countries from the sixties on, disasters that were clearly *somehow* connected with the stresses and strains accompanying development and "modernization."[20] These development disasters, ranging from civil wars to the establishment of murderous authoritarian regimes, could not but give pause to a group of social scientists, who, after all, had taken up the cultivation of development economics in the wake of World War II not as narrow specialists, but impelled by the vision of a better world. As liberals, most of them presumed that "all good things go together"[21] and took it for granted that if only a good job could be done in raising the national income of the countries concerned, a number of beneficial effects would follow in the social, political, and cultural realms.

When it turned out instead that the promotion of economic growth entailed not infrequently a sequence of events involving serious retrogression in those other areas, including the wholesale loss of civil and human rights, the easy self-confidence that our subdiscipline exuded in its early stages was impaired. What looked like a failure to mount a vigorous counterattack against the unholy alliance of neo-Marxists and neoclassicists may well have been rooted in increasing self-doubt, based on mishaps far more serious than either the "misallocation of resources" of the neoclassicists or the "new dependency" of the neo-Marxists.

Not that all the large and gifted group of development economists which had in the meantime been recruited into the new branch of knowledge turned suddenly silent. Some retreated from the position "all good things go together" to "good economics is good for people."[22] In other words, rather than assuming that economic development would bring progress in other fields, they thought it legitimate to operate on the basis of an implicit Pareto-optimality assumption: like plumbing repairs or improvements in traffic control, the technical efforts of economists would improve matters in one area while at worst leaving others unchanged, thus making society as a whole better off. Economic development policy was here in effect downgraded to a technical task exclusively involved with efficiency improvements. An illusion was created and sought that, by confining itself to smaller-scale, highly technical problems, development economics could carry on regardless of political cataclysms.

There was, however, another reaction that was to have a considerable impact. Experiencing a double frustration, one over the appalling political events as such, and the other over their inability to comprehend them, a number of analysts and practitioners of economic development were moved to look at the economic performance itself with a more critical eye than before. In a Freudian act of displacement, they "took out" their distress over the political side on the weaker aspects of the economic record. Within countries with authoritarian regimes, the displacement was often reinforced, unintentionally of course, by the official censorship that was much more rigorous with regard to political dissent than in matters of economic performance.

It was, in a sense, an application of the maxim "all good things go together" *in reverse.* Now that political developments had taken a resoundingly wrong turn, one had to prove that the economic story was similarly unattractive. Some economists were satisfied once the balance between political and economic performance had been restored in this fashion, be it at a wretchedly low level. But others were in a more activist mood. Impotent in the face of political injustice and tyranny, yet feeling a faint sense of responsibility, they were attempting to make amends by exposing *economic* injustice. In doing so, they paid little attention to John Rawls who argued, at just about that time, in *A Theory of Justice* that "a departure from the institutions of equal liberty . . . cannot be justified by or compensated for by greater social or economic advantage."[23] But perhaps it was fortunate—and a measure of the vitality of the development movement—that the disappointment over politics led to an attempt at righting at least those wrongs economists could denounce in their professional capacity.

Here then is one important origin of the concern with income distribution which became a dominant theme in the development literature in the early seventies. Albert Fishlow's finding, on the basis of the 1970 census, that income distribution in Brazil had become more unequal and that some low-income groups may even have come to be worse off in absolute terms, in spite of (because of?) impressive growth, was particularly influential.[24] An alarm based on this and similar data from other countries was sounded by Robert McNamara, the President of the World Bank, in his annual address to the Board of Governors meeting in 1972. A large number of studies followed, and an attempt was made to understand how development could be shaped in accordance with distributional goals, or to formulate policies that would combine the objectives of growth and distribution.

Before long, attention was directed not only to the relative aspects of income distribution, but to the absolute level of need satisfaction among the poorer groups of a country's population. Thus was born the concern with *basic needs*—of food, health, education, etc.—that is currently a principal preoccupation of development economics. Just as the construct of the "typical underdeveloped country" gave way to diverse categories of countries, each with characteristics of its own, so did the heretofore unique maximand of development economics (income per capita) dissolve into a variety of partial objectives, each requiring consultation with different experts—on nutrition, public health, housing, and education, among others.

There is of course much to be said for this new concreteness in development studies, and particularly for the concern with the poorer sections. Nevertheless, development economics started out as the spearhead of an effort that was to bring all-around emancipation from backwardness. If that effort is to fulfill its promise, the challenge posed by dismal politics must be met rather than avoided or evaded. By now it has become quite clear that this cannot be done by economics alone. It is for this reason that the decline of development economics cannot be fully reversed: our subdiscipline had achieved its considerable luster and excitement through the implicit idea that it could slay the dragon of backwardness virtually by itself or, at least, that its contribution to this task was central. We now know that this is not so; a consoling thought is that we may have gained in maturity what we have lost in excitement.

Looking backward, the whole episode seems curious. How could a group of social scientists that had just lived through the most calamitous "derailments of history" *in various major economically advanced* countries entertain such great hopes for economic development per se? Here I can perhaps offer some enlightenment by drawing on my recent work in the history of ideas. In *The Passions and the Interests* I showed that the rise of commerce and money-making activities in the seventeenth and eighteenth centuries was then looked upon as promising for political stability and progress; and I stressed that such optimistic expectations were not based on a new respect for these activities, but rather on *continuing contempt* for them: unlike the passionate, aristocratic pursuit of glory and power with its then well-recognized potential for disaster, the love of money was believed to be "incapable of causing either good *or evil* on a grand scale."[25] A similar perception may have been at work in relation to the less developed countries of Asia, Africa, and Latin America of the twentieth century. The Western economists who looked at them at the end of World War II were convinced that these countries were not all that complicated: their major problems would be solved if only their national income per capita could be raised adequately. At an earlier time, contempt for the countries designated as "rude and barbarous" in the eighteenth century, as "backward" in the nineteenth and as "underdeveloped" in the twentieth had taken the form of relegating them to permanent lowly status, in terms of economic and other prospects, on account of unchangeable factors such as hostile climate, poor resources, or inferior race. With the new doctrine of economic growth, contempt took a more sophisticated form: suddenly it was taken for granted that progress of these countries would be smoothly linear if only they adopted the right kind of integrated development program! Given what was seen as their overwhelming problem of poverty, the underdeveloped countries were expected to perform like wind-up toys and to "lumber through" the various stages of development single-mindedly; their reactions to change were not to be nearly as traumatic or aberrant as those of the Europeans, with their feudal residues, psychological complexes and ex-quisite high culture. In sum, like the "innocent" and *doux* trader of the eighteenth century, these countries were perceived to have only *interests* and *no passions*.

Once again, we have learned otherwise.

Notes

This retrospective essay, which is also to appear in the forthcoming collection in honor of Sir Arthur Lewis (London: George Allen and Unwin), is of course a highly selective review. In particular, it does not treat the development of our factual knowledge about the development process which has often included the testing of theories; here the main debt is owed to such figures as Simon Kuznets and Hollis Chenery. A number of other surveys of the sort here attempted have appeared recently. See, in particular, Paul Streeten, "Development ideas in historical perspective," in *Toward a New Strategy for Development,* Rothko Chapel Colloquium (New York: Pergamon Press, 1979), pp. 21–52, and Fernando Henrique Cardoso, "The originality of a copy: CEPAL and the idea of development," *CEPAL Review* (second half of 1977), UN Commission for Latin America, UN Publication E.77.II.G.5, pp. 7–40. See also the introductory section of Chapter 4 for a brief review of "theorizing on economic development in historical perspective" with a rather different focus.

1. See, for example, David Morawetz, *Twenty-Free Years of Economic Develop-ment:* 1950 to 1975 (Washington, D.C : World Bank, 1977).

2. B. Sutcliffe, "Imperialism and Industrialization in the Third World," in R. Owen and B. Sutcliffe, eds., *Studies in the Theory of Imperialism* (London: Longman, 1972), pp. 180–86, and P. Singer, "Multinacionais: internacional-ização e crise," Caderno CEBRAP No. 28 (São Paulo: Editora Brasiliense, 1977), pp. 50–56. On the complexity of Marx's views, even in the preface of *Capital* where the cited phrase appears, see "A Generalized Linkage Approach to Devel-opment, with Special Reference to Staples," *Essays in Trespassing: Economics to Politics and Beyond* (New York: Cambridge University Press, 1981), pp. 89–90.

3. Dudley Seers leaned on this established terminological usage with his article "The Limitations of the Special Case," *Bulletin of the Oxford University Institute of Economics and Statistics*, 25 (May 1963): 77–98, in which he pleaded for recasting the teaching of economics so as to make it more useful in dealing with the problems of the less-developed countries. The "special case" that had falsely claimed generality was, for Keynes, the fully employed economy; for Seers, it was the economy of the advanced capitalist countries, in contrast to conditions of underdevelopment.

4. See, for example, Jacob Viner, "Some Reflections on the Concept of 'Disguised Unemployment,'" in *Contribuições à Análise do Desenvolvimiento Econômico* (Essays in honor of Eugênio Gudin), (Rio de Janeiro: Agir, 1957), pp. 345–54.

5. His principal empirical argument was the actual decline in agricultural output suffered when the labor force suddenly diminished in a country with an allegedly redundant labor force in agriculture, as happened during the 1918–19 influenza epidemic in India. Arthur Lewis pointed out later that the consequences he had drawn from the assumption of zero marginal productivity in agriculture would remain fully in force provided only the supply of labor at the given wage in industry exceeds the demand, a condition that is much weaker than that of zero marginal productivity. See W. Arthur Lewis, "Reflections on Unlimited Labor," in *International Economics and Development: Essays in Honor of Raúl Prebisch* (New York and London: Academic Press, 1972), pp. 75–96.

6. New Haven: Yale University Press, 1958, p. 5.

7. C. P. Kindleberger, *Europe's Postwar Growth: The Role of Labor Supply* (Cambridge, Mass.: Harvard University Press, 1967).

8. *Economic Backwardness in Historical Perspective* (Cambridge, Mass.: Harvard University Press, 1962), p. 355.

9. A. O. Hirschman, "The Political Economy of Import-Substituting Industrialization in Latin America," published in 1968 and reprinted in Hirschman, *A Bias for Hope: Essays on Development and Latin America* (New Haven: Yale University Press, 1971), Chapter 3.

10. See "The Social and Political Matrix of Inflation: Elaborations on the Latin American Experience," *Essays in Trespassing*, pp. 177–208.

11. This was the title of a well-known League of Nations study stressing the benefits of multilateral trade which were being threatened in the thirties by the spread of bilateralism and exchange controls. Its principal author was Folke Hilgerdt, a Swedish economist. In the immediate postwar period, Hilgerdt, then with the United Nations, noted that trade, however beneficial, had not

adequately contributed to a narrowing of income differentials between countries. With Hilgerdt coming from the Heckscher-Ohlin tradition and having celebrated the contributions of world trade to welfare, this paper, which was published only in processed form in the proceedings of a congress (I have not been able to locate it), was influential in raising questions about the benign effects of international economic relations on the poorer countries.

12. An account of the emergence of the thesis is now available in Joseph Love, "Raúl Prebisch and the Origins of the Doctrine of Unequal Exchange," *Latin American Research Review* 15 (November 1980): 45–72. See also my earlier essay "Ideologies of Economic Development in Latin America" (1961), reprinted in *A Bias for Hope,* Chapter 13. The latest review of the ensuing controversy and related evidence is in two articles by John Spraos: "The Theory of Deteriorating Terms of Trade Revisited," *Greek Economic Review* 1 (December 1979): 15–42, and "The Statistical Debate on the Net Barter Terms of Trade between Primary Commodities and Manufactures," *Economic Journal* 90 (March 1980): 107–28.

13. G. Arrighi; "Labour Supplies in Historical Perspective: A Study of the Proletarianization of the African Peasantry in Rhodesia," *Journal of Development Studies* 6 (April 1970): 197–234.

14. W. Arthur Lewis, "Economic Development with Unlimited Supplies of Labour," published in 1954 and reprinted in A. N. Agarwala and S. P. Singh, ed.; *The Economics of Underdevelopment* (London: Oxford University Press, 1958), p. 410.

15. "It is hardly possible to overrate the value, in the present low state of human improvement, of placing human beings in contact with persons dissimilar to themselves, and with modes of thought and action unlike those with which they are familiar. . . . Such communication has always been, and is peculiarly in the present age, one of the primary sources of progress." J. S. Mill, *Principles of Political Economy,* Book III, Chapter 17, para. 5.

16. *Strategy,* pp. 173–5, 199–201.

17. This view has been aptly labeled "catastrofismo" by Anibal Pinto.

18. B. Warren, "Imperialism and Capitalist Accumulation," *New Left Review,* no. 81 (Sept.–Oct. 1973): 3–45, and "The postwar economic experience of the Third World," in *Toward a New Strategy for Development,* pp. 144–68.

19. This is stressed, for example, by Clive Y. Thomas, *Dependence and Transformation: The Economics of the Transition to Socialism* (New York: Monthly Review Press, 1974), passim.

20. On this subject, see also "The Changing Tolerance for Income Inequality in the Course of Economic Development" and "The Turn to Authoritarianism

in Latin America and the Search for its Economic Determinants," *Essays in Trespassing*, pp. 39–58 and 98–133.

21. See Robert Packenham, *Liberal America and the Third World* (Princeton: Princeton University Press, 1973), pp. 123–9.

22. An expression attributed to Arnold Harberger, in an article in the *New York Times* of February 7, 1980.

23. Cambridge, Mass.: Harvard University Press, 1971, p. 61.

24. "Brazilian Size Distribution of Income," *American Economic Review* 62 (May 1972): 391–402.

25. Princeton: Princeton University Press, 1977, p. 58.

THE CHANGING TOLERANCE FOR INCOME INEQUALITY IN THE COURSE OF ECONOMIC DEVELOPMENT

While caught in traffic heading through a tunnel to Logan Airport in Boston, Hirschman observed that people swung from being ecstatic when the line that they were in moved to being irate when the neighboring lane moved faster. It reminded him of a broader sense of malaise that was prevalent by the early 1970s, particularly the sense of envy that lurked behind social tensions around the world. By then, sociologists and political scientists were fretting over how inequality was unraveling the social fabric; economists worried about how it would affect growth. Hirschman had already plunged into the complicated relationship between perception and reality in development; he was now pivoting to the role of "expectational calculus" more generally. In this essay he explored the role of emotions and subjective forces more explicitly, especially envy; just as social scientists and policy makers should not confuse circumstantial setbacks with failure in development, he also warned that rising intolerance for inequality need not be seen as a sign of a crisis of capitalism, of having to choose between growth **or** equality. Psychological effects, like the "tunnel effect," were highly contingent, and one had to understand them carefully before jumping to big conclusions. By now Hirschman was willing to accept that development was indeed going awry in Pakistan and Mexico; but that did not mean that it did so for the same reasons—and with the same outcomes. A strong tunnel effect, by making social injustice more visible, could have positive repercussions.

—Jeremy Adelman

A DRASTIC TRANSVALUATION of values is in process in the study of economic and political development. It has been forced upon us by a series of disasters that have occurred in countries in which development seemed to be vigorously under way. The civil war in Nigeria and the bloody falling apart of Pakistan are only the most spectacular instances of such "development disasters."

As a result, one reads with increasing frequency pronouncements about the bankruptcy of the "old" development economics, with its accent on growth rates, industrialization, and international assistance, and about the need for a wholly new doctrine that would emphasize income distribution, employment, and self-reliance.[1]

The present paper is not written with the intention of stemming this tide, which surely represents a wholesome reaction and response to current problems. It is grounded, however, in the strong feeling and insistent recollection of one participant observer that the intellectual enthusiasm for development in the fifties and early sixties reflected elements of real hopefulness that were then actually present in many developing countries. What was not correctly perceived was the precarious and transitory nature of that early hopeful and even exuberant phase. This essay, then, is an effort to understand both where we were right and where we went wrong. It will proceed on a fairly abstract level, reach out into several fields other than economics, and stray, on occasion, from the immediate experience and concern that are at its origin.

Gratification over Advances of Others: The Tunnel Effect Introduced

I shall start by baldly stating my basic proposition. In the early stages of rapid economic development, when inequalities in the distribution of income among different classes, sectors, and regions are apt to increase sharply, it can happen that society's *tolerance* for such disparities will be substantial. To the extent that such tolerance comes into being, it accommodates, as it were, the increasing inequalities in an almost providential fashion. But this tolerance is like a credit that falls due at a certain date. It is extended in the expectation that eventually the disparities will narrow again. If this does not occur, there is bound to be trouble and, perhaps, disaster.

To make this proposition plausible, I shall first argue by analogy. Suppose that I drive through a two-lane tunnel, both lanes going in the same direction, and run into a serious traffic jam. No car moves in either lane as far as I can see (which is not very far). I am in the left lane and feel dejected. After a while the cars in the right lane begin to move. Naturally, my spirits lift considerably, for I know that the jam has been broken and that my lane's turn to move will surely come any moment now. Even though I still sit still, I feel much better off than before because of the expectation that I shall soon be on the move. But suppose that the expectation is disappointed and only the right lane keeps moving: in that case I, along with my left lane cosufferers, shall suspect foul play, and many of us will at some point become quite furious and ready to correct manifest injustice by taking direct action (such as illegally crossing the double line separating the two lanes).

It is easy to translate this situation into the language of welfare economics.[2] An individual's welfare depends on his present state of contentment (or, as a proxy, income), as well as on his expected future contentment (or income). Suppose that the individual has very little information about his future income, but at some point a few of his relatives, neighbors, or acquaintances improve their economic or social position. Now he has something to go on: expecting that his turn will come in due course, he will draw gratification from the advances of others—for a while. It will be helpful to refer to this initial gratification as the "tunnel effect."

This is a simple and, I believe, immediately persuasive proposition. While it has to be formulated with greater care so as to spell out the conditions under which it does or does not hold, perhaps I shall be allowed to dwell on it and to advertise its novelty. The tunnel effect operates because advances of others supply information about a more benign external environment; receipt of this information produces gratification; and this gratification overcomes, or at least suspends, *envy*. Though long noted as the most uninviting of the seven deadly sins because, unlike lust, gluttony, pride, etc., it does not provide any initial fun to its practitioners, envy is nevertheless a powerful human emotion. This is attested to by the writings of anthropologists, sociologists, and economists, who all have proclaimed, in general quite independently of one another, that if you advance in income or status while I remain where I was, I will actually feel worse off than before because my relative position has declined.

In economics this has been argued as the "relative income hypothesis," according to which the welfare of an individual varies inversely with the income or the consumption of those persons with whom he associates.[3] In sociology the topic has been profusely studied under the heading of "relative deprivation." While this term is sometimes used to denote any lag of real accomplishments behind expectations, its predominant meaning refers to the feelings experienced by a person or group of persons who are falling behind others or who see others catch up with them in regard to income, influence, and status.[4] Finally, anthropologists, who are less given to using jargon, speak unabashedly of the envy caused by isolated advances of individuals in small, poor communities; they view many institutions, such as fiestas, gift giving, and appointment of the rich to financially burdensome honorary positions, as social mechanisms designed to lessen the potentially destructive impact of envy on personal bonds and social cohesion.[5]

This is no doubt an impressive body of converging writings, and massive data have been gathered in their support. But relentless pursuit of this line of reasoning and research may have led to a trained incapacity to perceive the tunnel effect and its importance in a number of contexts.

A preliminary way of rekindling perception is to reverse the signs of the phenomenon under study. Suppose my neighbor or acquaintance, far from improving his position, experiences a bad setback such as losing his job while I am keeping mine: Do I now experience the opposite of relative deprivation, that is, the satisfaction of relative enrichment? This is unlikely, for one thing, because envy, mortal sin though it may be, is an altogether gentle feeling if compared to *Schadenfreude*, the joy at someone else's injury, which is the emotion that would have to come into play to make me happy in this situation. The more important reason is the tunnel effect in reverse: once again I shall take what is happening to my neighbor as an indication of what the future might have in store for me, and hence I will be apprehensive and worried—less well off than before, just as he. This reaction is well-known from the onset and spread of depressions.[6]

The opposite reaction will surely take place when the economy experiences a cyclical upturn. Now the news that someone I know is getting his job back while I am still unemployed gives me a pleasure that overwhelms any possible envy, for the event is hailed as a confirmation that better times are under way for me also. This is close to the situation in countries that experience a vigorous surge of development.

As long as the tunnel effect lasts, everybody feels better off, both those who have become richer[7] and those who have not. It is therefore conceivable that some uneven distribution of the new incomes generated by growth will be preferred to an egalitarian distribution by all members of the society.[8] In this eventuality, the increase in income inequality would not only be politically tolerable; it would also be outright desirable from the point of view of social welfare.

Some Evidence

But this possible consequence of the tunnel effect is a theoretical curiosum, whereas the effect itself definitely is not. In a number of countries its reality has impressed itself on careful observers. Interestingly enough, it was often stumbled upon by researchers who were looking for the opposite phenomenon, such as seething discontent and revolutionary fervor among the urban poor, and were surprised and sometimes not a little disappointed at what they actually found.

The following comments on a sample survey carried out over a decade ago in the *favelas* of Rio de Janeiro are a first case in point:

One way of testing the favelado's sense of sharing in what goes on in the nation is to ascertain the extent to which he perceives national economic growth as producing real gains to himself. When asked in February of 1961 whether things had improved, had remained about the same, or had become worse for him during the last five years, nearly one out of two favelados replied that his present situation is worse. Another three out of ten found that their situation remained much the same. . . . The general sensation that things have not improved noticeably for themselves has not created any great disillusion among favelados with the idea of industrialization as a road to prosperity. The favelado does not deny that the nation's industrial growth has produced benefits for people like himself; he only states that his own situation has not changed appreciably. Thus, when asked immediately after the above question whether the growth of industry had benefited people like themselves, most

answered affirmatively. Their explanation, however, was almost entirely in terms of the expansion of job opportunities *for others*—
friends, acquaintances, or simply other Brazilians.[9]

Writing also in the early sixties, a well-known Mexican political scientist coined the term "hope factor" to explain what by then amounted
to an astonishingly long record of political stability in his country.[10]
Even after this record had been shattered by the events of 1968 and the
Tlatelolco massacre, another observer wrote:

> Even though the perspectives of individual advance are limited,
> there is one reason for which one finds less disappointment with
> the development process among lower-class persons of all sectors
> than might be expected. With education spreading rapidly and with
> migration on the increase, there are a number of relatively easy ways
> of achieving personal advance. Thus even when an individual has
> been unable to get a new job or in general has not improved his
> income or position, it is nevertheless probable that *he knows one
> or several persons* who have been successful in these respects. . . .[11]

The contrast between the objective situation of low incomes, poor
working conditions, and general deprivation, on the one hand, and the
subjective mood of hopefulness, on the other, were also found to be
characteristic of the Puerto Rico of the late fifties:

> We suggest that Puerto Ricans feel far better off than the objective
> facts of incomes, education and occupations show. . . . Puerto Ri-
> cans perceive the existing marked inequalities. Yet they do not feel
> particularly depreciated by them, and certainly not overwhelmed
> by them; indeed, on some counts, their views of life and how good
> it is have often seemed to ignore the objective situation . . . on
> every visible count, these people at all levels are full of hopes for
> the future.[12]

In an article dealing with the continent as a whole, two Latin American sociologists catch the essence of these situations by asserting that
" . . . the patterns of deferred social mobility, even though somewhat
mythical, are nonetheless effective."[13]

Finally, we shall quote some revealing personal remarks about the general atmosphere of countries where mid-twentieth-century-style capitalist development suddenly "broke out." They come from an American anthropologist who reminisces about her stay in Venezuela, in an article in which she gives a sympathetic account of a recent trip to Cuba:

> I thought about what I had seen in Cuba, and about Venezuela, and about my own country. . . . I thought about how when I went to Venezuela, I felt that for the first time I realized something about my own country which I had not previously seen there: the idealism which is inherent in what I had experienced [in the United States] as materialism and individual self-seeking. I saw that for Venezuelans, for whom economic development had just begun . . . the democratizing of material consumption and the opening up of opportunities—for those able to seize them—was a truly exciting and liberating idea.[14]

This passage is of particular interest, first, because it sensitively renders the feeling of the early exuberant phase of development during which the tunnel effect operates; and, secondly, because it illustrates at the same time the considerable reluctance of social-justice-minded intellectuals to perceive the effect—it just goes too much against the grain of any but the most honest to speak of this deplorable "false consciousness" or of that vulgar frontier atmosphere as an "exciting and liberating idea"! Moreover, social scientists live in an intensely competitive atmosphere in which envy and "relative deprivation" are far more prevalent than hopefulness caused by someone else's advance; and although one hesitates to make these ad homines points, they may help explain why the tunnel effect, though widely noted, has not been dealt with in a systematic way in either economic or sociological theory.

Consequences for Integration and Revolution

A brief digression is in order. The various descriptions of the "hope factor" reported in the previous section strongly suggest that the subject of this paper shades over into a topic familiar to political sociologists: the effect of social mobility on political stability and social integration. This relationship has usually been examined from the point of view of the reactions of the socially mobile themselves, while our focus has thus far been on those who are left behind. With respect to the upwardly mobile, the economist, with his touching simplicity, would tend to think that there is no problem: being better off than before, these people are also likely to be more content with the world around them. Social history has shown, however, that matters are far more complicated: as de Tocqueville already noted, the upwardly mobile do not necessarily turn into pillars of society all at once, but may on the contrary be disaffected and subversive for a considerable time. The principal reason for this surprising development is the phenomenon of partial and truncated mobility: the upwardly mobile who may have risen along one of the dimensions of social status, such as wealth, find that a number of obstacles, rigidities, and discriminatory practices still block their continued ascent, particularly along other dimensions, as well as their all-round acceptance by the traditional elites, and consequently they feel that in spite of all their efforts and achievements, they are not really "making it."[15] Only as social mobility continues for a long period, and the traditional system of stratification is substantially eroded as a result, will the upwardly mobile become fully integrated—or "coopted."

Discrimination against *nouveaux riches* by the older elites is by no means the only reason for which the upwardly mobile may be critical of the society in which they live and advance. A more charitable interpretation would point to the possibility that convictions about social justice, once formed, acquire a life and staying power of their own so that they are not necessarily jettisoned when pressing personal problems of material welfare have been solved—not, in any way, until after a decent time interval.

This dynamic of the socially mobile is thus the reverse of the one that has been suggested here for those who are left behind: during a first and all-round paradoxical phase, frustration and continued alienation are the lot of the upward bound, while the nonmobile derive satisfaction from the anticipation that matters are bound to improve pretty soon. This earlier conclusion of ours can be maintained as the nonmobile see only the improvement in the fortunes of the mobile and remain totally unaware of the new problems being encountered by them. In a second phase there may then take place a symmetrical switch: the upwardly mobile become integrated, whereas the nonmobile lose their earlier hope of joining the upward surge and turn into enemies of the existing order. It is quite unlikely, however, that the beginning of the second phase will coincide for the two groups. Noncoincidence of these two changeovers will obviously be the norm. The upwardly mobile may become integrated, while the left-behind ones are still experiencing the tunnel effect. Alternatively and more interestingly, the nonmobile may experience the turnaround from hopefulness to disenchantment, while the mobile are still disaffected. This last situation clearly contains much potential for social upheaval. Its possible occurrence might even qualify as a theory of revolution.[16] At this point, however, I shall abandon the matter to the historians for I must return to the tunnel effect and its reversal.

From Gratification to Indignation

As was pointed out, gratification at the advances of others arises under the tunnel effect not from benevolence or altruism, but strictly from an expectational calculus: I expect that my turn to move will soon come. Nonrealization of the expectation will at some point result in my "becoming furious," that is, in my turning into an enemy of the established order. This change from supporter to enemy comes about purely as a result of the passage of time—no particular outward event sets off this dramatic turnaround. In this respect, the theory of social conflict here proposed is quite distinct from the "*J*-curve" hypothesis, which attributes revolutionary outbreaks to a sudden downturn in economic performance coming after a long upswing.[17] Such a downturn no doubt increases the likelihood of commotion, but it is by no means indispensable. Providential and tremendously helpful as the tunnel effect is in one respect (because it accommodates the inequalities almost inevitably arising in the course of development), it is also treacherous: the rulers are not necessarily given any advance notice about its decay and exhaustion, that is, about the time at which they ought to be on the lookout for a drastically different climate of public and popular opinion; on the contrary, they are lulled into complacency by the easy early stage when everybody seems to be enjoying the very process that will later be vehemently denounced and damned as one consisting essentially in "the rich becoming richer."[18]

Semantic inventions and inversions are perhaps the best portents of the turnaround. To give an example: in the fifties the term "pôle de croissance" (growth pole), coined by François Perroux, was widely used for the growing industrializing cities of the developing countries. At some point during the next decade, this expression, which suggested irradiation of growth, gave way to a new term, "internal colonialism," which was now said to be practiced by these same cities with regard to their zones of economic influence.

The Tunnel Effect: Social, Historical, Cultural, and Institutional Determinants of Its Strength

In what kind of societies does the tunnel effect arise and gather strength? What are the conditions under which it will last for a substantial time period or, on the contrary, decay rapidly and turn into the opposite, namely disappointment, alienation, and outrage at social injustice? Answering this question is crucial for bringing our hypothesis down to earth and for ascertaining its empirical and heuristic usefulness.

For the tunnel effect to be strong (or even to exist), the group that does not advance must be able to empathize, at least for a while, with the group that does. In other words, the two groups must not be divided by barriers that are or are felt as impassable. Thus, the fluidity or rigidity of class lines will have an obvious bearing on the intensity of the tunnel effect.

But stratification according to social class is a distinction of limited usefulness for our purpose. However unevenly economic growth proceeds, any strong advance is likely to mean gains or new and better jobs for members of several different classes. One might therefore conclude that the tunnel effect will always come into being as, within each social class, those who are not advancing empathize initially with those who are. But this need not happen if each class is composed of ethnic or religious groups that are differentially involved in the growth process. Hence, the contrast between fairly unitary and highly segmented societies is particularly relevant for our topic. If, in segmented societies, economic advance becomes identified with one particular ethnic or language group or with the members of one particular religion or region, then those who are left out and behind are unlikely to experience the tunnel effect: they will be convinced almost from the start of the process that the advancing group is achieving an unfair exploitative advantage over them. The nonmobile group may thus make the prediction opposite to that implied in the tunnel effect: as a result of another group's advance, it will expect to be *worse* off. The possibility of this reaction will be discussed in the next section. In any event, it appears that highly segmented societies will or should eschew strategies of development that are politically feasible elsewhere because of the availability of the tunnel effect.

More concretely, the capitalist road to development appears to be particularly ill-suited for highly segmented societies; if it is followed there, it will require a far greater degree of coercion than it did in the fairly unitary countries in which capitalist development scored its historic successes. On the other hand, rejection of the capitalist road does not yield a ready proven alternative, for the centralized decision making typical of socialist systems is unlikely to function at all well in segmented societies.[19]

A variant of a segmented society in which economic progress becomes largely identified with one domestic segment is a society where most emerging economic opportunities are created or seized by foreigners. Once again, the tunnel effect will not prosper in such a situation. The greater the role of foreign capital and of foreign skilled personnel in the development process, the less expectation of eventual participation in it will there be on the part of the local population, including large parts of the local elites. Hence, tolerance for the emerging inequalities of income will be low, and the need for coercion to maintain social and political stability correspondingly high, even at an early stage of the process.

In passably homogeneous societies where resources are largely owned domestically, the tolerance for economic inequalities may be quite large as no language, ethnic, or other barrier keeps those who are left behind from empathizing with those who are "making it."

It seems that, once again, "to him who hath shall be given," for the country that enjoys the manifold advantages of a nonsegmented citizenry gains thereby the additional latitude of being able to develop without having to impose the serious and perhaps crippling constraints arising from the need to make all portions of the community advance at a roughly even pace.

On the other hand, the greater tolerance of these more homogeneous countries for inequality has a real and possibly fearful price. As we know, the greater the tolerance, the greater is the *scope* for the reversal that comes once the tunnel effect wears off (unless the inequalities are corrected in time). In this fashion a somewhat counterintuitive conclusion is reached: the more homogeneous the country, the more prone will it be to violent social conflict in the course of development unless its leadership is uncommonly perceptive and able.[20] Once again I must leave it to the historians to ascertain whether any empirical sense can be made out of this purely deductive proposition; it might be mentioned, however, that part of the evidence favoring the hypothesis could come not from actual revolution, or similar civil strife, but from protracted lower class alienation such as is found in Argentina, France, and Italy.

National homogeneity is ordinarily defined in terms of static characteristics such as unity of race, language, and religion. But the most effective homogenizing agent is perhaps an intensive historical experience that has been shared by all members of a group.[21] Wars and revolutions typically can be frequently such experiences, and the tunnel effect is therefore at its most potent in postwar and postrevolutionary societies. The result can be an irony-laden historical cycle: revolutions are often made to eradicate a certain kind of inequality, but after such a revolution and because of it, society will have acquired a specially high tolerance for new inequalities if and when they arise. A particularly apt illustration is the Mexican Revolution and its subsequent "betrayal" through the sharply uneven development of recent decades. Similarly, the egalitarian or, rather, "born equal" heritage of the United States—the collective leaving behind of Europe with its feudal shackles and class conflicts—may have set the stage for the prolonged acceptance by American society of huge economic disparities.

The more or less unitary character of a country is probably the most important single criterion for appraising the likely strength and duration of the tunnel effect. But other distinctions are of interest. It can be argued, for example, that the strength of family bonds has a direct bearing on these matters. In many cases, the advances of others will generate hope not so much for oneself as for one's children. The prediction that my children will have a better life than I did should improve my own welfare in any event, but it will do so with particular force if I expect my grown-up children to be living with me, to share in the expenses of the household, and eventually to support me in my old age. From this point of view, then, traditional family arrangements facilitate the operation of the tunnel effect and turn out to have some development-promoting potential.[22]

Provided it is not highly segmented, "traditional" society is generally in a better position than its modern counterpart to take advantage of the tunnel effect. Members of traditional societies are typically tied to each other by a dense network of obligations that are both mutual and flexible: it is none too clear what it is that is owed nor when it falls due. Hence, when some members of such a society advance, their obligations are apt to expand, and many of those who remain behind expect to be benefited in due course and in some measure as a result of their pre-existing, if imprecise, claims on the former. La Rochefoucauld noted this effect in a maxim that in general is as fine a formulation of the tunnel effect as I have come across: "The immediate feeling of joy we experience when our friends meet with luck . . . is an effect . . . of our hope to be lucky in turn or to gain some advantage from their good fortune."[23]

Next, a distinction may be made between various "theories of success" that typically prevail in different societies or cultures. If individual advances are attributed primarily to chance, the success of others will occasion the tunnel effect; for the next time fortune strikes, I may well be the lucky one. Hence, the belief that the world is governed by chance, ordinarily considered so harmful to sustained development, has something to recommend itself to the extent that the tunnel effect is considered a valuable, if somewhat volatile, resource for an economy attempting to achieve growth. If, on the other hand, success of others is likely to be attributed from the outset to nepotism, favoritism, or similar unfair practices, then there will hardly be any initial feeling of anticipatory gratification among those who are not participating in the division of the spoils.

It is also conceivable, though perhaps not very likely, that success of others is attributed to their superior merit and qualities such as hard work. Those who are left out would then blame only themselves for their lack of advance. They could, as a result, either simply defer to the more successful members of their community, or they might envy them for being more richly endowed, or they could try to emulate them by redoubling their own effort. In this case, therefore, the result would be rather indeterminate, and one needs more information.[24]

A further possibility is that the success of others is attributed not to their qualities, but to their *defects*. One often rationalizes his own failure to do as well as others in the following terms: "I would not want to get ahead by stooping to his (ruthless, unprincipled, servile, etc.) conduct." This sort of attribution of success is not too dissimilar, in its consequences for the tunnel effect, from the one that concentrates on the merits of those who have risen. It makes it possible, of course, for those who are not advancing to rest content with their own station in life. But it could also happen that the next time around they will change their conduct and be a bit more ruthless, unprincipled, servile, etc., than hitherto. To the extent that it is easier to be servile and unprincipled than gifted and hardworking, attribution of success of others to their faults rather than to their qualities may actually facilitate the operation of the tunnel effect.

A distinction related to these theories of success is based on the various organizational ways in which individual advances are perceived to come about. Such perceptions depend fundamentally on the decision-making system. If decision making is perceived to be largely decentralized, individual advances are likely to be attributed to chance, or possibly to merit (or demerit). When decision making is known to be centralized, such advances will be attributed to unfair favoritism or, again, to merit. To the extent that merit is not a likely attribution, decentralized decision making, which permits success of others to be explained by chance, is therefore more conducive to giving full play to the tunnel effect. It is indeed characteristic of market economies. Centralized-decision-making economic systems have come typically into the world because of excessive inequalities existing in, or arising under, decentralized systems. It is interesting to note that they will strain to be more egalitarian not just because they want to, but also because they have to: centralization of decision making largely deprives them of the tolerance for inequality that is available to more decentralized systems.

Similar considerations apply as a *given* economic system evolves in the direction of greater centralization or decentralization. For example, the tolerance for inequality can be expected to decline when a capitalist economy becomes more oligopolized and bureaucratized. An upsurge in populist sentiment has usually been attributed to the greater concentration of wealth that has sometimes been characteristic of such a period. But the tolerance for inequality may decline even without such concentration, simply because those who are excluded from advances no longer perceive such exclusion as temporary bad luck, but as an inevitable or even calculated effect of the "system."

An Alternative Reaction:
Apprehension over Advances of Others

It is a basic idea of this essay that changes in the income of B lead to changes in A's welfare not only because A's relative position in the income scale has changed, but because changes in B's fortunes will affect

A's prediction of his own future income. The principal case that has been considered so far is the tunnel effect: B advances, and this leads A to predict an improvement in his own position as well. Mention has also been made of the diametrically opposite situation: a deterioration in B's situation leads A to be apprehensive about his own, as is the case in a spreading depression. Is a mixed case conceivable? In other words, could A come to feel under certain circumstances that an advance on the part of B is likely to affect his own welfare *negatively*?[25] Actually this sort of prediction is not too farfetched: it is likely to be made in a society whose members are convinced that they are involved in a zero-sum game because resources are available in strictly limited amounts. This representation of social reality has been called the Image of Limited Good by George Foster, who claims it to be typical of many peasant societies around the world.[26] Assume the Image prevails in a community and that, at one point, a number of its citizens (group B) improve their position, while the income of the rest of the people (group A) remains unchanged. One conclusion to be drawn from such a development would of course be for both A and B to give up the Image. But suppose the community is strongly committed to it as a result of past experiences: one way of maintaining the Image is then to dismiss what has happened as purely transitory. And if the advance of group B appears to be irreversible, then the Image can be held on to only by the prediction that A's fortunes will soon suffer decline.[27]

It is in fact possible that we have here come upon a better way of accounting for what has been described by Foster and others as the "prevalence of envy" in peasant societies.[28] It may well be that when B advances, this makes A unhappy not because he is envious, but because he is worried; on the basis of his existing world view, he must expect to be worse off in short order. In other words, A is unhappy not because of the presence of relative deprivation, but because of the anticipation of absolute deprivation.

The reinterpretation of institutionalized envy, which is suggested here, can actually be seen to be closely related to the tunnel effect. In a society without the experience of sustained growth, an initially emerging situation in which one group of people is improving its economic position while another group remains stationary is probably felt as essentially unstable: either available resources have not increased, and in that case group A will necessarily suffer a decline to compensate for B's rise; or some windfall gain has expanded total resources, and in this case group *A* will soon get its proper share of the windfall. Therefore, one or the other of these two outcomes is likely to be anticipated rather than the continuation of the current situation. Which one will be picked as most likely will of course make a great deal of difference to the course of social conflict in that society. The decision could often be narrowly balanced, as on a knife's edge, depending as it does on *A*'s perception of the causes of *B*'s initial advance. This perception will depend on the factors briefly reviewed in the preceding section. But it now appears that the alternative for those who are left behind is not merely between an expectation of sharing in the advances of others and the status quo, but between expectation of advance and anticipation of decline. This situation and the knife-edge character of the decision between these alternative expectations perhaps explain why the forecasting of social conflict is such hazardous business.

Concluding Remarks

The preceding argument suggests a few summary points and concluding remarks.

1. If growth and equity in income distribution are considered the two principal economic tasks facing a country, then these two tasks can be solved sequentially if the country is well supplied with the tunnel effect. If, because of existing social, political, or psychological structures, the tunnel effect is weak or nonexistent, then the two tasks will have to be solved simultaneously, a difficult enterprise and one that probably requires institutions wholly different from those appropriate to the sequential case.[29] To make matters worse, it may be impossible to tell in advance whether a given country is or is not adequately supplied with the tunnel effect: as was argued in the last section, it is conceivable that only development itself will tell.

2. On the basis of the distinction just made, it is possible to speak of two kinds of "development disasters." The first is characteristic of societies that have attempted to develop by means of a strategy implying the arising of new inequalities or the widening of

old ones; but, in view of their structure, these societies should never have done so. Nigeria and Pakistan are probably cases in point. The other kind of development disaster occurs in countries in which the above strategy is nicely abetted for a while by the tunnel effect, but where ruling groups and policy makers fail to realize that the safety valve, which the effect implies, will cease to operate after some time. This situation has been increasingly typical of a number of Latin American countries: Brazil and Mexico have already experienced disasters, and there are numerous portents of more to come.

3. In contrast with most conventional representations, the development process is here viewed as being exposed to crisis, and perhaps disaster, even after lengthy periods of forward movement. The view here proposed necessarily allocates a decisive role to politics. Its implications for the political evolution of countries where the tunnel effect operates are obvious. As long as the effect is strong, the developing country will be relatively easy to govern. It may even exhibit a surprising aptitude for democratic forms, which, alas, is likely to be ephemeral; for, after a while the tunnel effect will decay and social injustice will no longer go unperceived and unresisted. As a first reaction, the coercive powers of the state will then be used to restrict participation and to quell protest and subversion. More constructive programs of responding to crisis are easy to conceive, but seem to be extraordinarily difficult to bring into the world.

Mathematical Appendix

Consider a society composed of two types of people, labeled A and B. We assume that utilities are interdependent in two distinct ways. The utility of people of type A, besides being determined by their own present income, $Y^A(t)$, is affected by the present income of people of type B, $Y^B(t)$, and by their expected future income, $E^A(t)$ which depends on B's present income, among other things.[30] Hence we write

$$U^A(t) = V(Y^A(t), Y^B(t), E^A(t)). \tag{1}$$

It is natural to assume that A's utility increases with his present and future income or that[31]

$$V_1 > 0; \quad V_3 > 0. \tag{2}$$

The effect of B's income on A's utility is more complex. A evaluates it in two ways—first, according to whether B's success (or failure) *considered by itself* pleases or displeases him and, second, depending on what he thinks B's fate portends for him. Thus,

$$\frac{\partial U^A(t)}{\partial Y^B(t)} = V_2 + V_3 \frac{\partial E^A(t)}{\partial Y^B(t)}. \tag{3}$$

In this expression V_2 is the pure effect of compassion or envy and $V_3 \partial E^A(t)/\partial Y^B(t)$ reflects A's concern for B's income as an indication of his own future prospects.

The text of this paper focused on the second term of (3). The first part of this term is essentially the rate at which A discounts future income.[32] The second part of the term, $\partial E^A(t)/\partial Y^B(t)$, has not been well studied. It is determined by the method that A uses to form expectations of his future income. Neither formal economic theory nor the weight of historical and econometric evidence indicates that there is any one preferred way to model the complex processes that people use to form expectations. We are thus free to speculate on the implications of different plausible specifications. Not only is the form of the expectations function not clearly prescribed, but also the signs of its first partial derivatives can conceivably be either positive or negative. If the tunnel effect is present, $\partial E^A(t)/\partial Y^B$ will be positive. But A could also feel that an increase in B's income does not augur well for him. In that case $\partial E^A(t)/\partial Y^B(t) < 0$, and possibly $\partial U^A(t)/\partial Y^B(t) < 0$, even though A is a perfectly decent benevolent fellow ($V_2 > 0$). Conversely, if A is subject to the tunnel effect but is mean spirited, then his hopes of future good fortune may swamp his envy. That is, it is quite conceivable that $\partial U^A(t)/\partial Y^B(t)$ should be positive even though V_2 is negative.

The rest of this appendix consists of explicit models of possibilities mentioned in the text. First, we give an example of a society in which everyone is made "better off" by an unequal distribution of income. Then we show how an initial tolerance for income inequality may be reversed if the benefits of economic growth are not distributed equally.

1. Preferences for Inequality

Suppose that the utility function in (1) is linear,

$$
\begin{aligned}
V(Y^A(t), Y^B(t), E^A(t)) = \\
a_1 Y^A(t) + a_2 Y^B(t) + a_3 E^A(t),
\end{aligned}
\tag{4}
$$

and that A forms expectations by averaging his income with B's,[33] so that

$$
E^A(t) = \lambda Y^A(t) + (1 - \lambda) Y^B(t).
\tag{5}
$$

Society is composed of individuals of type A and type B in the ratio of N to 1. A sum of money is to be distributed among the populace. For political or administrative reasons, all people of each type must be treated exactly alike. Let us compare the utility accruing to persons of type A from a dollar spent on each of them,

$$
\frac{\partial V}{\partial Y^A(t)} = a_1 + a_3 \lambda,
\tag{6}
$$

to that from the same N dollars spent on B,

$$
N \frac{\partial V}{\partial Y^B(t)} = N(a_2 + a_3(1 - \lambda)).
\tag{7}
$$

If we presume that $a_2 = 0$, or that people of type A are indifferent to the well-being of B, then (7) becomes

$$
N \frac{\partial Y}{\partial Y^B(t)} = N a_3(1 - \lambda),
$$

which will exceed (6) whenever

$$
N > \frac{a_1 + a_3 \lambda}{a_3(1 - \lambda)}.
\tag{8}
$$

So far we have not mentioned B's preferences. There is no reason to suppose that A's preferring that B get additional income should imply that B will not also be made better off by distributions of income to himself than by distributions to A.[34] Suppose B's utility and expectations function are of the same linear form as A's. Thus, if b_1 and b_3 are the weights B assigns to the utility of present and expected future income (b_2, the weight given to A's income, is presumed equal to zero for simplicity and symmetry) and μ and $1 - \mu$ are the weights accorded B's and A's present income and in B's prediction of his own future income, then B will be made better off if he, rather than A, is given additional income whenever

$$\frac{1}{N} < \frac{b_1 + b_{3\mu}}{b_3(1 - \mu)}. \tag{9}$$

If both (8) and (9) hold, everybody will be happier if the benefits of growth are distributed noticeably and unevenly rather than equitably and imperceptibly. It is clear from (8) and (9) that this seemingly odd state of affairs is likely to obtain when N is large, λ small, and μ large. That is, the rich must be a relatively small segment of the population who themselves do not predicate their own good fortune on that of the masses (large N and μ). More crucially, the bulk of the population must find it sufficiently plausible that their fellow citizens' good fortune will spread to them (small λ).

It is interesting to speculate when λ is likely to be small. A plausible hypothesis is that people will be confident that their neighbors' good fortune will spread to them when (i) their neighbors are not obviously different from them and (ii) the inequality has not persisted for long. This is, in part, the basis of the assertion in the text that the tunnel effect is more available to unitary than segmented societies and that relying on it for too long may lead to rising discontent, if not disaster. An example of such a reversal is given in the next section in which a more explicitly dynamic model is analyzed.

2. The Reversal from Tolerance for Inequality to Intolerance

In this section we discuss an example of the sort of process that could lead to a development disaster. As development takes place, all its benefits are distributed to B whose income grows steadily while that of A remains constant. Initially A's utility rises as he expects to share in B's bounty. As time goes on and his situation remains stationary, he becomes discouraged. Eventually his utility falls. A's utility function is log-linear so that

$$V(Y^A(t), Y^B(t), E^A(t)) = \alpha \log Y^A(t) + \beta \log Y^B(t) + \gamma \log E^A(t), \quad (10)$$

while predicted future income is a geometric average of $Y^A(t)$ and $Y^B(t)$,

$$E^A(t) = [Y^A(t)]^{(1-\eta(t))} [Y^B(t)]^{(\eta(t))}$$

or[35]

$$\log E^A(t) = (1 - \eta(t)) \log Y^A(t) + \eta(t) \log Y^B(t). \quad (11)$$

A's utility as a function of $Y^A(t)$, $Y^B(t)$, and t may then be written

$$W^A(Y^A(t), Y^B(t), t) = (\alpha + \gamma(1 - \eta(t))) \log Y^A(t) + (\beta + \gamma\eta(t)) \log Y^B(t). \quad (12)$$

We may plot the time profile of A's utility if we know the course of his income, of B's income, and of $\eta(t)$. Suppose that initially the income of A and B is equal,

$$Y^A(O) = Y^B(O) = Y, \quad (13)$$

and that B's income begins to grow at a constant rate g, while A's remains static,

$$Y^A(t) = Y; \quad Y^B(t) = Ye^{gt}. \quad (14)$$

Suppose further that A initially hopes to share in B's good fortune but grows more discouraged as time goes on. Symbolically this is $\eta'(t) < 0$. A plausible specification is that

$$\eta(t) = \eta e^{-ht}. \quad (15)$$

Substituting (13), (14), and (15) into (12), we find that A's well-being at time t is given by

$$W^A(t) = (\alpha + \gamma(1 - \eta e^{-ht})) \log Y$$
$$+ (\beta + \gamma \eta e^{-ht})(\log Y + gt) \tag{16}$$
$$= (\alpha + \beta + \gamma) \log Y + (\beta + \gamma \eta e^{-ht}) gt.$$

Differentiating (16), we have

$$W^{A'}(t) = g(\beta + \gamma \eta e^{-ht}) - gt(h\gamma \eta e^{-ht}). \tag{17}$$

It follows that

$$W^{A'}(0) = g(\beta + \gamma \eta),$$

which will be positive whenever

$$\beta + \gamma \eta > 0. \tag{18}$$

Thus, if there is not too much envy ($-\beta$ is not too large), A's utility will rise even though his own income remains static. It is easy to see that if A is malevolent or indifferent to B's fate ($\beta \leq 0$), then this state of affairs cannot persist. This conclusion follows from the calculation of the limiting value of A's utility. If $\beta = 0$, then A eventually returns to a situation in which he was just as well off as he was initially,

$$(\lim_{t \to \infty} W^A(t) = W^A(0));$$

if A is envious, then he eventually becomes infinitely miserable,

$$(\lim_{t \to \infty} W^A(t) = -\infty).$$

If A is made better off by B's good fortune, then his asymptotic utility is infinite (as he accords a positive weight to B's infinite utility). However, even in this case it is possible that his fortunes will suffer a temporary reversal. If β is not too large and $\gamma \eta$ not too small, then the equation $W^{A'}(t) = 0$ has a solution, say τ. When that τ. is reached, A's utility will begin to decline. Society's tolerance for inequality will reverse.

We hope these examples illustrate how easy it is to incorporate the tunnel effect into formal models. Many other variants are possible. It is not difficult to write down and analyze models in which the strength of the tunnel effect depends on the absolute size of B's income or on the gap (absolute or relative) between the incomes of the two classes. Similarly, models with more than two classes of individuals are simple to construct. We are aware that the construction of formal models of the content of a theory is not equivalent to the detailing of testable empirical implications of that theory. However, it does seem a useful first step.

Notes

A preliminary version of this paper was presented as an invited lecture at the University of Puerto Rico at Rio Piedras in Feb. 1972. Discussions after that lecture and during subsequent seminars at Harvard and Yale led to a number of additions and reformulations. The author is grateful to Jorge Dominguez and Val Lorwin for detailed comments.

1. For a particularly forceful statement of this sort, see Mahbub ul Haq, "Employment and Income Distribution in the 1970's: A New Perspective," *International Development Review* (Dec. 1971), 9–13.

2. See Mathematical Appendix for a more formal statement and development of the argument.

3. James S. Duesenberry, *Income, Saving and Theory of Consumer Behavior* (Cambridge: Harvard University Press, 1949), Ch. III. A clear diagrammatical exposition is in Harvey Leibenstein, "Notes on Welfare Economics and the Theory of Democracy," *Economic Journal*, LXXII (June 1962), 300–05. Leibenstein considers three possible ways in which individuals make comparisons between their income and that of others: "(1) *Pure* Pareto comparisons in which each individual takes into account his own income but no one else's; (2) the 'share of the pie' comparisons in which each individual takes into account the income distribution from a relative point of view but not the absolute magnitude of his income; and (3) the 'compromise Pareto comparison' in which individuals take into account both the absolute magnitude of their income and their relative income position" (p. 301).

The "pure Pareto comparison," where an individual's utility is not decreased by the improving fortunes of his neighbor as long as his own income does not change, is a limiting case in this scheme. There is no room in it for the possibility of a positive interaction between my and my neighbor's utility.

4. For an excellent survey and bibliography, see Thomas F. Pettigrew, "Social Evaluation Theory: Convergences and Applications," *Nebraska Symposium on*

Motivation, 1967 (Lincoln: University of Nebraska Press, 1967), particularly pp. 261–73. The concept was introduced by S. A. Stouffer and his associates in the well-known monumental study of the American soldier in World War II (*The American Soldier, Vol. 1, Adjustment During Army Life*) Princeton, N.J.: Princeton University Press, 1949). See below, note 18.

For a development of the concept in its narrower and more useful meaning, see W. G. Runciman, *Relative Deprivation and Social Justice* (London: Routledge and Kegan Paul, 1966). The wider meaning, which practically equates relative deprivation with any form of discontent, is extensively used in Ted Robert Gurr, *Why Men Rebel* (Princeton, N.J.: Princeton University Press, 1970).

5. See Ch. 7 entitled "The Fear of Envy" in George M. Foster, *Tzintzuntzan: Mexican Peasants in a Changing World* (Boston: Little, Brown, 1967); also Frank Cancian, *Economics and Prestige in a Maya Community* (Cambridge, Mass.: Harvard University Press, 1963), p. 135 and passim.

6. See, however, note 24, below.

7. See, however, Section III below.

8. See Mathematical Appendix for an exploration of this case.

9. Frank Bonilla, "Rio's Favelas: The Rural Slum within the City," *The American Universities Field Staff Reports Service,* Vol. VIII, No. 3, New York, 1961, pp. 8–9.

10. Pablo González Casanova, *La democracia en México* (Mexico: Era, 1965, popular edition), p. 133.

11. David Barkin, "La persistencia de la pobreza en México: un análisis económico estructural," *Comercio Exterio,* Banco Nacional de Comercio Exterior, México, Aug. 1971, p. 673 (my translation and italics).

12. Melvin M. Tumin with Arnold Feldman, *Social Class and Social Change in Puerto Rico* (Princeton, N.J.: Princeton University Press, 1961), pp. 165–66.

13. Fernando Henrique Cardoso and Jorge Luis Reyna, "Industrialization, Occupational Structure, and Social Stratification in Latin America," in Cole Blasier, ed., *Constructive Change in Latin America* (Pittsburgh: University of Pittsburgh Press, 1968), p. 51.

14. Lisa Peattie, "Cuban Notes," *Massachusetts Review* (Autumn 1969), 673–74.

15. For an excellent survey with particular attention to this problem, see Gino Germani, "Social and Political Consequences of Mobility," in N. Smelser and S. M. Lipset, eds., *Social Structure and Mobility in Development* (Chicago: Aldine, 1966), pp. 371 ff. It is also possible, of course, that aspirations, once aroused, will outrun achievements, but this explanation of the discontent of the upwardly mobile is far less convincing than the one mentioned in the text.

16. It comes close to satisfying the criterion the French historian Ernest Labrousse has suggested for the arising of revolutionary situations: namely, that "the vast majority of the country is united in a total rejection of existing society and of the reigning order of things." Richard Cobb, *A Second Identity: Essays on France and on French History* (London: Oxford University Press, 1969), pp. 272–73.

17. James C. Davies, "Toward a Theory of Revolution," *American Sociological Review*, XXVII (Feb. 1962), 5–19.

18. It is tempting to suggest a reinterpretation, along the foregoing lines, of the famous and paradoxical findings about the morale in the American armed forces during World War II. While wartime promotions had of course been much more prevalent in the Air Corps than in the Military Police, the survey conducted by Stouffer and his associates found more frustration over promotions in the former than in the latter. This finding has been the origin and one of the mainstays of the theory of relative deprivation. The study argued that Air Corps promotions, though frequent in comparison with those in the other branches, lagged in relation to expectations and aspirations aroused within the Corps by the actual promotions of those who made rapid careers. While other social scientists have later proposed different explanations, not enough attention has perhaps been devoted to the time dimension. The survey was taken rather late in the war, in 1944. Is it not likely that if a similar survey had been taken earlier, the finding would have confirmed the common-sense expectation that promotion morale was higher in the Air Corps than in the Military Police? Early in the war the rapid advances of some most probably reinforced morale in line with the tunnel effect; only later on, as the various members of the Air Corps reached their level and failed to achieve quite what they had been led to expect, did frustration take over. See S. A. Stouffer *et al, op. cit.,* pp. 250 ff.

19. For a detailed argument, see the case study of centralized vs. decentralized decision making in a segmented society (rail vs. road in Nigeria) in my *Development Projects Observed* (Washington, D.C.: Brookings, 1967), pp. 139–48.

20. This point is similar to one that can be made about the economic consequences of the size of countries. While the literature of economic development has—quite properly—stressed the advantages of size, particularly in connection with import-substituting industrialization, large size also means that it is possible for a large backward region to fall cumulatively and hopelessly behind—as the progressive region absorbs for a long time virtually all of the country's industrial growth and develops a modern agriculture to boot. So wide, protracted, and dangerous a cleavage cannot arise as easily in a small

country, as, under most circumstances, economic growth there either has to spill over to the poorer regions or will come to a halt.

21. This important point was suggested to me by Katherine Auspitz.

22. For other arguments along this line, see my *A Bias for Hope: Essays on Development and Latin America* (New Haven: Yale University Press, 1971), Ch. 14. The proposition about family arrangements that is put forward in the text is a special case of a more general proposition: the tunnel effect will be the stronger, the weaker is the time preference for present over future income, i.e., the lower is the discount rate. The Mathematical Appendix shows that the discount rate enters explicitly into the expression relating changes in B's income to A's utility. This is intuitively obvious: even a very strong positive effect of B's income increase on A's expected income will make little difference to A's present utility if A attaches a steep discount rate to his expected income.

23. *Maximes,* 582. The phenomenon in reverse was pointed out at about the same time by Thomas Hobbes: "Griefe, for the Calamity of another, is PITTY; and ariseth from the imagination that the like calamity may befall himselfe; . . . therefore for Calamity arriving from great wickedness, the best men have the least Pitty; and for the same Calamity, those have least Pitty, that think themselves least obnoxious [= exposed] to the same." *Leviathan,* Part I, Ch. 6. La Rochefoucauld and Hobbes both came upon these insights in the course of their search for a rigorous, if unpleasant, science of human nature. Unpleasantness of findings almost became a test of rigor and truth for them. Naturally enough, it did not occur to them that, in the situations at hand, self-centeredness has the virtue of overcoming envy and *Schadenfreude,* respectively.

24. Attribution theory, a relatively new branch of social psychology, has attempted to throw light on this area of human behavior. Experiments have been devised to study the extent to which onlookers pin the blame for accidents on those who have been involved rather than on ill fate. Apparently the onlooker typically resorts to what has been called "defensive attribution": he looks for some good reason why the accident is one of the involved parties' own peculiar fault so as to gain the assurance that the mishap could not possibly happen to himself. (Only if no such good reason can be found, if in other words the person who might be blamed is and behaves very much like the onlooker, then and only then will the latter tend to exonerate the former and blame fate instead.) On the other hand, if another person, rather than being involved in an accident, experiences a lucky break, the onlooker will tend to credit chance rather than merit, thereby gaining some hope that a similar lucky break is in store for him. Besides being unflattering to human nature, these findings

introduce an asymmetry into the operation of the tunnel effect: it will be stronger in the forward than in the backward direction; that is, the expectation to share eventually in the advances of others will be more pronounced than the expectation to follow them in their setbacks. For an experimental confirmation of this asymmetry and for references to other research in this area, see Jerry I. Shaw and Paul Skolnick, "Attribution of Responsibility for a Happy Accident," *Journal of Personality and Social Psychology,* XVIII (1971), 380–83.

25. This question arose as a result of Michael Rothschild's mathematical formulation of the tunnel effect. See Appendix.

26. *Tzintzuntzan,* Ch. 6.

27. One reason for this prediction could be *A*'s feeling that *B*, as a result of his increased wealth, will also acquire more power, a good that is generally acquired at the expense of others, and that this redistribution of power, besides being in itself objectionable to *A*, will have in time an adverse effect on his economic position. Such a feeling is likely to arise particularly if *B* comes to be substantially better off than *A*. Oskar Morgenstern has pointed to this situation as one limitation to the doctrine of Pareto optimality. See his "Pareto Optimum and Economic Organization," in Norbert Kloten *et al.,* eds., *Systeme und Methoden in den Wirtschafts- und Sozialwissenschaften* (Tubingen: J. C. B. Mohr, 1964), p. 578.

28. *Tzintzuntzan,* pp. 153–55.

29. Political scientists have described the difficulties facing the new states of the twentieth century in these terms. Whereas, so they point out, the countries of Western Europe had centuries to solve, one after the other, the various problems of modernization and nation building—territorial identity, authority, mass participation, etc.—the new nations are faced with all of them at once. See Samuel P. Huntington, *Political Order in Changing Societies* (New Haven: Yale University Press, 1968), Ch. 2; Stein Rokkan, "Dimensions of State Formation and Nation Building," in Charles Tilly, ed., *The Formation of National States in Western Europe* (Princeton, N.J.: Princeton University Press, 1975). Various alternative sequential paths are explored in Dankwart A. Rustow, *A World of Nations* (Washington: Brookings, 1967), Ch. 4.

30. Symmetry and completeness would demand that $E^B(t)$, predicted future income of people of type *B*, be an argument of *A*'s utility function. Rigor would require recognizing that the expectations of future income, which will occur over several periods, cannot always be faithfully represented by a single number. These (and other) fine points will be ignored here.

31. Subscripts denote partial differentiation.

32. From this observation it follows immediately that the greater the discount rate, the greater the tunnel effect, as observed on p. 556, note 4 of the text.

33. Those who object to these simple forms are invited to think of them as approximations to whatever functional forms they find more plausible. Since the analysis is explicitly marginal, this is appropriate. To the objection that the weights accorded $Y^A(t)$ and $Y^B(t)$ need not sum to one, it should be noted that any deviation from unity is absorbed in the parameter a_3.

34. We do not consider the possibility that either A or B prefers an equal distribution to one in which A or B gets everything. Linearity precludes equality ever being preferred to inequality.

35. Again we have chosen γ so that the weights on log $Y^A(t)$ and log $Y^B(t)$ sum to unity. Since we are about to examine how $\eta(t)$, but not γ changes over time, more is implied than a harmless normalization.

THE POLITICAL ECONOMY
OF IMPORT-SUBSTITUTING
INDUSTRIALIZATION
IN LATIN AMERICA

Hirschman was known as the chief exponent of "unbalanced growth"—the view that economies should develop by prioritizing key sectors rather than relying on comprehensive, overarching plans. By the mid-1960s, one sector that had been seen as the engine for transformation, industry, was seen by many as "exhausted" and finished. In previous years, Latin American reformers had pinned so many of their hopes on a strategy of import substitution industrialization, to build manufacturing by replacing what used to be brought and bought from abroad. After so many years of exaggerated expectations, suddenly faced with difficulties, social scientists were now despondent. A witness and partisan in these big debates, Hirschman felt that enchantments and disenchantments reflected two propensities. The first was an assumption that industrialization in dependent economies would resemble the first industrializers based on universal theories. The second was a pendular tendency of Latin Americans to swing from despondency to euphoria and back. It was necessary to have a clear-eyed view of what "late-late" industrializing was; instead of exhaustion, he posited that Latin Americans were confronted with the growing pains of having industrialized without an industrial revolution (basic social and political changes). Rather than abandon hope, it was important to develop better theories and explore hidden links (like entrepreneurship) and opportunities (like exporting manufactures) that might point to possibilities instead of failures.

—*Jeremy Adelman*

Introduction: Disenchantment with Industrialization in Latin America

Not long ago, industrialization ranked high among the policy prescriptions which were expected to lead Latin America and other underdeveloped areas out of their state of economic, social and political backwardness. In the last few years, however, considerable disenchantment with this particular solution of the development problem has set in. The present paper will survey some characteristics of "import-substituting industrialization" (ISI) in an attempt to appraise its evolution and the principal difficulties it has encountered. Some purely economic aspects of the problem will be discussed, but particular attention has been directed to interrelations with social and political life. The ease with which such interrelations could be suggested—mostly in the form of tentative and untested hypotheses—indicates serious neglect by social scientists of a fertile terrain.

To set the stage for our inquiry it is useful to illustrate, through quotes from Latin America's most prominent economists, the change in attitude toward industrialization as a cure of the area's ills. In his well-known "manifesto" of 1949 Raúl Prebisch said:

> Formerly, before the great depression, development in the Latin-American countries was stimulated from abroad by the constant increase of exports. There is no reason to suppose, at least at present, that this will again occur to the same extent, except under very exceptional circumstances. These countries no longer have an alternative between vigorous growth along those lines and internal expansion through industrialization. Industrialization has become the most important means of expansion.[1]

Thirteen years later, Prebisch wrote another basic paper on Latin America, in a sense his farewell message to his Latin American friends upon assuming his new post as Secretary-General of the United Nations Conference on Trade and Development. Here industrialization is presented in a rather different light:

> An industrial structure virtually isolated from the outside world thus grew up in our countries. . . . The criterion by which the choice

was determined was based not on considerations of economic expediency, but on immediate feasibility, whatever the cost of production . . . tariffs have been carried to such a pitch that they are undoubtedly—on an average—the highest in the world. It is not uncommon to find tariff duties of over 500 per cent.

As is well known, the proliferation of industries of every kind in a closed market has deprived the Latin American countries of the advantages of specialization and economies of scale, and owing to the protection afforded by excessive tariff duties and restrictions, a healthy form of internal competition has failed to develop, to the detriment of efficient production.[2]

If we take a look at the writings of Celso Furtado, the shift in the climate of opinion stands out even more starkly. In 1960, after a decade or more of rapid industrial advance, Furtado celebrated the resulting "transfer of decision centers" from abroad to Brazil in almost lyrical terms:

By now the Brazilian economy could count on its own dynamic element: industrial investments supported by the internal market. Growth quickly became two-dimensional. Each new impulse forward would mean an increasing structural diversification, higher productivity levels, a larger mass of resources for investment, a quicker expansion of the internal market, and the possibility of such impulses being permanently surpassed.[3]

Only six years later, after Brazil had suffered a series of political and economic setbacks, a disillusioned Furtado wrote:

In Latin America . . . there is a general consciousness of living through a period of decline. . . . The phase of 'easy' development, through increasing exports of primary products *or through import substitution* has everywhere been exhausted.[4]

Considering these two pairs of quotes one could easily conclude that we have here an instance of the acceleration of history. The phase of export-propelled growth (*crecimiento hacia afuera*) in Latin America lasted roughly from the middle of the nineteenth century until the Great Depression; and it took another twenty years, from 1929 to the Prebisch manifesto of 1949, before the end-of-export-propelled-growth became official Latin American doctrine. Then came the next phase of Latin American growth, *crecimiento hacia adentro* or growth via the domestic market. It gathered strength during the Depression and World War II, flourished briefly in both theory and practice during the fifties and was pronounced either dead or a dud in the sixties. It looks, therefore, as though the acceleration of technical progress in the developed countries were matched in the underdeveloped ones by an increasingly rapid accumulation of failures in growth experiences!

As will be seen, there may be considerable exaggeration in the announced failure of import-substituting industrialization just as, in spite of the supposed demise of export-propelled growth, Venezuela, Ecuador, Peru, and Central America achieved notable economic gains in the two postwar decades through rapidly growing exports of petroleum, bananas, fishmeal, and cotton, respectively. While *fracasomania*, or the insistence on having experienced yet another failure, certainly has its share in the severity of the recent judgments on industrialization, the widespread criticism of ISI—in Pakistan and India very similar problems are being discussed—indicates that there is real substance to the concern that is being expressed. But the rapidity of the reversal in the climate of opinion makes one rather suspect that ISI had, *from its very onset*, both positive and negative aspects, with the latter simply coming into view a few years after the former. Our inquiry will therefore start out with a brief survey of the principal characteristics which set off ISI from other types of industrialization.

Four Impulses of Import-Substituting Industrialization (ISI)

Wars and depressions have historically no doubt been most important in bringing industries to countries of the "periphery" which up to then had firmly remained in the nonindustrial category. The crucial role of the two World Wars and of the Great Depression in undermining acceptance of traditional ideas about the international division of labor between advanced and backward countries is well known.[5] But industrialization has not only been the response to sudden deprivation of imports; it has taken place in many erstwhile nonindustrial countries as a result of the gradual expansion of an economy that grows along the export-propelled path. As incomes and markets expand in such a country and some thresholds at which domestic production becomes profitable are crossed, industries come into being without the need of external shocks or governmental intervention—a process I have described as "import-swallowing"[6] and which has been perhaps more aptly termed industrialization through "final demand linkage," as distinct from the continuation of the process via backward and forward linkage effects.[7] Gradual import substitution in response to the growth of domestic markets accounts for the widespread establishment of industries which have substantial locational advantages because of the weightiness of the product (cement, beer) and of those whose market is large even at low per capita incomes such as textiles.

Over the past two decades import-substituting industrialization has, of course, no longer been exclusively a matter of natural market forces reacting to either gradual growth of income or to cataclysmic events, such as wars and depressions. It has been undertaken in many countries as a matter of deliberate development policy, carried out no longer just by means of protective duties, but through a wide array of credit and fiscal policy devices, through pressures on foreign importing firms to set up manufacturing operations as well as through direct action: the establishment of state-owned industries or, increasingly, of development corporations or banks which are then entrusted with the promotion of specific ventures.

It is useful to keep in mind these distinct origins of ISI—wars, balance-of-payments difficulties, growth of the domestic market (as a result of export growth) and official development policy—in focusing on the distinctive characteristics of the process.

Clearly, there is not just *one* ISI process. An industrialization that takes place in the midst and as a result of export growth has a wholly different *Gestalt* from one that feeds on foreign exchange deprivation. For example, in the latter situation it seems much more likely that inflationary developments will accompany the industrialization process than in the former. Or, to proceed to one of the alleged—and often criticized—characteristics of the industrialization process itself, namely its tendency to concentrate on nonessential, luxury-type goods. This tendency to give importance to what is unimportant will be present only when the primary impulse to industrialization arises out of unexpected balance-of-payments difficulties which are fought routinely by the imposition of quantitative import controls. The controls will aim at permitting continued supply of the more essential goods traditionally imported at the cost of shutting out nonessentials and will thus cause domestic production of the latter to become especially profitable.

It is easy, however, to make too much of this situation. Of the four motive forces behind ISI—balance-of-payments difficulties, wars, gradual growth of income, and deliberate development policy—only the first leads to a bias in favor of nonessential industries. The last, deliberate development policy, is likely to produce exactly the opposite bias; and the remaining two causes are neutral with respect to the luxury character of the industry. Wars cause interruption of, or hazards for, *all* international commodity flows, essential or nonessential, and therefore provide a general unbiased stimulus to domestic production of previously imported goods. The same is true for the stimulus emanating from the gradual growth of markets. It seems likely, therefore, that the role of nonessential goods within the total ISI process has been exaggerated by the "new" critics who, in stressing this role, sound almost like the old-line Latin American laissez-faire advocates who were forever inveighing against the introduction of "exotic" industries into their countries.

Characteristics of the Initial Phase of ISI

Industrialization by Tightly Separated Stages

No matter what its original impulse, ISI starts predominantly with the manufacture of finished consumer goods that were previously imported and then moves on, more or less rapidly and successfully, to the "higher stages" of manufacture, that is, to intermediate goods and machinery, through backward linkage effects. The process can and does start here and there with capital or even intermediate goods insofar as such goods are imported prior to any industrialization because they are needed in connection with agricultural or transportation activities. Machetes, coffee hulling machines, trucks and fertilizers are examples. In the textile industry, the crushing superiority of machine spinning over hand spinning, combined with a lesser advantage of machinery in weaving, has made sometimes for the installation of spinning mills ahead of weaving mills, especially in countries where a strong handweaving tradition had not been previously destroyed by textile imports from the industrial leaders.

But the bulk of new industries are in the consumer goods sector and as they are undertaken in accordance with known processes, on the basis of imported inputs and machines, industrialization via import substitution becomes a *highly sequential,* or *tightly staged,* affair. Herein lies perhaps its principal difference from industrialization in the advanced countries. This aspect is so familiar and seemingly inevitable that it has not received quite the attention it deserves. It is the basic reason for which the ISI process is far smoother, less disruptive, but also far less learning-intensive than had been the case for industrialization in Europe, North America, and Japan.

This is not the place for renewing the discussion over the advantages or drawbacks of an early or late start in industrialization.

Suffice it to point out, however, that those who have stressed the advantages of a late start have often had in mind the ability of newcomers to jump with both feet into a newly emerging dynamic industrial sector (as Germany did with chemicals) instead of remaining bogged down in sectors that had long passed their prime (as England in textiles and railways construction). But the "late latecomers" with whom we are concerned here are not apt to jump in this fashion. Industrialization is here at first wholly a matter of imitation and importation of tried and tested processes. Consider by way of contrast the following description of the establishment of new industries in advanced countries:

> Young industries are often strangers to the established economic system. They require new kinds or qualities of materials and hence make their own; they must overcome technical problems in the use of their products and cannot wait for potential users to overcome them; they must persuade customers to abandon other commodities and find specialized merchants to undertake the task. These young industries must design their specialized equipment and often manufacture it. . . .[8]

Not much of this travail occurs when a new industry is introduced into the "late late" starting countries. It is in this connection that one must be on guard against studies purporting to show that the history of industrialization is substantially the same in all countries, working its way from light consumer goods industries, to heavy and capital goods industries, and eventually to consumer durables. The apparently similar pattern of the earlier and "late late" industrializers in this respect conceal an essential qualitative difference. Even when the earlier industrializers were predominantly in the light consumer goods stage (from the point of view of labor force or value added), they were already producing *their own* capital goods, if only by artisan methods. As Marx wrote: "There were mules and steam-engines before there were any labourers whose exclusive occupation it was to make mules and steam-engines; just as men wore clothes before there were tailors."[9] But the "late late" industrializers will *import*, rather than make, their clothes until such time as they are able to set up a tailor in business all by himself. This situation forecloses, of course, for a considerable time any fundamental adaptation of technology to the characteristics of the importing countries, such as the relative abundance of labor in relation to capital. Whether and to what extent such an adaptation is desirable is an idle question under these circumstances; given the sequential pattern of industrialization, there is remarkably little choice. ISI thus brings in complex technology, but without the sustained technological experimentation and concomitant training in innovation which are characteristic of the pioneer industrial countries.

"Late" vs. "Late Late" Industrialization

The "late late" industrialization sketched so far may be contrasted not only with that of the presently advanced industrial countries in general, but particularly with that of the so-called latecomers among them. The "late" industrialization of countries like Germany, Italy and Russia has been depicted by Gerschenkron through the following propositions:

1. The more backward a country's economy, the more likely was its industrialization to start discontinuously as a sudden great spurt proceeding at a relatively high rate of growth of manufacturing output.
2. The more backward a country's economy, the more pronounced was the stress in its industrialization on bigness of both plant and enterprise.
3. The more backward a country's economy, the greater was the stress upon producers' goods as against consumers' goods.

4. The more backward a country's economy, the heavier was the pressure upon the levels of consumption of the population.
5. The more backward a country's economy, the greater was the part played by special institutional factors designed to increase the supply of capital to the nascent industries and, in addition, to provide them with less decentralized and better informed entrepreneurial guidance; the more backward the country, the more pronounced was the coerciveness and comprehensiveness of those factors.
6. The more backward a country, the less likely was its agriculture to play any active role by offering to the growing industries the advantages of an expanding industrial market based in turn on the rising productivity of agricultural labor.[10]

Of these six characteristics only the last one applies unconditionally to the late late industrializers. Special institutions designed to supply capital and entrepreneurial guidance (point 5), became important in most of Latin America after the ISI process had already been underway as a result of private, decentralized initiative for a considerable time. As to the remaining four points, almost the opposite could be said to hold for our late latecomers. Their industrialization started with relatively small plants administering "last touches" to a host of imported inputs, concentrated on consumer rather than producer goods, and often was specifically designed to improve the levels of consumption of populations who were suddenly cut off, as a result of war or balance-of-payments crises, from imported consumer goods to which they had become accustomed. Even though the rates at which new plants were built and at which their output expanded were often respectable, the process thus lacked some of the essential characteristics of Gerschenkron's "great spurt."

As a result, late late industrialization shows little of the inspiring, if convulsive *élan* that was characteristic of the late industrializers such as Germany, Russia and Japan. This is perhaps the basic reason for the feelings of disappointment experienced by Latin American observers who had looked to industrialization for a thorough transformation and modernization of their societies.

Naturally, the difference between the two types of industrialization must not be overdrawn. At least one experience in Latin America, that of Brazil during the fifties, came fairly close to the picture drawn by Gerschenkron: sustained and rapid progress of steel, chemical and capital goods industries during this decade was here combined with a "special institutional factor designed to increase supply of capital," namely inflation, and even with the flowering of a "developmentalist" (*desenvolvimentista*) ideology.[11] But what looked like the hopeful beginning of a "Brazilian economic miracle" was thrown into disarray by the political crises and related economic and social setbacks of the sixties. The gloom that pervades the Latin American mood at present stems precisely from the convergence of frustrations over the unexciting character of late late industrialization in *most* Latin American countries with the despair felt over the stumblings of the *one* country whose advance had assumed the more inspiring characteristics of the "great spurt."

The Sources of Entrepreneurship

A number of important characteristics of late late industrialization remain to be surveyed. What has been said so far permits, first of all, some discussion of the sources of entrepreneurship. As industry is started primarily to substitute imports, those engaged in the foreign trade sector are likely to play a substantial role in the process. This is the reason for the industrial prominence of (a) the former importers of Lebanese, Jewish, Italian, German, etc. origin, and (b) of the large foreign firms intent on maintaining their market and therefore turning from exporters into manufacturers. Once again, however, it is useful to distinguish between an industrialization which is brought underway under conditions of expanding income from exports and one that is ignited by deprivation of previously available imports (due to war or balance-of-payments troubles). Only in the latter situation are local importers and foreign exporting firms likely to be the main promoters of industrial enterprise. When foreign exchange income is expanding, one may rather expect industrial opportunities to be exploited by indigenous entrepreneurship. Under such conditions, the importing interests are apt to be well satisfied with their lot and activity; industrial development will run clearly counter to their short-run interests, especially when it requires the imposition of even a moderate level of protection. Some evidence in support of our distinction may be cited: in both Brazil and Colombia, coffee booms in the late nineteenth and early twentieth centuries, respectively, gave rise to periods of industrial expansion led by domestic entrepreneurs who were in no way tied to the importing interests.[12] The latter, on the other hand, were prominent in these and other Latin American countries during the high pressure drives toward import substitution which marked the World Wars and the Great Depression.

The importance of foreigners, of minorities or, generally speaking, of non-elite-status groups in the total industrialization process has on occasion been held responsible for the fact that industrial interests do not wield in Latin America the political influence and social prestige which have been theirs in the older industrial countries. Insofar as the phenomenon is real, it can also be explained by the *kind* of industries most characteristic of the first phases of import-substituting industrialization: opinions of the owners of soft-drink bottling plants or of cosmetic or pharmaceutical industries are unlikely to command as much attention as those of steel and machinery manufacturers. In addition, the industrialists of the leading industrial countries always gained considerable influence by virtue of being exporters; as such they achieved prestige abroad, acquired contacts and gathered information—all accomplishments that were highly prized by their governments. This source of influence is quite unavailable to the import-substituting industrialists who are usually aiming only at supplying the domestic market.[13]

The Exuberant Phase of ISI and Its Political Consequences

A final characteristic of the early phases of import—substituting industrialization is the growth pattern of the newly established industries. It has been suggested that

> output curves in newly established import-substituting industries have tended to be kinked, rising rapidly when exports are being replaced, but flattening out when further growth of demand has been grounded in the growth of domestic income. Profits have also followed this kinked pattern. Thus industries have moved rapidly from high profit and growth to precocious maturity, at which point they fall back to monopolistic quiescence with lower profit rates, a reduced level of investment, and aging plant and equipment.[14]

The extent to which the kinked pattern of output growth is really a fact rather than an inference from the nature of import-substitution remains to be established. After all, newly established industries have to overcome initial production and organization problems, they encounter some sales resistance due to preference for the imported product so that the early portion of their sales data may still approximate the logistic curve which has given a good fit for the time shape of the expansion of many industries in the advanced countries.[15] Nevertheless, it is probably legitimate to speak of a particularly "easy" phase of import substitution when the manufacturing process is entirely based on imported materials and machinery while importation of the article is firmly and effectively shut out by controls. Under such conditions, the early experience of the new manufacturers is likely to be most gratifying.

It is this phase of import substitution that gives rise to the often noted exuberance and boom atmosphere during which demand is easily over-estimated. In any event, low duties or preferential exchange rates for machinery imports make for lavish orders. As a result, the new industry is likely to find itself saddled with excess capacity as soon as it reaches the kink.[16]

It is tempting to speculate about the psychological-political consequences of this pattern of industrialization. Progressive Latin Americans had long hoped that industry would introduce new, much needed disciplines into the behavior of their governments. The very nature of industrial operations—their precision, the need for exact timing, punctuality, reliability, predictability and all-around rationality—was expected to infuse these same qualities into policymaking and perhaps even into the political process itself. This sort of inference was based on the nature—or supposed nature—of industrial operations at the plant level. It disregarded, however, the larger financial and economic aspects of the process which had, of course, a much more direct and determining impact on politics. Thus the ease with which new industries were installed in spite of dire warnings and often in the midst of war and depression, the rapid growth they experienced and the handsome profits they realized during the first phases made import-substituting industry appear as a new incarnation of some primary product that would suddenly erupt with an old-fashioned world market boom. Little wonder, then, that the hoped for achievement of rationality in economic policymaking and in the political process in general failed to occur. On the contrary, the "exuberant" phase of import-substitution was accompanied by flamboyant public policies which badly overestimated the tolerance of the economy for a variety of ventures, be they income redistribution by fiat, the building of a new capital, or other extravaganzas. Here we can do no more than touch upon these matters; but it may be conjectured that in their very different ways, Perón, Kubitschek, Rojas Pinilla and Pérez Jiménez could all be considered victims of the delusions of economic invulnerability fostered by the surprising early successes and rapid penetration of industry into a supposedly hostile environment.

The Alleged Exhaustion of Import Substitution

Then, suddenly, the honeymoon was over and the recriminations began. Import-substituting industrialization was officially added, as we have seen, to the long list of certified *fracasos* in Latin American policymaking. We shall now attempt to sort out and evaluate some of the elements in this reversal of opinion.

Three principal accusations have been leveled against the industrialization process as it has appeared in Latin America:

1. Import-substituting industrialization is apt to get "stuck" after its first successes, due to the "exhaustion of easy import substitution opportunities"; it leaves the economy with a few relatively high-cost industrial establishments and with a far more vulnerable balance of payments since imports consist now of semifinished materials, spare parts and machinery indispensably required for maintaining and increasing production and employment.
2. Import-substituting industry is affected by seemingly congenital inability to move into export markets.
3. The new industries are making an inadequate contribution to the solution of the unemployment problem.

In the following we shall concentrate on the first two critiques; the third cannot be adequately discussed within the limits of the present essay.

A Naive and a Seminaive Exhaustion Model

The argument on ISI getting stuck is put forward in several forms. Most frequently and crudely, the assertion is made that the process faces "exhaustion" after a certain period during which the "easy" import substitution opportunities are taken up. Exhaustion evokes the image of a natural resource available in strictly limited quantities which is being depleted; and we must ask now to what extent the image is sensible. One model which could underlie the exhaustion concept is an exceedingly simple one: at any one point of time, a country imports commodities A, B, C . . . ; the annual import volumes of these commodities are M_A, M_B, M_C, . . . Next, one assumes the existence of economies of scale such that the minimum economic sizes of plants which are to produce these various goods can be unequivocally defined. If the annual capacities of such plants are designated by P_A, P_B, P_C, . . . then import substitution opportunities are limited to those products (say, A, C, E, . . .) for which imports (the M's) exceed the minimum economic sizes (the P's).

This would be a truly naive model rationalizing the exhaustion concept, and it is perhaps too much of a caricature of what the critics of import substitution have in mind. The more sophisticated among them, at least, do realize that the first steps of ISI open up new opportunities for the establishment of domestic manufactures through both income and backward linkage effects. In the first place, the domestic production of A, C, and E creates new incomes which may enlarge the market for a number of additional final demand goods to the point where their domestic production becomes, in turn, feasible. Secondly, domestic production of A, C, and E, which is *ex hypothesi* set up on the basis of imported inputs, opens up new opportunities for the establishment of domestic manufacturing facilities turning out these inputs.

The income effect is likely to result in a convergent series of new investment opportunities. Thus it postpones exhaustion in relation to the naive model, but does not overcome it. When backward linkage effects are taken into account, however, the exhaustion concept tends to evaporate unless it is bolstered by some additional assumptions.

Again a rather naive, let us call it "seminaive," exhaustion model could be built up as follows. Industry A requires imported inputs $a_1, a_2, a_3, \ldots$ $a_i \ldots$; industry C inputs $c_1, c_2, c_3, \ldots c_i \ldots$ and so on. It seems plausible that imports of any individual input, such as $M_{a_1}, M_{a_2}, M_{a_3}, \ldots M_{a_i} \ldots$ should be smaller than M_a had been before domestic production of A started. On the other hand, it could be surmised (and frequently is unquestioningly assumed) that minimum economic plant size *increases* as one ascends to "higher" stages of production. If this is so, then we have $P_{a_i} > P_a$ while $M_{a_i} < M_A$. Under these circumstances the chances that imports will exceed the minimum economic sizes for any large number of imported inputs for A, C and E decrease rapidly as one ascends via backward linkage toward the higher stages of production.

Criticism of the Seminaive Model: The Importance of Policy

I believe that something like this seminaive model is indeed in the minds of those who speak of exhaustion. For this reason it is useful to spell it out, for as soon as that is done, it is easy to perceive where such an exhaustion model goes wrong and what are, therefore, the requirements of an industrialization process that would "beat" exhaustion.[17]

Two modifications of the model serve to make it look both more realistic and less exhaustion-prone. In the first place, some of the inputs needed for the initial import-substitution industries are likely to be identically the same (steel, paper, glass are needed as intermediate inputs in a wide variety of final demand products). As a result of this *product convergence* of industrial processes the a_i's are not always distinct from the c_i's and e_i's, so that imports of a number of intermediate goods may well be larger than the previous imports of final demand goods.

Secondly, it is of course not necessarily true that minimum economic plant size increases regularly as one ascends toward the higher stages of production. I am not aware of any systematic study relating to this point. But it is well known, for example, that automobile assembly plants deal with a number of suppliers and subcontractors for many needed components, just as a single steel plant will draw for its supply of coal on several mines. Large capacity plants do characterize the technology of a few important intermediate and basic products; but at every stage—particularly in the machinery and equipment industries which, in a sense, represent the "highest" stage of production—small and medium-sized establishments are also to be found.[18]

If we put these two considerations together, one particularly favorable possibility appears: minimum economic size could providentially be, and in fact often is, large in those industries for whose products (steel, glass, paper) the convergence phenomenon is important. But even apart from such a happy coincidence, the preceding considerations make the exhaustion concept lose the physical and predictable definiteness it had assumed with the previous models. It appears instead that the difficulties that may well dog the backward linkage process are to a considerable extent a matter of *economic environments and policies,* instead of being determined exclusively by objective quantities such as market and minimum economic plant sizes.

We have a few more words to say on the latter topics before we turn to the economic and sociopolitical reasons for which the backward linkage process may or may not get stuck. It must be recognized that one implication of the above considerations is to stress even more the importance of market size. In the seminaive exhaustion model, market size sets definite limits to the number of industries which a given country can set up. With increasing market size, an additional number of industries, *all* of larger size than could be accommodated previously, become possible. But if one gives up the idea that minimum economic size and stage of production are closely correlated, the advantages of market size can become larger rather than smaller, for a larger market permits the installation not only of an industry requiring that market, but, *in its wake,* of a host of other plants supplying that industry; the required market size of these plants may be much smaller, but they could not be established without the prior establishment of the industry requiring the larger market and which might therefore be called the "bottleneck industry."

These considerations make us understand better the tremendous importance of market size (so well illustrated by the exceptional achievements in Latin America of Mexico and Brazil) if the backward linkage process is to be vigorous. But they also lead to some interesting policy conclusions: with the seminaive model, the industrialization process is bound to stop at a given point. It can be likened to the ascent of a mountain which gets steeper all the time; the country is the mountain climber and the larger it (or rather its market) is, the higher up the mountain it gets. If this were really so, there would not be much point in pushing it up a bit higher through special incentives or promotion of public enterprise, and any infant industry protection should be uniform. But if we abandon the seminaive model, the mountain alters its shape; at one point its slope does become forbiddingly steep, but then it flattens to turn up again only much later. Under those conditions it becomes exceedingly important to climb the forbidding portion (the bottleneck industry) of the mountain as then the traveling can be continued with ease for some time. In other words, the existence of the bottleneck industries is a powerful argument for special protection, or direct promotion, and even better, for efforts to export the portion of the industry's output that cannot be accommodated by the domestic market. In any event, public policy is very much back in the saddle with this view of the industrialization process.

A further remark along similar lines. The phenomenon of product convergence can also be utilized to help a country negotiate the steeper slopes of its bottleneck industries. When an intermediate product industry faces inadequate domestic demand and cannot therefore be established on an economic scale, it is possible to canvas possibilities for setting up industries which might generate additional demands for the bottleneck industry's output. While this may be difficult in practice, the argument leads to a counsel of caution in policies directed against so-called "nonessential" industries: the demands for intermediate products emanating from these industries can be very precious in permitting *essential* intermediate product industries to be established.

Economic, Political, and Technological Determinants of Backward Linkage

While the preceding considerations ended up by stressing the importance of policy, they were still focused on the *mechanism* of industrialization through backward linkages. We must now address ourselves directly to the political economy of the process.

The importance of market size and of an adequate supply of foreign exchange in setting some limits to the process is undoubted; nevertheless, the industrialization processes of countries which are not too dissimilar with respect to these constraints still displays considerable variation so that curiosity is aroused about the role of other factors, such as the behavior of private industrialists and of public authorities.

As is well known by now, the setting up of an industry based on imported inputs has two contradictory effects: it becomes possible, and in some to be defined ways attractive, to set up industries producing inputs for the initial industry; but at the same time, the very establishment of that industry sets up resistances against backward linkage investments. Several reasons for such resistances had already been noted in my *Strategy of Economic Development*:

The industrialist who has worked hitherto with imported materials will often be hostile to the establishment of domestic industries producing these materials. First, he fears, often with good reason, that the domestic product will not be of as good and uniform quality as the imported one. Secondly, he feels that he might become dependent on a single domestic supplier when he could previously shop around the world. Thirdly, he is concerned about domestic competition becoming more active once the basic ingredients are produced within the country. Finally, his location may be wrong once the source of supply of the materials he uses is thoroughly altered. For all these reasons, the interests of the converting, finishing, and mixing industries are often opposed to the establishment of domestic sources of supply for the products that they convert, finish, or mix.[19]

Another powerful factor making for resistance has since received much attention: high tariff protection for the initial industry combined with low or zero tariffs or preferential exchange rate treatment for the industry's inputs.[20] The greater the difference between the level of protection accorded to the import-substituting industry and that applying to its imported inputs, the more will the profit margin of the industry depend *on preventing* domestic production of the inputs. For it is a fair assumption that the backward linkage industries would, once established, be eligible for a level of protection similar to that benefiting the initial import-substituting industry, and it is at least doubtful whether the initial industry can obtain a compensatory tariff increase for its own output or, in general, whether the resulting increase in costs can be passed on to the consumers without loss in sales volume.

For those various reasons, the newly established industries may not act at all as the entering wedge of a broad industrialization drive. The high customs duties on their outputs, combined with low (or negative) duties on their inputs, could almost be seen as a plot on the part of the existing powerholders to corrupt or buy off the new industrialists, to reduce them to a sinecured, inefficient, and unenterprising group that can in no way threaten the existing social structure. Indeed, like the workers' aristocracy in Lenin's theory of imperialism, these pampered industrialists might go over to the enemy—that is, make common cause with agrarian and trading interests which had long been opposed to the introduction of "exotic" industries.

The possibility that the industrialists who first appear in nonindustrial countries may not be all that much in favor of dynamic industrial development leads to an interesting sociopolitical puzzle. Sociologists and political scientists have frequently deplored the weakness of the middle class and particularly of the industrialists in Latin America, its lack of self-assertion and its failure to influence public affairs. Earlier we have tried to account for this phenomenon by some characteristics of late late industrialization. But at this point, one begins to wonder whether it would really be a good thing if the new industrialists were much more self-assertive and powerful than they are—perhaps they would then really be able to choke off further industrialization, something which generally they have not been able to do! Considering what we have called the tightly staged character of late late industrialization it may in fact be preferable for the governments of the late late industrializing countries to be run by *tecnicos,* by groups of planner-technicians, rather than by the new industrialists themselves. It has been in fact due to the regulations issued by the *tecnicos* of the Kubitschek administration that backward linkage was *enforced* rapidly in the Brazilian automotive industry in the late fifties. In Mexico, on the other hand, assembly plants had existed for decades without any progress being made toward the local manufacture of motors and parts until measures similar to those in Brazil were adopted in the sixties. Thus the resistance of the initial industrialists to backward linkage combines with other already noted characteristics of late late industrialization to enhance the potential contribution of public policy to the process.[21]

But we dare not rely on such policies emerging simply because they are needed and because we issue a call for them. Could the resistance to backward linkage be overcome otherwise than by state action? While the resistances of the new industrialists are perfectly rational, one cannot but feel that they are based on a myopic, excessively short-run view of the development process. In this manner, we can supply a concrete justification for the view of a Brazilian sociologist according to which the traditional Western, Puritan-ethnic-imbued, rational, profit-maximizing businessman is not really the type that is most needed in the situation of Latin America; what is required, he feels, are entrepreneurs who can identify themselves with the general developmental aspirations of their society, be it even at the expense of some rationality in their everyday business operations.[22]

But, once again, one cannot rest content with issuing a call for the *desenvolvimentista* entrepreneur; it would be more useful to be able to explain his appearance or nonappearance by a series of economic and social factors. This will be our next task. While it is true that backward linkage meets with certain resistances and obstacles, we have yet to inquire about the existence of other forces working in the opposite direction, that is, in the direction of making backward linkage work. This appraisal of the comparative strengths of forces and counterforces is probably the key to understanding why industrialization has been more vigorous and continuous in some developing countries than in others—long before they ran up against any barriers of market size.

As is the case for the start of late late industrialization, so will the continuation of the process through backward linkage be strongly influenced by the industrializing country's balance of payments. The opposition of the initial industrialists to backward linkage investments is likely to be considerably reduced if they occasionally experience curtailments, due to foreign exchange shortages, in the flow of imported inputs; on the other hand, the backward linkage investments require availability of foreign exchange for the importation of machinery. Consequently it is likely that some alternation of foreign exchange stringency and abundance would be optimal from the point of view of generating both the motivation and the resources required for the process. I have previously made this point[23] and considerable attention has been paid to the foreign exchange constraint.[24] Hence, it will be more useful to focus here on other forces affecting the process. There surely exist many situations in which some backward linkage investments are neither impossible in the light of foreign exchange availabilities, nor wholly compelled because of previous searing experience with foreign exchange shortages. We are interested here in the conditions that make for vigorous continuation of industrialization in these situations.

In line with our previous arguments, we posit a certain level of resistance of the new industrialists to the manufacturing of currently imported inputs. The resistance, while rational on the part of the initial industrialists, is undesirable from the point of view of the economy in the sense that profitable production of some inputs is assumed to be possible provided some average or normal level of protection is extended to them. In other words, there is room for, but resistance against, further industrialization along reasonably efficient lines of comparative advantage.

We now inquire what conditions other than balance-of-payments developments could make this resistance weaken or disappear.

The principal point to be made here is very simple: the resistance is almost wholly premised on the supposition that manufacturing in the higher stages of production is going to be undertaken by entrepreneurs *other* than the already established initial industrialists (or other than members of his immediate family). For if he himself undertakes it, most of the listed objections to the expansion of manufacturing via backward linkage fall to the ground. Thus, the fear of unreliability and poor quality of the domestic article should abate and the fear of domination by a monopoly supplier will disappear entirely. True, domestically produced inputs may have to be purchased at a higher price than was paid for the previously imported product which was perhaps obtained duty free or bought at some preferential exchange rate. But even if the increase in input costs that comes with domestic manufacture cannot be passed on, vertical integration would take the sting out of it; for the decrease of profits in one operation of an integrated industrial concern does not seriously matter if that decrease is compensated by the emergence of profits in another, newly established operation. To realize such profits the industrialist who contemplates the manufacture of hitherto imported inputs will usually have to obtain for those inputs some "normal" level of protection. It must be assumed, therefore, that he does not consider existing customs duties and exchange rate preferences as unchanging parameters immune to his will and influence; the opposite assumption is sometimes made in the literature on import substitution (with pessimistic consequences for the prospects of ISI), but it is manifestly unrealistic for most investment decisions.

If the disposition of the initial industrialists *themselves* to move farther back into the industrial structure is an important element in overcoming obstacles to the backward linkage process, a brief inquiry into the factors making for a disposition of this sort is in order.

The economist can contribute a *general* reason for which backward linkage investments are likely to be carried on by the new industrialists themselves: the mere fact that they have been earning profits and are therefore presumably looking for new investment opportunities. Once the new industries have reached the point at which imports have been wholly substituted so that horizontal expansion is no longer profitable, vertical expansion into the "higher stages" of production may well offer

the best available and, in any event, the most obvious outlet for investment funds that have accumulated as a result of the profitable operation
of the existing industries. The availability of profits from the first phase
of import substitution thus provides a generalized incentive for the successful import-substituting industrialist to plunge once again, naturally
after appropriate modification of the tariff and exchange rate policies
affecting the products whose manufacture is to be undertaken. The likelihood that the new industrialist will look in this particular direction
is increased by two interrelated factors: one, by the special difficulty of
moving into export markets, to be commented on in the next section;
and secondly by what we have called the sequential or "tightly staged"
character of late late industrialization. The industrialist manufacturing a
final demand good during earlier cycles of industrialization was likely to
call into life domestic producers of inputs and of the required machinery; therefore, once he was no longer able to expand his domestic sales
volume, he found the higher stages already *occupied* by others and was
therefore impelled to look elsewhere, including to exports, for further
expansion. The situation is very different when production is undertaken wholly on the basis of imported inputs.

The availability of profits and resulting search for new profitable investment opportunities act, as has been said, as a general counterweight
to the hostility toward backward linkage investments on the part of new
industrialists. Whether or not this counterweight will outweigh the hostility is difficult to say. Under the worst of circumstances the combination of the two forces may result in a dog-in-the-manger situation: the
new industrialists are able to prevent others from entering the backward
linkage arena, but are not sufficiently motivated to enter it themselves.

To carry the analysis a bit further and to account for the different degrees of strength which the backward linkage dynamic has displayed in
different countries, it is tempting to make a brief foray into the realm of
sociology. The eagerness of an industrialist to move into related fields of
activity instead of being satisfied with his existing operation based on
imported inputs, may, for example, be reinforced if he has the feeling
that his sons are locked into his own class and career. If an industrialist's sons are able and eager to enter the professions or the government,
there is no need for father to think about finding new industries for
the sons to expand into and to manage (preferably one for each son so
they won't fight). But if industrialists look down on government and the

professions, or if the latter look down upon the former, or, as happens frequently, if dislike and disdain are mutual, or simply, if the social distance between the industrialists and other groups is considerable, then the advantage of providing jobs for the family may fully compensate for the inconveniences, headaches, and even for minor monetary sacrifices that may be entailed by backward linkage investments. It appears once again, although from a rather different angle, that it is perhaps not a bad thing for the initial entrepreneurs to belong to a group of immigrants or of some other outsiders, with no immediate prospects of joining the established upper class or of moving into politics or the professions.

Social distance is bred by geographical distance. For this reason, one might expect that an industrialization process which, at least in its beginnings, is strongly identified with one or several centers other than the national capital stands a better chance to spill over vigorously from one industry to another than one which has its base in the capital city itself. The importance of having a somewhat isolated, inbred and self-consciously proud industrial center during the early stages of industrialization is demonstrated by the roles played by São Paulo, Monterrey, and Medellín. No similar pioneering center outside the capital city arose in Chile and Argentina, and it is perhaps not a coincidence that these two countries have provided the critics of the ISI process with far better examples of its alleged irrationality and propensity to exhaustion than Brazil, Mexico, and Colombia.

A final subject of speculation is the differential impact of technology on the comparative strength of the linkage process in different industries. When a backward linkage effect points to an industry which is technologically quite distinct from the one requiring the input, the input-utilizing industrialist is less likely to be attracted to the input-producing industry than if the latter is closely related to processes and techniques with which the industrialist is already familiar. For example, the backward (and forward) linkage dynamic may show more spontaneous vigor in the "inbred" metalworking and chemical industries than in, say, the textile industry whose inputs come in large part from technological strangers such as, precisely, the chemical industry. Thus the backward linkage dynamic may be held back at some point simply by "technological strangeness." This point is of particular importance for the machinery industry since machinery is usually a technological stranger to the industry in which it is utilized. An inquiry into the technological determinants of the differential propensity of different industries toward linkage investments could be of considerable value. To identify and then to remove this sort of bottleneck should be a principal task of public agencies concerned with industrial development.

The purpose of the preceding observations was to convince the reader that there is far more to the vigor or weakness which late late industrialization displays in various countries than minimum economic size of plants, market size and even foreign exchange availabilities. We have left the naive and seminaive exhaustion models far behind and have instead generated a highly complex "field" of forces and counterforces. If the reader feels a bit confused, we have achieved our purpose: for essentially we wished to show that the process is not nearly so straightforward and constrained as it has recently been made to look, and that it depends far more on public and private acts of volition than has sometimes been granted as well as on numerous economic, sociological and technological factors which remain to be investigated.

The Inability to Export Manufactures: "Structural" Causes and Remedies

It is hardly necessary to stress how desirable it would be for our late late industrializing countries to become exporters of the outputs of their new industries:

1. Through exports they would overcome whatever obstacles of market size limit their growth or prevent their establishment.
2. Through exports they would loosen the balance-of-payments constraint which may otherwise prevent capacity operation of existing industries as well as establishment of new industries.
3. Finally, by competing in world markets, industries would be forced to attain and maintain high standards of efficiency and product quality and would thereby acquire defenses against oligopolistic collusion and decay to which they often succumb in highly protected, small local markets.

Unfortunately, the intensity with which one would wish for exports of manufacturers from the late late industrializers is matched by the solidity of the arguments which appear to foreclose any real prospects of success in this direction.

Once again, the arguments are familiar: The new industries have been set up exclusively to substitute imports, without any export horizon on the part of either the industrialists themselves or the government; the foreign branch plants and subsidiaries, which have taken an important part in the process, often are under specific instructions not to compete abroad with the products of the parent company; even more decisive than these obstacles deriving from attitudes and institutions, is the fact that the new industries, set up behind tariff walls, usually suffer from high production costs in countries that are, moreover, permanently subject to strong inflationary pressures—hence there is no real possibility of these industries competing successfully in international markets even if they were disposed to do so.

These are weighty arguments and they seem to meet the test of a satisfactory explanation in that they put one's mind to rest. But do they?

After all, there are many industries which started out producing for the home market and eventually spilled over into foreign markets. Prior, successful acceptance of a manufactured commodity in the home market has even been considered to be a prerequisite for successful exporting.[25]

Secondly, foreign firms have been known to be quite adaptable in their manufacturing and export policies. Just as they have been coaxed by national policies to produce or procure domestically a larger proportion of their inputs, so they could be induced to engage on export drives.

Finally, even the most impressive explanation of the inability to export—the cost disadvantage of new industries set up under tariff protection—loses some of its persuasiveness when one remembers that protection of industries in Germany and the United States has not prevented considerable success of those protected industries in world markets. Industrialization of the nineteenth century latecomers was in fact frequently accompanied by both tariff protection and a vigorous export drive which threatened the previous dominant position of the old established industrial countries in a number of important markets. Again, the behavior of the late late industrializers could not be more different and it now begins to appear that we may be in need of some further, perhaps more fundamental explanations of the inability to export that afflicts them. While such a "structuralist" strategy of problem-solving may show the problem to be even more deeply rooted than had been thought, it can also uncover new, hitherto unsuspected ways of attacking it.[26]

One additional explanation of the difficulty of exporting has already been given in the preceding section. It was asserted that in view of the sequential character of industrialization, late late industrialists looking for new profitable business opportunities will frequently have the option between investing in backward linkage industries and expanding into export markets, whereas late industrialists had primarily the latter course open to them since the backward linkage industries were already in existence. Little wonder, then, that the late late industrialists decide to stay cozily at home much longer than the late industrialists who were under a far greater compulsion to make the plunge into foreign markets if they were going to expand. It would therefore be unrealistic to expect an industry to become an exporter before it has truly taken root in the country through a variety of the more obvious backward linkage investments. And the expeditious undertaking of these investments is therefore desirable not only per se, but also as a necessary way-station to the opening of the export phase.

Another structural reason for the inability to export derives from the circumstances under which resources have been channeled into the industrial sector in many Latin American countries. Industrial investments became attractive not only because of customs protection, but additionally because of the combination of internal inflation, overvaluation of the currency, and exchange controls. In effect, maintaining an overvalued exchange rate meant that the exporters of traditional primary products would receive a smaller real income than with an equilibrium or undervalued exchange rate. At the same time, the overvalued exchange rate permitted the acquisition at favorable prices (in domestic currency) of those imports that were let in by the control authorities. And since machinery and essential industrial materials enjoyed preferential status, the overvalued exchange rate acted in effect as a mechanism to transfer income from the traditional export sector to the new industries.[27]

At the same time, however, the overvalued exchange rate acted as a bar to exports from these industries. This probably was not a serious drawback and certainly was not felt as such during the earlier stages of import-substituting industrialization when exports on the part of the nascent industries were not a real prospect. But as a vigorous industrial establishment grew up in various countries one may well ask the question why a different institutional arrangement was not chosen. For example, why not tax the export sector, subsidize the new industries and do away with the overvalued exchange rate so that industrial exports are encouraged? To ask this question is to answer it: in most Latin American countries such a course would have been politically impossible. The power of the groups tied to the primary export sector would hardly have permitted so direct an assault, as is attested by the strong, permanent and occasionally successful pressures that were exerted against the indirect squeeze of the sector which Latin American monetary authorities had more or less inadvertently stumbled on. The great advantage of the inflation-cum-overvaluation arrangement was in fact not only that it resulted in an indirect rather than direct squeeze of politically and socially powerful groups, but that this mechanism was an *unintended* and, for a long time, an *unnoticed* by-product of a course of action which had the perfectly respectable objective of "defending the national currency against depreciation."[28]

Viewed in this way, the inability to export manufactures appears as the price which had to be paid for building up an industrial sector under adverse sociopolitical conditions. Should we then perhaps be simply gratified that industrialization was contrived at all, and be happy to pay the price? Not necessarily. As industrialization proceeded, the desirability of the overvaluation device became increasingly questionable *from the point of view of industry itself.* For overvaluation not only impeded exports, but interfered, in ways already analyzed, with the vigorous exploitation of the backward linkage dynamic. Moreover, in several countries, industries became sufficiently vigorous and integrated so that the help stemming from the procurement of a few imported inputs at bargain prices (via the overvalued exchange rate) was bound to be more than offset, for an increasing number of firms, by the loss of potential profits that could have been realized through exports at a nonovervalued rate of exchange. It could thus be suggested that, at a certain point, overvaluation of the currency turned from a stimulus to industrial progress into a drag on it.

It appears that the much advertised noncompetitiveness of Latin American industry may be rooted more in the failure to modify institutions than in any inability to bring down real costs. The question then arises why the industrial interests have not vigorously pressed for institutional arrangements—export subsidies, preferential exchange rates, or more radically, an exchange rate that is undervalued rather than overvalued—that would make exporting profitable. Are there some grounds on which industrialists could be basically *reluctant* to commit substantial resources to an export drive?

This question leads to a third structural reason for—or speculation about—the difficulties of exporting. It has to do, once again, with the distribution of power in Latin American societies. To stage an export drive, an industrialist must frequently make special investments in research, design and packaging; he must assemble a specialized sales force, delegate considerable authority, launch an entirely different advertising campaign; in short, he incurs special risks and new overhead costs which will be recoverable only over a comparatively long period of successful exporting. Therefore, an industrialist will consider exporting only when he can be sure either that the basic institutions and policies which vitally affect his foreign operations are highly stable or, as a minimum, that his interests will be given the most serious attention when these institutions and policies are altered.

In effect, we have just spelled out a "prerequisite" for a determined and successful export drive for manufactures: to undertake such a drive with all its risks and special costs, the industrialist class must feel reasonably sure that it can control certain crucial fiscal and monetary policies of its government. Differently put: only a cohesive, vocal, and highly influential national bourgeoisie is likely to carry industrialization beyond relatively safe import-substitution to the risky export-oriented stage. It will be noted that this assertion—the industrialists do not export because they are not influential—completes the second half of a vicious circle whose first half, given on pages 96–97, asserted that the ISI industrialists are lacking in influence because they are not "conquering foreign markets." Obviously we should not take inordinate pride in having fashioned a new vicious circle or in having identified a new prerequisite to the economic progress of the developing countries. Rather, we shall consider in a moment ways of breaking out of the circle and of doing without the prerequisite or of finding, à la Gerschenkron, a substitute for it. But we must nevertheless pause at this point in our reasoning and take notice that conditions for a strong export drive by the private sector are highly unfavorable in Latin America: in no country of that continent do the industrialists feel securely in control of vital economic policies affecting them. Policymakers positively cultivate unpredictability and distance from interest groups; at the same time, they are highly manipulative. Changes in fiscal, monetary, and foreign exchange policies are therefore frequent while communication about these changes with the affected interest groups is infrequent. These are the sociopolitical traits that account, perhaps more fundamentally than the cost-price structure of the new industries, for their poor export performance.

Having uncovered ever more cogent reasons for the inability to export, have we encountered by the same token a "fundamental" remedy? One way of staking such a claim would be to expect that, as a result of our analysis, Latin America will change the nature of its politics and that its powerholders will henceforth become less manipulative and more communicative. Unfortunately analysis is not likely to act as so powerful a solvent. But is it really necessary to wait until a trusting and intimate relationship between the industrialists and the policymakers emerges or is it conceivable that countries which find it difficult to establish such a relationship could travel an alternative road?

A radical reaction to the problem would be for the state itself to take over the foreign merchandising function. The spectacle of the state rendering difficult or impossible the performance of an important function by the private sector and then taking over that function because the private sector is ostensibly falling down on the job, is by no means uncommon. If this course of action has not been taken so far for the export of manufactures, one reason is that the importance of this function is only beginning to be appreciated. Also, state enterprise is hardly likely to be at its best in selling a wide variety of manufactures in foreign markets; for, by its nature, this task requires levels of initiative, flexibility, risk-taking and decentralized decisionmaking which it has been difficult for state enterprise to attain.

A less radical and more promising solution would be for the state simply to take an active role in promoting exports by private enterprise. As already mentioned in connection with exports from foreign-owned branch plants and subsidiaries, the state could very well tie the granting of tax and other incentives to the attainment of export targets in a manner analogous to that with which backward linkage has been enforced in the Brazilian automobile industry. From the point of view of the industrialists, such a policy would have the advantage that one sector of the bureaucracy would become committed to the export drive and could then be relied on to do battle with those sectors whose policies interfere with the success of the drive.

Quite a different solution consists in leaving alone, at first, the obstacles to exporting that derive from the actions of one's own government and in concentrating instead on those that are caused by other governments. This is in fact what is being attempted at present through the United Nations Conference on Trade and Development and its campaign for preferences for the manufactures of developing countries in the markets of developed countries. Perhaps this request can be viewed more sympathetically than it has been if it is considered as a *compensation* to the exporters of the newly industrializing countries for some of the extra burdens they must bear because of the policies and frequent policy changes of their own governments. In this reasoning, one may also discern a hope that such preferences would be temporary: once exports in volume would have been achieved, the first half of the vicious circle we have identified—industrialists are not influential because they do not export, and they do not export because they are not influential—would have been shattered. There would then be hope that government policies would become more finely attuned to the needs of the exporting industrialists who might therefore dispense in due course with the special privileges obtained from *other* governments.

The need for common markets among developing countries can also be better appreciated from this perspective. The common markets would not only provide preferential treatment for the industrialists of the participating countries; for these mutual arrangements to be durable, monetary and foreign exchange policies would have to become more uniform and stable than they have been; and such a development would be even more important than the customs preferences themselves in promoting exports from the common market countries, *not only to each other, but also to third* countries.

It is, however, precisely the prospect of less freedom of movement in monetary and foreign exchange policies which makes national governments so skittish about entering effective common market commitments.

Finally our problem could be alleviated by developments in the structure of international trade in manufactures. According to some observers, countries of recent industrialization should be acquiring a comparative advantage in certain types of highly *standardized* industrial products.[29] To sell such goods abroad may not be possible, in a number of lines, without special international market and firm connections, but it does not require either expensive advertisement campaigns or any special adaptation to foreign tastes and conditions. As a result, the overhead cost of exporting would be cut and the risks deriving from the instability or unpredictability of official economic policies would be correspondingly reduced.

Conclusion

In the preceding pages an attempt has been made to describe the varieties and characteristic features of import-substituting industrialization, and to derive from them sociopolitical consequences which in turn affect the process. Among the characteristics of ISI the possibility of proceeding sequentially, in tightly separated stages, because of the availability of imported inputs and machinery, plays, as was shown, a particularly commanding and complex role, direct and indirect, positive and negative.

Thus, the sequential or staged character of the process is responsible not only for the ease with which it can be brought underway, but also for the lack of training in technological innovation and for the resistances to both backward linkage investments and to exporting that are being encountered. The most important consequence of sequentiality, however, is the fact that it has become possible for industrialization to penetrate into Latin America and elsewhere among the late latecomers without requiring the fundamental social and political changes which it wrought among the pioneer industrial countries and also among the earlier group of latecomers. The repercussions of this situation on the industrialization process itself are ambivalent: on the one hand, the lack of political power of the new industrialists means, as we have just seen, that exporting meets with political and institutional, rather than purely economic, obstacles; on the other hand, this very lack of power neutralizes in various ways some of the possible adverse effects of sequentiality, for example, the resistance of the new industrialists to backward linkage.

In addition, the fact that import-substituting industrialization can be accommodated relatively easily in the existing social and political environment is probably responsible for the widespread disappointment with the process. Industrialization was expected to change the social order and all it did was to supply manufactures! Hence one is only too ready to read evidence of total failure into any trouble it encounters.

This paper has by no means denied the various difficulties which the ISI process is apt to experience; in fact, they have on occasion been shown to be more deepseated than had been thought. At the same time, our exploration of the characteristics of the process has made it possible to discern avenues toward continued industrial growth that remain open to the late latecomers.

Notes

A preliminary version of this paper formed the subject of public lectures given in the summer of 1967 at Rio de Janeiro under the auspices of the Sociedade Brasileira de Instrucção and at Bogotá under those of Colombia's National Planning Department and Harvard's Development Advisory Service. I am grateful to Christopher Clague, Gottfried Haberler, Nathan Rosenberg, Henry Rosovsky, Daniel Schydlovsky, Judith Tendler, and Raymond Vernon for detailed comments.

1. *The Economic Development of Latin America and Its Principal Problems* (New York: United Nations, 1950), p. 6.

2. *Towards a Dynamic Development Policy for Latin America* (New York: United Nations, 1963), p. 71.

3. Celso Furtado, "The Brazilian Economy in the Middle of the Twentieth Century," Industrial Conference on Science in the Advancement of New States, Israel, 1960 (mimeo), p. 5.

4. "U.S. Hegemony and the Future of Latin America," *The World Today,* Vol. 22 (Sept. 1966), p. 375. My italics.—Detailed critiques of the ISI process in Latin America can be found in two influential articles: "The Growth and Decline of Import Substitution in Brazil," and Santiago Macario, "Protectionism and Industrialization in Latin America," both in *Economic Bulletin for Latin America, IX* (Mar. 1964), 1–61 and 62–102.

5. Apparently even earlier crises had positive effects on industrial growth in Latin America. The following quote is instructive: "There is no ill wind that does not blow some good . . . the crisis the country is going through is tremendous—and yet this is a perfect wind for national industry. Many of our industries have had a more or less vigorous protection through customs duties. But all of this would not have been enough had it not been for the crisis of 1875 which gave the impulse to industry and for that of 1890 which strengthened

and diffused it." Quoted from *El Nacional* in Adolfo Dorfman, *Desarrollo industrial en la Argentina* (Rosario, 1941), p. 11. My translation.

6. *The Strategy of Economic Development* (New Haven: Yale University Press, 1958), Chap. 7.

7. See Melville H. Watkins, "A Staple Theory of Economic Growth," *Canadian Journal of Economics and Political Science*, Vol. 29 (May 1963), pp. 141–58, and Richard E. Caves, "Vent-for-Surplus Models of Trade and Growth" in *Trade, Growth and the Balance of Payments*, Essays in honor of Gottfried Haberler (Chicago: Rand-McNally, 1965), pp. 95–115.

8. George Stigler, "The Division of Labor is Limited by the Extent of the Market," *Journal of Political Economy*, LIX (June 1951), 190.

9. *Kapital*, I, (Wien-Berlin, 1932), 399. This passage and the previous one by Stigler were brought to my attention by Nathan Rosenberg's article "Capital Goods, Technology, and Economic Growth," *Oxford Economic Papers*, Vol. 15 (Nov. 1963), pp. 223–24.

10. Alexander Gerschenkron, *Economic Backwardness in Historical Perspective* (Cambridge, Mass.: Harvard University Press, 1962), pp. 343–44.

11. While not included in the six points cited above, support by a vigorous movement of ideas has been stressed elsewhere by Gerschenkron as a characteristic of late industrialization. See, for example, *op. cit.,* pp. 22–26. For a survey of developmentalist-nationalist ideas in Brazil during the fifties, see Frank Bonilla, "A National Ideology for Development: Brazil" in K. H. Silvert (ed.), *Expectant Peoples: Nationalism and Development* (New York: Random, 1963) pp. 232–64.

12. Warren Dean, "The Planter as Entrepreneur: The Case of São Paulo," *The Hispanic American Historical Review,* XLVI (May 1966), 138–52; Luis Ospina Vásquez, *Industria y próteccion en Colombia (1810–1930),* (Medellín: E. S. F., 1955), Chap. 8.

13. The proposition that the comparative *lack* of political power of the industrialists can be explained by the *lack* of industrial exports becomes perhaps more convincing when one states its positive counterpart: namely that the continuing political influence of the land-owning interests throughout the period of industrialization in Latin America is explained by the continuing almost total dependence of the capacity to import on exports of primary products. This point is made for Brazil in Francisco C. Weffort, "Estado y masas en el Brasil," *Revista Latinoamericana de Sociologia,* I (Mar. 1965), 53–71.

14. David Felix, "Monetarists. Structuralists and Import-Substituting Industrialization:" in W. Baer and I. Kerstenetzky (eds.), *Inflation and Growth in Latin America* (Homewood, Illinois: Irwin, 1964), p. 384.

15. Simon S. Kuznets, *Secular Movements in Production and Prices* (Boston: Houghton Mifflin, 1930). Arthur F. Burns, *Production Trends in the United States since 1870* (New York: National Bureau of Economic Research, 1934).

16. Even if expansion plans of competing firms are known all around and there is no excessive optimism, demand tends to be overestimated for two special reasons: with protection the price of the domestically produced product is going to be higher than that of the imported one; and market studies based on import statistics often overestimate the domestic market for the new domestic industry also because the statistics usually include a fair volume of specialty products which the domestic industry is unable to supply.

17. One way of staving off the exhaustion predicted by the naive or seminaive model would be to enlarge total market size, either for *all* products through the amalgamation of several national markets, or for *some* products particularly important for industrial progress, through appropriate income redistribution within a given national market. Accordingly the formation of common markets and a redistribution of income which would result in larger domestic markets for mass-produced articles have held an important place in the discussions that arose after the "exuberant" phase of ISI was over. There can be no doubt that the creation of a larger market through either or both of these moves would contribute much to dynamic industrial growth. But we wish to argue here that they are not the only available instruments or, in other words, that market size is not as rigid and definite a barrier as the exhaustion thesis claims.

18. For striking evidence on the smallness of the typical machine tool firm in the United States and on low concentration ratios in the industry, see Murray Brown and Nathan Rosenberg, "Prologue to a Study of Patent and Other Factors in the Machine Tool Industry," *The Patent, Trademark and Copyright Journal of Research and Education*, IV (Spring 1960), 42–46. One reason for this situation is that capital/labor ratios are typically low in the machinery industry.

19. *Op. cit.*, p. 118. I am quoting myself here because the critics of ISI have sometimes taken me to task for having overrated the power and automaticity of the backward linkage process.

20. See, for example, Santiago Macario, *op. cit.*, and R. Soligo and J. J. Stern, "Tariff Protection, Import Substitution and Investment Efficiency" in *Pakistan Development Review*, V (Summer 1965), 249–70. A general critique of import substitution on the grounds that the concentration on, and strong protection of, consumers goods it usually implies make for misallocation of resources, for obstacles to further industrial growth, and for a bias in favor of consumption

is in John H. Power, "Import Substitution as an Industrialization Strategy" (mimeo.), Jan. 1966.

21. That a policy of forcing backward linkage investments has problems and pitfalls of its own is shown in Leland L. Johnson, "Problems of Import Substitution: The Chilean Automobile Industry," *Economic Development and Cultural Change*, XV (Jan. 1967), 202–16.

22. Fernando H. Cardoso, "The Industrial Elite" in S. M. Lipset and A. Solari (eds.), *Elites in Latin America* (New York: Oxford University Press, 1967), pp. 96–99.

23. *Strategy, op. cit.,* pp. 173–76.

24. See, for example, Carlos F. Diaz-Alejandro, "On the Import Intensity of Import Substitution," *Kyklos*, XVIII (1965), 495–511.

25. S. B. Linder, *An Essay on Trade and Transformation* (New York: Wiley, 1961), pp. 87 ff.

26. A general plea for "structuralist" analysis of Latin America economic problems along with a good bibliography is to be found in Osvaldo Sunkel, "El trasfondo estructural de los problemas del desarrollo latinoamericano," *Trimestre Economico,* XXXIV (Jan–Mar. 1967), 11–58. For an interpretation of structuralism as a strategy for problem-solving, see my *Journeys Toward Progress* (New York: Twentieth Century Fund, 1963) pp. 210–16 and 231–35.

27. Alexandre Kafka, "The Theoretical Interpretation of Latin American Economic Development," in H. S. Ellis (ed.), *Economic Development in Latin America* (New York: St. Martin's Press, 1961), p. 21, and Celso Furtado, "Industrialization and Inflation," *International Economic Papers,* XII (1967), 101–19.

28. The policy originated, ironically enough, in an attempt to *defend* the export interests, e.g., in the case of Brazil, to maintain the cruzeiro price of coffee in the face of falling world market prices during the Great Depression. This policy led to an increase in the money supply, and thereby caused domestic inflationary pressures which would eventually result in the inflation-cum-overvaluation arrangement. Cf. Furtado, *ibid.,* p. 103.

29. Raymond Vernon, "International Investment and International Trade in the Product Cycle," *The Quarterly Journal of Economics,* LXXX (May 1966), 202–07.

THE SEARCH FOR PARADIGMS AS A HINDRANCE TO UNDERSTANDING

Though Hirschman was a leading figure in North American social sciences, he was becoming more vocal about mainstream tendencies—especially the application of analytical techniques to social contexts without much interest in the context themselves. This represented an unfortunate "cognitive style" that got in the way of understanding social realities in favor of "theoretical" preference for predictability. Two books exemplified the options in cognitive styles, one a study of the Mexican revolution by Hirschman's young colleague at Harvard, John Womack, and the other a study of violence in Colombia by the political scientist James L. Payne. Hirschman had little sympathy for the latter and reserved some unflattering words for what he saw as a disease in the social sciences, the search for models and paradigms that aim to prove theories rather than understand realities; among other things, the tendency collapsed into old failurist nostrums Hirschman was combating in Latin America, and that were now infecting North American social science. The study of social change, if it is to be helpful, he felt, should rethink the typical reliance on ex ante predictions according to laws of change and consider instead the analysis of possibilities and alternatives for social change. This at least would close the unfortunate gap that had widened between professionalized social scientists from the north and their subjects in the south.

—*Jeremy Adelman*

IN A RECENT ISSUE of this journal, Oran Young argued forcefully against the "collection of empirical materials as an end in itself and without sufficient theoretical analysis to determine appropriate criteria of selection."[1] The present paper issues a complementary critique of the opposite failing. Its target is the tendency toward *compulsive and mindless theorizing*—a disease at least as prevalent and debilitating, so it seems to me, as the one described by Oran Young.

While the spread of mindless number-work in the social sciences has been caused largely by the availability of the computer, several factors are responsible for the compulsion to theorize, which is often so strong as to induce mindlessness. In the academy, the prestige of the theorist is towering. Further, extravagant use of language intimates that theorizing can rival sensuous delights: what used to be called an interesting or valuable theoretical point is commonly referred to today as a "stimulating" or even "exciting" theoretical "insight." Moreover, in so far as the social sciences in the United States are concerned, an important role has no doubt been played by the desperate need, on the part of the hegemonic power, for shortcuts to the understanding of multifarious reality that must be coped with and controlled and therefore be understood *at once*. Interestingly enough, revolutionaries experience the same compulsion: while they are fond of quoting Marx to the approximate effect that interpreting the world is not nearly as important as changing it, they are well aware of the enormous strength that is imparted to revolutionary determination by the conviction that one has indeed fully understood social reality and its "laws of change." As a result of these various factors, the quick theoretical fix has taken its place in our culture alongside the quick technical fix.

In the following pages, I do not have a central epistemological theorem to offer that would permit us to differentiate between good and bad theorizing, or between fruitful and sterile paradigmatic thinking. My accent throughout is on the kind of *cognitive style* that hinders, or promotes, understanding. I introduce the topic by a critical look at two books that exemplify opposite styles. Subsequently, I make an attempt to delineate various areas in which an impatience for theoretical formulation leads to serious pitfalls. Theorizing about Latin American society and economy, on the part of both Latin Americans and outside observers, receives special attention because it has been particularly marked by the cognitive style I find unfortunate.

I

John Womack's *Zapata and the Mexican Revolution*[2] and James L. Payne's *Patterns of Conflict in Colombia*[3] are the two books I shall use to open the argument. They have in common that they are both by young North American scholars; both, in fact, were originally written as doctoral dissertations; and they were both published early in 1969. But this is where any possible resemblance ends. At this point I should state that both books aroused in me unusually strong feelings: I found Womack's way of telling the Zapata story extraordinarily congenial, while I was strongly repelled by Payne's book in spite of its crispness, cleverness, and occasional flashes of wit. There are of course many striking contrasts between the two books that can account for these opposite reactions, not the least perhaps being that Womack obviously fell in love with revolutionary Mexico and the Zapatistas whereas Payne's treatment exudes dislike and contempt for Colombians in general, and for Colombian politicians in particular. But the more important, and not necessarily related, difference is in the cognitive styles of the two authors. Within the first few pages of his book Payne presents us triumphantly with the key to the full and complete understanding of the Colombian political system. The rest of the book is a demonstration that the key indeed unlocks all conceivable doors of Colombian political life, past, present, and future. Womack, on the other hand, abjures any pretense at full understanding right in the Preface, where he says that his book "is not an analysis but a story because the truth of the revolution in Morelos is in the feeling of it which I could not convey through defining its factors but only through telling of it." "The analysis that I could do," so he continues, "and that I thought pertinent I have tried to weave into the narrative, so that it would issue at the moment right for understanding it" (p. x).

And indeed what is remarkable about the book is the continuity of the narrative and the almost complete, one might say Flaubertian, absence from its pages of the author who could have explained, commented, moralized, or drawn conclusions. Yet whoever reads through the book will have gained immeasurably in his understanding not only of the Mexican Revolution, but of peasant revolutions everywhere, and Womack's very reticence and self-effacement stimulate the reader's curiosity and imagination. Payne's book, on the contrary, obviously explains far too much and thereby succeeds only in provoking the reader's resistance and incredulity; the only curiosity it provokes is about the kind of social science that made an obviously gifted young man go so wrong.

Here, then, is the experience behind the title of this paper: understanding as a result of one book without the shadow of a paradigm; and frustration as a result of another in which one paradigm is made to spawn 34 hypotheses (reproduced, for the convenience of the reader, in the book's appendix) covering all aspects of political behavior in Colombia and, incidentally, the United States as well.

Perhaps I should explain briefly what Mr. Payne's basic "insight" or paradigm consists in: politicians in Colombia, he has found out through questionnaires, interviews, and similar devices, are motivated primarily by status considerations rather than by genuine interest in programs and policies, as is predominantly and fortunately the case in the United States. He uses the neutral-sounding terms "status incentive" and "program incentive"; the former characteristically motivates Colombian political leaders whereas the latter animates their North American counterparts. In plain language, occasionally used by the author, Colombian politicians are selfish (p. 70), ambitious, unscrupulous, unprincipled, exceedingly demagogic—interested exclusively in increasing their own power, always ready to betray yesterday's friends and allies, and, to top it all, incapable of having friendly personal relations with anyone because they feel comfortable only with abject supplicants (p. 12). On the other hand, there is the politician with a program incentive whose preferred habitat is the United States of America. *He* enjoys working on concrete policies and achieving a stated goal; hence he is principled, willing to defend unpopular causes, always ready to come to constructive agreements, hard-working, and generally lovable.

For a North American to contrast Colombian and United States politicians in terms of such invidious stereotypes is, to say the least, a distasteful spectacle. We must of course allow for the possibility that truth, as unearthed by the scholar, turns out to be distasteful. But Payne does not betray any sense of realizing the unpleasantness of his discovery. On the contrary, he evidently draws much satisfaction from the edifice he has built and takes good care to make sure that there will be no escape from it. At various points he assures us that Colombians are like that; that, as he put it in a subtitle, they are not "on the brink of anything"; that it is futile to expect any change in the pattern of Colombian politics from such incidental happenings as industrialization or urbanization or agrarian reform: like the three characters in Sartre's *Huis Clos,* the 20 million Colombians will just have to go on living in their self-made hell while Mr. Payne, after his seven-month diagnostic visit (from February to September, 1965, as he informs us in the preface), has returned to his own, so much more fortunate section of the hemisphere.

It is easy to show that the Payne model is as wrong as it is outrageous. In the first place, it is unable to explain the very wide swings of Colombian politics; after all, during almost all of the first half of the twentieth century Colombia stood out as a "stable" democracy with peaceful transfers of power from one party to another; throughout the Great Depression of the thirties when almost all other Latin American countries experienced violent political convulsions, constitutional government continued in spite of much social unrest.

This experience is hard to explain by a theory that holds that vicious political in-fighting, untrammeled by any concern with programs or loyalty, holds continuous sway throughout the body politic. Moreover, such a theory ought to take a good look at—and give a special weight to—the body's head: if Payne had done that he might have noticed that his stereotype, the politician with a status incentive, simply does not apply to a number of the most outstanding leaders and recent presidents of Colombia—there is no need to mention names, but it is amusing to quote, in contrast, from a recent portrait of a contemporary President of the United States: "His preoccupation seems to have been success—in this case the achievement of power rather than its use for political purposes."[4]

Supposing even that the diagnosis is essentially correct and that politicians in Colombia are more interested in the quest for power *per se* than in the use of this power for the carrying out of specific programs—what does this "insight" explain? Suppose that we find, as Payne indeed does, that those self-seeking politicians frequently switched sides or vote for demagogic measures, does this finding teach us anything fundamental about the political system, its ability to accommodate change, to solve newly arising problems, to assure peace, justice, and development? It does nothing of the sort, but at best leaves us with the proposition, which incidentally is both platitudinous and wrong, that if the politicians are vicious, the ensuing politics are likely to be vicious too!

Let us pass now from the paradigms of James Payne to John Womack, who has rigorously excluded from his universe any semblance of a paradigm. It is of course impossible to do justice to his narrative. I shall refer here only to one particular turn of the events he describes in order to show how he invites speculation and thereby contributes to the possibility of understanding.

It has perhaps not been sufficiently remarked that the book has *two* protagonists: Zapata dominates the action during the first nine chapters, but in the important last two chapters (80 pages) the leading figure is Gildardo Magaña who became Zapata's ranking secretary after mid-1917 and, after a brief fight for the succession, the chief of the Zapatista movement following Zapata's death in April, 1919. Womack honors Magaña with one of his too-rare character portraits: "From these stresses [of his youth] Gildardo Magaña somehow emerged strong and whole. What he had learned was to mediate: not to compromise, to surrender principle and to trade concessions, but to detect reason in all claims in conflict, to recognize the particular legitimacy of each, to sense where the grounds of concord were, and to bring contestants into harmony there. Instinctively he thrived on arguments, which he entered not to win but to conciliate" (p. 290).

Womack then relates the exploits of Magaña as a resourceful negotiator of ever new alliances and contrasts him with the rigid and sectarian Palafox, Zapata's earlier principal secretary, who "seemed in retrospect the individual responsible for the Zapatistas' present plight—the man they could blame for their disastrous involvement with Villa in 1914, their alienation of worthy chiefs in the constitutionalist party, and their abiding reputation as the most intransigent group in the revolutionary movement" (p. 306).

After the murder of Zapata, Magaña maneuvered tactfully and successfully among the various chiefs. After six months, the succession crisis was over and Magaña was recognized as commander-in-chief, with the movement virtually intact. Womack then traces the complex events through which the Zapatistas, as he puts it in the title of his last chapter, "Inherit Morelos"—that is manage, by alternately fighting and negotiating and by backing Obregón at the right moment, to pass from outlaws into local administrators and members of a national coalition. "So ended the year 1920, in peace, with populist agrarian reform instituted as a national policy, and with the Zapatista movement established in Morelos politics. In the future through thick and thin these achievements would last. This was the claim Zapata, his chiefs, and their volunteers had forced, *and Magaña had won and secured*" (p. 369; italics added).

Twice Womack implies that this outcome was due not only to the presence of Magaña, but perhaps also to the absence of Zapata from the scene. There is first the "extraordinary maneuver" by which Magaña offered the Carranza government the Zapatistas' support when United States intervention threatened in the Jenkins case in 1919. Womack says here flatly, "Had Zapata lived, Zapatista strategy could not have been so flexible" (p. 348). Then again at the celebration of Obregón's victory, on June 2, 1920, "twenty thousand Agua Prieta partisans marched in review through the Zócalo, among them the forces from Morelos. And watching with the honored new leaders from a balcony of the Palacio National . . . stood the squat, swarthy de la O, frowning into the sun. From an angle he looked almost like Zapata, dead now for over a year. (If de la O had been killed and Zapata had lived, Zapata would probably have been there in his place, with the same uncomfortable frown, persuaded by Magaña to join the boom for Obregón but probably worrying, as Magaña was not, about when he might have to revolt again.)" (p. 365).

Out of these bits and pieces, there emerges a proposition or hypothesis that must have been on Womack's mind, but that he allows the reader to formulate: did the comparative success of the Morelos uprising within the Mexican Revolution rest on the *alternating* leadership, first of the charismatic, revolutionary Zapata and then of the skillful, though highly principled, negotiator Magaña? And what are the "lessons" of this story for other revolutions and, in particular, for revolutionary movements that are confined to a limited portion or sector of a nation-state?

The historian is probably ambivalent about such questions. He revels in the uniqueness of the historical event, yet he constantly intimates that history holds the most precious lessons. And I believe he is right on both counts! Perhaps the rest of this paper will show why this is not a self-contradictory position.

II

First let me return briefly to the comparison of Payne and Womack. What strikes the reader of the two books most is, as I said before, the difference in cognitive style: Payne, from the first page to the last, breathes brash confidence that he has achieved complete understanding of his subject, whereas Womack draws conclusions with the utmost diffidence and circumspection. His respect for the autonomy of the actors whose deeds he recounts is what gives his book its special appeal and probably contributed to the spectacular accolade he received from Carlos Fuentes in the *New York Review of Books*.[5] For it is today a most unusual restraint. I believe that the countries of the Third World have become fair game for the model-builders and paradigm-molders, to an intolerable degree. During the nineteenth century several "laws" were laid down for the leading industrial countries whose rapid development was disconcerting to numerous thinkers who were strongly affected by what Flaubert called "la rage de vouloir conclure."[6] Having been proven wrong by the unfolding events in almost every instance, the law-makers then migrated to warmer climes, that is, to the less developed countries. And here they really came into their own. For the less developed, dependent countries had long been objects of history—so that to treat them as objects of iron laws or rigid models from whose working there is no escape came naturally to scholars who turned their attention to them. Soon we were witnesses to a veritable deluge of paradigms and models, from the vicious circle of poverty, low-level equilibrium traps, and uniform stage sequences of the economist, to the traditional or non-achievement-oriented or status-hungry personality of the sociologist, psychologist, or political scientist. A psychologist may find it interesting some day to inquire whether these theories were inspired primarily by compassion or by contempt for the underdeveloped world. The result, in any case, is that the countries of Latin America, for example, appear to any contemporary, well-read observer far more constrained than, say, the United States or France or the USSR. Latin American societies seem somehow less complex and their "laws of movement" more intelligible, their medium-term future more predictable or at least formulable in terms of clearcut simple alternatives (such as "reform or revolution?"), and their average citizens more reducible to one or a very few stereotypes. Of course, all of this is so exclusively because our paradigmatic thinking makes it so. Mr. Payne is merely the latest in a long line of "law"-makers, model-builders, and paradigm-molders who have vied with one another in getting an iron grip on Latin American reality. And it must now be said that Latin American social scientists have themselves made an important contribution to this headlong rush toward the all-revealing paradigm.

Elsewhere I have described as "the age of self-incrimination" one phase of the efforts of Latin Americans at understanding their own reality and the lag of their countries behind Europe and the United States. Incidentally, traces of this phase can be found in a few contemporary Latin American intellectuals, and they, jointly with their bygone confrères, provide Payne with some telling quotations about the despicable character of Colombian politicians and politics. By and large, the phase has fortunately passed; it has, however, been replaced by a somewhat related phase that might be called the age of the *action-arousing gloomy vision*: on the basis of some model or paradigm, the economic and social reality of Latin America is explained and the laws of movement of economy and society are formulated in such a way that current trends (of terms of trade, or of income distribution, or of population growth) are shown to produce either stagnation or, more usually, deterioration and disaster. The art of statistical projection has made a potent contribution to this type of forecast, which is then supposed to galvanize men into action designed to avert the threatened disaster through some fairly fundamental "structural changes."

Now I believe that this strategy for socioeconomic change has sometimes been and can on occasion again be extremely useful in just this way. But for several reasons I would caution against the exclusive reliance on it that has recently characterized Latin American social and economic thought.

There is a world of difference, by the way, between this action-arousing gloomy vision and the Marxian perspective on capitalist evolution. In the Marxian perspective, events in the absence of revolution were not at all supposed to move steadily downhill. On the contrary, capitalist development, while punctuated by crises and accompanied by increasing misery of the proletariat, was nevertheless expected to be going forward apace. It was in fact the genius of Marxism—which explains a large part of its appeal—that it was able to view both the advances and the setbacks of economic development under the capitalist system as helping toward its eventual overthrow.

My first criticism of the vision ties in directly with my dislike of paradigms laying down excessive constraints on the conceivable moves of individuals and societies. Why should all of Latin America find itself constantly impaled on the horns of some fateful and unescapable dilemma ? Even if one is prepared to accept Goldenweiser's "principle of limited possibilities" in a given environment, any theory or model or paradigm propounding that there are only two possibilities—disaster or one particular road to salvation—should be *prima facie* suspect. After all, there *is*, at least temporarily, such a place as purgatory!

The second reason for which I would advocate a de-emphasis of the action-arousing gloomy vision is that it creates more gloom than action. The spread of gloom is certain and pervasive, but the call to action may or may not be heard. And since the theory teaches that in the normal course of events things will be increasingly unsatisfactory, it is an invitation *not* to watch out for possible positive developments. On the contrary, those imbued with the gloomy vision will attempt to prove year by year that Latin America is going from bad to worse; a year like 1968— and this may hold for 1969 as well—when the economic performance of the three large and of several small countries was little short of brilliant, will come as a distinct embarrassment.

Frequently, of course, the theories I am criticizing are the result of wishful thinking: wouldn't it be reassuring if a society that has been unable to meet some standard of social justice or if an oppressive political regime were *ipso facto* condemned to economic stagnation and deterioration? For that very reason we should be rather on our guard against any theory purporting to *prove* what would be so reassuring.

But the propensity to see gloom and failure everywhere is not engendered only by the desire to reprove further an oppressive regime or an unjust society. It may also be rooted in the fact that one has come to expect his country to perform poorly because of its long history of backwardness and dependence; hence any evidence that the country may possibly be doing better or may be emerging from its backwardness is going to be dissonant with previous cognitions and is therefore likely to be suppressed; on the contrary, evidence that nothing at all has changed will be picked up, underlined, and even greeted, for it does not necessitate any change in the preexisting cognitions to which one has become comfortably adjusted. This is so because people who have a low self-concept and expect failure apparently feel some discomfort when they suddenly perform well, as psychologists have shown.[7] In this manner, social psychology provides a clue to a Latin American phenomenon that has long puzzled me, yet has struck me with such force that I have invented a name for it—the "failure complex" or "fracasomania."

Finally the paradigm-based gloomy vision can be positively harmful.

When it prevails, hopeful developments either will be not perceived at all or will be considered exceptional and purely temporary. In these circumstances, they will not be taken advantage of as elements on which to build. To give an example: the rise of the fishmeal industry in Peru and the similarly spectacular growth of banana planting in Ecuador from about 1950 to the mid-sixties contradicted the doctrine that the era of export-promoted growth had ended in Latin America. As a result, economists first ignored these booms, then from year to year predicted their imminent collapse. It is quite possible that particularly the latter attitude held down the portion of the bonanza that the two countries might otherwise have set aside for longer-term economic and social capital formation; for why bother to exert oneself and, in the process, antagonize powerful interests if the payoff is expected to be so limited and short-lived? More recently, another theory of gloom has been widely propagated: it seems that now the opportunities for import-substituting industrialization have also become "exhausted" even though it can be argued that, just as earlier in the case of *desarrollo hacia afuera,* there is still much life left in *desarrollo hacia adentro.*[8] Again, if the exhaustion thesis is wholly accepted it may weaken the search for and prevent the discovery of new industrial opportunities.

In all these matters I would suggest a little more "reverence for life," a little less straitjacketing of the future, a little more allowance for the unexpected—and a little less wishful thinking. This is simply a matter, once again, of cognitive *style.* With respect to actual socioeconomic analysis, I am of course not unaware that without models, paradigms, ideal types, and similar abstractions we cannot even start to think. But cognitive style, that is, the kind of paradigms we search out, the way we put them together, and the ambitions we nurture for their powers—all this can make a great deal of difference.

III

In trying to spell out these notions in greater detail I shall now make three principal points. In the first place, I shall explain why the gloomy vision is in a sense the first stage of any reflections about a backward reality and shall make a plea for not getting stuck in that stage. I shall then attempt to show that in evaluating the broader social and political consequences of some ongoing event we must be suspicious of paradigms that pretend to give a clearcut answer about the desirable or undesirable nature of these consequences. And finally I shall suggest that large-scale social change typically occurs as a result of a unique constellation of highly disparate events and is therefore amenable to paradigmatic thinking only in a very special sense.

The initial effort to understand reality will almost inevitably make it appear more solidly entrenched than before. The immediate effect of social analysis is therefore to convert the real into the rational or the contingent into the necessary. Herein, rather than in any conservatism of "bourgeois" social scientists, probably lies the principal explanation of that much commented-upon phenomenon—the conservative bias of social science in general, and of functional analysis in particular. This very conservatism takes, however, a strange turn when the target of the social scientist is a society that is viewed *from the outset* as backward or unjust or oppressive. For analysis will then make it appear, at least to start with, that the backwardness, injustice, and oppression are in reality far more deep-rooted than had been suspected. This is the origin of all the vicious-circle and vicious-personality theories that seem to make any change impossible in the absence of either revolution, highly competent central planning with massive injection of foreign aid, or massive abduction of the young generation so that it may be steeped elsewhere in creativity and achievement motivation.[9] Interestingly enough, then, the same analytical turn of mind that leads to a conservative bias in the case of a society that we approach *without* a strong initial commitment to change, leads to a revolutionary or quasi-revolutionary stance in the case of societies that are viewed from the outset as unsatisfactory. In the case of the former, the analyst, like the ecologist, often becomes enamored of all the fine latent functions he uncovers, whereas in the latter case he despairs of the possibility of change (except for the most massive and revolutionary varieties) because of all the interlocking vicious circles he has come upon.

Fortunately these initial effects of social science analysis wear off after a while. In the case of the backward countries, the realization will dawn that certain so-called attributes of backwardness are not necessarily obstacles, but can be lived with and sometimes can be turned into positive assets. I have elsewhere attempted to bring together the accumulating evidence for this sort of phenomenon.[10] This evidence, then, should make us a bit wary when *new* vicious circles or *new* development-obstructing personality types or *new* deadends are being discovered. Though such discoveries are bound to occur and can be real contributions to understanding, they carry an obligation to look for ways in which they may play not a reinforcing but a neutral or debilitating role in so far as system maintenance is concerned. Perhaps social scientists could pass a rule, such as has long existed in the British Parliament, by which an M.P. proposing a new item of public expenditure must also indicate the additional revenue through which he expects the nation to finance it. Similarly it might be legislated by an assembly of social scientists that anyone who believes he has discovered a new obstacle to development is under an obligation to look for ways in which this obstacle can be overcome or can possibly be lived with or can, in certain circumstances, be transformed into a blessing in disguise.

IV

A related element of the cognitive style I am advocating derives from the recognition of one aspect of the unfolding of social events that makes prediction exceedingly difficult and contributes to that peculiar *open-endedness* of history that is the despair of the paradigm-obsessed social scientist. Situations in which the expertise of the social scientist is solicited frequently have the following structure: some new event or bundle of events such as industrialization, urbanization, rapid population growth, etc., has happened or is happening before our eyes, and we would like to know what its consequences are for a number of social and political system characteristics, such as integration of marginal or oppressed groups, loss of authority on the part of traditional elites, political stability or crisis, likely level of violence or of cultural achievement, and so on. Faced with the seemingly reasonable demand for enlightenment on the part of the layman and the policy-maker, and propelled also by his own curiosity, the social scientist now opens his paradigm-box to see how best to handle the job at hand. To his dismay, he then finds, *provided he looks carefully,* that he is faced with an embarrassment of riches: various available paradigms will produce radically different answers. The situation can be compared, in a rough way, with the quandary the forecasting economist has long experienced: the magnitudes that are of most interest to the policy-makers, such as the prospective deficit or surplus in the balance of payments or the budget, or the inflationary or deflationary gap, or the rate of unemployment, are usually—and maddeningly—*differences* between gross magnitudes. Hence even if the gross magnitudes are estimated with an acceptable margin of error, the estimate of the difference may be off by a very large percentage and may easily be even of the wrong sign. The hazards in forecasting qualitative social events on the basis of perfectly respectable and reliable paradigms can be rather similar. Take the question: what is the effect of industrialization and economic development on a society's propensity for civil war, or for external adventure, or for genocide, or for democracy? As with the effect, say, of accelerated growth on the balance of payments, the answer must be: it depends on the *balance* of the contending forces that are set in motion. Industrialization creates new tensions, but may allay old ones; it may divert the minds of the elite from external adventure while creating new capabilities for such adventure, and so forth. Thus the outcome is here also a *difference* whose estimate is necessarily subject to a particularly high degree of error. This ambiguous situation, incidentally, characterizes also less crucial, more "middle-range" causal relationships. An example is the effect of bigness and diversity of an organization on innovation. As James Q. Wilson has argued, bigness and diversity increase the probability that members will conceive of and propose major innovations; but they also increase the probability that any one innovation that is proposed will be turned down. Again the net effect is in doubt.[11]

Wilson's dilemma is the sort of cognitive style in paradigmatic thinking that is not often met with; ordinarily social scientists are happy enough when they have gotten hold of *one* paradigm or line of causation. As a result, their guesses are often farther off the mark than those of the experienced politician whose intuition is more likely to take a variety of forces into account.

V

Finally, the ability of paradigmatic thinking to illuminate the paths of change is limited in yet another, perhaps more fundamental way. In the context of most Latin American societies, many of us are concerned with the bringing about of *large-scale* change to be carried through in a fairly brief period of time. But ordinarily the cards are stacked so much against the accomplishment of large-scale change that when it happens, be it a result of revolution or reform or some intermediate process, it is bound to be an unpredictable and nonrepeatable event, unpredictable because it took the very actors by surprise and nonrepeatable because once the event has happened everybody is put on notice and precautions will be taken by various parties so that it won't happen again. The uniqueness and scientific opaqueness of the large-scale changes that occur when history "suddenly accelerates" have often been remarked upon. Womack brings them out as well as anyone in his narrative of the Mexican Revolution. I shall invoke the authority of two recent commentators belonging to rather different camps. The first is the anthropologist Max Gluckman, who addresses himself to "radical change" after having defended anthropology against the charge that it is not interested in change. He writes, "The source of radical change escapes these analyses [of other kinds of change]. Perhaps this is inevitable because social anthropology aims to be scientific. Scientific method cannot deal with unique complexes of many events. The accounts of the actual course of events which produce change therefore necessarily remain historical narratives. . . ."[12]

Perhaps a more significant witness, because as a Marxist he should be an inveterate paradigm-lover, is Louis Althusser. In his remarkable essay, "Contradiction and Over-determination," Althusser makes much of some striking statements of Lenin's about the unique constellation of events that made possible the Russian Revolution of 1917. The key passage from Lenin is: "If the revolution has triumphed so rapidly it is exclusively because, as a result of a historical situation of extreme originality, a number of completely distinct currents, a number of totally heterogeneous class interests, and a number of completely opposite social and political tendencies have become fused with remarkable coherence."[13]

On the basis of Lenin's testimony Althusser then proceeds to explain that revolutions never arise purely out of the basic economic contradictions that Marx stressed, but only when these contradictions are "fused" in some unique manner with a number of other determinants. This fusion or embedding is the phenomenon he calls "overdetermination" of revolutions. Actually this is a poor term (as he himself recognizes) for it could imply that, had one of the many circumstantial factors not been present, the revolution would still have taken place.

But the whole context of the essay, and certainly the quotations from Lenin, exclude this interpretation. On the contrary, it is quite clear that even with all these converging elements the revolution won by an exceedingly narrow margin. *Thus, while a surprising number of heterogeneous elements almost miraculously conspired to bring the revolution about, every single one of them was still absolutely indispensable to its success.* Uniqueness seems a better term for this phenomenon than overdetermination.

Incidentally, this interpretation of revolutions undermines the revolutionary's usual critique of the advocacy of reform. This critique is generally based on the *high degree of improbability* that a ruling group will ever tolerate or even connive at the elimination or destruction of its own privileges; the only way to achieve this end is by smashing the "system" through revolutionary assault. But with the view of revolutions as overdetermined or unique events, it turns out to be a toss-up which form of large-scale change is more unlikely—so we may as well be on the lookout for whatever rare openings in either direction appear on the horizon.

In sum, he who looks for large-scale social change must be possessed, with Kierkegaard, by "the passion for what is possible" rather than rely on what has been certified as probable by factor analysis.

This view of large-scale social change as a unique, nonrepeatable, and *ex ante* highly improbable complex of events is obviously damaging to the aspirations of anyone who would explain and predict these events through "laws of change." Once again, there is no denying that such "laws" or paradigms can have considerable utility. They are useful for the apprehending of many elements of the complex and often are stimuli to action before the event and indispensable devices for achieving a beginning of understanding after the event has happened. That is much but that is all. The architect of social change can never have a reliable blueprint. Not only is each house he builds different from any other that was built before, but it also necessarily uses new construction materials and even experiments with untested principles of stress and structure. Therefore what can be most usefully conveyed by the builders of one house is an understanding of the experience that made it at all possible to build under these trying circumstances. It is, I believe, in this spirit that

Womack makes that, at first sight rather shocking, statement, "the truth of the revolution in Morelos is in the feeling of it." Perhaps he means not only the truth, but also the principal lesson.

Notes

The substance of this paper was originally presented at a Conference on Social Science Research and Political Change in Latin America organized by the Centro de investigaciones sociopolíticas para América Latina (CISAL) at Pacific Grove, California, May 9–11, 1969. It was written while the author was a Fellow at the Center for Advanced Study in the Behavioral Sciences, Stanford, California. David Riesman contributed extensive comments.

1. Oran R. Young, "Professor Russett: Industrious Tailor to a Naked Emperor," *World Politics,* XXI (April 1969), 489–90.

2. New York.

3. New Haven and London.

4. Nora Beloff and Michael Davie, "Getting to Know Mr. Nixon," *The Observer,* February 23, 1969.

5. March 13, 1969.

6. I have long looked for a good translation of this key concept into English. It now strikes me that an apt, if free, rendering of Flaubert's meaning would be "the compulsion to theorize"—which is the subject and might have been the title of the present paper.

7. Elliott Aronson, "Dissonance Theory: Progress and Problems," in R. P. Abelson and others, eds., *Theories of Cognitive Consistency: A Source Book* (Chicago 1968), 24.

8. See my article, "The Political Economy of Import-Substituting Industrialization in Latin America," *Quarterly Journal of Economics,* LXXXII (February 1968), 1–32. The Spanish terms *desarrollo hacia afuera* and *desarrollo hacia adentro* are convenient shorthand expressions for growth through the expansion of exports and of the domestic market, respectively.

9. It is only fair to note that, in his more recent work on achievement motivation, David McClelland has changed his earlier views on these matters. Thus he writes (after having given cogent reasons for doing so): "To us it is no longer a self-evident truth that it is easier to produce long-range personality transformations in young children than it is in adults." David C. McClelland and David G. Winter, *Motivating Economic Achievement* (New York 1969), 356.

10. "Obstacles to Development: A Classification and a Quasi-Vanishing Act," *Economic Development and Cultural Change,* XIII (July 1965), 385–93.

11. James Q. Wilson, "Innovation in Organization: Notes Toward a Theory," in James D. Thompson, ed., *Approaches to Organizational Design* (Pittsburgh 1966), 193–218.

12. *Politics, Law and Ritual in Tribal Society* (Oxford 1965), 286.

13. As quoted in Althusser, *Pour Marx* (Paris 1967), 98.

A GENERALIZED LINKAGE APPROACH TO DEVELOPMENT, WITH SPECIAL REFERENCE TO STAPLES

Hirschman had written an influential book in 1958 called *The Strategy of Economic Development*. There he proposed that growth sectors could change the rest of the economy through "linkage effects." This was a powerful analytical device, and economists and economic historians ran with it—some going so far as to tout it as a generalized "theory." Some even went so far as to show that the absence of linkages in dependent economies was the cause of underdevelopment. By 1976 there was a full-blown debate over whether development had led to underdevelopment in the periphery. For Hirschman, engaged in deep discussions with Latin American scholars over the causes of authoritarianism, and ever the skeptic of grand claims, this was a chance to return to his own coinage of linkage effects to offer some clarifications and expansions, especially in relation to how primary exports, "staples" shaped development. Refining what he called "micro-Marxism"—to examine the local, smaller-scale fusions of technology and production that had larger-scale social effects—he laid out a complex inventory of linkage effects. Some were even more than just economic; they could be social and political as well. The result was the expansion of variables that could account for the varieties of pathways to capitalist development.

—*Jeremy Adelman*

Theorizing on Economic Development
in Historical Perspective

The career of development economics in the last twenty-five years illustrates one of the crucial differences between the natural and the social sciences. In the natural sciences, as Thomas Kuhn has shown, the formulation of a new paradigm is followed by an extended period in which the paradigm is fully accepted and the labors of "normal science" are devoted to its verification, application, and further extension. In the social sciences, on the other hand, the enunciation of a new paradigm not only gives rise to similar sympathetic labors, but is often followed almost immediately by a persistent onslaught of qualification, criticism, and outright demolition that is very much part of normal social science. This situation explains the distinctive intellectual climate of the social sciences: here the confident belief in a genuine cumulative growth of knowledge, so characteristic of the natural sciences, hardly ever has a chance to arise.

The story of development economics since 1950 is a case in point: it tells of progress on the condition that intellectual progress is defined as the gradual loss of certainty, as the slow mapping out of the extent of our ignorance, which was previously hidden by an initial certainty parading as paradigm. The main purpose of the present paper is not to trace the progressive disintegration of the initial paradigm; it is rather to build on one specific critical approach that was elaborated in the course, and for the purpose, of this disintegration. Nevertheless, if that approach is to be extended, a brief account of the movement of ideas within which it originated is perhaps a useful prologue.

From the point of view of intellectual history, one of the important, though hardly ever mentioned, dates in the emergence of development economics was the publication, in 1948–49, of two definitive articles by Paul Samuelson on the pure theory of international trade.[1] The articles proved that under certain largely traditional assumptions (no factor movements, zero transport costs, etc.) free trade could be relied on to equalize not the relative but the absolute factor prices in the various trading countries and that trade could thus function as a perfect substitute for the movement of factors of production across national borders. The classical theory of international trade has of course long taught that trade could lead to mutual gains for all trading countries, but Samuelson's results were much stronger and pointed to trade as a potential force toward the equalization of incomes around the world.

This brilliant theoretical capstone of the classical and neoclassical theory was put into place just as consciousness of the persistent and widening international inequality of incomes was becoming acute in the postwar years. While in Kuhn's scientific revolution sequence, the accumulating facts are supposed to gradually contradict the paradigm, here the theory contributed to the contradiction by resolutely walking away from the facts. As a result, Samuelson's findings—even though they have been put forward with all due warnings about the unrealistic and demanding nature of the assumptions on which they rested—acted as a devastating boomerang for the traditional theory and its claim to usefulness in explaining the problems of the real world. The challenges put forward at around the same time by Raùl Prebisch and Hans Singer were far less polished than Samuelson's theory and were immediately contested on statistical and analytical grounds, but they achieved a degree of credibility both because they took these problems seriously and because of the self-inflicted wound from which the classical theory was now suffering.

But Western economics avoided the charge of being incompetent to deal with the problems of underdevelopment by advances in another one of its branches. The fledgling growth theory, in its Harrod-Domar version, jumped into the breach and supplied for a while a much-needed paradigm for the purpose of understanding and, hopefully, remedying the poverty of Asia, Africa, and Latin America. It became an article of faith, reinforced by the rapid postwar recovery and growth (as then understood) of both Western and Eastern Europe, that growth depended critically on the injection of an adequate amount of capital, domestic or foreign. A generation of planners and foreign aid officials came to believe in the reality and manipulability of the Propensity to Save and the Capital-Output Ratio, and they stuck to this faith over an astonishingly long period of time for the good reason that the representation of the world in terms of these concepts was essential to their status as experts—it was "the only game in town."

A revolutionary or radical variant of the same theory made its appearance not long after the elaboration of the Harrod-Domar growth model and its first application to underdeveloped countries. In an influential article published in 1952, Paul Baran argued that, without social revolution, growth in these countries was impossible: foreign private capital was exploitative, parasitic or *comprador* local elites were unable and unwilling to invest productively, and foreign aid only had the effect of shoring up the existing growth-defeating power structure. This representation of reality did not reject the logic of the orthodox paradigm which had installed productive capital investment as the prime mover. But it argued that the sociopolitical characteristics of the poor countries and their relations to the centers of capitalist-imperialist expansion were such as to make capital investment there both inadequate and unproductive.[2]

Between the thesis, which sees development as certain provided capital is injected in the right amounts, and the antithesis, which views development as impossible given the social and political status quo, there was a great deal of room for intermediate positions. In fact, once evidence accumulated on actual economic developments in the periphery, the two extreme positions looked unsatisfactory.

The first attempts at moving away from the excessive simplicities of the paradigmatic growth model took the form of showing that the amount of investment depended not only on the total income earned during the preceding period but also on the distribution of income, a concept almost as familiar to economists as that of aggregate income flow. What is remarkable—though it has remained unnoticed—is that the two major contributions that were made along these lines in 1955 and 1956 reached opposite conclusions. One paper, by Walter Galenson and Harvey Leibenstein, argued that the greater the capital intensity of new production the greater would be the share of profits in the ensuing income stream and therefore the higher the reinvestment out of profits in the next period. The other article, by Robert Baldwin, suggested that an equalitarian distribution of income would make for rapid growth because domestic markets would then more easily reach the size necessary for the establishment and profitable operation of consumer goods industries.[3] Clearly, the two sets of authors had different circumstances in mind: Galenson-Leibenstein wrote in terms of an industrialization process that is already powerfully under way, whereas Baldwin was assessing the comparative ability of countries operating at a much earlier stage to attract basic consumer goods industries. Looked at in this way, the two theories are no longer contradictory, for it is possible and even likely that the patterns of income distribution that are supportive of rapid growth are different at different stages of development. In fact, the economic history of the United States during the nineteenth century outside of the South bears considerable resemblance first to the Baldwin and then to the Galenson-Leibenstein pattern, moving from a comparatively egalitarian to a highly concentrated income distribution, with industrial development proceeding apace throughout.

The articles just noted were valuable in puncturing the ruling paradigm and its excessive aggregation, but they continued to emphasize the income side of the economy. The pace of economic development was made to depend, not on total income, but on the way in which income was divided among different groups. A more radical break with the paradigm came through suggestions that a determining influence on growth may issue from the production side of the economy. Sociologists like Bert Hoselitz and others took this point of view when they focused on the conditions for the emergence of entrepreneurship. As an economist, I preferred to simply assume an insufficiency of entrepreneurial motivation and then to systematically search for such constellations of productive forces as would move private or public decision makers to "do something" through special pressures—pressures that are more compelling than those that are expected to move the rational decision maker of received economic theory.[4]

One suggestion along this line was that development is accelerated through investment in projects and industries with strong forward or backward linkage effects.[5] I argued that entrepreneurial decision making in both the private and the public sectors is not uniquely determined by the pull of incomes and demand, but is responsive to special push factors, such as the linkages, emanating from the product side.

Backward and forward linkages have become part of the language of development economics. Looking at this success from the point of view of the sociology of knowledge, I suspect that it owes much to my having presented the linkages as intimately tied to input-output analysis, that is, to the existing technical corpus of economic knowledge. As such they seemed more operational, less fuzzy than, for example, Perroux's propulsive industry or Rostow's leading sector. Actually, of course, input-output analysis is by nature synchronic, whereas linkage effects need time to unfold. This basic difference has bedeviled various ingenious attempts at comprehensive, cross-section measurement of linkage effects and at thereby "testing the linkage hypothesis."[6] The more illuminating uses of the concept are perhaps to be found in a number of historically oriented studies which paid close attention to the sequence of development in individual countries.[7]

I now wish to propose some extensions and generalizations of the linkage concept along several lines. First I shall consider processes that, because of their similarities to the backward and forward variety, also deserve to be called linkages and have indeed been so labeled already. Then I shall suggest a more inclusive linkage concept and use it to look at selected development sequences. Finally, in the course of some methodological observations, I shall discuss, among other things, the relation of the generalized linkage approach to the staple and development-of-underdevelopment theses as well as its affinity to what I shall call micro-Marxism.

A brief personal comment on how this essay came to be written is in order here. For a number of years I have assembled notes, references, and ideas on the topics to be discussed and have taught seminars around them. All along I felt that to deal with them adequately required a vast amount of further research eventually to be incorporated in a book. Yet that research and that book were postponed from year to year as new interests claimed increasing portions of my time or as the task seemed too formidable. Then came the invitation to contribute a paper for a special occasion. At that point I decided to write an article rather than a book about the matters I have been carrying around with me. Thus the following pages should be read as an outline and preview of what the book might have been or may yet be.

Linkage Effects—Some Further Varieties and Some Interactions

I have defined the linkage effects of a given product line as investment-generating forces that are set in motion, through input-output relations, when productive facilities that supply inputs to that line or utilize its outputs are inadequate or nonexistent. Backward linkages lead to new investment in input-supplying facilities and forward linkages to investment in output-using facilities.

Consumption and Fiscal Linkages

The linkage concept was put forward with industry and industrialization primarily in mind because here it was possible to conceive of linkages of considerable variety and depth in both the backward and forward directions. Nevertheless, the concept has also had useful applications to primary production, where its close connection with the staple thesis soon became evident. The staple thesis, as originated by Harold Innis and further developed by Canadian economists and economic historians, has attempted to show how the growth experience of a "new" country is concretely shaped by the specific primary products which it successively exports to world markets. It is an attempt to discover in detail how "one thing leads to another" through the requirements and influence of the staple, from transportation facilities and settlement patterns to the establishment of new economic activities. The original linkage concept captures of course only one aspect of this overall process, the one that is most directly tied to the procurement and elaboration of the staple itself. But some important additional aspects can be encompassed by the concept once it has been appropriately stretched by bringing the income side into the picture. For one thing, the new incomes earned in the process of staple production and export may be spent initially on imports, but these imports, once grown to a sufficient volume, could eventually be substituted by domestic industries. The somewhat roundabout mechanism through which certain import-substituting industries are called into life by the staple in this manner has been aptly called consumption linkage .[8] In contrast, the more direct backward and forward linkages might be subsumed under the name of production linkages. A notable characteristic of the consumption linkages is that they can be outright negative rather than merely weak or nonexistent. It is now widely recognized that during the first phase of export expansion in the countries of the periphery an important effect is, not the creation of new industries to satisfy rising consumer demand, but the destruction of established handicraft and artisan activities as labor is withdrawn from them for staple production and as new imports of consumer goods compete successfully against them.[9] It is at this point, among others, that the linkage approach and the staple thesis make contact with the development-of-underdevelopment thesis which will be discussed briefly below.

Another important way in which one thing may lead to another is through the ability of the state to tap the income stream accruing from the staple to various parties, particularly to the owners of the mines and plantations. If the state levies taxes on these incomes and channels the proceeds into productive investment, it is possible to speak of fiscal linkages of the staple to be contrasted with the, again, more direct physical (or production) linkages described in my *Strategy of Economic Development*.[10]

A comparative appraisal of the existence, strength, and reliability of these various linkage effects for different staples in various socioeconomic settings is one way toward an understanding of the growth process in the countries of the periphery, during the period of export-led growth. A considerable advantage of this approach is that it points from the outset to the possibility of characteristically different experiences in line with different linkage constellations.

Conditions Favoring Fiscal Linkage

The most favorable constellation would of course be one in which a staple was simultaneously endowed with strong production, consumption, and fiscal linkages. Unfortunately, this ideal situation is not likely to occur: a little reflection suggests that one kind of linkage is often to be had only at the expense of another. For example, the fiscal linkages have made a strong showing in those mining and petroleum activities that had all the earmarks of the "enclave." But the enclave is defined by the absence of involvement with the rest of the economy, that is, by the absence of other kinds of linkages. It is precisely because of this absence of links that the enclave becomes an obvious and comparatively easy target of the fiscal authorities. Being a foreign body, often owned by foreigners to boot, the enclave has few defenders of its interests once the state acquires the will and authority to divert toward its own ends a portion of the income stream originating therein.

Let us consider, on the other hand, a productive activity with many direct links to the rest of the economy, either because of strong backward and forward linkages or, more simply, because it is carried on in the central region of a country by producers with intimate ties to a dense network of traders and townspeople. Clearly, with so many friends in court this activity is not likely to be subjected to significant special taxation.

The situation that is brought to mind here is that of coffee-growing countries such as Brazil and Colombia. In both countries, coffee has been crucial for the creation of settlement patterns, transportation networks, and consumption linkages, but it has yielded a fiscal contribution only quite late in its history as an export staple, and then only as the unintended result of economic policies originally directed to quite different and sometimes even opposite ends. In both Africa and Latin America, policies that had been adopted for the purpose of helping the growers of coffee, cocoa, and other staples by insulating them from depressed world market prices later turned into instruments that permitted taxation of the same growers, and these tax proceeds were then partly devoted to the financing of development ventures.

If it is correct that fiscal linkages are usually associated with the lack of physical and consumption linkages and vice versa, the question of which set of linkage endowments is more favorable arises. The answer is complex, as it depends on the speed and strength with which the various linkages are likely to make their appearance. Only a few of the factors relevant to such a comparison can be discussed here.

Fiscal linkage depends on the willingness and ability of national governments to tax, or otherwise to claim participation in, the incomes originating in mining and similar enclave-type enterprises. This propensity to tax—and to own—has of course grown spectacularly since decolonization and other political developments have established the state in Asia, Africa, and Latin America as an actor with some autonomy. As a result, the development prospects of countries with nonrenewable natural resources are now very different from what they were under colonialism and earlier capitalist expansion.

As I have already hinted, fiscal linkage has a better chance to emerge if the enclave resources are owned by foreigners, for the same reason that an enclave is taxed more readily than an activity with a dense linkage network: taxing a foreign company comes more easily than assessing nationals who, besides owning the resources, are likely to run or "own" the government as well. The foreign-owned nitrate and copper mines of Chile, for example, yielded substantial revenues to the Chilean state during the early decades of the century, while the large, locally owned cocoa plantations of Ecuador created a bonanza that profited primarily a handful of Guayaquil families who controlled the Ecuadorean government from Paris, where they had settled to spend their fortunes pleasantly and rapidly.[11]

But the Chilean part of this story brings to mind that the ability to tax the enclave is hardly a sufficient condition for vigorous economic growth. For the fiscal linkage to be an effective development mechanism, the ability to tax must be combined with the ability to invest productively. Here lies precisely the weakness of fiscal linkage in comparison with the more direct production and consumption linkages. In the case of the latter, existing production lines or imports to be substituted point to the tasks to be undertaken next, whereas no such guidance is forthcoming when a portion of the income stream earned in the enclave is siphoned off for the purpose of irrigating other areas of the economy. Hence the possibility of either faulty investment or a great deal of leakage on the way—for example, the siphoned-off funds may simply lead to an enlarged bureaucracy. The pre-1930s Chilean experience with nitrates and copper has been analyzed in the latter terms,[12] while a reexamination of Peru's abortive mid-nineteenth-century guano boom has pointed to ill-considered railroad investments as the main culprit.[13] No matter how adept governments have become at taxing the income stream originated by the export staple, the success of fiscal linkage continues to be daunted by similar difficulties. This is so, to repeat, not because funds in the hands of governments are always "wasted," but because the tasks taken on by governments through fiscal linkage are intrinsically more difficult than those that are assumed, frequently by private capital, in conjunction with physical and consumption linkages.

As long as the ability to tax and the ability to invest productively are both required for fiscal linkage to qualify as an effective mechanism, it would be easy to make a pronouncement to the effect that both of these abilities must be acquired by the state pari passu. Having stressed both the likelihood and the uses of unbalanced growth, I would rather refrain from that sort of advice and examine instead the comparative problems and advantages of the more likely unbalanced growth paths. It is possible to distinguish, as I did in *Strategy*, between an orderly, or permissive, and a disorderly, or compulsive, sequence.[14]

The unbalanced path can be said to be more orderly when the ability to tax develops ahead of the ability to invest: fiscal revenue is collected before the authorities have prepared a well-considered and commensurate shelf of investment projects. In extreme cases of this imbalance much of the revenue accumulates as foreign exchange, as is currently happening in small countries that are large petroleum producers. In less affluent cases, such as that of Chile earlier in the century, the disproportion between the accruing revenue and the ability to invest it productively in the domestic economy is likely to be reflected by an enlarged bureaucracy, by more plentiful and frequently unrealistic social services, by spending on armaments and other wasteful investments, and, in the balance of payments, by an increase in the imports of consumer goods. The trouble with this imbalance is that it is not self-correcting: bureaucracy, social services, and even unproductive public investments can go on expanding for a considerable time, and little pressure is brought on the government to develop its entrepreneurial capabilities instead. Insofar as the expansion of the bureaucracy and of social services is concerned there is at least the possibility that the increased imports of consumer goods which this expansion is likely to bring will eventually result in some consumption linkages. In this manner, spending of the tax proceeds for such "unproductive" purposes can be a lesser evil than their expenditure for supposedly productive investment projects that turn out to be failures.

In the opposite model, the government's motivation to develop some sector of the economy other than the staple outpaces its ability to extract taxes from the exporting interests. The obvious outcome of this situation is inflation induced by deficit spending or credit expansion. Although fraught with social and political dangers, this sort of disequilibrium situation contains at least some stimulus in the direction of balance at a higher level: the inflation itself can act as a powerful argument for the generation of more fiscal resources and for the procurement of foreign finance. This more compulsive unbalanced path is characteristic of countries where the export staple is owned by nationals that are proficient at resisting taxation. It finds indeed a prototypical illustration in the Brazilian experience of the fifties.

As discussed so far, fiscal linkage is restricted to the direct participation of the state in the income stream generated by the export sector. A more roundabout way for the state to extract revenue is through the levying of customs duties on the manufactures that are imported into a country with an expanding export trade in primary products. This indirect extraction has been the more common way for the state to raise revenue and has in fact been the mainstay of public finance at the early stage of export-led growth whenever the state has been too weak, vis-à-vis the staple producers, to insist on direct fiscal linkage. On the whole, the revenues raised by means of the indirect route have paid for an expansion of government functions and services. They also have often served to provide infrastructure investments for the further expansion of primary exports; in this manner they have accentuated the colonial character of the economies concerned, whereas direct fiscal linkage investments have typically been undertaken for the opposite purpose, that is, to diversify the economy away from the dominant export staple.[15]

Forward Linkages as Handicaps

Though less problematic than fiscal linkages, production and consumption linkages are by no means wholly straightforward and uniformly reliable. In my original treatment of the subject, the relation between market size and the economic size of plant was singled out as the key variable that would trigger the private or public entrepreneurship needed to take up opportunities for backward- and forward-linkage investments as well as for import substitution. Further reflection and observation have made it clear, however, that other variables are also at work and help explain the differential speed with which these investments come into being.

One such variable is the degree of technological "strangeness" or "alienness" of the new economic activities in relation to the ongoing ones. In an environment in which backward linkages originate primarily among the owner-operators of the ongoing activity, such linkages can be expected to be rather weak if the required input comes from an industry whose process and technique is totally unfamiliar to these operators. The linkage dynamic may thus be held back by the difficulties of making a technological leap whose size differs with different industries—it is bigger in the case of textiles, for example, than in metalworking and chemicals.[16]

In the case of agricultural and industrial raw materials, the size of the technological jump is almost always big for backward linkage since, under modern conditions, the technique of growing wheat or coffee or sugarcane has very little in common, except for the seeds or cuttings, with the technique of fabricating the tools or synthetic fertilizers that are used as inputs by the growers. The same is true for many of the forward linkages that are potentially so significant for staple-based economic development. The milling, refining, and other processing industries are usually technological strangers to the staple. Perhaps the principal reason why it is difficult to establish backward and forward linkage industries around the staples is not so much that, as I argued originally, there are fewer linkage effects in agriculture than in industry, but that they largely point to industries whose technologies are alien to the grower of the staple.[17] Hence, for a very long time these industries are carried on abroad, where, moreover, they are usually protected through the well-known tariff pattern making for stiff effective rates.

Processing industries have of course been established near the growing areas when they were indispensable to preparing the harvested product for world markets. The existence of forward linkages of this sort has depended more on compelling technical characteristics of the product than on entrepreneurial choice. An obvious example is sugarcane which, in the interest of maximizing sugar yield, must be crushed as soon as possible after cutting, and which is far too bulky to be transported for any distance. An even better example is the shipping of bananas in cardboard cartons, which was begun during the sixties. Previously the fruit had always been shipped on the stem, making the banana the export staple with possibly the smallest added postharvest value. Shipping in cartons turned out to be a considerable convenience in terms of speed of loading and unloading; it also saved on shipping space and weight, partly because the weight of the useless center stalk alone comes to about 15 percent of the total. In addition, the packaging of bananas in cartons provided employment to the exporting countries, and the need for cartons meant a stimulus for their pulp and paper industries. But the decision to go to cartons was exclusively dictated by the need to find a way of avoiding bruising the fruit during transport after the tough Gros Michel had been widely replaced by the more delicate Cavendish variety. The switch to the latter had in turn been made necessary by the destructive Panama disease, against which the Gros Michel proved to be defenseless in spite of protracted and expensive efforts at control.[18]

The normal and quite justified reaction to this story is to lament the developing country's inability to exploit such simple, obvious, and useful opportunities for forward linkages except under conditions of utter technological necessity and to look for institutional arrangements and economic incentives that would facilitate the perception and grasping of such, opportunities. But the earlier example of sugarcane points to a rather different moral: because processing operations and forward linkages in general tend to be technological strangers to the staple, these operations, when they do come into existence because of compelling requirements of the staple's export technology, tend to be undertaken and controlled by groups distinct from the grower of the staple, who is thus relegated more firmly to his agricultural role. The sugarcane grower or rice farmer who delivers his crop to the sugar refinery or rice mill owned and operated by "others" is effectively cut off from any further economic activities on behalf of his product. From this point of view, it begins to appear paradoxically that the less of these forward linkages exist in the case of staples, the better. Conditions for the development of entrepreneurial initiative on the part of the staple grower may be more favorable if the staple requires only a few simple operations such as drying and bagging to prepare it for the market and if it does not have to rely on alien transportation. For example, the higher the staple's value per unit of weight the more worthwhile it is for the grower or a member of his family to take it to market. In the absence of elaborate forward linkage industries based on alien technology and probably run by alien entrepreneurs, the grower of the staple may himself become involved in the more accessible nonindustrial forwarding operations, such as transportation, commerce, and finance; he or a member of his family may become specialized in these functions; and from a strong base here he can eventually contribute to industrial development through the exploitation of opportunities for consumption linkages that may appear in the wake of the staple boom. This corresponds substantially to the history of commercial, urban, and eventual industrial expansion via import substitution following upon coffee exports in the São Paulo and Antioquia regions of Brazil and Colombia. The lack of cumulative development that has marked the career of such staples as sugarcane, groundnuts, and cotton also fits into the picture: in these cases the alien forward linkage industries of refining and ginning, or the need for specialized—hence alien—transportation because of distance and bulk of the staple (groundnuts), cut off the producer of the staples from any further involvement with them.[19]

I have shown that fiscal linkage has the best chance of coming into play when a staple is a true enclave and is therefore poor in other linkages of whatever kind. Now it appears similarly that the absence of one linkage—technologically complex, hence alien, forward linkage—creates favorable conditions for another, more diffuse kind of linkage as staple growers develop the entrepreneurial initiative needed for the cumulative growth of commerce and other economic activities around the staple. Forcing matters only a little, one might say that both fiscal and consumption linkages are more likely to appear if some other linkages are absent.

Linkages—A Broader Definition and a New Subdivision

By now, the various linkages and their interaction have taken on a new character and importance. They appear to constitute a structure that is capable of generating alternative paths toward development or underdevelopment for the different staple exporters. In other words, some of the principal features of a country's development in the period of export-led growth can be described in terms of linkages deriving from its staple. The question arises, therefore, why this is so and how the structure can be further developed.

The linkages capture much of the development story for a reason that has already been given: development is essentially the record of how one thing leads to another, and the linkages are that record, from a specific point of view. They focus on certain characteristics inherent in the productive activities already in process at a certain time. These ongoing activities, because of their characteristics, push or, more modestly, invite some operators to take up new activities. Whenever that is the case, a linkage exists between the ongoing and the new activity. All our previous linkages fall within this definition.

With this generalization of the linkage concept a new subdivision may be suggested. On the one hand, there are situations in which the same economic operators who are already engaged in the ongoing activity are impelled to undertake the additional activity; this is linkage due to insiders or "inside linkage." On the other hand, the push to take up new activities may be felt not so much by those who are involved in the ongoing activity as by other parties. For example, the ongoing activity might be carried on by indigenous economic operators, while the new activity would be taken up by foreigners or by the state. This is linkage through outsiders or "outside linkage."

Except for fiscal linkage, which is outside linkage by definition, the new subdivision cuts across all previous linkage categories. Forward and backward linkages, in particular, can be either outside or inside. In the latter case, one is in the presence of vertical integration. With this new terminology, it is possible to give a compact formulation of various propositions about development patterns and to generate new hypotheses in the process. To illustrate: (a) if the new activity is technologically alien to the ongoing activity, inside linkage will meet with special difficulties; (b) twentieth-century latecomers tend to have a particularly marked preference for inside over outside linkage; hence the conjecture arises that (c) the industrialization process of those latecomers is subject to special problems and perhaps discontinuities whenever the next steps of the development process require, or are believed to require, a massive injection of alien technology.[20]

A more general use of the new linkage categories is to look at the developmental advantages and drawbacks that may be associated with each. Thus, outside linkage has the advantage of mobilizing new agents and of preventing an excessive concentration of economic wealth and power, while the advantage of inside linkage is that it develops the entrepreneurial initiatives of the older agents and permits them to break out of their existing pursuits. The balance of these advantages and corresponding disadvantages in each case is likely to reveal a great deal about different development profiles and about missed or captured opportunities. In the following discussion, some further varieties of inside and outside linkages will be reviewed.

Inside Linkage: Invitation to Spatial Mobility

A linkage exists whenever an ongoing activity gives rise to economic or other pressures that lead to the taking up of a new activity. But how is newness to be defined? Until now, as in the cases of forward and backward linkage, newness has been understood as a new kind of productive activity and, specifically, as one yielding a new product. With the broader linkage concept, a new activity could also be defined as one that yields the same product as before but is carried on in a new place. An inside linkage can therefore be said to exist when some characteristics of the ongoing activity compel or invite some or all of its operators to move to another place even though they may not plan, at least initially, to undertake a new activity.

A considerable contribution to the analysis of this kind of process is made by Clifford Geertz in his observations on Indonesia.[21] The Javanese rice farmer, living in the midst of paddies that have been carefully terraced over many generations, clings to his parcel of land with the utmost tenacity. Geertz has contrasted the resulting immobility of the Javanese farmer with the mobility of the cultivators on the Outer Islands who typically engage in slash-and-bum agriculture. Two very different patterns of colonial exploitation resulted: in Java it was possible to force the rice farmer to devote some of his land to the cultivation of sugarcane for delivery to Dutch-owned refineries, whereas in the Outer Islands the colonizers were unable to take advantage of this convenient system of indirect production. Instead, they established and managed their own plantations of coffee, tea, and rubber. The preexisting mode of agricultural production thus had important consequences for the form of colonial exploitation: in Java the colonizer penetrated virtually every peasant household, whereas in the Outer Islands he made his presence felt through the creation of enclaves. These differences also determined differences in decolonization: in Java it took the form of letting most of the land in sugarcane revert to paddy; the plantations of the Outer Islands, on the other hand, were expropriated, but continued to produce the same crops, mostly for export, as before.

While primarily helpful for the understanding of the specific patterns of colonization and decolonization, the characteristics noted by Geertz also have importance for gauging development perspectives. The tenacity with which the Javanese rice farmer clings to his land is due in part to his expectation that some extra care in maintaining the terraces, irrigation ditches, and bunds, as well as special efforts at weeding and other labors, will produce increases, in yield sufficient to feed his growing family. While the rice plant, with its elaborate infrastructure, has received over the centuries and still receives and needs "tender, loving care" it also responds to such care almost indefinitely. In economic terms this amounts to saying that the marginal productivity of labor used in paddy rice farming declines only very slowly and is probably perceived as having an even smaller downward slope than turns out to be the case in fact. These characteristics have contributed to the immobility of the Javanese rice farmer and to the enormous accumulation of population in the countryside. They also help one understand the ease with which opportunities for trade and other services on the island have been appropriated by foreigners, mostly Chinese.

A product or staple with the opposite characteristics would be one whose output per unit of labor input would fall off rapidly as more labor is supplied. In the case of such a product, a population increase in the countryside cannot be absorbed in the existing area of settlement and is likely to lead rapidly to migration to the cities or to the opening up of new lands. An example is the tree crops such as coffee and cocoa which, once planted, require, besides harvesting, only a moderate and not highly variable amount of pruning and weeding (fertilizer being primarily a capital input).

In some cases, moreover, coffee has led to soil exhaustion, which causes the productivity of labor to decline unexpectedly without any increase in labor input. In Brazil, there is a striking contrast between the soil exhaustion of the coffee plantations in the Paraíba Valley near Rio de Janeiro in the second half of the nineteenth century and the century-long undiminished productivity of the cane lands in the *zona da mata* of the northeast. It explains, in part, why the sugar barons of the northeast never became involved in other economic activities, while the coffee planters near Rio, in spite of their expectation and full intention to turn into sedentary plantation owners leading a life of leisure, were forced to look farther afield, to found new plantations in the state of São Paulo, and in the process to become involved in tasks of transportation, communication, and commerce.[22]

The lesson implicit in these examples is not that erosion is good for development—although it can work out that way if fertile lands remain to be opened up fairly close to the eroded ones. Rather it is that the deeply rooted Western value judgment which sees sedentary agriculture as a huge step forward from more mobile ways of life must be questioned when it is applied outside of its original context, the neolithic revolution. At the very least, it certainly is not true that the more sedentary, the better. This is shown by the comparison of the migrant coffee and cocoa farmers of Colombia, Brazil, Nigeria, and Ghana with situations where the staple fitted right into the existing mode of agricultural production.[23] The latter condition is characteristic of sugarcane in Java, as just mentioned, as well as of cotton in Egypt, groundnuts in northern Nigeria, perhaps coffee in Uganda, and so on. In these situations the staple is grown by an already well-settled peasantry that makes a place for it on land previously uncultivated or devoted to food crops, and techniques of cultivation are rather similar to those that are already in use.[24] The staple fits into the existing production, settlement, and skill pattern with a minimum of disruption, and also with a minimum, of cumulative development. Depending on the social, demographic, and political circumstances, the result for the cultivators ranges widely, from the Javanese pattern of impoverishment to "once-over" development. Whatever the actual outcome, the initiative for cumulative development, if any, has to originate elsewhere, that is, in outside linkage.

Outside Linkage: Provision of Public Goods by the State

At first sight, it may seem that it is asking too much of our approach to make a contribution to this topic. How specific characteristics of export staples can contribute to the propensity and ability of the staple growers themselves to engage in further development moves is easy enough to see. But how could such characteristics be related to the behavior of other actors, such as the commercial and industrial classes, foreign investors, or the state? Actually, it will be recalled that one type of developmental behavior on the part of the state, its propensity to tax the staple, has already been related to such characteristics of staples as lack of direct linkages to the rest of the economy. Taxing is of course not all that one wants a development-minded state to do. As I have shown, a state that only knows how to tax a staple may be very far from making an effective contribution to development.

It is in fact conceivable that the opposite kind of involvement is a better way for the state to acquire an ability to promote development. In other words, instead of taxing the staple growers, the state may somehow be pushed into assisting them. If this happens, a new actor comes onto the development stage. This could be yet another case of once-over development: it is conceivable that the state will undertake a specific job which it is uniquely suited to perform and that this will be the end of the story. But it is also possible, and in certain circumstances probable, that the state, as a result of having intervened successfully in one sector of the economy, will acquire the capability and the appetite to tackle advances for other sectors or for the economy in general.[25]

What are the conditions, then, under which the state will be impelled into such assistance activities? This is most likely to occur in connection with services that the staple growers need, but find it difficult or impossible to supply individually or even cooperatively. These conditions point to the domain of public goods that must be supplied by the state if they are to be supplied at all.

There are many well-known public or semipublic goods of this sort, from power, transportation, and irrigation to education and public health. Often designated as "infrastructure," as though they were preconditions for the more directly productive activities, these goods have more usually been provided in response to urgent demands emanating from such activities and from their need for consolidation, greater profitability, and further expansion.[26] For staples, the more important of such public goods are transportation and irrigation, as well as disease and pest control. The latter is particularly typical of the linkage phenomenon here described: a characteristic of the staple—that is, its susceptibility to disease and infestation—combined with the fact that success in eradication or control requires remedial action over a large area, means that whenever many producers are involved such action can be undertaken only by an authority with coercive powers. This was precisely the situation that led to an expansion of the role of government in Egypt during the late nineteenth century when cotton, the country's principal staple, was threatened by cotton-worm infestation. According to a recent study, this expansion in the role of government took place even though it went "much against the inclination of many of the British administrators, particularly Lord Cromer. . . ."[27] Naturally, when the expansion of the role of the state takes place under colonial conditions with the colonizers having a set image of their responsibility and its limits, the cumulative effects otherwise to be expected from such a new involvement of the state in the economy will be severely stunted.

In the case of irrigation, the hypothesis that the state may become more development oriented and public serving as a result of practice in providing certain useful public services for staple producers runs up against the well-known Wittfogel thesis which sees state-organized irrigation works as a determinant of "Oriental despotism" in its various forms.[28] This conflict of hypotheses makes it possible to appreciate that the Wittfogel thesis has plausibility only under very special circumstances: that is, when irrigation is essential to the growing of basic food crops, so that state and society come into being jointly as a result of the state's assuming the life-giving function of building, managing, and maintaining the irrigation works. On the other hand, in the numerous situations in which the state has long been in existence as an administrative-bureaucratic entity and then comes to undertake an irrigation activity with the comparatively modest aim of improving the incomes of the staple growers, this new activity on the part of the state may well mean that an otherwise largely parasitic bureaucracy will acquire a development-minded component. While this component may come to exhibit some technocratic traits, it is unlikely to have either the propensity or the power to develop an autocratic style.[29]

A particularly interesting linkage, leading from the staple and its characteristics to state action designed to provide a service which producers are incapable of supplying themselves, is that of price stabilization. Through exchange-rate policy or the institution of marketing boards, the state can, within limits, divorce the international price of a staple from its domestic price; it even can manipulate the staple's international price if the country produces a sufficiently large share of total supplies so as to hold some monopoly power in world markets. In the case of staples grown by many producers, a special need and clamor for this type of state intervention will arise whenever the staple is subject to violent price declines. These conditions point to tropical tree crops such as coffee and cocoa. Because of the 5-year delay between planting and first full crop, supply is particularly likely to be out of phase with demand in cobweb-like fashion. Also, the trees, once in place, keep yielding a crop even if no fertilizing, pruning, or weeding is practiced, so that supply response to lower prices is small in the short run. Finally, the fact that the number of producers is usually quite large makes it unlikely that they will engage in organized remedial action except to join in an interest group that will insistently invoke help from the state.

These characteristics and the resulting special vulnerability of coffee and cocoa prices to world-market disturbances have long been thought of as a liability. They are now seen to have some compensating advantages because of the state action they predictably trigger. The help proffered by the state through the various arrangements just mentioned is in a sense the exact obverse of the extraction of revenue from the staple that has been called fiscal linkage. (Indeed, the staples most likely to elicit fiscal linkage-minerals and petroleum enclaves-are least likely to be the recipients of stabilization assistance as they usually respond to price declines through swift cuts in ouput.) Yet, ironically and dialectically, once the state has provided stabilization assistance it has also established the institutional framework and perhaps acquired the frame of mind which will enable it to extract fiscal revenue from the staple at some future time when prices will have recovered. And at that point the staple will be just as defenseless against state taxation, because of its low price elasticity of supply, as it was earlier against drops in world market prices.

Price stabilization assistance is therefore a particularly interesting variety of state intervention from the point of view of how one thing leads to another. Whereas assistance categories such as disease control and irrigation may give the state a new taste for developmental activities, price stabilization supplies both the taste and, at some future time, the institutional mechanism to indulge it.

Further Observations, Mostly Methodological
On the Nature of the Generalized Linkage Approach

Not long ago a new theory of consumption attempted to look behind the individual consumable commodities which had long stood in the center of traditional theory. The new theory considered each commodity as a bundle of qualities (say, sweetness, juiciness, peelability, and appearance in the case of oranges) and each consumer as demanding various combinations of such qualities.[30] A number of interesting new results were obtained by this approach. Similarly, metallurgists have long given up thinking of metals as discrete, nature-given materials. They have identified each metal as a bundle of properties (such as hardness, porosity, conductivity, etc.) and have systematically fashioned alloys and substitutes for the purpose of supplying combinations of such properties that happened to be in demand for various industrial purposes.[31]

The focus on linkages to delineate the development prospects of different staple exporters has something in common with these approaches. It is an attempt to look behind such staples as sugarcane, coffee, rice, or tobacco and to identify some general characteristics of these products that influence and condition the kind of development experienced by the countries specializing in them. Such an attempt at finding meaningful classification criteria is not new. Economic geographers and others have sometimes grouped staples into various natural or botanical categories for the purpose of showing that differences in economic and sociopolitical destinies can be made intelligible in this way.

This sort of scheme—mineral products, tropical agricultural products, temperate agricultural products—has been adopted in an influential essay by Fernando Henrique Cardoso and Enzo Faletto on the economic and political development of Latin America.[32] The integration of economic with sociological and political analysis and the demonstration that characteristic differences could be established between the development or underdevelopment experiences of different groups of Latin American countries made this into a pathbreaking work. Nevertheless, in searching for general properties of staples that are likely to impart distinctive characteristics to the development process, the appropriate method is not to borrow these properties from some alien field, such as botany or climatology, but to look for properties that arise out of the development process itself and then to conduct the analysis in terms of these properties. For appraising a country's development prospects, the knowledge that its export staple is endowed with a certain constellation of linkages is obviously more revealing than the information that the staple is a tropical agricultural product.

The system laid out here makes it possible to translate technical information into a language that points directly toward development possibilities. For example, both the availability of tubewells and the addition of a highway to a rail link tend to make for substitution of inside for outside linkage as farmers install their own tubewells and ship their produce to market in their own trucks instead of, having to rely on state-managed irrigation and railroad systems.[33] A number of possible consequences can immediately be visualized as a by-product of these substitutions: they could enhance private entrepreneurship, concentrate income, and complicate the extraction of fiscal revenue. So far so good; but there remains much room for enriching this language and for substantially modifying the hypotheses thus far generated in the process. A good example of a modification that has already taken place is found earlier in the present essay: in the case of staples, forward linkages that imply considerable industrial processing were shown to act as developmental handicaps rather than as propellants because they tend to be technologically alien and therefore lock the producers of the staple into their agricultural activity.

A major general caveat follows: the various characteristics of staples and ensuing linkages, however neatly arranged in an apparently comprehensive system, have been extracted from the observation of actual experience. They therefore constitute no more than a useful arrangement of our present knowledge of development mechanisms. The way in which linkages have proliferated since the concept was first proposed makes it likely that this process of knowledge gathering is by no means at an end. It is therefore most important to consider the preceding schemes as open-ended and to use them primarily for heuristic purposes while remaining receptive to new information.

Relation to the Staple and Development-of-Underdevelopment Theses

The approach set out here has several points of contact with other attempts to account for the development experience of the countries of the periphery in the period of export-led growth.

The close relation of the linkage approach to the staple thesis will be evident by now. The former is essentially an attempt to supply the somewhat scattered insights of the latter with a conceptual framework that makes a more systematic exploration possible, with the just-noted proviso that the framework here proposed is not to be taken as an exhaustive explanatory scheme.

The question remains of how the approach set out here relates to another interpretation that has been put forward in recent years and that is perhaps best referred to as the "development-of-underdevelopment" thesis. At first sight, it seems difficult to conceive of a greater contrast than that between the linkage approach and the neo-Marxist writings of, say, André Gunder Frank who is responsible for the above phrase.[34] For "development of underdevelopment" means essentially that one thing did *not* lead to another in the countries of the periphery; that, in fact, things there have constantly been going from bad to worse. The impact of capitalism and imperialism on the periphery has been to extract surplus and, in the process, to impoverish the people, destroy local industry, deplete the soil and subsoil, and emasculate and corrupt the local elites. To the extent that a certain amount of capitalist development in the form of industrialization cannot be denied, it is attributed exclusively to lack of contact with the imperialist center on the part of certain privileged regions and during certain exceptional periods.[35]

From the point of view of the linkage approach, some of the assertions of this kind of writing are not particularly shocking. It is implicit in what has been said that contact with the capitalist center through exports of staples may well result for the countries of the periphery in an impoverished population with exhausted natural resources. This would be the case as long as the particular staple is not activating fiscal linkage, is endowed only with technologically alien forward linkage, and leads to the competition of imported consumer goods driving local industry and handicraft out of existence, rather than to consumption linkages. Even when fiscal linkage is present, but the state is unable to invest productively the revenue it extracts, the ensuing situation may not be better than if the revenue generated by the staple were largely accruing to absentee owners. Many of the propositions of this essay point to the possibility of particularly unfortunate combinations of circumstances: while fiscal linkage is predicated on the absence of forward and backward linkages, it is perfectly conceivable that during a prolonged period neither physical nor fiscal linkages will put in an appearance. In this manner the present approach, while admittedly originating in the attempt to understand how development can happen, is equally able to account for lack of development or for periods of development of underdevelopment. It has no blind spot with respect to the possibility of immiserization and is in this respect quite unlike the classical theory of international trade which can at worst conceive of a zero gain from trade for any country participating in world commerce.

At the same time, of course, the present approach is fully alive to the possibilties of development, particularly to those that may be wholly unintended on the part of exploitative operators and authorities who are responsible for the development of underdevelopment. Most of the linkages that were reviewed here—consumption linkages, the extraction of revenue from the staple, or the provision of pest control and price stabilization by the state—are in the nature of events that are originally unintended on the part of those who got staple production under way. The present approach makes it possible to understand such potentially positive events as already contained in a preceding exploitative phase. Therefore, it has a claim to being more truly dialectical than the development-of-underdevelopment thesis, which misses altogether the intimate connection between the various phases of what ought to be understood as a dynamic process.[36]

One of the great merits of the development-of-underdevelopment thesis has been the devastating and definitive critique of the concept of "traditional society," an unhistorical construct endemic in much of the previous development literature, that supposedly prevailed wherever dynamic development had not yet taken hold.[37] It is too bad that some of the critics have substituted for this construct the equally unhistorical notion of a uniform downward slide which all countries outside the capitalist-imperialist center are supposed to have experienced or to be experiencing until such time as they throw off the imperialist or neoimperialist yoke.

From Linkages to Micro-Marxism

Having taken my distance from contemporary neo-Marxist theorizing about the periphery, I shall now claim for my own approach a degree of intellectual kinship with the Marxian system. To this end something must first be said about the nature of the properties or characteristics of staples that have been singled out as giving rise to linkages.

Some of the linkages, such as the backward and forward ones, are directly tied to the technical conditions of production of the staple. Technological change will of course affect the number and kinds of such linkages, but they are invariant to social and political change. If attention is focused instead on, say, the fiscal linkages, the importance of the political context is immediately manifest. For fiscal linkage actually to happen the state must have evolved the will and ability to stake a claim, for purposes of reinvestment elsewhere in the economy, on the resources that are being exploited in its territory. Fiscal linkage does not therefore inhere in petroleum like a certain percentage of sulphur; it becomes associated with that product in certain historical circumstances. Nevertheless, the point is that fiscal linkage does not happen just because the state becomes modern, autonomous, development oriented, or antiimperialist. For a number of reasons tied to its mode of production— lack of physical linkages plus the likelihood of foreign ownership at a certain historical period—the presence of petroleum predisposes the state to develop the propensity to tax far more than if its staple consisted of some agricultural product grown by many local farmers on their own land in the central region of the country. In this manner it is after all possible to trace influences that go from the product and its technology—that is, from the "productive forces"—to a specific shape of economic development and to certain sociopolitical happenings, like nationalism and taxation, which define that shape.

There is obviously something here that has a considerable affinity with Marxism and historical materialism, but the difference is also striking. Marxist thought has traditionally focused on a very few constellations of productive forces—such as the feudal or capitalist modes of production—that are dominant over wide geographical areas and persist over long periods of time; social and political configurations are seen as deriving from these macromodes. The linkage approach also takes characteristic features of technology and production processes as points of departure for understanding social events, but it does so on a much smaller scale, in much more minute detail, and for a much more limited time frame. Hence, "micro-Marxism" might be a good term for this attempt to show how the shape of economic development, including its social and political components, can be traced to the specific economic activities a country takes up.

Marx and the more perceptive Marxists moved themselves in the micro direction when they were dealing with specific events and country experiences. Marx in particular oscillated between the grand generalization with which to characterize an entire epoch or process and the discriminating analysis of events which made differences between countries and subperiods stand out in richly textured detail. An example that is relevant for present purposes is in the preface of *Capital*, where at first we meet with the frequently cited phrase, "the industrially most developed country does nothing but hold up to those who follow it on the industrial ladder the image of their own future." Here Marx seems to suggest that capitalist industrial development is bound to exhibit uniform features and stages in all countries no matter how late they will step on the "ladder." But one only needs to read on in order to realize that Marx had a very acute sense of small and critical differences. For in the very next paragraph (which is apparently never read by those who quote the above sentence), Marx predicts a very different path for Germany and continental Europe in relation to England because of the absence of factory laws and in general because of a variety of social and political residues from feudalism that did not exist in England. In this manner Marx presents elements for a comparative analysis that considerably qualifies and in effect contradicts the generalization with which he starts out.[38]

It is remarkable—and characteristically un-Marxist—that Marx differentiated between England and Germany on the basis of certain elements in Germany's juridical institutions and historical heritage. In projecting likely differences in historical outcome he thus appeals to differences in the "superstructure" while apparently perceiving the infrastructure—industrial development under capitalism—as being identical for England and Germany. In this respect later students of comparative capitalist development were to be more Marxist than Marx. In explaining differences between the development pattern of England and that of latecomers such as Germany and Russia, Gerschenkron, for example, did not invoke residues from the previous historical experiences of the latter two countries; rather, he concentrated on the different rates of development of agriculture and industry during the period of industrial expansion and on the different roles of consumer goods and capital goods production.[39] In looking at countries of even more recent industrialization, I have similarly attempted to show that the "tightly staged" pattern of import-substituting industrialization, the importance of foreigners in the process, and the long-continued absence of any industrial production for export could explain much about some outstanding features of political development in these countries, such as the weakness of the national bourgeoisie.[40]

It is characteristic of this micro-Marxist approach to derive important differences in sociopolitical development from comparatively small and initially difficult-to-perceive differences in the structure of the "productive forces" within what had generally been considered a uniform historical phase or a homogeneous mode of production. Much more can be done along these lines for the period of industrialization.[41] But micro-Marxism comes particularly into its own when one deals with the development of the countries of the periphery during the so-called period of export-led growth which for most of these countries occupies the second half of the nineteenth century and the first 2 or 3 decades of the twentieth, but goes on even today in some cases. The countries of the periphery were cast by the capitalist center in the role of providers of agricultural and mineral raw products, and most of them specialized along one or a very few individual product lines. With substantial differences existing between the characteristics and linkages of different staples, the productive forces prevailing in these countries were probably more heterogeneous during the stage of export-led growth than at any other preceding or subsequent historical period. Little wonder, then, that the micro-Marxist approach is particularly suitable and revealing for that stage.

A Final Puzzle

There exists a literature that has much in common with the generalized linkage or micro-Marxist approach as presented here. In addition to the writings of Harold Innis and other contributors to the staple thesis, this literature consists of a fairly scattered and often impressionistic group of writings that focuses on one or, more often, two products, generally of a single country, in order to derive a great deal of the country's fortunes, misfortunes, and general history from these products and their properties. The archetypical representative of this genre is Ortiz's *Cuban Counterpoint*,[42] where the contrast between the beneficent tobacco and the pernicious sugarcane is lyrically portrayed from every conceivable angle. Such comparisons of the contrasting performances of two staples have proven to be intellectually attractive; similar, if less baroque, portrayals have been attempted for sugarcane versus coffee in Brazil, tobacco versus coffee in Colombia, and sugarcane versus tree crops in Indonesia.[43]

As will be obvious, I have taken a great deal from this literature and its insights. It has, nevertheless, one fairly pervasive characteristic that arouses intellectual suspicion: in almost all of these pairwise comparisons one staple is assigned the role of all-around villain, while the other is the all-around hero (the exception is Geertz's treatment of cane versus tree crops in Indonesia, where the former is the villain, all right, but there is no true hero). In Cuba sugarcane is the villain and tobacco the hero, in Colombia tobacco is the bad guy while coffee is the good guy, and in Brazil sugarcane is once again the villain while coffee is the good guy (note that as a result of these three pairwise comparisons, the ordering of the three staples is actually transitive!). In all of these comparisons the staples are looked at from a wide variety of angles, and one of the two staples scores consistently over the other. The same kind of convergence of pluses in one direction and minuses in the other is observed when economic activities other than staples are looked at from the point of view of their indirect, other-than-output contribution to economic development. Judith Tendler's studies of thermal energy versus hydropower and of generation versus distribution of power in Brazil and Argentina accumulated an impressive number of arguments demonstrating the all-around superiority of hydropower over thermal power and of generation over distribution. Similarly, my own observations on the comparative suitability of road and railroad to postindependence Nigeria resulted in singling out highways and trucking as being consistently superior to railroads, on a large number of diverse counts.[44]

It is of course possible that this strange convergence is due to some selective perception of reality, with the latter being caused in turn by the underlying questions that are being asked. To give an example: the nineteenth-century coffee boom in Brazil led without any doubt to the rise of São Paulo and eventually to the preeminence of that city as an industrial center, while the growing of sugarcane in the country's northeast ever since the sixteenth century left little behind but the most populous depressed area of Latin America. This contrast impels one to find numerous reasons for pinning praise on coffee and blame on sugarcane.

Nevertheless, we must allow for the possibility that the convergence phenomenon is not just something that is forced by our minds upon a recalcitrant reality for the reason just given: it is illegitimate to discard the hypothesis that the phenomenon may truly "exist in nature" just because we can think of good psychological reasons for which we may want to believe in its existence.

That the convergence phenomenon *may* exist is obvious. The properties which have been found relevant to the analysis of development effects—say, absence or presence of elaborate, technologically alien forward linkage, high or low price per unit of weight, gradually or steeply declining marginal productivity of labor, rapid or slow supply response to price changes—all of these could be so combined in a staple as to make for a cumulation of either pluses or minuses. For example, the botanical-economic nature of many tropical tree crops is such that they score along each of the above dimensions. From many points of view coffee cultivation has resulted in the stimulation of development in a number of countries: it has encouraged the individual cultivators to migrate or to undertake entrepreneurial tasks outside of coffee cultivation, it has led to the formation of strong pressure groups of cultivators and to the consequent intervention of the state to stabilize prices, because of the slow supply response to price it has eventually been possible to tax the coffee farmer during a prolonged period in favor of industry, and so on.

There is, then, nothing intrinsically inconceivable in one particular commodity acting as a multidimensional conspiracy in favor of or against development within a certain historical and sociopolitical setting. But how likely is it that such conspiracies have really existed? For an answer to this question, a brief excursion into a different historical period and event, the emergence of massive slavery in the New World, is revealing. It seems evident that a number of characteristics of sugarcane cultivation—the heavy, largely unskilled work in tropical climates, the availability of free land close to the plantations, the need to keep the labor force together during the slack season, and the possibility of using that force, including women and children, in minor tasks—conspired with the "sugar hunger" in post-Renaissance Europe to create a special affinity between sugarcane and slavery.[45] Obviously it was not sugarcane that created slavery, but it is fairly safe to suggest that slavery would not have become as extended as it did after the sixteenth century without that particular staple and its peculiar bundle of characteristics. A confirmation of the hypothesis is supplied in a way by the absence of slavery from New England, which was surely due in large part to lack of opportunity to engage in slavery, that is, to the poor soils and harsh climate of that region which made it unfit for the introduction of any slave-grown staple and relegated it to small-scale, owner-operated subsistence agriculture.

Generalizing from this historical example, it is possible to conjecture that the emergence of a new mode of production is more intimately tied to the availability, at the proper time, of a specific economic activity with a strong affinity for that mode than is realized later on when the mode has become ubiquitous and dominant and therefore appears to be and has in fact become independent from the activity. This sort of relationship, where a specific economic activity is, to paraphrase Marx, the midwife of a new mode of production, can probably be shown to have prevailed also between the textile industry and the Industrial Revolution. If our conjecture is correct, then the appearance of a new mode of production is prima facie evidence that an activity with that special, intellectually suspect multiple affinity for the mode must have been around—the new mode could not have made it otherwise.

Having made the case for the possible existence of the convergence phenomenon, I must qualify it in two quite different ways. In the first place, it is easy to claim too much for the connection between the characteristics of a specific staple and the sociopolitical environment. Depending as it does on the exact technical conditions of production, that connection is closely bound up with a particular time and place. It has already been noted that relatively small changes in technique—for example, the substitution of tubewell irrigation for a centrally managed system—may substantially change existing social roles and relations. One of the merits of the generalized linkage or micro-Marxist approach is that it invites the analyst to be constantly on the lookout for technological "news" that may have considerable economic and sociopolitical repercussions. In short, coffee production today in Colombia may have an entirely different social and developmental meaning from coffee production tomorrow in Uganda.

On the other hand, there is not necessarily a one-to-one correspondence between a staple and "its" sociopolitical environment. Strangely enough, a staple that has played an important reinforcing role in relation to a given social and political environment could come to perform this role once again in a very much changed environment. A striking example of such a repeat performance under drastically changed circumstances has been supplied in recent years by sugarcane cultivation in Cuba: some of the same characteristics that once created the affinity between cane and slavery—the large incidence of unskilled labor and the seasonal nature of the demand for labor—now made out of sugarcane the ideal economic activity for the periodic demonstration of community spirit and of the dignity of physical labor as young men and women leave their city pursuits during the cutting season to help out in the fields for short periods. Just as sugarcane magnified the extent of slavery, so it was now enhancing socialism in Cuba as it enabled that country to engage in experiments and pursue directions that are not nearly as readily available to other socialist countries.

"The flax looks just as before. Not one of its fibers is changed, but a new social soul has slipped into its body." This phrase from *Capital* seems nicely to the point, but the somewhat puzzling aspect of the matter is brought out, in a very different context, by Pascal: "Just as all things tell of God to those who know Him and just as they reveal Him to those who love Him, so these same things hide Him from those who do not know Him."[46] In other words, the same factual evidence may fit and even foster opposite interpretations of the world. Analogously, the same staple, its characteristics, and mode of production, may unexpectedly lend

strength to two totally different social arrangements and political regimes. At this point, then, my micro-Marxism takes a rather un-Marxist
turn. For in Marxist terminology I have just been saying that an identical
set of productive forces could not only be compatible, but could entertain a collusive, mutually reinforcing relationship with more than one set
of relations of production.

Actually this finding is all to the good, for I am very far from wishing
to lay down a new kind of reductionism or determinism. My point has
been, not that a staple will determine the sociopolitical environment in
any unique and exhaustive way, but that each time it will imprint certain
patterns of its own on whatever environment happens to be around and
that it is possible and worthwhile to study the imprinting process. A related point is that there are different degrees of affinity or compatibility
between specific economic activities, on the one hand, and varieties of
sociopolitical environments on the other. At one end of the scale, we
have discussed activities that stand in the just-noted collusive and mutually reinforcing relationship with such an environment. And while it is
possible for the same activity to entertain such a relationship with more
than one sociopolitical environment, there exist at the other end of the
scale economic activities that have a very low degree of compatibility
with certain sociopolitical frameworks; for example, certain fruits and
vegetables that require tender loving care appear to be poorly suited to
collectivist agriculture.

But the argument in defense of the convergence phenomenon has carried me too far. To explore these matters systematically would require
a much longer work. The present essay has had as its principal aim to
explore lines of compatibility of staples, not with sociopolitical regimes,
but with economic development at a given historical period and within
the social and political patterns characteristic of that period. And even
this topic has barely been opened up for discussion here, as I warned in
the opening section.

Notes

Reprinted from *Economic Development and Cultural Change* 25 (Supplement
1977): 67–98, by permission of the University of Chicago Press. © 1977 by the
University of Chicago. All rights reserved.

1. Paul A. Samuelson, "International Trade and the Equalization of Factor Prices," *Economic Journal* 58 (June 1948): 163–84, and "International Factor-Price Equalisation Once Again," ibid., 59 (June 1949): 181–97.

2. Paul A. Baran, "On the Political Economy of Backwardness," *Manchester School of Economics and Social Studies* 20 (January 1952): 66–84.

3. Walter Galenson and Harvey Leibenstein, "Investment Criteria, Productivity and Economic Development," *Quarterly Journal of Economics* 69 (August 1955): 343–70; Robert E. Baldwin, "Patterns of Development in Newly Settled Regions," *Manchester School of Economics and Social Studies* 24 (May 1956): 161–79.

4. For an exploration of similar "extra" pressures in the area of technological change, see Nathan Rosenberg, "The Direction of Technological Change; Inducement Mechanisms and Focusing Devices," *Economic Development and Cultural Change* 18 (October 1969): 1–24.

5. See my *Strategy of Economic Development* (New Haven, Conn.: Yale University Press, 1958), Chapter 6. The first rough outline of the idea is in a paper written in 1954 and republished as Chapter 1 in *A Bias for Hope: Essays on Development and Latin America* (New Haven, Conn.: Yale University Press, 1971), pp. 59–61.

6. Werner Baer and Isaac Kerstenetzky, "Import Substitution and Industrialization in Brazil," *American Economic Review* 54 (May 1964): 411–25; Pan A. Yotopoulos and Jeffrey B. Nugent, "A Balanced Growth Version of the Linkage Hypothesis," *Quarterly Journal of Economics* 87 (May 1973): 157–72. The latter article has led to a regular symposium on linkage effect measurement, with contributions by Prem S. Laumas, Michel Boucher, James Riedel, Leroy P. Jones, and a reply by Yotopoulos and Nugent in *Quarterly Journal of Economics* 90 (May 1976): 308–43. The paper by Jones is particularly noteworthy for solving, at last, the problem of how to measure total (direct and indirect) forward linkage effects.

7. Albert Fishlow, *American Railroads and the Transformation of the Ante-Bellum Economy* (Cambridge, Mass.: Harvard University Press, 1965); Judith Tendler, *Electric Power in Brazil: Entrepreneurship in the Public Sector* (Cambridge, Mass.: Harvard University Press, 1968); Michael Roerner, *Fishing for Growth: Export-led Development in Peru, 1950–1967* (Cambridge, Mass.: Harvard University Press, 1970); Scott R. Pearson, *Petroleum and the Nigerian Economy* (Stanford, Calif.: Stanford University Press, 1970). See also Richard Weisskoff and Edward Wolff, "Linkages and Leakages: Industrial Tracking in an Enclave Economy," *Economic Development and Cultural Change* 25 (July 1977): 607–28.

8. By Melville H. Watkins in his well-known paper, "A Staple Theory of Economic Growth," *Canadian Journal of Economics and Political Science*

29 (May 1963): 141–58. In Chapter 7 of *Strategy*, I had described the same phenomenon—the "swallowing up" through industrialization of successive categories of expanding imports in the course of export-led growth—but had not characterized it as a linkage.

9. Staffan B. Linder, *Trade and Trade Policy for Development* (New York: Praeger Publishers, 1967), pp. 143–49 and 171–72; Stephen H. Hymer and Stephen A. Resnick, "A Model of an Agrarian Economy with Non-agricultural Activities," *American Economic Review* 59 (September 1969): 493–506; Stephen A. Resnick, "The Decline of Rural Industry under Export Expansion: A Comparison among Burma, Philippines, and Thailand, 1870–1938," *Journal of Economic History* 30 (March 1970): 51–73.

10. See Pearson, *Petroleum*, pp. 46–50 and passim. When the incomes from the staple accrue primarily to domestic parties who save a substantial portion of these incomes, a centralized national banking system can accomplish a redirection of the income stream that would be similar to that achieved by fiscal linkage. According to a communication from Juan Linz, in Spain this "banking linkage" has been of some importance and has served to channel funds from the citrus-fruit and mineral-ore exporters toward the industrial sector. Another note: the opposition between fiscal and physical linkages is not absolute, for it is perfectly conceivable that a government would use the revenues accruing from a given economic activity to establish an industry that is linked, in backward and forward fashion, to that activity.

11. See also below.

12. The history of this episode remains to be written. My sources are conversations with Professor Frank Fetter and with some descendants of the cocoa planters in Guayaquil—their fathers and grandfathers had to return to Ecuador after having been ruined by the witches' broom disease that destroyed the cocoa plantations, as well as by the depression of the thirties.

13. Anibal Pinto, *Tres ensayos sobre Chile y América Latina* (Buenos Aires: Solar, 1971), pp. 71ff.; that nitrate mining led to substantial nonfiscal linkages is demonstrated and stressed in a paper by Carmen Cariola and Osvaldo Sunkel, "La expansiíon salitrera y sus repercusiones sobre la economia agraria en el período 1880–1930" (October 1974), written for the Economic History Project of the Joint Committee on Latin American Studies (Social Science Research Council and American Council on Learned Societies).

14. See Shane J. Hunt, "Growth and Guano in Nineteenth-Century Peru" (discussion paper no. 34, Research Program in Economic Development, Princeton University, February 1973). This paper is written in part in rebuttal

of the earlier view, put forward in chap. 2 ("Peru in the Guano Age") of Jonathan V. Levin, *The Export Economies* (Cambridge, Mass.: Harvard University Press, 1960), that the revenues from guano were largely dissipated through luxury imports and profit remittances.

15. Hirschman, *Strategy,* pp. 78–83, 86–96, and passim.

16. See Thomas B. Birnberg and Stephen A. Resnick, *Colonial Development: An Econometric Study* (New Haven, Conn.: Yale University Press, 1975).

17. I have explained this matter at greater length in "The Political Economy of Import-substituting Industrialization in Latin America" (1968), reprinted in *Bias for Hope* (see p. 114). In the case of agriculture, technological strangeness is often combined with other obstacles to backward or forward linkages being taken up by the producers themselves; among those obstacles are the need for large amounts of capital due to scale requirements and the lack of marketing access and knowledge.

18. There are exceptions, of course: in many areas where coffee is grown the bags in which the beans are shipped are made from the fibers of the agave family of plants which are grown by the coffee farmer along the borders of his coffee plantings.

19. See R. E. Evenson, J. P. Houck, Jr., and V. W. Ruttan, "Technological Change and Agricultural Trade: Three Examples—Sugarcane, Bananas, and Rice," in *The Technology Factor in International Trade,* ed. R. Vernon (New York: Columbia University Press, for the National Bureau of Economic Research, 1970), pp. 442–51.

20. During earlier discussions, some observers noted that in many underdeveloped areas specialization in the production of staples for exports led to "onceover," noncumulative development. This intermediate possibility-a reality in many countries-has been lost sight of as the discussion has centered on the alternatives: immiserization or cumulative development. See, in particular, H. Myint, *Economic Theory and the Underdeveloped Countries* (London: Oxford University Press, 1971), chaps. 3 and 4 (originally published as articles in 1954).

21. Proposition (*a*) was put forward earlier in this essay; proposition (*b*) is in my "Political Economy of Import—Substituting Industrialization in Latin America"; and proposition (*c*) plays an important role in Guillermo O'Donnell's analysis of the economic foundations of bureaucratic authoritarianism in Latin America. See his "Reflexiones sobre las tendedas generales de cambio en el Estado Burocratico-autoritario," mimeographed (Buenos Aires: CEDES, August 1975). A somewhat different English version is in *Latin American Research Review* 13 (1978): 3–38.

22. Clifford Geertz, *Agricultural Involution: The Processes of Ecological Change in Indonesia* (Berkeley: University of California Press, 1963).

23. Pedro Calmon, *História do Brasil* (São Paulo: Companhia editora national, 1947), 4: 384–86, cited in Warren Dean, "The Planter as Entrepreneur: The Case of São Paulo," *Hispanic American Historical Review* 46 (May 1966): 146.

24. This is the factor stressed by Robert Baldwin in an article in which he examines the question, primarily for Africa, of why export staples have not led to cumulative growth. The alternative—or rather the dilemma—he describes is that between the mineral enclaves, where a skill ladder exists but is available only to a very small population group, and the agricultural staples, which do not provide for the acquisition of new skills. In my view, Baldwin overrates the importance of the acquisition of specific skills and overlooks the increase in overall competence, versatility, and entrepreneurial drive that can result from migration and geographical mobility. With mobility rather than skill acquisition as the crucial factor, the outlook for development looks somewhat more hopeful (see Robert E. Baldwin, "Export Technology and Development from a Subsistence Level," *Economic Journal* 73 [March 1963]: 80–92).

25. For the evidence from Ghana and Nigeria, see Polly Hill, *Migrant Cocoa Farmers of Southern Ghana* (Cambridge: Cambridge University Press, 1963), and Sara S. Berry, *Cocoa, Custom, and Socio-Economic Change in Rural Western Nigeria* (London: Oxford University Press, 1975), which, on pp. 75–78, spells out a number of advantages migrants have over local farmers.

26. See Judith Tendler, "Technology and Economic Development: The Case of Hydro vs. Thermal Power," *Political Science Quarterly* 80 {June 1965): 236–53.

27. A particularly striking demonstration that railroads in the United States were built piecemeal in this fashion and not "ahead of demand" is in Fishlow (n. 7 above).

28. E. R. J. Owen, *Cotton and the Egyptian Economy, 1820–1914* (London: Oxford University Press, 1969), p. 215.

29. Karl Wittfogel, *Oriental Despotism* (New Haven, Conn.: Yale University Press, 1957).

30. See Albert O. Hirschman, *Development Projects Observed* (Washington, D.C.: Brookings Institution, 1967), pp. 166–68.

31. Kelvin Lancaster, *Consumer Demand: A New Approach* (New York: Columbia University Press, 1971).

32. Anthony Scott, "The Development of the Extractive Industries," *Canadian journal of Economics and Political Science* 28 (February 1962): 81.

33. Fernando Henrique Cardoso and Enzo Faletto, *Dependencia y desarrollo en América Latino* (Mexico City: Siglo XXI, 1969), available in English as *Dependency and Development in Latin America* (Berkeley: University of California Press, 1979). A further important development of this typology is in Osvaldo Sunkel and Pedro Paz, *El subdesarrollo latino-americano y la teoría del desarrollo* (Mexico City: Siglo XXI, 1970), pp. 317–43. For a good survey of the related literature, see Norman Girvan, "The Development of Dependency Economics in the Caribbean and Latin America: Review and Comparison," *Social and Economic Studies* 22 (March 1973): 1–33.

34. For this and other development-related contrasts between road and railroad (in Nigena), see my *Development Projects Observed,* pp. 139–48.

35. Andre Gunder Frank, "The Development of Underdevelopment," *Monthly Review* 18 (September 1966): 17–31, and *Capitalism and Underdevelopment in Latin America* (New York: Monthly Review Press, 1967); see also Samir Amin, *L'Accumulation à l'échelle mondiale* (Paris: Anthropos, 1971).

36. For critiques of these views from within the left and/or the periphery, see Fernando Henrique Cardoso, *As contradições do desenvolvimento associado,* Estudos CEBRAP (Sao Paulo: CEBRAP, April–June 1974); also published as chapter 1 of his *Autoritarismo e democratização* (Rio de Janeiro: Paz e Terra, 1975); and Bill Warren, "Imperialism and Capitalist Industrialization," *New Left Review,* no. 81 (September/October 1973), pp. 3–45.

37. There is no intention here to suggest that the development story always has a happy end, that after a period of exploitation development's turn may surely be expected to come. For one thing, the opposite sequence, from a spurt of development to a period of stagnation and exploitation, can frequently be encountered, as 1 have attempted to show in discussing the positive and negative effects of foreign investment (see "How to Divest in Latin America, and Why," in *Bias for Hope,* Chapter 11). The need is for an analysis that can account for turnarounds of either kind.

38. The argument that the backwardness and poverty of the periphery is not a "state of nature," but is closely related to the development and enrichment of the center, is of course much older than the development-of-underdevelopment thesis of A. G. Frank, and is in fact implicit in Marx's theory of primitive accumulation. Even without plunder or exploitation, close economic contact between advanced and less advanced regions or countries can make for cumulatively divergent paths of development and impoverishment because of "backward" or "polarization" effects, as was shown in Gunnar

Myrdal, *Economic Theory and Under-developed Regions* (London: Duckworth, 1957) and in my *Strategy,* chap. 10. An early criticism of the concepts of "traditional society" and "modernization" is in Fernando Henrique Cardoso, *Empresario industrial e desenvolvimento economico* (São Paulo: Difusão Européia do Livro, 1964), pp. 65–72.

39. Alexander Gerschenkron, *Economic Backwardness in Historical Perspective* (Cambridge, Mass.: Harvard University Press, 1962)

40. "The Political Economy of Import-substituting Industrialization in Latin America, in *Bias for Hope.*

41. See, for example, Cardoso, "As contradições"; O'Donnell, "Reflexiones"; and James R. Kurth, "Patrimonial Authoriity, Delayed Development, and Mediterranean Politics" (paper presented at the annual meeting of the American Political Science Association, New Orleans, 1973), and "Industrial Structure and Comparative Politics," unpublished paper, May 1975.

42. Fernando Ortiz Fernandez, *Contrapunteo cubano del tabaco y el azucar* (Havana: Jesus Montero, 1940); the English version, with a foreword by B. Malinowski, is entitled *Cuban Counterpoint: Tobacco and Sugar* (New York: Knopf, 1947). The Spanish work was reedited by the Consejo Nacional de Cultura in 1963. A related treatment, primarily centered on sugar, is in Ramiro Guerra y Sánchez, *Sugar and Society in the Caribbean,* foreword by Sidney W. Mintz (New Haven, Conn.: Yale University Press, 1964). The original Spanish edition of this influential work was published in 1927.

43. Celso Furtado, *The Economic Growth of Brazil* (Berkeley: University of California Press, 1963), pp. 123–26; Luis Eduardo Nieto Arteta, *Economia y cultura en la historia de Colombia* (Bogotá: Ediciones Tercer Mundo, 1962; first edition in 1942), and particularly his *El café en la sociedad colombiana* (Bogotá: Breviarios de orientación colombiana, 1958); William Paul McGreevey, *An Economic History of Colombia, 1845–1930* (Cambridge: Cambridge University Press, 1971), chap. 9; Geertz, *Agricultural Involution.*

44. Tendler, *Electric Power in Brazil* and "Technology and Economic Development: The Case of Hydro vs. Thermal Power"; and my *Development Projects Observed,* pp. 139–48.

45. H. J. Nieboer, *Slavery as an Industrial System* (The Hague: Martinus Nijhoff, 1900), pp. 420–22; Sidney W. Mintz, "Foreword," in Sanchez; *Cambridge Economic History of Europe* (Cambridge: Cambridge University Press, 1967), 4: 290–1, 311–14; Evsey D. Domar, "The Causes of Slavery or Serfdom: A Hypothesis," *Journal of Economic History* 30 (March 1930): 18–32; Keith

Aufhauser, "Slavery and Technological Change," *Journal of Economic History* 34 (March 1974): 36–50, and passages from Ortiz and Tocqueville there cited.

46. Karl Marx, *Das Kapital* (Vienna: Verlag für Literatur und Politik, 1932), 1:785; Blaise Pascal, letter to his sister dated April 1, 1648, in *Oeuvres completes* (Paris: NRF-Pleiade, 1969), p. 484.

THE CONCEPT OF INTEREST
From Euphemism to Tautology

Few words in public debate have been burdened with more baggage than "self-interest." By the early 1980s, right-wingers were slinging it around to make the case for unfettering individuals from intrusive states; critics called them naive. They extolled the importance not of self-interest but of social purpose. Hirschman, as ever, found the exchange between ideologues unhelpful to say the least. His friend Pierre Bourdieu invited him to return to Paris, this time to deliver a series of keynote lectures at the Collège de France; Hirschman chose the theme of an enlarged political economy (*une économie politique élargie*), hoping to turn a dialogue of the deaf into fruitful conversation between adversaries. His goal was to show that the idea—the concept—of "interest" had a history and had been the battleground for economists since the seventeenth century. It was linked, however, not just to the concept of the self, but so importantly to the idea of political power itself. His point to the audience gathered in Paris was to show that personal welfare and statecraft were raveled together from the start. The effort to narrow the definition threatened to separate behaviors and activities from one domain of life from others, selfish or "interested" motivations from altruistic or "ethical" actions. This trend drained the concept itself of its great analytical power.

—*Jeremy Adelman*

"INTEREST" OR "INTERESTS" is one of the most central and controversial concepts in economics and, more generally, in social science and history. It is also extremely versatile, not to say ambiguous, and its meaning has been shifting a great deal. Since coming into widespread use, in various European countries around the latter part of the sixteenth century as essentially the same Latin-derived word (*intérêt, intéresse*, etc.), the concept has stood for the fundamental forces, based on the drive for self-preservation and self-aggrandizement, that motivate or should motivate the actions of the prince or the state, of the individual, and, later, of groups of people occupying a similar social or economic position (classes, interest groups). When related to the individual, the concept has at times had a very inclusive meaning, encompassing interest in honor, glory, self-respect, and even afterlife, while, at other times, it became wholly confined to the drive for economic advantage. Correspondingly, "pursuing one's interests" can cover—to the point of tautology—all of human action while it will more usefully designate a specific manner or *style* of conduct, known variously as "rational" or as "instrumental" action.

The esteem in which interest-motivated behavior is held has also varied drastically. The term was originally pressed into service as a euphemism serving, already in the late Middle Ages, to make respectable an activity, the taking of interest on loans, that had long been considered contrary to divine law and known as the sin of usury. In its wide meanings, the term achieved at times enormous prestige as key to a workable, peaceful, and progressive social order. But it has also been attacked as degrading to the human spirit and as dangerously disruptive and corrosive of the foundations of society. An inquiry into these multiple meanings and appreciations is in effect an exploration of much of economic history and in particular of the history of economic and political doctrine in the West over the past four centuries.

Moreover, the concept is still central in contemporary economics and political economy: the construct of the self-interested, isolated individual who chooses freely and rationally between alternative courses of action after computing their prospective costs and benefits to him- or herself, that is, while ignoring costs and benefits to other people and to society at large, underlies much of welfare economics; and the same perspective has yielded important, if disturbing, contributions to a broader science of social interactions, showing how the unfettered pursuit of private interest can lead to inefficient and harmful outcomes: examples are the decision problem known as the Prisoner's Dilemma, the obstacles to collective action because of free riding, and the problems of ensuring an adequate supply of public goods in general.

Two essential elements appear to characterize interest-propelled action: *self-centeredness*, that is, predominant attention of the actor to the consequences of any contemplated action for himself; and *rational calculation*, that is, a systematic attempt at evaluating prospective costs, benefits, satisfactions, and the like. Calculation could be considered the dominant or fundamental element: once action is supposed to be informed only by careful estimation of costs and benefits, with most weight necessarily being given to those that are better known and more quantifiable, it tends to become self-referential by virtue of the simple fact that each person is best informed about his or her own desires, satisfactions, disappointments, and sufferings.

Interest and Statecraft

Rational calculation was also preponderant in the emergence of the concept of interest-motivated action on the part of the prince in the sixteenth and seventeenth centuries. Self-centeredness was then either hidden from view, as the interest of the prince was assumed to be identical with that of his subjects, or treated as a matter of course, rather than of choice; in relation to other princes, the absence of interests in common and the hazards of antagonistic coexistence were considered to be unalterable facts of nature.

It was probably this stress on rational calculation that accounts for the high marks that interest (interest-governed behavior) received during the late sixteenth- and early seventeenth-century phases of its career in politics. The term actually did duty on two fronts. First, it permitted the emergent science of statecraft to assimilate the important insights of Machiavelli. The author of *The Prince* had almost strained to advertise those aspects of politics that clashed with conventional morality. He dwelt on instances where the prince was well-advised or even duty-bound to practice cruelty, mendacity, treason, and so on. Just as, in connection with money lending, the term interest came into use as a euphemism for the earlier term usury, so did it impose itself on the political vocabulary as a means of anesthetizing, assimilating, and developing some of Machiavelli's shocking insights. "Reason of state" was another such term, which as Meinecke later showed explicitly referred to the new practical rationality that came into favor.

But in the early modern age, "interest" was not only a label under which a ruler was given new latitude or was absolved from feeling guilty about following a practice he had previously been taught to consider as immoral: the term also served to impose new restraints, as it enjoined the prince to pursue his interests with a rational, calculating spirit that would often imply prudence, and moderation. At the beginning of the seventeenth century, the interests of the sovereign were contrasted with the wild and destructive passions, that is, with the immoderate and foolish seeking of glory and other excesses involved in pursuing the by then discredited heroic ideal of the Middle Ages and the Renaissance. This disciplinary aspect of the doctrine of interest was particularly driven home in the influential essay *On the Interest of Princes and States of Christendom* by the Huguenot statesman, the Duke of Rohan (1579–1638).

The interest doctrine thus served to release the ruler from certain traditional restraints (or guilt feelings) only to subject him to new ones that were felt to be far more efficacious than the well-worn appeals to religion, morals, or abstract reason. Genuine hope arose that, with princely or national interest as guide, statecraft would be able to produce a more stable political order and a more peaceful world. A distinct nineteenth-century echo of these seventeenth-century notions is heard in various pronouncements of Bismarck, and particularly in a famous foreign policy speech of 1888 where he contrasted legitimate *Interessenpolitik* with arrogant *Machtpolitik*, which he defined as a policy "that seeks to influence and press upon the policy of other countries and to call the tune *outside* of one's own sphere of interests.[1]

Interest and Individual Behavior

The early career of the interest concept with regard to statecraft finds a remarkable parallel in the role it played in shaping behavior codes for individual men and women in society. Here also a new license went hand in hand with a new restraint.

The new license consisted in the legitimation and even praise that was bestowed upon the single-minded pursuit of material wealth and upon activities conducive to its accumulation. Just as Machiavelli had opened up new horizons for the prince, so did Mandeville two centuries later lift a number of don'ts for the commoner, in this case primarily in relation to moneymaking. Once again, a new insight into human behavior or into the social order was first proclaimed as a startling, shocking para-dox. Like Machiavelli, Mandeville presented his thesis on the beneficial effects on the general welfare of the luxury trades (which had long been strictly regulated) in the most scandalous possible fashion, by referring to the activities, drives, and emotions associated with these trades as "private." Here again, his essential message was eventually absorbed into the general stock of accepted practice by changing the language with which he had proclaimed his discovery. For the third time, euphemistic resort was had to "interest," this time in substitution for such terms as "avarice," "love of lucre," and so on. The transition from one set of terms to the other is nicely reflected by the first lines of David Hume's 1742 essay "On the Independency of Parliament":

> Political writers have established it as a maxim, that, in contriving any system of government and fixing the several checks and bal-ances of the constitution, every man ought to be supposed a *knave*, and to have no other end, in all his actions, than private interest. By this interest we must govern him, and, by means of it, make him, notwithstanding his insatiable avarice and ambition, cooperate to public good.[2]

Here interest is explicitly equated with knavishness and "insatiable av-arice." But soon thereafter the memory of these unsavory synonyms of interest was suppressed, as in Adam Smith's famous statement about the butcher, the brewer, and the baker who are driven to supply us with our daily necessities through their interest rather than their benevolence. Smith thus did for Mandeville what the Duke of Rohan had done for Machiavelli His doctrine of the Invisible Hand, which held that the gen-eral welfare is best served by everyone catering to his private interests, le-gitimated total absorption of the citizens in their own affairs and thereby served to assuage any guilt feelings that might have been harbored by the many Englishmen who were drawn into commerce and industry during the eighteenth century but had been brought up under the civic humanist code enjoining them to serve the public interest *directly*. They were now reassured that by pursuing their private gain they were doing so *indirectly*.

In fact, Adam Smith was not content to praise the pursuit of private gain. Prefiguring Milton Friedman's hostility to corporations contribut-ing funds to charities and community improvements, he berated citizens' involvement in public affairs, by adding that he had "never known much good done by those who affected to trade for the public good." This may be just one of Smith's ill-humored sideswipes, but ten years before Sir James Steuart, in his *Inquiry into the Principles of Political Oeconomy*, had supplied an interesting explanation for a similar aversion toward citizens' involvement in public affairs:

> . . . were everyone to act for the public, and neglect himself, the statesman would be bewildered . . . were a people to become quite disinterested, there would be no possibility of governing them. Everyone might consider the interest of his country in a different light, and many might join in the ruin of it, by endeavoring to promote its advantages.[3]

In counterpart to the new area of authorized and recommended behavior, these statements point to the important restraints that accompanied the doctrine of interest. For the individual citizen or subject as for the ruler, interest-propelled action meant originally action informed by rational calculation in any area of human activity—political, cultural, economic, personal, and so on. In the seventeenth century and through part of the eighteenth, this sort of methodical, prudential, interest-guided action was seen as vastly preferable to actions dictated by the violent and unruly passions—the French liked to speak about *la violence et le désordre des passions*. Hope was held out that the steady, if self-centered, pull of the interests might serve more efficiently as a brake on passionate behavior than the traditional appeals to reason, duty, morals, and religion. At the same time, the interests of the vast majority of people, that is, of those outside of the highest reaches of power, came to be more narrowly defined as economic, material, or "moneyed" interests, probably because the non-elite was deemed to busy itself primarily with scrounging a living with no time left to worry about honor, glory, and the like. In this manner, the infatuation with interest helped to bestow legitimacy and prestige on commercial and related private activities that had hitherto ranked rather low in public esteem; correspondingly, the Renaissance ideal of glory, with its implicit celebration of the public sphere, was downgraded and debunked as a mere exercise in the destructive passion of self-love.[4]

Adam Smith and Sir James Steuart echo this feeling of mistrust toward, and disaffection from, activities that are aimed at achieving the public good directly. This change in attitude toward public involvement may have reflected a general mood: it is perhaps significant that only in the course of the eighteenth century did the verb "to meddle" firmly acquire its present-day derogatory sense.[5] The meaning of the French *se mêler de* has had a similar evolution. Previously these terms had a neutral and sometimes even a positive connotation: after all, to meddle is to care for somebody or something outside of one's own immediate circle or area of interest, an attitude and activity that became offensive only in an era when to mind one's own business had become enthroned as a general rule of conduct.

The Political Benefits of an Interest-Based Social Order

The idea that the interests, understood as the methodical pursuit and accumulation of private wealth, would bring a number of benefits in the political realm took various distinct forms. There was, first of all, the expectation that they would achieve at the macrolevel what they were supposed to accomplish for the individual: hold back the violent passions of the "rulers of mankind." Here the best known proposition, voiced early in the eighteenth century, says that the expansion of commerce is incompatible with the use of force in international relations and, would gradually make for a peaceful world. Still more utopian—and therefore perhaps half-forgotten—hopes were held out for the effects of commerce on domestic politics: the web of interests delicately woven by thousands of transactions would make it impossible for the sovereign to interpose his power brutally and wantonly through what was called "grands coups d'autorité" by Montesquieu or "the folly of despotism" by Sir James Steuart. This thought was carried further in the early nineteenth century when the intricacies of expanding industrial production compounded those of commerce: in the technocratic vision of Saint-Simon the time was at hand when economic exigencies would put an end, not just to *abuses* of the power of the state, but to any power whatsoever of man over man: politics would be replaced by administration of "things." As is well known this conjecture was taken up by Marxism with its prediction of the withering away of the state under communism. In this manner, an argument that a century earlier had been advanced on behalf of emergent capitalism was refurbished for a new, *anti*capitalist utopia.

Another line of thought about the political effects of an interest-driven society looks less at the disciplines and constraints such a society will impose upon those who govern than at the difficulties of the task of governing. As already noted, a world where people methodically pursue their private interests was believed to be far more predictable, and hence *more governable,* than one where the citizens are vying with each other for honor and glory. There was thought to be a huge common gain here, quite apart from the proposition that voluntary acts of exchange necessarily imply the existence of mutual benefits.

The stability and lack of turbulence that were expected to characterize a country where men pursue single-mindedly their material interests were very much on the minds of some of the "inventors" of America, such as James Madison and Alexander Hamilton. The enormous prestige and influence of the interest concept at the time of the founding of America is well expressed in Hamilton's statement: "The safest reliance of every government is on man's interests. This is a principle of human nature, on which all political speculation, to be just, must be founded."[6]

Finally, at the most naive level, a number of writers essentially extrapolated from the putative personality traits of the individual trader, as the prototype of interest-driven man, to the general characteristics of a society where traders would predominate. In the eighteenth century, perhaps as a result of some continuing, if unavowed, disdain for economic pursuits, commerce and moneymaking were often described as essentially innocuous or "innocent" pastimes, in contrast no doubt with the more violent or more strenuous ways of the upper or lower classes. Commerce was to bring "gentle" and "polished" manners. In French, the term innocent appended to commerce was often coupled with *doux* (sweet, gentle), or *adoucir* (soften, render gentle), and what has been called the thesis of the *doux commerce* held that commerce was a powerful civilizing agent diffusing prudence, probity, and similar virtues within and among trading societies. Only under the impact of the French Revolution did some doubt arise on the direction of the causal link between commerce and civilized society: taken aback by the outbreak of social violence on a large scale, Edmund Burke suggested that the expansion of commerce depended itself on the *prior* existence of "manners" and "civilization" and on what he called "natural protecting principles" grounded in "the spirit of a gentleman" and "the spirit of religion."[7]

It was inevitable that the celebration of the interests should have enhanced the esteem accorded to those social groups that were primarily involved in commerce and industry. An early expression of this tendency is in *Robinson Crusoe* where Crusoe's father explains to his son—to dissuade him from his plans—that the "middle state" is "the most suited to human happiness, not exposed to the miseries and hardships, the labour and sufferings of the mechanic part of mankind, and not embarrassed with the pride, luxury, ambition and envy of the upper part of mankind."

Similar expressions of admiration for what was later often called the "middling rank of men" or simply "middle ranks" (rather than middle class) can be found in the writings of David Hume, Adam Smith, Adam Ferguson, and of the other exponents of the Scottish Enlightenment. In the nineteenth century James Mill waxed remarkably eloquent on this subject.[8] In France, the praise of the bourgeoisie as such was never quite so unreserved, but some of its constituent parts, such as the commercial community, rose in prestige as a result of the praise for the *doux commerce*.

The Invisible Hand

The capstone of the doctrine of self-interest was of course Adam Smith's Invisible Hand. Even though this doctrine, being limited to the economic domain, was more modest than the earlier speculations on the beneficent *political* effects of trade and exchange, it soon came to dominate the discussion. An intriguing paradox was involved in stating that the *general* interest and welfare would be promoted by the self-interested activities of numerous decentralized operators. To be sure, this was not the first nor the last time that such a claim of identity or coincidence or harmony of interests of a part with those of a whole has been put forward. Hobbes had advocated an absolute monarchy on the ground that this form of government brings about an identity of interests between ruler and ruled; as just noted, the writers of the Scottish Enlightenment saw an identity of interest between the general interests of British society and the interests of the middle ranks; such an identity between the interests of one class and those of society later became a cornerstone of Marxism, with the middling ranks having of course been supplanted by the proletariat; and finally, the American pluralist school in political science returned essentially to the Smithian scheme of harmony between many self-interests and the general interest, with Smith's individual economic operators having been replaced by contending "interest groups" on the political stage.

All these *Harmonielehren* (and I have probably been omitting some) have two factors in common: the "realistic" affirmation that we have to deal with men and women, or with groups thereof, "as they really are"; and an attempt to prove that it is possible to achieve a workable and progressive social order with these highly imperfect subjects, and, as it were, behind their backs. The mixture of paradoxical insight and alchemy involved in these constructs makes them powerfully attractive, but also accounts for their ultimate vulnerability. Perhaps social scientists ought to be advised to use caution in the construction of any further harmony-of-interests doctrines.

The Interests Attacked

The infatuation of the seventeenth and eighteenth centuries with the new insights offered by the concept of interest was remarkable. From the seventeenth-century English proverbs "Interest will not lie" or "Interest governs the world" to the late eighteenth-century dictum of the French *philosophe* Helvétius, "As the physical world is ruled by the laws of movement so is the moral universe ruled by the laws of interest," and to Hamilton's already noted similar pronouncement, interest was perceived as the key that unlocks the secrets of the social universe.

The seventeenth century was perhaps the real heyday of the interest doctrine. Governance of the social world by interest was then viewed as an alternative to the rule of destructive passions; that was surely a lesser evil, and possibly an outright blessing. In the eighteenth century, the doctrine received a substantial boost in the economic domain through the doctrine of the Invisible Hand, but it was indirectly weakened by the emergence of a more optimistic view of the passions: such passionate sentiments and emotions as curiosity, generosity, and sympathy were then given detailed attention, the latter in fact by Adam Smith himself in his *Theory of Moral Sentiments*. In comparison to such fine, newly discovered or rehabilitated springs of human action, interest no longer looked nearly so attractive. Here was one reason for the reaction against the interest paradigm that unfolded toward the end of the eighteenth century and was to fuel several powerful nineteenth-century intellectual movements, starting with romanticism.

Actually the passions did not have to be wholly transformed into benign sentiments to be thought respectable and even admirable by a new generation. Once the interests appeared to be truly in command with the vigorous commercial and industrial expansion of the age, a general lament went up for "the world we have lost." The French Revolution brought another sense of loss and Edmund Burke joined the two when he exclaimed, in his *Reflections on the Revolution in France*, "the age of chivalry is gone; that of sophisters, economists and calculators has succeeded; and the glory of Europe is extinguished forever." This famous statement came a bare fourteen years after the *Wealth of Nations* had denounced the rule of the "great lords" as a "scene of violence, rapine and disorder" and had celebrated the benefits flowing from everyone catering to his interests through orderly economic pursuits. Now Burke was an intense admirer of Adam Smith and took much pride in the identity of views on economic matters between himself and Smith. His "age of chivalry" statement, so contrary to the intellectual legacy of Smith, therefore signals one of those sudden changes in the general mood and understanding from one age to the next of which the exponents themselves are hardly aware. Burke's lament set the tone for much of the subsequent romantic protest against an order based on the interests which, once it appeared to be dominant, was seen by many as lacking nobility, mystery, and beauty.

This nostalgic reaction merged with the observation that the interests, that is, the drive for material wealth, were not nearly so "innocuous," "innocent," or "mild" as had been thought or advertised. To the contrary, it was now the drive for material advantage that suddenly loomed as a subversive force of enormous power. Thomas Carlyle thought that all traditional values were threatened by "that brutish god-forgetting Profit-and-Loss Philosophy" and protested that "cash payment is not the only nexus of man with man."[9] The phrase "cash nexus" was taken over by Marx and Engels, who used it to good effect in the first section of the *Communist Manifesto* where they painted a lurid picture of the moral and cultural havoc wrought by the conquering bourgeoisie.

In the same vein Proudhon saw property as a boundless revolutionary force. Trying to snatch good from evil, he conceived of the modern idea that the power of property might serve to check the equally terrifying power of the state: human liberty would be founded on this tension.[10] But such constructive or optimistic thoughts were exceedingly rare. Among the critics of capitalist society the accent was in general on the destructiveness of the new energies that were released by a social order in which the interests were given free rein. In fact, the thought arose that these forces were so wild and out of control that they might undermine the very foundations on which the social order was resting, that they were thus bent on self-destruction. In a startling reversal, feudal society, which had earlier been treated as "rude and barbarous" and was thought to be in permanent danger of dissolution because of the unchecked passions of violent rulers and grandees, was perceived in retrospect to have nurtured such values as honor, respect, friendship, trust, and loyalty, that were essential for the functioning of an interest-dominated order, but were relentlessly, if inadvertently, undermined by it. This argument was already contained in part in Burke's assertion that it is civilized society that lays the groundwork for commerce rather than vice versa; it was elaborated by a large and diverse group of authors, from Richard Wagner via Schumpeter to Karl Polanyi and Fred Hirsch.[11]

The Interests Diluted

While the interest doctrine thus met with considerable opposition and criticism in the nineteenth century, its prestige remained nevertheless high, particularly because of the vigorous development of economics as a new body of scientific thought. Indeed, the success of this new science made for attempts to utilize its insights, such as the interest concept, for elucidating some noneconomic aspects of the social world. In his "Essay on Government" (1820), James Mill formulated the first "economic" theory of politics and based it—just as was later done by Schumpeter, Anthony Downs, Mancur Olson, and others—on the assumption of rational self-interest. But this widening of the use of the concept turned out to be something of a disservice. In politics, so Mill had to recognize, the gap between the "real" interest of the citizen and "a false supposition [i.e., perception] of interest" can be extremely wide and problematic. This difficulty provided an opening for Macaulay's withering attack in the *Edinburgh Review* (1829). Macaulay pointed out that Mill's theory was empty: interest "means only that men, if they can, will do as they choose . . . it is . . . idle to attribute any importance to a proposition which, when interpreted, means only that a man had rather do what he had rather do."

The charge that the interest doctrine was essentially tautological acquired greater force as more parties climbed on the bandwagon of interest, attempting to bend the concept to their own ends. Like so many key concepts used in everyday discourse, "interest" had never been strictly defined. While individual self-interest in material gain predominated, broader meanings were never completely lost sight of, as appears from the expression "narrow" self-interest, which is presumably distinguished from another kind of self-interest. An extremely inclusive interpretation of the concept was put forward at a very early stage of its history: Pascal's Wager—his demonstration that it is "rational" to act as though God existed, in the absence of certain knowledge about the matter—was nothing but an attempt to demonstrate that belief in God (hence, conduct in accordance with His precepts) was strictly in our (long-term) self-interest. Thus the concepts of *enlightened self-interest* or *intérêt bien compris* have a long history. But they received a boost and special, concrete meaning in the course of the nineteenth century. With the contemporary revolutionary outbreaks and movements as an ominous backdrop, advocates of social reform were able to argue that a dominant social group is well advised to surrender some of its privileges or to improve the plight of the lower classes so as to ensure social peace ("give up something not to lose everything"). "Enlightened" self-interest of the upper classes and conservative opinion was appealed to, for example, by the French and English advocates of universal suffrage or electoral reform at mid-century (the introduction of universal manhood suffrage in France after the 1848 Revolution was expected to "close the era of revolutions");[12] it was similarly invoked by the promoters of the early social-welfare legislation in Germany and elsewhere toward the end of the century, and again by Keynes and the Keynesians who favored limited intervention of the state in the economy through countercyclical policy and "automatic stabilizers" resulting from welfare-state provisions. These appeals were often made by reformers who, while fully convinced of the intrinsic value and social justice of the measures they advocated, attempted to enlist the support of important groups by appealing to their "longer-term" rather than short-term and therefore presumably shortsighted interests. But the advocacy was not only tactical. It was sincerely put forward and testified to the continued prestige of the notion that interest-motivated social behavior was the best guarantee of a stable and harmonious social order.

Whereas enlightened self-interest was something the upper classes of society were in this manner pressed to ferret out and to pursue, the lower classes were similarly exhorted, at about the same epoch but from different quarters, to raise their sights above day-to-day interests and pursuits. Marx and the Marxists invited the working class to become aware of its *real interests* and to shed the "false consciousness" from which it was said to be suffering as long as it did not throw itself wholeheartedly into the class struggle. Once again, the language of interests was borrowed for the purpose of characterizing and signifying a type of behavior a group was being pressed to follow.

Here, then, was one way in which the concept of interest-motivated behavior came to be diluted. Another was the progressive loss of the sharp distinction an earlier age had made between the passions and the interests. Already Adam Smith had used the two concepts jointly and interchangeably. Even though it became abundantly clear in the nineteenth century that the desire to accumulate wealth was anything but the "calm passion" as which it had been categorized and commended by some eighteenth-century philosophers, there was no return to the earlier distinction between the interests and the passions or between the wild and the mild passions. Perhaps this was so because moneymaking had once and for all been identified with the concept of interest so that all forms of this activity, however passionate or irrational, were automatically thought of as interest-motivated. As striking new forms of accumulation and industrial or financial empire-building made their appearance, new concepts were introduced, such as Schumpeter's entrepreneurial leadership and intuition or Keynes's "animal spirits" (of the capitalists.) But they were not contrasted with the interests, and were rather assumed to be one of their manifestations.

In this manner the interests came to cover virtually the entire range of human actions, from the narrowly self-centered to the sacrificially altruistic, and from the prudently calculated to the passionately compulsive. In the end, interest stood behind anything people do or wish to do, and to explain human action by interest thus did turn into the vacuous tautology denounced by Macaulay. It so happened that, at about the same time, other key and time-honored concepts of economic analysis, such as utility and value, became similarly drained of their earlier psychological or normative content. The positivistically oriented science of economics that flourished during much of this century felt it could do without any of these terms and replaced them by the less value- or psychology-laden "revealed preference" and "maximizing under constraints." And thus it came to pass that interest, which had rendered such long, faithful, and multiple services as a euphemism (for usury, for cruelty and other types of amoral princely behavior, and for avarice and love of lucre), was now superseded by various even more neutral and colorless neologisms.

It may be conjectured that the development of the self-interest concept and of economic analysis in general in the direction of positivism and formalism was related to the discovery, toward the end of the nineteenth century, of the instinctual-intuitive, the habitual, the unconscious, the ideologically and neurotically driven—in short, to the extraordinary vogue for the nonrational that characterized virtually all of the influential philosophical, psychological, and sociological thinking of the age. It was out of the question for economics, all based on rationally pursued self-interest, to incorporate the new findings into its own apparatus. So that discipline reacted to the contemporary intellectual temper by withdrawing from psychology to the greatest possible extent, by emptying its basic concepts of their psychological origin—a survival strategy that turned out to be highly successful. It is of course difficult to prove that the rise of the nonrational in psychology and sociology and the triumph of positivism and formalism in economics were truly connected in this way. Some evidence is supplied by the remarkable case of Pareto: he made fundamental, *interrelated* contributions both to a sociology that stressed the complex "nonlogical" (as he put it) aspects of social action and to an economics that is emancipated from dependence on psychological hedonism.

Current Trends

Lately there have been signs of discontent with the progressive evisceration of the concept of interest. On the conservative side, there was a return to the orthodox meaning of interest and the doctrine of enlightened self-interest was impugned. Apart from the discovery, first made by Tocqueville, that reform is just as likely to unleash as to prevent revolution, it was pointed out that most well-meant reform moves and regulations have "perverse" side effects which compound rather than alleviate the social ills one had set out to cure. It was best, so it appeared, not to stray from the narrow path of narrow self-interest, and it was confusing and pointless to dilute this concept.

Others agreed with the latter judgment, but for different reasons and with different conclusions. They also disliked the maneuver of having every kind of human action masquerade under the interest label: But they regarded as relevant for economics certain human actions and activities which cannot be accounted for by the traditional notion of self-interest: actions motivated by altruism, by commitment to ethical values, by concern for the group and the public interest and, perhaps most important, the varieties of noninstrumental behavior. A beginning has been made by various economists and other social scientists to take these kinds of activities and behavior seriously, that is, to abandon the attempt to categorize them as mere variants of interest-motivated activity.[13]

One important aspect of these various forms of behavior which do not correspond to the classical concept of interest-motivated action is that they are subject to considerable variation. Take actions in the public interest as an example. There is a wide range of such actions, from total involvement in some protest movement down to voting on Election Day and further down to mere grumbling about, or just commenting on, some public policy within a small circle of friends or family—what Guillermo O'Donnell has called "horizontal voice" in contrast to the "vertical" voice directly addressed to the authorities. The actual degree of participation under more or less normal political conditions is subject to constant fluctuations along this continuum, in line with changes in economic conditions, government performance, personal development, and many other factors. As a result, with total time for private *and* public activity being limited, the intensity of citizens' dedication to their private affairs is also subject to constant change. Near-total privatization occurs only under certain authoritarian governments, for, as Benjamin Constant acutely noted, "the art of oppressive government is to keep all its citizens separated from each other."[14] The most repressive regimes not only do away with the free vote and any open manifestation of dissent, but also manage to suppress, through their display of terrorist power, all *private* expressions of inconformity with public policy, that is, all those manifestations of "horizontal voice" that are actually important forms of public involvement.

An arresting conclusion follows. That vaunted ideal of predictability, that alleged idyll of a privatized citizenry paying busy and exclusive attention to its economic interests and thereby serving the public interest indirectly, but never directly, becomes a reality only under wholly nightmarish political conditions! More civilized political circumstances necessarily imply a less transparent and less predictable society.

Actually, this outcome of the current inquiries into activities not strictly motivated by traditional self-interest is all to the good: for the only certain and predictable feature of human affairs is their unpredictability and the futility of trying to reduce human action to a single motive—such as interest.

Bibliographical References

Ball, Terence. "The Ontological Presuppositions and Political Consequences of a Social Science." In *Changing Social Science*, edited by D. R. Sabia, Jr., and J. T. Wallulis. Albany: State University of New York Press, 1983.

Boulding, Kenneth E. *The Economy of Love and Fear: A Preface to Grant Economics*. Belmont, Calif.: Wadsworth, 1973.

Burke, Edmund. *Reflections on the Revolution in France*. 1790.

Carlyle, Thomas. *Past and Present*. 1843. New York: New York University Press, 1977.

Collard, David. *Altruism and Economy: A Study in Non-selfish Economics*. Oxford: Robertson, 1978.

Collini, Stefan; Winch, Donald; and Burrow, John. *That Noble Science of Politics: A Study in Nineteenth-Century Intellectual History*. Cambridge: Cambridge University Press, 1983.

Constant, Benjamin. *Principes de Politique*. Edited by Etienne Hofmann. Geneva: Droz, 1980.

Defoe, Daniel. *Robinson Crusoe*. 1719.

Hamilton, Alexander. "Letters from Phocion." 1784. Number 1. In *The Works of Alexander Hamilton*, edited by John C. Hamilton, vol. 2, p. 322. New York: C. S. Francis, 1851.

Himmelfarb, Gertrude. *The Idea of Poverty: England in the Early Industrial Age*. New York: Knopf, 1984.

Hirschman, Albert O. *The Passions and the Interests: Political Arguments for Capitalism before Its Triumph*. Princeton, N.J.: Princeton University Press, 1977.

————. *Shifting Involvements: Private Interest and Public Action.* Princeton, N.J.: Princeton University Press, 1982.

Holmes, Stephen. *Benjamin Constant and the Making of Modern Liberalism.* New Haven, Conn.: Yale University Press, 1984.

Hume, David. *Essays Moral, Political and Literary.* 1742. Edited by T. H. Green and T. H. Grose. London: Longmans, 1898.

Keynes, John Maynard. *The General Theory of Employment Interest and Money.* London: Macmillan, 1936.

Koselleck, Reinhart. "Der Interessebegriff im Wandel des sozialen und politische Kontexts." In *Geschichtliche Grundbegriffe.* Stuttgart: Klett-Cotta, 1982, III, 344–62.

Macaulay, Thomas B. "Mill's Essay on Government." 1829. In *Utilitarian Logic and Politics,* edited by J. Lively and J. Rees. Oxford: Clarendon, 1978.

McPherson, Michael S. "Limits on Self-seeking: The Role of Morality in Economic Life." In *Neoclassical Political Economy,* edited by D. C. Colander, pp. 71–85. Cambridge, Mass.: Ballinger, 1984.

Margolis, Howard. *Selfishness, Altruism, and Rationality.* Cambridge: Cambridge University Press, 1982.

Meinecke, Friedrich. *Die Idee der Staatsräson in der neueren Geschichte.* Munich: Oldenburg, 1924.

Mill, James. "Essay on Government." 1820. In *Utilitarian Logic and Politics,* edited by J. Lively and J. Rees. Oxford: Clarendon, 1978.

O'Donnell, Guillermo. "On the Convergences of Hirschman's *Exit, Voice, and Loyalty* and *Shifting Involvements.*" In *Development, Democracy, and the Art of Trespassing: Essays in Honor of Albert O. Hirschman,* edited by A. Foxley et al. Notre Dame, Ind.: University of Notre Dame Press, 1986.

Phelps, Edmund S., ed. *Altruism, Morality and Economic Theory.* New York: Russell Sage Foundation, 1975.

Pizzorno, Alessandro. "Sulla razionalità della scelta democratica." *Stato e Mercato,* April 1983. English version in *Telos,* Spring 1985.

Pocock, John G. A. "The Political Economy of Burke's Analysis of the French Revolution." *Historical Journal,* June 1982.

Rohan, Henri, Due de. *De l'interest des princes et estats de la chrestiente.* 1638.

Schelling, Thomas C. *Choice and Consequence.* Cambridge, Mass.: Harvard University Press, 1984.

Schumpeter, Joseph. *The Theory of Economic Development.* 1911. Cambridge, Mass.: Harvard University Press, 1951.

Sen, Amartya. "Rational Fools: A Critique of the Behavioral Foundations of Economic Theory." *Philosophy and Public Affairs,* Summer 1977.

Smith, Adam. *An Inquiry into the Nature and Causes of the Wealth of Nations.* 1776.

Steuart, Sir James. *Inquiry into the Principles of Political Oeconomy.* 1761. Edited by A. S. Skinner. Chicago: University of Chicago Press, 1966.

Winch, Donald. "The Burke-Smith Problem and Late Eighteenth-Century Political and Economic Thought." 1984. *Historical Journal*, March 1985.

Notes

1. Cited in Koselleck, p. 349.

2. See Hume, pp. 117–118.

3. See Steuart, pp. 243–44.

4. See my *The Passions and the Interests*, pp. 31–42.

5. I owe this to a personal communication from Quentin Skinner.

6. Cited in Ball, p. 45.

7. Cited by Pocock.

8. See Collini, Winch and Burrow, p. 122.

9. *Past and Present*, p. 187.

10. See my *The Passions and the Interests*, p. 120.

11. See my "Rival Views of Market Society," *Rival Views of Market Society and Other Recent Essays* (New York: Viking Press, 1986), pp. 105–139.

12. See my *Shifting Involvements*, pp. 112–117.

13. Among many other works, reference should be made to writings (cited in the Bibliographical References) by Boulding, Collard, Margolis, McPherson, Phelps, Pizzorno, Schelling, and Sen; see also my "Against Parsimony: Three Easy Ways of Complicating Some Categories of Economic Discourse," *Rival Views of Market Society.*

14. Cited in Holmes, p. 247.

RIVAL VIEWS OF MARKET SOCIETY

The beginning of the 1980s saw Hirschman reaching his prime. He was a global figure. His work transcended the boundaries of academic disciplines and was shaping fields as wide apart as psychology and intellectual history. In 1977 he had published *The Passions and the Interests: Political Arguments for Capitalism before its Triumph*, a book that registered him as one of the great humanist thinkers of his age. *Passions and the Interests*, however, was unusual for Hirschman. He once noted that it was a kind of "retreat" into history, away from the current-day struggles over policy and political economy that consumed him from the 1940s. Without losing sight of contemporary issues, what he sought was to excavate the multiple ways in which economists had thought about capitalism, and so to illuminate in the 1970s the range of possible ways in which one might think about markets and property just as a certain kind of orthodoxy associated with "free markets" was gaining strength. An invitation from the École des Hautes Études en Sciences Sociales to deliver the Marc Bloch lectures in Paris in 1982 afforded the right opportunity for Hirschman to take the historical arguments of *The Passions and the Interests* and use them to inform debates that were heating up in the age of Ronald Reagan and Margaret Thatcher.

—Jeremy Adelman

ONCE UPON A TIME, not all that long ago, the social, political, and economic order under which men and women were living was taken for granted. Among the people of those idyllic times many of course were poor, sick, or oppressed, and consequently unhappy; no doubt, others managed to feel unhappy for seemingly less cogent reasons; but most tended to attribute their unhappiness either to concrete and fortuitous happenings—ill luck, ill health, the machinations of enemies, an unjust master, lord or ruler—or to remote, general, and unchangeable causes, such as human nature or the will of God. The idea that the social order—intermediate between the fortuitous and the unchangeable—may be an important cause of human unhappiness became widespread only in the modern age, particularly in the eighteenth century. Hence Saint-Just's famous phrase: "The idea of happiness is new in Europe"—it was then novel to think that happiness could be *engineered* by changing the social order, a task he and his Jacobin companions had so confidently undertaken.

Let us note in passing that the idea of a perfectible social order arose at about the same time as that of human actions and decisions having unintended effects. The latter idea was in principle tailor-made to neutralize the former: it permitted one to argue that the best intentioned institutional changes might lead, via those unforeseen consequences or "perverse effects," to all kinds of disastrous results. But two ideas were not immediately matched up for this purpose. In the first place, the idea of the perfectibility of the social order arose primarily in the course of the French Enlightenment, while that of the unintended consequences was a principal contribution of contemporary Scottish moralists. Also, the form that the latter idea took initially stressed the happy and socially desirable outcome of self-serving individual behavior that was traditionally thought to be reprehensible, rather than uncovering the unfortunate consequences of well-intentioned social reforms. In any event, the idea of a perfectible society was not to be nipped in the bud; to the contrary, it experienced a most vigorous development and, soon after the French Revolution, reappeared in the guise of powerful critiques of the social and economic order—capitalism—emerging at the beginning of the nineteenth century.

Here I am concerned with several such critiques and their interrelations. First I shall show the close relationship and direct contradiction between an early argument *in favor of* market society and a subsequent principal *critique* of capitalism. Next, I shall point to the contradictions between this critique and another diagnosis of the ills from which much of modern capitalist society is said to suffer. And finally the tables will be turned on this second critique by yet another set of ideas. In all three cases, there was an almost total lack of communication between the conflicting theses. Intimately related intellectual formations unfolded at great length, without ever taking cognizance of each other. Such ignoring of close kin is no doubt the price paid by ideology for the self-confidence it likes to parade.

The *Doux-Commerce* Thesis

To begin, let me briefly evoke the complex of ideas and expectations that accompanied the expansion of commerce and the development of the market from the sixteenth to the eighteenth centuries. Here I must return to a principal theme of my book *The Passions and the Interests* (1977), with the hope of placating at least partially those of my readers who complained that, while I traced ideological developments in some detail up to Adam Smith, they were left guessing what happened next, in the age—our own—that *really* mattered to them. My book dwelt on the favorable side effects that the emerging economic system was imaginatively but confidently expected to have, with respect to both the character of citizens and the characteristics of statecraft. I stressed particularly the latter—the expectation, entertained by Montesquieu and Sir James Steuart, that the expansion of the market would restrain the arbitrary actions and excessive power plays of the sovereign, both in domestic and in international politics. Here I shall emphasize instead the expected effects of commerce on the *citizen* and *civil society.* At mid-eighteenth century it became the conventional wisdom—Rousseau of course rebelled against it—that commerce was a civilizing agent of considerable power and range. Let me again cite Montesquieu's key sentence, which he placed at the very beginning of his discussion of economic matters in the *Spirit of the Laws*: "It is almost a general rule that wherever manners are gentle [*moeurs douces*] there is commerce; and wherever there is commerce, manners are gentle." The relationship between "gentle manners" and commerce is presented as mutually reinforcing, but a few sentences later Montesquieu leaves no doubt about the predominant direction of the causal link: "Commerce . . . polishes and softens [*adoucit*] barbaric ways as we can see every day."[1]

This way of viewing the influence of expanding commerce on society was widely accepted throughout most of the eighteenth century. It is stressed in two outstanding histories of progress—then a popular genre—William Robertson's *View of the Progress of Society, in Europe* (1769) and Condorcet's *Esquisse d'un tableau historique du progrés de l'esprit humain* (1793–94). Robertson repeats Montesquieu almost word by word—Commerce . . . softens and polishes the manners of men"— and Condorcet, while elsewhere critical of Montesquieu's political ideas, also followed his lead in this area quite closely:

> Manners [*moeurs*] have become more gentle [*se sont adoucies*] . . . through the influence of the spirit of commerce and industry, those enemies of the violence and turmoil which cause wealth to flee.[2]

One of the strongest statements comes in 1792, from Thomas Paine, in *The Rights of Man*,

> [Commerce] is a pacific system, operating to cordialise mankind, by rendering Nations, as well as individuals, useful to each other . . . The invention of commerce . . . is the greatest approach towards universal civilization that has yet been made by any means not immediately flowing from moral principles.[3]

What was the concrete meaning of all this *douceur*, polish, gentleness, and even cordiality? Through what precise mechanisms was expanding commerce going to have such happy effects? The eighteenth-century literature is not very communicative in this regard, perhaps because it all seemed so obvious to contemporaries. The most detailed account I have been able to find appears in a technical book on commerce by one Samuel Ricard first published in 1704, which must have been highly successful as it was reprinted repeatedly through the next eighty years.

> Commerce attaches [men] one to another through mutual utility. Through commerce the moral and physical passions are superseded by interest . . . Commerce has a special character which distinguishes it from all other professions. It affects the feelings of men so strongly that it makes him who was proud and haughty suddenly turn supple, bending and serviceable. Through commerce, man learns to deliberate, to be honest, to acquire manners, to be prudent and reserved in both talk and action. Sensing the necessity to be wise and honest in order to succeed, he flees vice, or at least his demeanor exhibits decency and seriousness so as not to arouse any adverse judgement on the part of present and future acquaintances;

he would not dare make a spectacle of himself for fear of damaging his credit standing and thus society may well avoid a scandal which it might otherwise have to deplore.[4]

Commerce is presented as a powerful moralizing agent which brings many nonmaterial improvements to society even though a bit of hypocrisy may have to be accepted into the bargain. Similar modifications of human behavior and perhaps even of human nature were later credited to the spread of commerce and industry by David Hume and Adam Smith: the virtues they specifically mention as being enhanced or brought into the world by commerce and manufacturing are industriousness and assiduity (the opposite of indolence), frugality, punctuality, and, most important perhaps for the functioning of market society, probity.[5]

There is here, then, the insistent thought that a society where the market assumes a central position for the satisfaction of human wants will not only produce considerable new wealth because of the division of labor and consequent technical progress, but generate as a by-product, or external economy, a more "polished" human type—more honest, reliable, orderly, and disciplined, as well as more friendly and helpful, ever ready to find solutions to conflicts and a middle ground for opposed opinions. Such a type will in turn greatly facilitate the smooth functioning of the market. According to this line of reasoning, capitalism, which in its early phases led a rather shaky existence, having to contend with a host of precapitalist mentalities left behind by the feudal and other "rude and barbarous" epochs, will create, in the course of time and through the very practice of trade and industry, a set of compatible psychological attitudes and moral dispositions, that are both desirable in themselves and conducive to the further expansion of the system. And at certain epochs, the speed and vigor displayed by that expansion lent considerable plausibility to this conjecture.

The Self-Destruction Thesis

Whatever became of this brave eighteenth-century vision? I shall reserve this topic for later and turn now to a body of thought which is far more familiar to us than the *doux-commerce* thesis—and happens to be its obverse. According to it, capitalist society, far from fostering *douceur* and other fine attitudes, exhibits a pronounced proclivity to undermining the moral foundations on which any society, including its own, must rest. I shall call this the self-destruction thesis.

This thesis has a fairly numerous ancestry among both Marxist and conservative thinkers. Moreover, a political economist who was neither has recently given it renewed prominence and sophisticated treatment. In his influential book *Social Limits to Growth*, Fred Hirsch dealt at length with what he called "The Depleting Moral Legacy" of capitalism. (This is the general heading of chaps. 8–11.) He argues that the market *undermines* the moral values that are its own essential underpinnings, values that, so he asserts, have been inherited from *preceding* socioeconomic regimes, such as the feudal order. The idea that capitalism depletes or "erodes" the moral foundation needed for its functioning is put forward in the following terms:

> The social morality that has served as an understructure for economic individualism has been a legacy of the precapitalist and preindustrial past. This legacy has diminished with time and with the corrosive contact of the active capitalist values—and more generally with the greater anonymity and greater mobility of industrial society. The system has thereby lost outside support that was previously taken for granted by the individual. As individual behavior has been increasingly directed to individual advantage, habits and instincts based on communal attitudes and objectives have lost out. The weakening of traditional social values has made predominantly capitalist economies more difficult to manage.[6]

Once again, one would like to know in more detail how the market acts on values, this time in the direction of "depletion" or "erosion," rather than *douceur*. In developing his argument Hirsch makes the following principal points:

1. The emphasis on self-interest typical of capitalism makes it more difficult to secure the collective goods and cooperation increasingly needed for the proper functioning of the system in its later stages (chapter 11).
2. With macromanagement, Keynesian or otherwise, assuming an important role in the functioning of the system, the macromanagers

must be motivated by "the general interest" rather than by their self-interest, and the system, being based on self-interest, has no way of generating the proper motivation; to the extent such motivation does exist, it is a residue of previous value systems that are likely to "erode."

3. Social virtues such as "truth, trust, acceptance, restraint, obligation,"needed for the functioning of an "individualistic, contractual economy," are grounded, to a considerable extent, in religious, belief, but "the individualistic, rationalistic base of the market undermines religious support."[7]

The last point stands in particularly stark contrast to the earlier conception of commerce and of its beneficial side effects. In the first place, thinkers of the seventeenth and eighteenth centuries took it for granted that they have to make do with "man as he really is" and that meant to them with someone who has been proven to be largely impervious to religious and moralistic precepts. With this realistic-pessimistic appraisal of human nature, those thinkers proceeded to discover in "interest" a principle that could replace "love" and "charity" as the basis for a well-ordered society. Second, and most important in the present context, to the extent that society is in need of moral values such as "truth, trust, etc." for its functioning, these values were confidently expected to be *generated*, rather than eroded, by the market, its practices and incentives.

Hirsch is only the latest representative of the idea that the market and capitalism harbor self-destructive proclivities. Let us now trace it back, if only to find out whether contact was ever made between these two opposite views about the moral effects of commerce and capitalism.

The idea that capitalism as a socioeconomic order somehow carries within itself the seed of its own destruction is of course a cornerstone of Marxian thought. But for Marx, this familiar metaphor related to the social and economic working of the system: some of its properties, such as the tendency to concentration of capital, the falling rate of profit, the periodic crises of overproduction, would bring about, with the help of an ever-more numerous and more class-conscious and combative proletariat, the socialist revolution. Thus Marx had little need to discover a more indirect and insidious mechanism that would operate as a sort of fifth column, undermining the moral foundations of the capitalist system from within. Marx did, however, help in forging one key link in the chain of reasoning that eventually led to that conception: in the *Communist Manifesto* and other early writings, Marx and Engels make much of the way in which capitalism corrodes all traditional values and institutions such as love, family and patriotism. Everything was passing into commerce; all social bonds were dissolved through money. This perception is by no means original with Marx. Over a century earlier it was the essence of the *conservative* reaction to the advance of market society, voiced during the 1730s in England by the opponents of Walpole and Whig rule, such as Bolingbroke and his circle. The theme was taken up again, from the early nineteenth century on, by romantic and conservative critics of the Industrial Revolution. Coleridge, for example, wrote in 1817 that the "true seat and sources" of the "existing distress" are to be found in the "Overbalance of the Commercial Spirit" in relation to "natural counter-forces" such as the "ancient feelings of rank and ancestry."[8]

This ability of capitalism to "overbalance" all traditional and "higher" values was not taken as a threat to capitalism itself, at least not right away. The opposite is the case: even though the world shaped by it was often thought to be spiritually and culturally much impoverished, capitalism was viewed as an all-conquering, irresistible force, its rise widely expected to lead to a thorough remaking of society: custom would be replaced by contract, gemeinschaft by gesellschaft, the traditional by the modern; all spheres of social life, from the family to the state, from traditional hierarchy to longtime cooperative arrangements, would be vitally affected. Metaphors often used to describe this action of capitalism on ancient social forms ranged from the outright "dissolving" to "erosion," "corrosion," "contamination," "penetration," and "intrusion" by what Karl Polanyi was to call the "juggernaut market."

But once capitalism was thus perceived as an unbridled force, terrifyingly successful in its relentless forward drive, the thought arose naturally enough that, like all great conquerors, it just might break its neck. Being a blind force (recall the expression "blind market forces") as well as a wild one, capitalism might corrode not only traditional society and its moral values, but even those essential to its own success and survival.

To credit capitalism with extraordinary powers of expansion, penetration, and disintegration may in fact have been an adroit ideological maneuver for intimating that it was headed for disaster. The maneuver was especially effective in an age that had turned away from the idea of progress as a leading myth and was on the contrary much taken with various myths of self-destruction, from the Nibelungen to Oedipus.[9]

The simplest model for the self-destruction of capitalism might be called, in contrast to the self-reinforcing model of *doux commerce*, the *dolce vita* scenario. The advance of capitalism requires, so this story begins, that capitalists save and lead a frugal life so that accumulation can proceed apace. However, at some ill-defined point, increases in wealth resulting from successful accumulation will tend to enervate the spirit of frugality. Demands will be made for *dolce vita*, that is, for instant, rather than delayed, gratification, and when that happens capitalist progress will grind to a halt.

The idea that successful attainment of wealth will undermine the process of wealth generation is present throughout the eighteenth century from John Wesley to Montesquieu and Adam Smith. With Max Weber's essay on *The Protestant Ethic and the Spirit of Capitalism*, reasoning along such lines became fashionable once again: any evidence that the repressive ethic, alleged to be essential for the development of capitalism, may be faltering was then interpreted as a serious threat to the system's survival. Observers as diverse as Herbert Marcuse and Daniel Bell have written in this vein, unaware, it would appear, that they were merely refurbishing a well-known, much older morality tale: how the republican virtues of sobriety, civic pride, and bravery—in ancient Rome—led to victory and conquest which brought opulence and luxury, which in turn undermined those earlier virtues and destroyed the republic and eventually the empire.

While appealing in its simple dialectic, that tale has long been discredited as an explanation of Rome's decline and fall. The attempt to account for or to predict the present or future demise of capitalism in almost identical terms richly deserves a similar fate, and that for a number of reasons. Let me just point out one: the key role in this alleged process of capitalism's rise and decline is attributed first to the generation and then to the decline of personal savings so that changes in much more strategic variables, such as corporate savings, technical innovation, and entrepreneurial skill, not to speak of cultural and institutional factors, are totally left out of account.

There are less mechanical, more sophisticated forms of the self-destruction thesis. The best known is probably the one put forward by Joseph Schumpeter in *Capitalism, Socialism and Democracy*, whose second part is entitled *Can Capitalism Survive?* Schumpeter's answer to that question was rather negative, not so much, he argued, because of insuperable economic problems encountered or generated by capitalism as because of the growing hostility capitalism meets with on the part of many strata, particularly among intellectuals. It is in the course of arguing along these lines that Schumpeter writes:

> . . . capitalism creates a critical frame of mind which, after having destroyed the moral authority of so many other institutions, in the end turns against its own; the bourgeois finds to his amazement that the rationalist attitude does not stop at the credentials of kings and popes but goes on to attack private property and the whole scheme of bourgeois values.[10]

In comparison to the *dolce vita* scenario, this is a much more general argument on self-destruction. But is it more persuasive? Capitalism is here cast in the role of the sorcerer-apprentice who does not know how to stop a mechanism once set in motion—so it demolishes itself along with its enemies. This sort of vision may have appealed to Schumpeter, who, after all, came right out of the Viennese fin-de-siècle culture for which self-destruction had become something totally familiar, unquestioned, *selbstverstandlich*. Those not steeped in that tradition might not find the argument so compelling and might timidly raise the objection that, in addition to the mechanism of self-destruction, elementary forces of reproduction and *self-preservation* also ought to be taken into account. Such forces have certainly appeared repeatedly in the history of capitalism, from the first enactments of factory legislation to the introduction of social security schemes and the experimentation with countercyclical macroeconomic policies.

Schumpeter's point is made more persuasive if it can be argued that the ideological currents unleashed by capitalism are corroding the moral foundations of capitalism *inadvertently*. In other words, if the capitalist order is somehow beholden to previous social and ideological formations to a much greater extent than is realized by the conquering bourgeoisie and their ideologues, then their demolition work will have the *incidental* result of weakening the foundation on which they themselves are sitting. This idea was developed at about the time Schumpeter wrote by a very different group of European intellectuals who had also come to the United States during the 1930s: the critical theorists of the Frankfurt School, while working in the Marxist tradition, paid considerable attention to ideology as a crucial factor in historical development. In fact, a purely idealistic account of the disasters through which Western civilization was passing at the time is given by Max Horkheimer, a leading member of the group, in wartime lectures subsequently published under the title *Eclipse of Reason*.

According to Horkheimer, the commanding position of self-interest in capitalist society and the resulting agnosticism with regard to ultimate values downgraded reason to a mere instrument that would decide about the *means* to be used for reaching arbitrarily given ends, but would have nothing to say about those ends. Previously, reason and revelation had been called upon to define the ends as well as the means of human action and reason was credited with being able to shape such guiding concepts as liberty or equality or justice. But with utilitarian philosophy and self-interest-oriented capitalist practice in the saddle, reason came to lose this power, and thus " . . . the progress of subjective reason destroyed the theoretical basis of mythological, religious, and rationalistic ideas [and yet] *civilized society has up until now been living on the residue of these ideas*."

And Horkheimer speaks movingly of "all these cherished ideas" and values, from freedom and humanity, to "enjoyment of a flower or of the atmosphere of a room . . . that, in addition to physical force and material interest, hold society together . . . but have been *undermined* by the formalization of reason."[11]

Here, then, are some early versions of Hirsch's thesis on the "depleting moral legacy" of capitalism. It is no mystery why the idea was almost forgotten in the thirty-year interval between Schumpeter-Horkheimer and Hirsch: during that era the Western world passed through a remarkably long period of sustained growth and comparative political stability. Capitalist market society, suitably modified by Keynesianism, planning, and welfare-state reforms, seemed to have escaped from its self-destructive proclivities and to generate, once again, if not *douceur*, at least considerable confidence in its ability to solve the problems that it would encounter along its way. But the sense of pervasive crisis that had characterized the 1930s and 1940s reappeared in the 1970s, in part as an after-effect of the still poorly understood mass movements of the late 1960s and in part as an immediate reaction to contemporary shocks and disarray.

Moreover, the analytical exploration of social interaction along the logic of self-interest had by then uncovered situations, such as the Prisoners' Dilemma, in which strict allegiance to self-interest was shown to bring far-from-optimal results *unless* some exogenous norms of cooperative behavior were adhered to by the actors. Now, since human behavior, allegedly guided by self-interest, had not yet had clearly disastrous effects, it was tempting to conclude that: (a) such norms, in effect, have been adhered to tacitly; (b) they must somehow predate the market society in which self-interest alone rules; and (c) their survival is now threatened. In the circumstances, the idea that capitalism lived on time (and morals) borrowed from earlier ages surfaced naturally enough once again.

What is surprising, then, is not that these somber ideas about self-destruction arose at the more difficult and somber moments of our century, but that there was a failure to connect them with earlier, more hopeful expectations of a market society bringing forth its own moral foundation, via the generation of *douceur*, probity, trust, and so on. One reason for this lack of contact is the low profile of the *doux-commerce* thesis in the nineteenth century, after its period of self-confidence in the preceding century. Another is the transfiguration of that thesis into one in which it was hard to recognize. The story of that low profile and that transfiguration must now be told.

Eclipse of the *Doux-Commerce* Thesis after the Eighteenth Century

The most plausible explanation for the eclipse of the *doux-commerce* thesis in the nineteenth century is that it became a victim of the Industrial Revolution. The commercial expansion of the preceding centuries had of course often been violent and had created a great deal of social and human havoc, but this violence and havoc primarily affected the societies that were the objects of European penetration in Africa, Asia, and America. With the Industrial Revolution, the havoc came home. As traditional products were subjected to competitive pressure from ever new "trinkets and baubles," as large groups of laborers were displaced, and their skills became obsolete, and as all classes of society were seized by a sudden passion for enrichment, it was widely felt that a new revolutionary force had arisen in the very center of capitalist expansion.

As I have noted, that force was often characterized as wild, blind, relentless, unbridled—anything but *doux*. Only with regard to international trade was it still asserted from time to time, usually as an afterthought, that expanding transactions would bring, not only mutual material gains, but also some fine by-products in the cultural and moral realms, such as intellectual cross-fertilization and mutual understanding and peace.[12] Within the boundaries of the nation, the expansion of industry and commerce was widely viewed as contributing to the breakdown of traditional communities, and to the loosening and disintegration of social and affective ties, rather than to their consolidation.

To be sure, here and there one can still find echoes of the older idea that civil society is largely held together by the dense network of mutual relations and obligations arising from the market and from its expansion, which in turn is fueled by an increasingly fine division of labor. In fact, as soon as the matter is put this way one's thoughts travel to Emile Durkheim and his *Division of Labor in Society*. Durkheim argued, at least in part, that the advanced division of labor in modern society functions as a substitute for the "common consciousness" that so effectively bonded more primitive societies: "it is principally [the division of labor] which holds together social aggregates of the higher type." But in Durkheim's subtle thought, the transactions arising from the division of labor were not by themselves capable of this substitution. The decisive role was played by the many often *unintended* ties that people take on or fall into in the wake of market transactions and contractual commitments. Here are some 'formulations of this thought that recur throughout the book:

> We cooperate because we wanted to do so, but our voluntary cooperation creates duties which we did not intend to assume. . . .
>
> The members [of societies with a fine division of labor] are united by ties that go well beyond the ever so brief moments during which exchange actually takes place . . . Because we exercise this or that domestic or social function, we are caught in a network of obligations which we do not have the right to forsake. . . .
>
> If the division of labor produces solidarity, this is not only because it makes of each person an exchanger [*échangiste*] to speak the language of the economists; it is because the division of labor creates among men a comprehensive system of rights and duties which tie them to one another in a durable fashion.[13]

So Durkheim's construction is a great deal more complex and round-about than Montesquieu's (or Sir James Steuart's): society is *not* held together directly nor is it made peaceful and *doux* by the network of self-interested market transactions alone; for that sort of doctrine Durkheim has some harsh words that contrast sharply with the seventeenth and eighteenth centuries' doctrine about interest:

> While interest brings people closer together, this is a matter of a few moments only; it can only create an external tie among them . . . The consciences are only in superficial contact; they do not penetrate one another . . . every harmony of interest contains a latent or delayed conflict . . . for interest is what is least constant in the world.[14]

Durkheim was thus caught between the older view that interest-oriented action provides a basis for social integration and the more contemporary critique of market society as atomistic and corrosive of social cohesion. He never spelled out in concrete detail how he conceived a "solidary" society to emerge from the division of labor and eventually moved on to a more activist view that no longer counted on this mechanism to achieve social cohesion and instead stressed moral education and political action.[15] But, as I shall argue later, there may be considerable virtue in his ambivalent stance; and the idea that social bonds can be grafted onto economic transactions if conditions are favorable remains to be explored in depth.

An ambivalence similar to that of Durkheim characterized the work of his German contemporary Georg Simmel. While no one has written more powerfully on the alienating properties of money, Simmel stressed in other writings the integrating functions of various conflicts in modern society. In this connection he gave high marks to competition as an institution that fosters empathy and the building of strong social ties, not of course among the competitors but between them and an important and often overlooked third party—the customer:

> The aim for which competition occurs within a society is presumably always the favor of one or more third persons. Each of the competing parties therefore tries to come as close to that third one as possible. Usually, the poisonous, divisive, destructive effects of competition are stressed and, in exchange, it is merely pointed out

that it improves economic welfare. But in addition, it has, after all, this immense sociating effect. Competition compels the wooer . . . to go out to the wooed, come close to him, establish ties with him, find his strengths and weaknesses and adjust to them . . .

Innumerable times (competition] achieves what usually only love can do: the divination of the innermost wishes of the other, even before he himself becomes aware of them. Antagonistic tension with his competitor sharpens the businessman's sensitivity to the tendencies of the public, even to the point of clairvoyance, in respect to future changes in the public's tastes, fashion, interests . . . Modern competition is described as the fight of all against all, but at the same time it is the fight *for* all . . .

. . . In short, [competition] is a web of a thousand sociological threads by means of conscious concentration on the will and feeling and thinking of fellowmen . . . Once the narrow and naive solidarity of primitive social conditions yielded to decentralization . . . man's effort toward man, his adaptation to the other seems possible only at the price of competition, that is, of the simultaneous fight against a fellowman for a third one.[16]

Simmel's thought here comes close to that of Durkheim's, in that he also uncovers in the structure and institutions of capitalist society a functional equivalent for the simple bonds of custom and religion that (allegedly) held traditional society together. Elsewhere he shows that the advanced division of labor in modern society, and the importance of credit for the functioning of the economy, rest on, and promote, a high degree of truthfulness in social relations.[17] With his effusiveness and vivid imagery, Simmel is perhaps more successful than the austere Durkheim in convincing the reader that some features of market society make for social integration rather than the opposite.

Thus was a minority position affirmed by eminent and somewhat protean figures whose *major* contribution to social thought—through such concepts as anomie in the case of Durkheim, for example—definitely strengthened the majority view. For a counterpoint to the European sociologists' generally somber analysis of capitalism's social impact, it is tempting to look to the American scene. There we find an important group of late nineteenth- and early twentieth-century sociologists—from George Herbert Mead, Charles Cooley, and Edward Ross to the young

John Dewey—who, less haunted than their European colleagues by problems of social disintegration, were simply seeking to understand how and why society coheres as well as it does. But in explaining what they called "social control," they attributed key roles to small-scale, face-to-face relationships, as well as to the ability of various social groups to make norms and rules effective.[18] Significantly, economic relationships are hardly ever mentioned as sources of socially integrative behavior in this literature.

This also holds true for the sociological system that Talcott Parsons later built up. In his thought, the rules of conduct that keep fraudulent behavior at bay in the marketplace derive from what he calls "collectivity-orientation," which must somehow be present in every society; he does not see such rules arising in any way out of the market itself. Given the rigid dichotomies within which the Parsonian system is conceived, there could not be much communication between market transactions, classified as "universalistic," and such "particularistic" and "diffuse" phenomena as friendship and social ties in general.[19]

So much for sociology. What about the economists? After all, they had a tradition of either outspokenly criticizing the capitalist system or defending and praising it. Should not the praisers, at least, have had an interest in keeping alive the thought that the multiple acts of buying and selling characteristic of advanced market societies forge all sorts of social ties of trust, friendliness, sociability, and thus help to hold society together? In actual fact, this sort of reasoning is conspicuously absent from professional economics literature. The reasons are several. First, economists, in their attempt to emulate, in rigor and quantitative precision, the natural sciences, had little use for the necessarily imprecise ("fuzzy") speculations about effects of economic transactions on social cohesion. Second, those trained in the tradition of classical economics had only scorn for the concern of sociologists over the more disruptive and destructive aspects of capitalism. They saw in such phenomena a short-run cost necessary to achieve superior long-run gains and were not impelled by that sort of critique of capitalism to search for or invoke any compensating positive effects which the expansion of the market might have on social life and ties.

But the principal explanation is supplied by yet another point. Economists who wish the market well have been *unable*, or rather have tied their own hands and denied themselves the opportunity, to exploit the argument about the integrative effect of markets. This is so because the argument cannot be made for the ideal market with perfect competition.

The economists' claims of allocative efficiency and all-round welfare maximization are strictly valid only for this market. Involving large numbers of price-taking anonymous buyers and sellers supplied with perfect information, such markets function without any prolonged human or social contact among or between the parties. Under perfect competition there is no room for bargaining, negotiation, remonstration or mutual adjustment, and the various operators that contract together need not enter into recurrent or continuing relationships as a result of which they would get to know each other well. Clearly this latter tie-forming effect of markets can be important only when there are substantial departures or "lapses" from the ideal competitive model. But the fact is that such lapses are exceedingly frequent and important. Nonetheless, pro-market economists either have singled out ties among suppliers and, like Adam Smith, castigated them as "conspiracies against the public"; or, much more frequently, have belittled the various lapses in an attempt to present the reality of imperfect competition as coming close to the ideal. In this manner, they have endeavored to endow the market system with *economic* legitimacy. But, by the same token, they have sacrificed the *sociological* legitimacy that could rightfully have been claimed for the way, so unlike the perfect-competition model, most markets function in the real world.[20]

Only in recent years have economists developed a number of approaches that do not look at departures from the competitive model as either sinful or negligible. To the contrary, with their stress on transaction costs, limited information and imperfect maximization, these approaches explain and justify the widespread existence of continuing relationships between buyers and sellers, the frequent establishment of hierarchies in preference to markets partly as a result of such "relational exchange," the use of "voice" rather than "exit" to correct mutual dissatisfaction, and similar phenomena that make for meaningful tie-forming interaction between parties to transactions. The stage could thus be set for a partial rehabilitation of the *doux-commerce* thesis.

The Feudal-Shackles Thesis

With all due respect for these new developments, it remains true that the *doux-commerce* thesis about the beneficial effects of expanding capitalism on social relations, so popular in the eighteenth century, all but disappeared from the intellectual stage during the protracted subsequent period which saw the full development of capitalist society and, concurrently, the deployment of a far more critical argument about its social impact. But the ways of ideology are intricate: upon looking closely it appears that the optimistic *doux-commerce* thesis does reemerge after all in the nineteenth and twentieth centuries, but as part and parcel of an important *critical* view of capitalist development. It is as though the thesis, faced with the widespread critical attitude toward capitalism, managed to survive by changing camp.

So far we have become acquainted with one kind of critical analysis of capitalism's impact on the social order. What I called the self-destruction thesis views capitalism as an extraordinarily powerful force that dissolves all previous social formations and ideologies and even chips away at capitalism's own moral foundations. But a very different, almost opposite, critique has also been prominently voiced: here the real grudge against capitalism and its standard-bearer, the bourgeoisie, is their *weakness* vis-à-vis traditional social forces, their unwillingness to stage a frontal attack, and often their submissiveness and "spineless" subservience toward the well-entrenched aristocrats of the ancien régime. As in the case of the self-destruction thesis, this is not a unified theory, but a series of contributions from different authors, for different purposes, and in different contexts. Nevertheless, there is a common theme: a number of societies that have been penetrated by capitalism are criticized and considered to be in trouble because this penetration has been too partial, timid, and halfhearted, with substantial elements of the previous social order being left intact. These elements are referred to variously as feudal overhang, shackles, remnants, residues, ballast, or relics and they turn out to retain considerable influence and power. Inasmuch as the societies in question are criticized for not having liquidated this feudal overhang, it has also often been said of them that they have "failed to complete the bourgeois revolution." In short, this group of ideas can be referred to as the feudal-shackles or unfinished-bourgeois-revolution thesis.

While the feudal-shackles thesis is clearly opposed to the self-destruction thesis, it is but an inverted version of the *doux-commerce* thesis. This is not hard to see. Things would have worked out famously, so the feudal-shackles thesis asserts implicitly, *if only* commerce, the market, capitalism had been able to unfold freely, if only they had not been reined in by precapitalist institutions and attitudes. The civilizing work of the market might be done either directly, according to the original script of the *doux-commerce* thesis, or indirectly, by opening the way to the proletarian revolution and to fraternal socialism, after the rapid sweep of capitalism. Here the *douceur* brought by the market would come at one remove. But, alas, neither one nor the other of these happy outcomes was to materialize as hostile forces of bygone social formations retained unexpected strength. The feudal-shackles thesis thus rests on the *doux-commerce* thesis—without, of course, acknowledging the affiliation. It is the *doux-commerce* thesis in negative disguise, in critical garb, stood on its head.

We now have two major critiques of capitalism, the self-destruction and the feudal-shackles theses. Each points to some "contradictions" of capitalism, but it is already apparent that the two views also violently contradict one another.

There is here then a contradiction between contradictions, or, to borrow a mathematical term, a second-order contradiction of capitalism. The nature of this contradiction will become clearer as the historical development and the various shapes of the feudal-shackles thesis are reviewed briefly.

However contradictory, the two theses can both be traced—as might be expected: after all, they are both critiques of capitalism—to the writings of Karl Marx. That he prepared the ground for the self-destruction thesis because of his emphasis on the all-corrosive properties of capitalism has already been noted. Similarly, the feudal-shackles thesis is adumbrated in Marx when he writes in the preface of *Capital* that in comparison to England the Germans suffer not only from all the modern woes of capitalist expansion, but from a "long series of inherited afflictions, resulting from the persistence of antiquated modes of production that have outlived their usefulness, with their sequel of adverse social and political relations."[21]

From this kind of observation it is not a big jump to assert that the persistence and unexpected strength of precapitalist forms, together with the correlative *weakness* of capitalist structures, could become a major problem in certain societies. In which ones? The German example suggests that it might be in those where capitalist development is delayed, the delay being precisely due to the resilience of precapitalist forms, to the fact that the feudal "cobwebs" have not been neatly "swept away" by a thoroughgoing "bourgeois revolution." On the contrary, so the story goes, the indigenous bourgeoisie in such countries was not only weak but servile, supine, craven, wishing to make it within the old order and submissive to its code and values. This results in the "distortion" or "stunting" of capitalist structures. In other words, the trouble with capitalism, suddenly, is not that it is so strong as to be self-destructing but that it is too weak to play the "progressive" role history has supposedly assigned to it.

The fullest development of these ideas has occurred in our time with some neo-Marxist analyses of the countries of the capitalist periphery. But there are earlier important applications, and Schumpeter's well-known theory of imperialism is a case in point. As already noted, one of the fondest hopes expressed in the seed-time of capitalist development was that worldwide trade and investment consequent upon capitalist development would make war impossible and lay a solid foundation for peace and friendship among nations. When, around the beginning of the twentieth century, the illusory nature of this hope became only too obvious, it was attractive to argue, along exactly opposite lines, that capitalism itself inevitably leads to great-power rivalry and war. This, with some variants, was indeed affirmed by the economic theories of imperialism proposed around that time by J. A. Hobson, Rosa Luxemburg, Rudolf Hilferding, and Lenin. But Schumpeter, writing during World War I, came to the rescue of the earlier optimistic view by arguing that capitalism, in and of itself, could lead only to peace. To him, the rational, calculating spirit of capitalism was wholly incompatible with the reckless gambling characteristic of warmaking in the modern age or any age. What had gone wrong? Precisely that capitalism had not proven vigorous enough, had not been able to alter decisively either the social structure or the mentality of the precapitalist age with its disaster-bound addiction to heroic antics.

Strangely enough, Schumpeter therefore became an articulate spokesman—far more so than Marx—both for the feudal-shackles thesis, according to which the trouble with capitalism was its *weakness* (vis-à-vis precapitalist forms), and for the self-destruction thesis which emphasizes capitalism's corrosive strength. To explain this apparent inconsistency, it must first be pointed out that the texts containing the two theses were written more than twenty years apart from one another. Second, the two theses, in spite of their contradiction, have various characteristics in common: both underline the importance of ideology and mentality and thereby are self-consciously critical of Marxism; and both take an obvious pleasure in stressing the key role of the irrational in human affairs, once again in line with the contemporary intellectual climate due to such figures as Freud, Bergson, Sorel, and Pareto.

In the meantime, however, the Marxists were also picking up the hints dropped by the master. Naturally enough, when they criticized the experience of certain countries under capitalism for lack of dynamism, they stressed structural rather than ideological factors. In Italy, for example, Antonio Gramsci and Emilio Sereni analyzed the Risorgimento as an "incomplete" or "failed" bourgeois revolution because political unification in the second half of the nineteenth century was not accompanied by agrarian reform or revolution. The weakness of the Italian bourgeoisie and its lack of Jacobin energies were thus proclaimed as the aboriginal flaw, or *vizio d'origine*, of modern Italian history, the root cause of all subsequent woes, from weak economic development to the advent of Fascism.[22]

Some of this analysis at least was later controverted by economic historians who pointed out that the so-called "failure to complete the bourgeois revolution" by land reform actually permitted capital accumulation to proceed in the north. So the alleged failure had its positive side in that it made possible the vigorous industrial push that did take place in the country's north prior to World War I.[23]

But to return to the failed or incomplete-revolution thesis: In Italy, the principal objective pursued by leaders of the Risorgimento was national unification and it was accomplished. To characterize that movement as a failed bourgeois revolution therefore amounted to *inventing* a failure by substituting some imaginary telos or historical geist for the real intentions of human agents. In nineteenth-century Germany, on the other hand, the failures of the political movements of 1848 were all too real, and they did expose the political weakness of the German bourgeois liberals. These events lent themselves to a straightforward interpretation, along feudal-remnants lines. "It is the tragedy of the bourgeoisie that it has not yet defeated its predecessor, that is, feudalism, when its new enemy, the proletariat, has already appeared on the stage of history." Clearly, this elegant formulation of Georg Lukács applied particularly to Germany and Central Europe, where the battle with the bourgeoisie's alleged historical "predecessors," the aristocratic and military power-holders, was never really joined. After some skirmishes, circa 1848, the bourgeoisie was ready for a compromise with the powerful "feudal remnants" and it is this compromise, according to numerous observers, which deserves much of the blame for the disasters of modern German history.

In spite of the historical importance of the Italian and German cases, the notion that the bourgeois class, which emerges with the rise of commerce and industry, does not necessarily sweep away all precapitalist formations had to be rediscovered, with great fanfare, again and again. This was so, for example, in Latin America. During the growth years following World War II, social scientists looking at the "periphery" generally set out with the unspoken assumption that capitalism was (and always has been) performing faultlessly in the center; hence, so they concluded, the difficulties of the periphery must be due to some deviation from the pattern the center had followed. Within this conceptual framework the feudal-shackles thesis—or close analogues—provided an appealing explanation.

Coining an expressive and successful metaphor, the political scientist Charles Anderson described the Latin American social and political scene as a "'living museum' in which all the forms of political authority of Western historic experience continue to exist and operate," implying that in the West these forms followed one another in an orderly sequence.[24]

Latin American societies, it was concluded, somehow did not manage to extirpate superannuated relations of production and this was why they were in trouble. Once more the culprit was the weakness of the indigenous bourgeoisie, ever ready to sell out to the old landowning elites or to foreign investors and preferably to both. Such was the essence of much neo-Marxist analysis, which, this time, did not bother to blame the bourgeoisie for not playing its "historic role." Rather, it was now denied that, given the peripheral position of Latin American societies, their bourgeoisie could ever come to play any constructive developmental role at all; this congenital incapacity was meant to be conveyed by the coining of insulting terms such as *"comprador bourgeoisie"* (Paul Baran) and *"lumpenbourgeoisie"* (Andre Gunder Frank). Quite consistently with this position, what industrialization and capitalist development have taken place in Latin America and elsewhere in the periphery were systematically belittled and berated.

This is not the place to discuss the truth value of these conceptions and assertions except to state that I have my doubts and have expressed them elsewhere.[25] I must go on and call attention to a strange turn taken quite recently by the feudal-shackles theorists.

Until now it always served to explain why one particular backward or latecoming country's economic development was experiencing difficulties *in comparison to* a leading country or countries; where development was believed to have proceeded smoothly and vigorously. Now, suddenly, a number of people are telling us that, at least in Europe, no such blessed country ever existed and that the bourgeoisie was weak, craven, and spineless all along. The strongest assertion of this sort is made in *The Persistence of the Ancien Régime* by Arno Mayer. According to him, the situation in all of Europe was, at least until World War I, very much like what it has been alleged to be today in the Latin American periphery: capitalist development was anything but dynamic and penetrative, the bourgeoisie was everywhere subservient to the established nobility, and the elites of the ancien régime retained not only economic and political power, but cultural hegemony as well. And, in a light variant of the Schumpeter thesis on imperialism, Mayer attributes the outbreak of World War I to the reaction of these traditional power-holders, when they perceived for the first time some distant rumblings of troubles for their hitherto uncontested dominion.

This near universalization of the feudal-remnants thesis represented a particularly surprising and daring proposition for England and France, the two major countries where, so it had long been thought, total victories had been achieved by the bourgeoisie and capitalism as a result of political revolution in France and industrial revolution in England. Now, it must be noted that this questioning of the status of France and England as model countries occurred when the golden "growth years" of the 1950s and 1960s were definitely behind us and new questions were being asked about the health of capitalist economy and society. In fact, Mayer's book, with its generalization of the feudal-shackles thesis to countries hitherto outside its reach, does not stand alone. According to a related volume by Martin Wiener on England, that country's industrial spirit had only the briefest flowering circa 1850 and from then on was in eclipse as middle-class intellectuals imbued with gentry ideals staged a successful counterrevolution of values.[26] Carrying this genre to extremes—and becoming a *succès de scandale* in the process—is *L'idéologie francaise* by Bernard-Henri Lévy. According to this author, French social and political thought was dominated, from the mid-nineteenth century to World War II and from one end to the other of the ideological spectrum, by a repulsive amalgam of racist and protofascist drivel!

My purpose here is not to criticize these works, but to show how the feudal-shackles thesis has lately been applied to countries, such as England and France, that had been almost by definition excluded from it. The reason is, of course, that the most advanced capitalist countries were generally thought to be suffering from contradictions that arose from capitalism's strength, rather than from its weakness.

In sum, the generalization of the feudal-shackles thesis pulls out two rugs simultaneously: one from under common conceptions about the specific nature and problems of capitalism in the periphery (and among European latecomers); and the other from under the self-destruction thesis, whose favorite terrain must surely be found, if anywhere, in the most advanced countries:

America, or the Perils of Not Having a Feudal Past

To get over our puzzlement and to complete our pageant of theories, it will be helpful, at this point, to turn to the United States, a preeminent outpost of capitalism that has remained unmentioned up to now. The reason is that this country alone has escaped from the generalization of the feudal-shackles thesis. No one has yet argued that the United States is or has ever been in the grip of some ancien règime or that its capitalist development has been hampered and distorted by tenacious gentlemanly values or entrenched feudal institutions except for the South and slavery. Rather, the United States has generally been taken to be the confirmation *a contrario* of the feudal-shackles thesis: its vigorous capitalist development, combined with sturdy political pluralism, has often been attributed precisely to the absence of a feudal background. This idea that the United States is uniquely blessed because, unlike old Europe, it is not weighed down by the shackles of the past was expressed as early as 1818 by Goethe in the poem "To the United States," whose opening lines read:

> Amerika, Du hast es besser
> Als unser Kontinent, der Alte,
> Hast keine verfallenen Schlösser . . .[27]

Tocqueville gave this same comparative appraisal its classic expression, of course, with the single, oft-quoted sentence: "The great advantage of the Americans is that they have come to democracy without having to endure democratic revolutions; and that they are born equal, instead of becoming so."[28] Many American commentators have been eager and happy to make these flattering insights their own. Thus arose what has become known as the thesis of "American exceptionalism," which holds that America is exceptionally fortunate among nations because of its peculiar historical background (plus a few other factors, such as abundant natural resources and size) and is therefore free from the unending internal conflicts of other Western countries.

But now comes a surprise, even a *coup de théâtre*. A major contributor to this literature is Louis Hartz with his classic *The Liberal Tradition in America*. Hartz fully accepts the idea that the United States is uniquely exempt from feudal relics. He duly cites Goethe's poem and even uses the Tocquevillian sentence as his epigraph: Yet, upon reading the book with some attention, one notices something that he never tells you outright: namely, he is in intimate disagreement with both Goethe and Tocqueville! His book is, in effect, a long lament about the many *evils* that have befallen the United States because of the *absence* of feudal remnants, relics, and the like. Throughout, this vaunted absence is shown to be a mixed blessing at best, and is most frequently depicted as a poisoned gift or a *curse* in disguise.

Hartz's reasoning is basically very simple—this is why it is so powerful. Having been "born equal," without any sustained struggle against the "father"—that is, the feudal past—America is deprived of what Europe has in abundance: social and ideological diversity. *But such diversity is one of the prime constituents of genuine liberty.* According to Hartz, the lack of ideological diversity in America has meant the absence of an authentic conservative tradition, is responsible for the often noted weaknesses of socialist movements, and has even made for the protracted sterility of liberal political thought itself. What is still more serious, this lack of diversity stimulates the ever-present tendencies toward a "tyranny of the majority" inspired by America's "irrational Lockianism" or its "colossal liberal absolutism."[29]

This state of affairs is shown to have numerous implications, mostly deplorable, in both domestic and international affairs. I shall cite only one observation, because of its relevance to present-day events. Analyzing the New Deal and its considerable departures from the traditional liberal credo, Hartz notes that Roosevelt put across his innovative reforms as an exercise in "pragmatism" and in "bold and persistent experimentation": " . . . the crucial thing was that, lacking the socialist challenge and of course the old corporate challenge on the right such as the European conservatisms still embodied, he did not need to spell out any real philosophy at all."[30]

According to Hartz, Roosevelt owed much of his success to this manner of presenting his policies as just a "sublimated 'Americanism.'" Today, of course, we can appreciate the high cost of the maneuver. The New Deal reforms, as well as the welfare-state schemes that were added later, were never truly consolidated as an integral part of a new economic order or ideology. Unlike similar policies in other economically advanced countries, these reforms failed to achieve full legitimacy and remained vulnerable, as is currently evident, to attack from revivalist forces adhering strictly to the aboriginal "colossal liberal absolutism."

Hartz's analysis achieved or permitted substantial insights by reversing the conventional lament about the presence and influence of feudal remnants in capitalist societies. He shows that other, perhaps no less troublesome, kinds of difficulties can plague a nation, just *because* it is in the "enviable," "exceptional" situation of not having a feudal past. Hartz's position, I should add, has been strengthened and extended by recent macrosociological speculations that tend to view feudal society, with its complex institutional structure and built-in conflicts, as the indispensable seedbed of both Western democracy and capitalist development.[31] Conversely, Claudio Véliz's essay on Latin America argues, very much in the spirit of Louis Hartz, that the lack of genuine feudal structures in that continent's historical experience accounts for its "centralist tradition," which in turn is held to be responsible for its principal troubles.

Toward a *Tableau Idéologique*

The focus of my extended *tour d'horizon* of interpretations of capitalist development has been not on what is right or wrong with capitalism (from the points of view of justice, efficiency, or growth), but on what *goes* right or wrong; that is, on ideas about the likely economic and noneconomic (moral, social, political) dynamics of the system. In case the reader feels bewildered by the seeming jumble of theses that I have paraded, I shall now demonstrate, by a two-by-two table, that the structure of my argument has really been quite simple as well as beauti-fully symmetrical.

I have essentially dealt with four types of theses or theories and have presented them in a sequence such that each successive thesis is in some respect the negation of the preceding one. According to the *doux-commerce* thesis of the eighteenth century, with which I started out, the market and capitalism were going to create a moral environment in which a good society as well as the market itself were bound to flourish. But soon there arose, in counterpoint, the self-destruction thesis, which asserts that, to the contrary, the market, with its vehement emphasis on individual self-interest, corrodes all traditional values, including those on the basis of which the market itself is functioning. Next, the feudal-shackles thesis demonstrates instead how capitalism is coming to grief, not because of its own excessive energies, but because of powerful res-idues of precapitalist values and institutions. This thesis is in turn con-tradicted by the demonstration that calamitous results follow from the *absence* of a feudal past. This is the thesis of Louis Hartz, which can also be called the *feudal-blessings thesis,* as it implies that a feudal background is a *favorable* factor for subsequent democratic-capitalist development. Thus we end up with a position that is in obvious conflict with the initial *deux-commerce* thesis; for, in the latter, the market and self-interested behavior are viewed as a benign force that is in fact destined to emanci-pate civil society from "feudal shackles."

Dominance of market vs. influential persistence of precapitalist forms:
Their effects on market society

	Positive effects	Negative effects
Dominance of market	Doux-commerce thesis (DC)	Self-destruction thesis (SD)
Influential persistence of precapitalist forms	Feudal-blessings thesis (FB)	Feudal-shackles thesis (FS)

A schematic presentation or mapping makes it easy to perceive the relationship between these theses. It promotes a principal aim of this essay, which has been to establish contact between a number of ideolog-ical formations that are in fact closely related but have evolved in total isolation from one another. Rather wondrously, the various ideologies, even though secreted in such isolation, end up composing a complete pattern, as shown in the table; it is as though four blindfolded children did a perfect job jointly coloring a coloring book.

So far I have essentially been, or pretended to be, a spectator and chronicler of that considerable portion of the Human Comedy which is involved with the production of ideologies. Faced with the highly diverse views here outlined, I confess, however, to a moderate interest in the question as to which one is *right*. And here the simple *tableau idéologique* I have presented can also be of use. First of all; it suggests that, however incompatible the various theories may be, each might still have its "hour of truth" and/or its "country of truth" as it applies in a given country or group of countries during some stretch of time. This is actually how these theses arose, for all of them were fashioned with a specific country or group of countries in mind.

But the table is especially useful if one wishes to pursue a more complex (and, I think, more adequate) way of giving each contending view its due. It is conceivable that, even at one and the same point in space and time, a simple thesis holds only a portion of the full truth and needs to be complemented by one or several of the others, however incompatible they may look at first sight. The table then invites us to try out systematically the various possible combinations of the four theses. In the following, I shall limit this exercise to the three "contradictions" with which we are already familiar.[32] But now the task is to explore whether it is at all possible and useful to combine the theses that constitute those contradictions.

Clearly there are degrees of incompatibility among points of view or doctrines that are contradictory on the face of it. As already noted, a highly irreconcilable contradiction is that between the self-destruction thesis and the feudal-shackles thesis. The former views capitalism as a wild, unbridled force which, having swept away everything in its path, finally does itself in by successfully attacking its own foundations. The feudal-shackles thesis, on the other hand, sees capitalists as weak and subservient and easily overpowered, distracted, or distorted by precapitalist forms and values: a determined eclectic or lover of reconciliations could still argue that capitalism has the knack of doing away with all in its "legacy" that is good and functional (that is, with such values as truth and honesty, not to speak of *gemütlichkeit*) while leaving intact, and utterly succumbing to, all in precapitalist society that is pernicious. But is it conceivable that any historical formation would have such an unerring, schlemiel-like instinct for going wrong?

Here, then, is our most genuine, most irreducible "second-order contradiction." It remains possible, of course, that each of these accounts—the self-destruction and the feudal-remnants theses—is valuable in explaining the difficulties capitalism is experiencing in different settings. In other words, I do not wish to intimate that these two theses checkmate each other, so that we can happily conclude that capitalism is wholly exempt from trouble on account of either of them.

By now, however, we know that these two accounts are contradicted not only by each other but also by points of view that evaluate as *positive* the very factors these accounts view negatively. I am referring to the *doux-commerce* and the feudal-blessings theses, which will now be brought into play.

Take, first, the feudal-shackles and the feudal-blessings theses. As soon as we examine the likelihood that both may be true at the same time, it becomes obvious that nothing stands in the way of that sort of amalgam, which, on the contrary, seems immediately more probable than the eventuality that just one of the theses holds to the total exclusion of the other. Mixing the two means that precapitalist forms and values hamper the full development of capitalism while also bequeathing something precious to it. A mature appraisal surely needs to be aware of both lines of influence, and the balance is likely to be different in each concrete historical situation.

This conclusion applies even more to our last remaining pair: the *doux-commerce* and self-destruction theses. Once one inquires whether both these theses could hold at the same time it becomes obvious that this is not only possible but overwhelmingly likely. For capitalism to be both self-reinforcing and self-undermining is not any more "contradictory" than for a business firm to have income and outgo at the same time! Insofar as social cohesion is concerned, for example, the constant practice of commercial transactions generates feelings of trust, empathy for others, and similar *doux* feelings; but on the other hand, as Montesquieu already knew, such practice permeates all spheres of life with the element of calculation and of instrumental reason. Once this view is adopted, the moral basis of capitalist society will be seen as being constantly depleted and replenished at the same time. An excess of depletion over replenishment and a consequent crisis of the system is then, of course, possible, but the special circumstances making for it would have to be noted, just as it might be possible to specify conditions under which the system would gain in cohesion and legitimacy.

It is now becoming clear why, in spite of our lip service to the dialectic, we find it so hard to acknowledge that contradictory processes might actually be at work in society. It is not just a question of difficulty of perception, but one of considerable psychological resistance and reluctance: to accept that the *doux-commerce* and the self-destruction theses (or the feudal-shackles and feudal-blessings theses) might both be right makes it much more difficult for the social observer, critic, or "scientist" to impress the general public by proclaiming some inevitable outcome of current processes.

But after so many failed prophecies, is it not in the interest of social science to embrace complexity, be it at some sacrifice of its claim to predictive power?

Bibliographical References

Anderson, Charles W. *Politics and Economic Change in Latin America.* Princeton, N.J.: Van Nostrand, 1967.

Anderson, Perry. "Origins of the Present Crisis," *New Left Review* (January–February 1964): 26–53.

———. *Lineages of the Absolutist State.* London: NLB, 1974.

Baechler, Jean. *Les origines du capitalisme.* Paris: Gallimard, 1974.

Baker, Keith MichaeL *Condorcet: From Natural Philosophy to Social Mathematics.* Chicago, Ill.: Chicago University Press, 1975.

Bell, Daniel. *The Cultural Contradictions of Capitalism.* New York: Basic Books, 1976.

Benjamin, Walter. *Deutsche Menschen.* Frankfurt: Suhrkamp, 1962.

Coleridge, Samuel Taylor. *Collected Works.* Vol. 6, *Lay Sermons.* London: Routledge and Kegan Paul; Princeton, N.J.: Princeton University Press, 1972.

Condorcet, Marquis de. *Esquisse d'un tableau historique du progrès de l'esprit humain.* Paris, 1795.

Durkheim, Émile. *De la division du travail social.* 1893. Paris: F. Alcan, 1902.

Eugène, Eric. *Les idées politiques de Richard Wagner.* Paris: Publications Universitaires, 1973.

Gerschenkron, Alexander. *Economic Backwardness in Historical Perspective.* Cambridge, Mass.: Harvard University Press, 1962.

Gramsci, Antonio. *Il risorgimento.* Turin: G. Einaudi, 1949.

Hartz, Louis. *The Liberal Tradition in America.* New York: Harcourt, Brace, 1955.

Hirsch, Fred. *Social Limits to Growth.* Cambridge, Mass., and London: Harvard University Press, 1976.

Hirschman, Albert O. *Exit, Voice, and Loyalty: Responses to Decline in Firms, Organizations, and States.* Cambridge, Mass.: Harvard University Press, 1970.

———. *A Bias for Hope: Essays on Development and Latin America.* New Haven, Conn.: Yale University Press, 1971.

———. *The Passions and the Interests: Political Arguments for Capitalism before Its Triumph.* Princeton, N.J.: Princeton University Press, 1977.

———. *Essays in Trespassing: Economics to Politics and Beyond.* Cambridge: Cambridge University Press, 1981.

Horkheimer, Max. *Eclipse of Reason.* New York: Oxford University Press, 1947.

Lévy, Bernard-Henri. *L'idéologie française.* Paris: Bernard Grasset, 1981.

Lukács, Georg. *Geschichte und Klassenbewusstsein.* Neuwied, Germany: Luchterhand, 1968.

Lukes, Steven. *Emile Durkheim: His Life and Work.* New York: Harper and Row, 1972.

Marcuse, Herbert. "Industrialization and Capitalism." *New Left Review* (March–April 1965): 3–17.

Marx, Karl *Das Kapital.* 1872. Vienna and Berlin: Verlag für Literatur und Politik, 1932.

Mayer, Arno. *The Persistence of the Ancien Régime.* New York: Pantheon Books, 1981.

Mill John Stuart. *Principles of Political Economy.* 1848. Vols. 2, 3 of *Collected Works.* Toronto: University of Toronto Press, 1965.

Montesquieu, Charles Louis. *De l'esprit des lois.* 1748. Paris: Garnier, 1961.

Paine, Thomas. *The Rights of Man.* 1792. New York: E. P. Dutton, 1951.

Parsons, Talcott. *The Social System.* Glencoe, Ill: Free Press, 1951.

Rather, L. J. *The Dream of Self-Destruction: Wagner's Ring and the Modern World.* Baton Rouge: Louisiana State University Press, 1979.

Ricard, Samuel. *Traité général du commerce.* Amsterdam: Chez E. van Harrevelt Soeters, 1781.

Robertson, William. *View of the Progress of Society in Europe.* 1769. Edited by Felix Gilbert. Chicago, Ill.: Chicago University Press, 1972.

Romeo, Rosario. *Risorgimento e capitalismo.* Bari, Italy: Laterza, 1959.

Rosenberg, Nathan. "Neglected Dimensions in the Analysis of Economic Change." *Oxford Bulletin of Economics and Statistics* 26, no. 1 (1964): 59–77.

Schumpeter, Joseph A. *Capitalism, Socialism and Democracy.* New York: Harper, 1942.

———. "The Sociology of Imperialisms." *Imperialism and Social Classes.* 1917. Edited by Paul Sweezy. New York: Kelley, 1951.

Sereni, Emilio. *Il capitalismo nelle campagne. 1860—1900.* Turin: G. Einaudi, 1947.

Silver, Allan. "Small Worlds and the Great Society: The Social Production of Moral Order." MS, 1980.

Simmel, Georg. *Soziologie.* 1908. Leipzig: Duncker and Humblot, 1923.

———. *Conflict and the Web of Group Affiliations.* Translated by Kurt H. Wolff. Glencoe, Ill.: Free Press, 1955.

Smith, Adam. *The Wealth of Nations.* 1776. New York: Modern Library Edition, 1937.

Tocqueville, Alexis de. *De la démocratie en Amérique.* 1840. Paris: Gallimard, 1961.

Véliz, Claudio. *The Centralist Tradition of Latin America.* Princeton, N.J.: Princeton University Press, 1980.

Il vizio d'origine. Biblioteca della Libertà. Florence, Italy, April–September 1980.

Weber, Max. *The Protestant Ethic and the Spirit of Capitalism.* 1904–5. New York: Scribner's, 1958.

Wiener, Martin J. *English Culture and the Decline of the Industrial Spirit, 1850–1980.* Cambridge: Cambridge University Press, 1981.

Williamson, Oliver E. "The Modem Corporation: Origins, Evolution, Attributes." *Journal of Economic Literature* (December 1981): 1537–68.

Notes

1. See Montesquieu, *De l'esprit des lois*, p. 8.

2. See Condorcet, p. 238.

3. See Paine, p. 215.

4. See Ricard, p. 463.

5. See Rosenberg, pp. 59–77.

6. See Hirsch, pp. 117–18.

7. See Hirsch, p. 143.

8. See Coleridge, pp. 169–70.

9. On the important place the theme of self-destruction held in Richard Wagner's political and economic thought, see Rather, and Eugène.

10. See Schumpeter, p. 143.

11. See Horkheimer, pp. 34, 36; my italics.

12. For example, John Stuart Mill writes in *Principles of Political Economy*: "It is hardly possible to overrate the value, in the present low state of human improvement, of placing human beings in contact with persons dissimilar to themselves, and with modes of thought and action unlike those with which they are familiar . . . Such communication has always been, and is peculiarly in the present age, one of the primary sources of progress." (Collected Works, Vol. 3, p. 594)

13. See Durkheim, pp. 148, 192, 207, 402–3.

14. See Durkheim, pp. 180–81. Compare this text with the exactly opposite seventeenth- and eighteenth-century statements on the constancy and predictability of interest which I reported in *The Passions and the Interests,* pp. 48–55.

15. See Lukes, p. 178.

16. See Simmel, *Conflict and the Web of Group Affiliations,* pp. 61–63.

17. See Simmel, *Soziologie,* pp. 260–61.

18. See Silver.

19. See Parsons, pp. 98, 125–27.

20. I made a similar point in *Exit, Voice, and Loyalty* (p. 22). In the same vein, Williamson has recently written about the "inhospitality tradition" of economists with regard to organizational innovations of business enterprise: such innovations were always suspected of entailing departures from the competitive model (p. 1540).

21. See Marx, p. 7.

22. A collection of articles around the concept, fortunately critical for the most part, is in *Il vizio d'origine.*

23. See Romeo, and Gerschenkron, chapter 5.

24. I am not denying, *of course,* that industrialization in Latin America had characteristics of its own; in fact, I have tried to set them forth in some detail.

25. See Hirschman, Albert O., *A Bias for Hope,* chapter 3.

26. An early argument on the historical weakness of the English bourgeoisie is in Anderson, Perry, "Origins of the Present Crisis."

27. "America, you are better off / Than our old continent / You have no castles in ruins . . ."

28. Tocqueville, vol. 2, p. 108. This sentence concludes a short chapter entitled "How it comes about that individualism is stronger after a democratic revolution than at other times" where Tocqueville lists the many conflicts and problems afflicting societies, such as the French, that have had to "suffer a democratic revolution."

29. Hartz, pp. 140–42, 11, 285.

30. See Hartz, p. 263.

31. For converging analyses along these lines, it is possible to cite the works of two authors with very different ideological positions: *Les origines du capitalisme* by Baechler, and *Lineages of the Absolutist State by* Perry Anderson.

32. Given the four theses, there are altogether six such pairwise combinations and we already know that four of them are "full of contradictions." The remaining two, that is, the diagonal pairs DC-FS and SD-FB, should be nicely compatible as, say, the *doux-commerce* thesis is here coupled with the negation of its negation. This is indeed the case. I pointed out that the feudal-shackles thesis could be understood as the *doux-commerce* thesis in disguise. To combine these two theses therefore does not really yield new information or interpretation.

If we look at the other diagonal pair, the self-destruction and the feudal-blessings theses, a similar conclusion follows. In Hartz's argument about the dire consequences of the lack of a feudal past, there is implicit a concern that a society wholly dominated by the market would face considerable dangers. The two theses are eminently compatible and to bring them together does not add much to either one or the other.

I shall not deal in the text with the DC-FB pair. These two do add up to a real contradiction, for they are two very different accounts of the reasons for capitalism's health and strength. But, in this manner, the pair is little more than the mirror image of the SD-FS pair with its two contrasting accounts of the difficulties encountered by market society. I discuss this latter pair in the text, along with the remaining two pairs, DC-SD and FS-FB.

AGAINST PARSIMONY

Three Easy Ways of Complicating Some Categories of Economic Discourse

Hirschman's second Marc Bloch lecture turned more squarely to the ways in which his fellow economists argue. Words had always fascinated Hirschman, and he loved to play with them because they allowed him to illustrate multiple, shifting meanings and complex patterns. He once admitted that had he had better mathematical training, he might see that equations could accomplish the same. But he was more than satisfied with words. His second Bloch lecture tackled the core vocabulary of economics: if there was to be an expanded economics, it would need a more complex vocabulary or discourse. This would also mean giving up one of the sacred cows of the discipline: the preference for parsimony—simple explanations of even complex phenomena, simple so they could be more easily tested under conditions of the intellectual's making. Doing this might allow economists to admit otherwise forbidden topics for analysis—like love, avarice, jealousy. Hirschman anticipated, in this sense, the importance of bridging the divide between emotions and behavior. This has become an important cornerstone in the recent turn in behavioral economics. Hirschman's essay is a pioneer.

—*Jeremy Adelman*

E CONOMICS AS A SCIENCE of human behavior has been grounded in a remarkably parsimonious postulate: that of the self-interested, isolated individual who chooses freely and rationally among alternative courses of action after computing their prospective costs and benefits. In recent decades, a group of economists has shown considerable industry and ingenuity in applying this way of interpreting the social world to a series of ostensibly noneconomic phenomena, from crime to the family, and from collective action to democracy. The "economic" or "rational-actor" approach has yielded some important insights, but its onward sweep has also revealed some of its intrinsic weaknesses. As a result, it has become possible to mount a critique which, ironically, can be carried all the way back to the heartland of the would-be conquering discipline. That the economic approach presents us with too simpleminded an account of even such fundamental economic processes as consumption and production is my basic thesis here.

I am not alone in this view. Schelling has noted that "the human mind is something of an embarrassment to certain disciplines, notably economics . . . that have found the model of the rational consumer to be powerfully productive." And in a well- known article, significantly entitled "Rational Fools: A Critique of the Behavioral Foundations of Economic Theory," Sen has asserted not long ago that "traditional [economic] theory has *too little* structure."[1] Noting that individual preferences and actual choice behavior are far from being always identical, he introduced novel concepts, such as commitment and second-order preferences. Like any virtue, so he seemed to say, parsimony in theory construction can be overdone, and something is sometimes to be gained by making things more complicated. I have increasingly come to feel this way. Some years ago, I suggested that criticism from customers, or "voice," should be recognized as a force keeping management of firms and organizations on their toes, along with competition or "exit," and it took a book to cope with the resulting complications. Here I deal with various other realms of economic inquiry that stand similarly in need of being rendered more complex. In concluding, I examine whether the various complications have some element in common: that would in turn simplify and unify matters.

Two Kinds of Preference Changes

A fruitful distinction has been made, by Sen and others, between first-order and second-order preferences, or between preferences and metapreferences, respectively. I shall use the latter terminology here.

Economics has traditionally dealt only with (first-order) preferences, that is, those that are revealed by agents as they buy goods and services. The complex psychological and cultural processes that lie behind the actually observed market choices have generally been considered the business of psychologists, sociologists, and anthropologists.

There were some good reasons for this self-denying ordinance. Nevertheless, one aspect in the formation of choice and preference must be of concern to the economist, to the extent that he claims an interest in understanding processes of economic change. That aspect has nothing to do with the cultural conditioning of tastes and choice behavior, at least at a first level of inquiry; its starting point is rather a very general observation on human nature (and should therefore be congenial to economics with its eighteenth-century moorings): men and women have the ability to step back from their "revealed" wants, volition, and preferences, to ask themselves whether they really want these wants and prefer these preferences and, consequently, to form metapreferences that may differ from their preferences. Unsurprisingly, it was a philosopher who first put matters this way. Harry Frankfurt argued that this ability to step back is unique in humans, but is not present in all of them. Those who lack this ability he called "wantons": they are entirely, unreflectively, in the grip of their whims and passions. (The terminology is quite apt as it conforms to common usage: wanton murder is precisely murder "for no good reason," i.e., murder that has not been preceded by the formation of any metapreference for murder.)

It is easy to see that there is a close link between preference change and the concept of metapreferences; for, as I have pointed out before, certainty about the existence of metapreferences can only be gained through changes in actual choice behavior. If preferences and metapreferences always coincide, so that the agent is permanently at peace with himself no matter what choices he makes, then the metapreferences hardly lead an independent existence and are mere shadows of the preferences. If, on the other hand, the two kinds of preference are permanently at odds, so that the agent always acts against his better judgment, then again, the metapreference cannot only be dismissed as wholly ineffective, but doubts will arise whether it is really there at all. In such cases, the situation is best characterized as a "tie-in purchase": along with the preferred commodity the consumer insists on acquiring unhappiness, regret, and guilt over having preferred it.

The notion of metapreference does not tell us much about the way actual change in choice behavior comes about. The battle to impose the metapreference is fought out within the self and is marked by all kinds of advances and reverses as well as by ruses and strategic devices. I am not concerned here with this topic, which Schelling has made his own, only with pointing out that an occasional success in changing choice behavior is essential for validating the concept of metapreferences.

Conversely, this concept illuminates the varied nature of preference change, for it is now possible to distinguish between two kinds of preference changes. One is the reflective and tortuous kind, preceded as it is by the formation of a metapreference at odds with the observed and hitherto practiced preference. But preference changes also take place without any elaborate antecedent development of metapreference. Following Frankfurt's terminology, the unreflective changes in preferences might be called wanton. These are the preference changes economists have primarily focused on: impulsive, uncomplicated, haphazard, publicity-induced, and generally minor (apples vs. pears) changes in tastes. In contrast, the nonwanton change of preference is not really a change in tastes at all. A taste is almost defined as a preference about which you do not argue—*de gustibus non est disputandum*. A taste about which you argue, with others *or yourself*, ceases ipso facto being a taste—it turns into a *value*. When a change in preferences has been preceded by the formation of a metapreference, much argument has obviously gone on within the divided self; it typically represents a change in values rather than a change in tastes.

Given the economists' concentration on, and consequent bias for, wanton preference changes, changes of the reflective kind have tended to be downgraded to the wanton kind by assimilating them to changes in tastes: thus Becker ascribed patterns of discriminatory hiring to a "taste for discrimination," and Johnson similarly analyzed increases in protectionism as reflecting an enhanced "taste for nationalism." Such interpretations strike me as objectionable on two counts: first, they impede a serious intellectual effort to understand what are strongly held values and difficult to achieve changes in values rather than tastes and changes in tastes; second, the illusion is fostered that raising the cost of discrimination (or nationalism) is the simple and sovereign policy instrument for getting people to indulge less in those odd "tastes."

There is a more general point here. Economists often propose to deal with unethical or antisocial behavior by raising the cost of that behavior rather than by proclaiming standards and imposing prohibitions and sanctions. The reason is probably that they think of citizens as consumers with unchanging or arbitrarily changing tastes in matters of civic as well as commodity-oriented behavior. This view tends to neglect the possibility that people are capable of changing their values. A principal purpose of publicly proclaimed laws and regulations is to stigmatize antisocial behavior and thereby to influence citizens' values and behavior codes. This educational, value-molding function of the law is as important as its deterrent and repressive functions.[2] Accordingly, as Kelman has shown, the resistance of legislators to the economists' proposals to deal with pollution exclusively through effluent charges and similar devices becomes intelligible and, up to a point, defensible.[3] The propensity to pollute of industrialists and corporations is not necessarily like a fixed demand schedule, so that all one can do is to make them pay their way for the pollution they are presumed to be bent on causing: that propensity is likely to be affected (the demand curve could shift) as a result of a general change in the civic climate that is signaled—in part—by the proclamation of laws and regulations against pollution.

In the light of the distinction between wanton and nonwanton preference changes, or between changes in tastes and changes in values, it also becomes possible to understand—and to criticize—the recent attempt of Becker and Stigler to do without the notion of preference changes for the purpose of explaining changes in behavior. Equating preference changes to changes in what they themselves call "inscrutable, often capricious tastes," they find, quite rightly, any changes in those kinds of tastes (our wanton changes) of little analytical interest.[4] But in their subsequent determination to explain all behavior change through price and income differences, they neglect one important source of such change: autonomous, reflective change in values. For example, in their analysis of beneficial and harmful addiction they take the elasticity of the individual's demand curve for music or heroin as given and, it would seem, immutable. May I urge that changes in values do occur from time to time in the lives of individuals, within generations, and from one generation to another, and that those changes and their effects on behavior are worth exploring—that, in brief, *de valoribus est disputandum*?

Two Kinds of Activities

From consumption I now turn to production and to human activities such as work and effort involved in achieving production goals. Much of economic activity is directed to the production of (private) goods and services that are then sold in the market. From the point of view of the firm, the activity carries with it a neat distinction between process and outcome, inputs and outputs, or costs and revenue. From the point of view of the individual participant in the process, a seemingly similar distinction can be drawn between work and pay or between effort and reward. Yet there is a well-known difference between the firm and the individual: for the firm any outlay is unambiguously to be entered on the negative side of the accounts whereas work can be more or less irksome or pleasant—even the same work can be felt as more pleasant by the same person from one day to the next. This problem, in particular its positive and normative consequences for income differentials, has attracted the attention of a long line of economists starting with Adam Smith. Most recently Winston has drawn a distinction between "process utility" and "goal utility," making it clear that the means to the end of productive effort need not be entered on the negative side in a calculus of satisfaction.[5] At the same time, this distinction keeps intact the basic instrumental conception of work, the means-end dichotomy on which our understanding of the work and production process has been essentially—and, up to a point, so usefully—based.

But there is a need to go further if the complexity and full range of human activities, productive and otherwise, are to be appreciated. Once again, more structure would be helpful. The possible existence of wholly *noninstrumental* activities is suggested by everyday language, which speaks of activities that are undertaken "for their own sake" and that "carry their own reward." These are somewhat trite, unconvincing phrases: after all, any sustained activity, with the possible exception of pure play, is undertaken with some idea about an intended outcome. A person who claims to be working exclusively for the sake of the rewards yielded by the exertion itself is usually suspect of hypocrisy: one feels he is really after the money, the advancement, or—at the least—the glory, and thus is an instrumentalist after all.

Some progress can be made with the matter by looking at the varying predictability of the intended outcome of different productive activities. Certain activities, typically of a routine character, have perfectly predictable outcomes. With regard to such tasks, there is no doubt in the individual's mind that effort will yield the anticipated outcome—an hour of labor will yield the well-known, fully visualized result as well as entitle the worker, if he has been contracted for the job, to a wage that can be used for the purchase of desired (and usually also well-known) goods.

Under these conditions, the separation of the process into means and ends, or into costs and benefits, occurs almost spontaneously and work appears to assume a wholly instrumental character.

But there are many kinds of activities, from that of a research scientist to that of a composer or an advocate of some public policy, whose intended outcome cannot be relied upon to materialize with certainty. Among these activities there are some—applied laboratory research may be an example—whose outcome cannot be predicted for any single day or month; nevertheless, success in achieving the intended result steadily gains in likelihood as the time of work is extended. In this case, the uncertainty is probabilistic, and one can speak of a certainty equivalent with regard to the output of the activity in any given period so that, once again, the separation of the process into means and ends is experienced, and work of this sort largely retains its instrumental cast. The combination of uncertainty about the result of work for a short stretch of time with near certainty of achievement over a longer period confers to these kinds of nonroutine activities an especially attractive, "stimulating," "exciting" quality that tends to be absent both from wholly routine activities whose outcome never fails to materialize no matter how short the work period, and from very different kinds of nonroutine activities, to be discussed presently.

From their earliest origins, men and women appear to have allocated time to undertakings whose success is simply unpredictable: the pursuit of truth, beauty, justice, liberty, community, friendship, love, salvation, and so on. As a rule, these pursuits are, of course, carried on through a variety of exertions for apparently limited and specific objectives (writing a book, participating in a political campaign, etc.). Nevertheless, an important component of the activities thus undertaken is best described not as labor or work, but as *striving*—a term that precisely intimates the lack of a reliable relation between effort and result. A means-end or cost-benefit calculus is impossible under the circumstances.

These activities have sometimes been referred to, in contrast to the instrumental ones, as "affective" or "expressive."[6] But labeling them does not contribute a great deal to understanding them, for the question is really why such activities should be taken up at all. It is important to note that by no means are these activities always pleasant in themselves; in fact, some of them are sure to be quite strenuous or highly dangerous. Do we have here, then, another paradox or puzzle, one that relates not just to voting (why do rational people bother to vote?) but to a much wider and most vital group of activities? I suppose we do—from the point of view of instrumental reason, noninstrumental action is bound to be something of a mystery. But I have proposed an at least semirational explanation: these noninstrumental activities whose outcome is so uncertain are strangely characterized by a certain fusion of (and confusion between) striving and attaining.

According to conventional economic thinking, utility accrues to an individual primarily upon reaching the goal of consumption, that is, in the process of actually consuming a good or enjoying its use. But given our lively imagination, things are really rather more complicated. When we become sure that some desired good is actually going to be ours or that some desired event is definitely going to happen—be it a good meal, a meeting with the beloved, or the awarding of an honor—we experience the well-known pleasure of *savoring* that future event in advance (the term *savoring* was suggested to me by George Loewenstein). Moreover, this premature hauling in of utility is not limited to situations where the future event is near and certain, or is believed to be so. When the goal is distant and its attainment quite problematic, something very much like savoring can occur, provided a determined personal quest is undertaken. He who strives after truth (or beauty) frequently experiences the conviction, fleeting though it may be, that he has found (or achieved) it. He who participates in a movement for liberty or justice frequently has the experience of already bringing these ideals within reach. In Pascal's formation:

> The hope Christians have to possess an infinite good is mixed with actual enjoyment . . . for they are not like those people who would hope for a kingdom of which they, as subjects, have nothing; rather, they hope for holiness, and for freedom from injustice, and they partake of both.[7]

This savoring, this fusion of striving and attaining, is a fact of experience that goes far to account for the existence and importance of noninstrumental activities. As though in compensation for the uncertainty about the outcome, and for the strenuousness or dangerousness of the activity, the striving effort is colored by the goal and in this fashion makes for an experience that is very different from merely agreeable, pleasurable, or even stimulating: in spite of its frequently painful character it has a well-known, intoxicating quality.

The foregoing interpretation of noninstrumental action is complemented by an alternative view which has been proposed by the sociologist Pizzorno. For him, participation in politics is often engaged in because it enhances one's feeling of belonging to a group. I would add that noninstrumental action in general makes one feel more human. Such action can then be considered, in economic terms, as an *investment in individual and group identity*. In lieu of Pascal, those who advocate this alternative way of explaining noninstrumental action might invoke Jean-Paul Sartre as their patron saint, given the following lines from Sartre's posthumously published wartime diary:

> Throughout his enterprises [man] aims not at self-preservation, as has often been said, or at self-aggrandizement; rather, he seeks to *found* himself. And at the end of every one of these enterprises, he finds that he is back where he started: purposeless, through and through. Hence those well-known disappointments subsequent to effort, to triumph, to love.[8]

In other words, the feeling of having achieved belongingness and personhood is likely to be just as evanescent as the fusion of striving and attaining which I stressed earlier. The two views are related attempts at achieving an uncommonly difficult insight: to think instrumentally about the noninstrumental.

But why should economics be concerned with all this? Is it not enough for this discipline to attempt an adequate account of man's instrumental activities—a vast area indeed—while leaving the other, somewhat murky regions alone? Up to a point such a limitation makes sense. But as economics grows more ambitious, it becomes of increasing importance to appreciate that the means-end, cost-benefit model is far from covering all aspects of human activity and experience.

Take the analysis of political action, an area in which economists have become interested as a natural extension of their work on public goods. Here the neglect of the noninstrumental mode of action was responsible for the inability of the economic approach to understand why people bother to vote and why they engage from time to time in collective action. Once the noninstrumental mode is paid some attention, it becomes possible to account for these otherwise puzzling phenomena. It is the fusion of striving and attaining, as well as the urge to invest in individual or group identity, that leads to a conclusion exactly opposite to the "free ride" argument with respect to collective action: As I wrote in *Shifting Involvements*, "since the output and objective of collective action are . . . a public good available to all, the only way an individual can raise the benefit accruing to him from the collective action is by stepping up *his own input*, his effort on behalf of the public policy he espouses. Far from shirking and attempting to get a free ride, a truly maximizing individual will attempt to be as activist as he can manage."

The preceding argument does not imply, of course, that citizens will never adopt the instrumental mode of action with respect to action in the public interest. On the contrary, quite a few may well move from one mode to the other, and such oscillations could help explain the observed instability both of individual commitment and of many social movements.

A better understanding of collective action is by no means the only benefit that stands to flow from a more open attitude toward the possibility of noninstrumental action. As I have argued earlier, a strong affinity exists between instrumental and routine activities on the one hand, and between noninstrumental and nonroutine activities on the other. But just as I noted the existence of nonroutine activities that are predominantly instrumental (in the case of an applied research laboratory), so can routine work have more or less of a noninstrumental component, as Veblen stressed in *The Instinct of Workmanship*. Lately the conviction has gained ground that fluctuations in this component must be drawn upon to account for variations in labor productivity and for shifts in industrial leadership. It does make a great deal of difference, so it seems, whether people look at their work as "just a job" or also as part of some collective celebration.

Contact can now be made with my earlier plea for complicating the analysis of choice behavior with the concept of metapreferences. One important application of this concept can precisely be found in an individual's deliberation whether to devote more of his time and energy to instrumental activities at the expense of the noninstrumental ones, or vice versa. Shifts of this sort may mean an actual shift from one kind of activity to another (e.g., from public action to private pursuits); they will often involve a two-stage sequence in which an actor first decides to look, say, at some public involvement through instrumental rather than noninstrumental lenses, and then comes to feel that he should cut down on the public activity or give it up altogether. Quite possibly, what I was really after (or should have been after) in *Shifting Involvements* was to describe an oscillation between the instrumental and noninstrumental modes of action, with the pursuits of the private and of the public happiness serving as concrete manifestations of these two basic modes.

"Love": Neither Scarce Resource
nor Augmentable Skill

My next plea for complicating economic discourse also deals with the production side, but more specifically with the role of one important prerequisite or ingredient known variously as morality, civic spirit, trust, observance of elementary ethical norms, and so on. The need of any functioning economic system for this "input" is widely recognized. But disagreement exists over what happens to this "input" as it is used.

There are essentially two opposite models of factor use. The traditional one is constructed on the basis of given, depletable resources that get incorporated into the product. The scarcer the resource the higher its price and the less of it will be used by the economizing firm in combination with other inputs. Arrow's more recent model recognizes the possibility of "learning by doing"; use of a resource such as a skill has the immediate effect of improving the skill, of enlarging (rather than depleting) its availability. The recognition of this sort of process—a considerable, strangely belated insight—also leads to important unorthodox policy conclusions, such as the desirability of subsidizing certain "scarce" inputs, since a subsidy-induced increase in their use will lead to the increased supply which, according to the more traditional model, was expected to be produced on the contrary by raising their price. I shall now attempt to show that neither of these two models is able to deal adequately with the nature of the factor of production that is under discussion here.

Because the "scarce resource" model has long been dominant, it has been extended to domains where its validity is highly dubious. Some thirty years ago, Robertson wrote a characteristically witty paper entitled "What Does the Economist Economize?" His often cited answer was: love, which he called "that scarce resource." Robertson explained, through a number of well-chosen illustrations from the contemporary economic scene, that it was the economist's job to create an institutional environment and pattern of motivation where as small a burden as possible would be placed, for the purposes of society's functioning, on this thing called "love," a term he used as a shortcut for morality and civic spirit. In so arguing, he was of course at one with Adam Smith, who celebrated society's ability to do without "benevolence" (of the butcher, brewer, and baker) as long as individual "interest" was given full scope. Robertson does not invoke Smith, quoting instead a telling phrase by Alfred Marshall: "Progress chiefly depends on the extent to which the strongest and not merely the highest forces of human nature can be utilized for the increase of social good."[9] This is yet another way of asserting that the social order is more secure when it is built on interest rather than on love or benevolence. But the sharpness of Robertson's own formulation makes it possible to identify the flaw in this recurrent mode of reasoning.

Once love and particularly public morality are equated with a scarce resource, the need to economize it seems self-evident. Yet a moment's reflection is enough to realize that the analogy is not only questionable but a bit absurd—and therefore funny. Take, for example, the well-known case of the person who drives in the morning rush hour and quips, upon yielding to another motorist: "I have done my good deed for the day; for the remainder, I can now act like a bastard." What strikes one as funny and absurd here is precisely the assumption, on the part of our driver, that he comes equipped with a strictly limited supply of good deeds; that, in other words, love should be treated as a scarce resource—as Robertson claimed. We know instinctively that the supply of such resources as love or public spirit is not fixed or limited as may be the case for other factors of production. The analogy is faulty for two reasons: first of all, these are resources whose supply may well increase rather than decrease through use; second, these resources do not remain intact if they stay unused— like the ability to speak a foreign language or to play the piano, these moral resources are likely to become depleted and to atrophy if not used.

In a first approximation, then, Robertson's prescription appears to be founded on a confusion between the *use of a resource* and the *practice of an ability*. While human abilities and skills are valuable economic resources, most of them respond positively to practice, in a learning-by-doing manner, and negatively to nonpractice. (Just a few skills— swimming and bicycle riding come to mind—seem to stay at the same level in spite of prolonged nonpractice: once acquired, it is virtually impossible to lose or forget them. In counterpart, such skills often are not notably improved beyond one's level by practice.)

It was on the basis of this atrophy dynamic—the less the requirements of the social order for public spirit, the more the supply of public spirit dries up—that the United States' system for obtaining an adequate supply of human blood for medical purposes, with its only partial reliance on voluntary giving, was criticized by the British sociologist Richard Titmuss. And the British policial economist Fred Hirsch generalized the point: once a social system, such as capitalism, convinces everyone that it can dispense with morality and public spirit, the universal pursuit of self-interest being all that is needed for satisfactory performance, the system will undermine its own viability, which is in fact premised on civic behavior and on the respect of certain moral norms to a far greater extent than capitalism's official ideology avows.

How is it possible to reconcile the concerns of Titmuss and Hirsch with those seemingly opposite, yet surely not without some foundation, of Robertson, Smith, and Marshall? The truth is that, in his fondness for paradox, Robertson did his position a disservice: he opened his flank to easy attack when he equated love with some factor of production in strictly limited supply that needs to be economized. But what about the alternative analogy that equates love, benevolence, and public spirit with a skill that is improved through practice and atrophies without it? This, too, has its weak points. Whereas public spirit will atrophy if too few demands are made upon it, it is not at all certain that the practice of benevolence will indefinitely have a positive feedback effect on the supply of this "skill." The practice of benevolence yields satisfaction ("makes you feel good"), to be sure, and therefore feeds upon itself up to a point, but this process is very different from practicing a manual (or intellectual) skill: here the practice leads to greater *dexterity*, which is usually a net addition to one's abilities, that is, it is not acquired at the expense of some other skill or ability. In the case of benevolence, on the other hand, the point is soon reached where increased practice does conflict with self-interest and even self-preservation: our quipping motorist, to go back to him, has not exhausted his daily supply of benevolence by yielding once, but there surely will be *some* limit to his benevolent driving behavior, in deference to his own vital—perhaps even ethically compelling—displacement needs.

Robertson had a point, therefore, when he maintained that there could be institutional arrangements that make excessive demands on civic behavior, just as Titmuss and Hirsch were right in pointing to the opposite danger: the possibility that society makes insufficient demands on civic spirit. In both cases, there is a shortfall in public spirit, but in the cases pointed to by Robertson et al., the remedy consists in institutional arrangements placing less reliance on civic spirit and more on self-interest, whereas in the situations that have caught the attention of Titmuss and Hirsch, there is need for increased emphasis on, and practice of, community values and benevolence. These two parties argue along exactly opposite lines, but both have a point. Love, benevolence, and civic spirit neither are scarce factors in fixed supply nor do they act like skills and abilities that improve and expand more or less indefinitely with practice. Rather, they exhibit a complex, composite behavior: they atrophy when not adequately practiced and appealed to by the ruling socioeconomic regime, yet will once again make themselves scarce when preached and relied on to excess.

To make matters worse, the precise location of these two danger zones—which, incidentally, may correspond roughly to the complementary ills of today's capitalist and centrally planned societies—is by no means known, nor are these zones ever stable. An ideological-institutional regime that in wartime or other times of stress and public fervor is ideally suited to call forth the energies and efforts of the citizenry is well advised to give way to another that appeals more to private interest and less to civic spirit in a subsequent, less exalted period. Inversely, a regime of the latter sort may, because of the ensuing "atrophy of public meanings,"[10] give rise to anomie and unwillingness ever to sacrifice private or group interest to the public weal so that a move back to a more community-oriented regime would be called for.

Conclusion

I promised to inquire whether the various complications of traditional concepts that have been proposed have any common structure. The answer should be obvious: all these complications flow from a single source—the incredible complexity of human nature, which was disregarded by traditional theory for very good reason but which must be spoon-fed back into the traditional findings for the sake of greater realism.

A plea to recognize this complexity was implicit in my earlier insistence that "voice" be granted a role in certain economic processes alongside "exit," or competition. The efficient economic agent of traditional theory is essentially a silent-scanner and "superior statistician," as Arrow put it, whereas I argued that she also has considerable gifts of verbal and nonverbal communication and persuasion that will enable her to affect economic processes.

Another fundamental characteristic of humans is that they are self-evaluating beings, perhaps the only ones among living organisms. This simple fact forces the intrusion of metapreferences into the theory of consumer choice and makes it possible to distinguish between two fundamentally different kinds of preference changes. The self-evaluating function may be considered a variant of the communication or voice function: it also consists in a person addressing, criticizing, or persuading someone, but this someone is now the self rather than a supplier or an organization to which one belongs. But let us beware of excessive parsimony!

In addition to being endowed with such capabilities as communication, persuasion, and self-evaluation, humanity is beset by a number of fundamental, unresolved, and perhaps unresolvable tensions. A tension of this kind is that between instrumental and noninstrumental modes of behavior and action. Economics has, for very good reasons, concentrated wholly on the instrumental mode. I plead here for a concern with the opposite mode, on the grounds that it is not wholly impervious to economic reasoning; and that it helps us understand matters that have been found puzzling, such as collective action and shifts in labor productivity.

Finally, I have turned to another basic tension humanity must live with, this one resulting from the fact that we live in society. It is the tension between self and others, between self-interest, on the one hand, and public morality, service to community, or even self-sacrifice, on the other, or between "interest" and "benevolence" as Adam Smith put it. Here again, economics has concentrated overwhelmingly on one term of the dichotomy, while putting forward simplistic and contradictory propositions on how to deal with the other. The contradiction can be resolved by closer attention to the special nature of public morality as an "input."

In sum, I have complicated economic discourse by attempting to incorporate into it two basic human endowments and two basic tensions that are part of the human condition. To my mind, this is just a beginning.

Notes

1. See Schelling, p. 342, and Sen, p. 335.

2. "Lawgivers make the citizen good by inculcating [good] habits in them, and this is the aim of every lawgiver; if he does not succeed in doing that, his legislation is a failure. It is in this that a good constitution differs from a bad one." Aristotle, *Nicomachean Ethics*, 1103b.

3. See Kelman, pp. 44–53.

4. See Becker and Stigler, p. 76.

5. See Winston, pp. 193–97.

6. See Smelser, and Parsons (cited by Smeller).

7. See Pascal, 540.

8. See Sartre, p. 141; my emphasis.

9. See Robertson, pp. 154, 148.

10. Taylor, p. 123.

Bibliographical References

Aristotle. *Nicomachean Ethics*. Translated by Martin Ostwald. Indianapolis: Bobbs-Merrill, 1962.

Arrow, Kenneth J. "The Economic Implications of Learning by Doing." *Review of Economic Studies* 29 (1962): 155–73.

———. "The Future and the Present in Economic Life." *Economic Inquiry* 16: (1978): 160.

Becker, Gary S. *The Economies of Discrimination*. Chicago: Chicago University Press, 1957.

Becker, Gary S., and Stigler, George. "De Gustibus Non Est Disputandum." *American Economic Review* 67 (1977): 76–90.

Frankfurt Harry G. "Freedom of the Will and the Concept of a Person." *Journal of Philosophy* 68 (1971): 5–20.

Hirsch, Fred. *Social Limits to Growth*. Cambridge, Mass.: Harvard University Press, 1976.

Hirschman, Albert O. Exit, *Voice, and Loyalty: Responses to Decline in Firms, Organizations, and States*. Cambridge, Mass.: Harvard University Press, 1970.

———. *Shifting Involvements: Private Interest and Public Action*. Princeton, N.J.: Princeton University Press, 1982.

Johnson, Harry G. "A Theoretical Model of Economic Nationalism in New and Developing States." *Political Science Quarterly* 80 (1965); 169–85.

Kelman, Steven. *What Price Incentives? Economists and the Environment.* Boston, Mass.: Auburn House, 1981.

Loewenstein, George F. "Expectations and Intertemporal Choice." Ph. D. Diss., Department of Economics, Yale University, 1985.

Parsons, Talcott. "Toward a Common Language for the Area of Social Science." In *Essays in Sociological Theory, Pure and Applied.* Glencoe, Ill.: Free Press, 1949.

———. "Pattern Variables Revisited." *American Sociological Review* 25 (1960): 467–83.

Pascal, Blaise. *Pensées.* Brunschvicg edition.

Pizzorno, Alessandro. "Sulla razionalità della scelta democratica." *Stato e Mercato* (1983): 3–46; English version in *Telos.* Spring 1985.

Robertson, Dennis H. "What Does the Economist Economize?" In *Economic Commentaries,* pp. 147–55. London: Staples Press, 1956.

Sartre, Jean-Paul. *Les Carnets de la drôle de guerre.* Paris: Gallimard, 1983.

Schelling, Thomas C. *Choice and Consequence.* Cambridge, Mass.: Harvard University Press, 1984.

Sen, Amartya K. "Rational Fools: A Critique of the Behavioral Foundations of Economic Theory." *Philosophy and Public Affairs* 6 (1977): 317–44.

Smelser, Neil J. "Vicissitudes of Work and Love in Anglo-American Society." In *Themes of Work and Love in Adulthood,* edited by Neil J. Smelser and Erik H. Erikson, pp. 105–19. Cambridge, Mass.: Harvard University Press, 1980.

Taylor, Charles. *The Pattern of Politics.* Toronto: McClelland and Stewart, 1970.

Titmuss, Richard M. *The Gift Relationship.* London: Allen and Unwin, 1970.

Veblen, Thorstein. *The Instinct of Workmanship and the State of the Industrial Arts.* New York: Macmillan, 1914.

Winston, Gordon C. *The Timing of Economic Activities.* Cambridge: Cambridge University Press, 1982.

THREE USES OF POLITICAL ECONOMY
IN ANALYZING EUROPEAN
INTEGRATION

With the end of the Second World War, Hirschman was demobilized from the US Army like millions of others. But unlike most of his fellow veterans, Hirschman was a multilingual European, a specialist in trade policy with a PhD in economics. He went to work for the Federal Reserve Board and was a member of the brain trust guiding policy on the Marshall Plan and European reconstruction. In late 1951 he would be purged from the civil service, his loyalties under suspicion. Many years later, as a member of the Institute for Advanced Study, he led a group of scholars thinking about the crisis of the welfare state, especially in Europe—thus returning to old concerns. An invitation from the European University Institute in Florence to talk about European integration enabled him to return to a seemingly forgotten theme, which he had discussed in *National Power and the Structure of Foreign Trade* (1945). In fact, a rising movement of international political economists was rediscovering this book and adopting it as one of its classics. Now Hirschman was determined to draw out more explicitly the interconnectedness of political and economic considerations that were more latent in his thinking almost four decades earlier. Lessons from development and insights from the exit, voice, and loyalty trilogy helped him build a new scaffolding for thinking about sovereignty above and beyond the nation state.

—Jeremy Adelman

WE HAVE RECENTLY BEEN TAUGHT by several works of large-scale historical interpretation that a group of competing states—such as France, Spain, and the other European powers that emerged after the Middle Ages—may acquire, augment, and maintain its collective influence over outlying areas precisely because of its divisions and interstate conflicts, because, that is, the group is *not* integrated into an imperial unit.[1]

If this conjecture has merit, some of our most hackneyed phrases and proverbs will have to be revised and inverted to read "be divided and rule!" or "*La désunion fait la force*" (Disunity makes for strength), etc. It is of course unlikely that these paradoxes can totally substitute for the older wisdom, but I can see at least one other field of application for the new insight: the influence and prestige of social science as a whole may owe much to the *lack* of integration and communication among the individual disciplines of economics, sociology, political science, and so on. It is this lack which may be responsible for the widespread conviction that *some* social science must hold the key to a full understanding of an ongoing and puzzling social process. When one discipline does not give too good an account of itself it is possible to appeal to another one, which, being totally isolated from the first, sets out, so to speak, with a clean sheet and honeymoonlike expectations.

Something of this sort may be happening with regard to the study of European integration. An attractive political science model of integration that was put forward in the fifties has been badly eroded, both by the evolving facts and by rival interpretations. The idea that political science is able to illuminate the dynamics of integration is owed in good measure to the 1958 book by Ernst Haas, *The Uniting of Europe*, and to its guiding concept of "spillover."[2] With this concept, which will be briefly discussed later in this essay, Haas essentially articulated what was the unspoken strategy—the "thinkful wishing"—of such architects of European integration as Jean Monnet. But already in the 1968 preface to the second edition of his book, Haas saw fit to qualify his earlier "neo-functionalist" analysis and enthusiasm. Another seven years later, he issued a paper whose very title, "The Obsolescence of Regional Integration Theory,"[3] appeared to deprecate the attempt to make sense of integration through the conceptual tools available to political scientists. In general, the literature on political integration, which was burgeoning in the fifties and sixties, has considerably abated in the seventies.

But this experience did not lead to a general stocktaking about the ability of social science to furnish explanations of certain processes and to formulate "laws of motion." The prestige of one social science discipline is not tarnished by the misadventures of another, so that it is possible for, say, economists to claim that they can "handle" a problem that has perplexed the political scientists. In recent years, this relay effect has in fact occurred in a number of areas long thought to be the exclusive province of political science as some economists, aided and abetted strangely enough by not a few political scientists, have asserted that their approach (based on the assumption of rational action in the service of individual self-interest) is applicable over a much wider field than it has traditionally occupied.

Now I must right away take my distance from this particular claim. As I wrote a few years ago:

> . . . there are serious pitfalls in any transfer of analytical tools and modes of reasoning developed within one discipline to another. As the economist, swollen with pride over the comparative rigor of his discipline, sets out to bring the light to his heathen colleagues in the other social sciences, he is likely to overlook some crucial distinguishing feature of the newly invaded terrain which makes his concepts and apparatus rather less applicable and illuminating than he is wont to think. [As in the case of] imported ideologies, the distance between reality and intellectual schema is here likely to be both wider and more difficult to detect than was the case as long as the scheme stayed safely "at home."[4]

Nevertheless, economists and economic reasoning can contribute a great deal to the understanding of the obviously interrelated processes of economic and political integration. The field for such explorations is in fact so rich that I propose to subdivide it into three distinct categories.

In the first place, we shall note a case—the economic theory of customs unions—in which the very distinctions made and concepts created for the purpose of analyzing the economics of integration have implications that throw light on the politics of the process. The economist who moves with ease among his own distinctions has of course a comparative advantage in getting hold of these unexpected dividends of his analysis. But often he fails to exploit his advantage, for lack of interdisciplinary motivation. Perhaps also, it is a sound, if partisan, instinct that makes him reluctant to venture onto the terrain of the political implications of his analysis: for once these implications have been spelled out, the policy conclusion of the economic analysis considered in isolation may have to be substantially modified, as will soon be shown.

The second category of useful interaction between economics and politics has to do with situations where economic and political phenomena are perceived to have analogical structures. In such cases—my example will here be economic development in comparison with economic-political integration—exploring the analogy can be conducive to a better understanding of both phenomena involved. Some years ago an analogy of this sort was drawn between money and power and political scientists were quite excited about the possibility of learning something new about power—that perennial black box—by asking questions about the "earning," "accumulation" and "spending" of power. In such cases, one discipline serves essentially as a metaphoric language for the other and in the process matters are often seen in an entirely new light. In the end, however, every metaphor, illuminating though it may be, has its limitations. Coming up against them will actually be also useful, for it will lead to a better appreciation of the uniqueness of each of the two phenomena.

It is my belief that the major contributions economists can make to an understanding of the politics of integration fall within the two just noted categories which have the common characteristic of respecting the autonomy of the political. But I do not want to deny that occasionally there may be a third category: Here the economist would transfer concepts and modes of analysis originally elaborated for the purpose of understanding the economy to the political terrain. This is clearly a case of "imperialistic" expansion of one discipline and, as I have already stated, I have serious doubts about the practice (for reasons other than mere dislike of imperialism). In the third part of this paper, I shall nevertheless engage in this sort of enterprise which will, however, have the redeeming feature that the basic conceptual structure that will be transferred and applied—the exit-voice model—is itself a mixture of economic and political elements.

The Politics of Trade Creation and Trade Diversion

Returning for a moment to the self-proclaimed demise of political science in relation to the analysis of integration, I feel that economists can offer some consolation to their distraught colleagues. Haas and his co-workers need not really have become so despondent over their inability to predict correctly the meandering movement and dynamics of integration: Economists make wrong forecasts all the time and have learned how to thrive on them! One of the principal excuses they have for their wrong predictions is the unfortunate fact that, just as in the case of private profit calculations, the most critical macroeconomic magnitudes, such as the prospective deficit or surplus in the balance of payments, or the rate of unemployment or inflation, are differences between gross values, such as foreign payments and receipts, total and employed labor force, etc. Hence, even if these values are estimated with an acceptable margin of error, the estimate of the critical difference may be off by a very large percentage and may even carry the wrong sign. Forecasting the progress of integration is similarly risky business: For that progress is the net outcome of opposing forces. Haas's "spillover" effect no doubt exists and has been felt continuously since the European Coal and Steel Community was first formed. But counterforces have also been at work and have in fact been aroused by the very successes of integration so that the net outcome or balance is continually in doubt.[5] Perhaps it is appropriate to recall here Paul Valéry's definition of peace as a "virtual, mute, continuous victory of the possible forces over the probable appetites."[6] Thus the outlook for peace, along with that for full employment, and the progress of integration, can all be viewed as depending on the *difference* between two gross magnitudes and all are subject to the same difficulty of prediction.

This does not mean that our whole enterprise is futile, but rather that prediction is not an appropriate test of the usefulness of social science analysis. The feeling that we have acquired a better *understanding* of a social process—even though, as is quite conceivable, it could become more *un*predictable as a result—is sufficient justification for the enterprise, particularly if, as is often the case, new ways of influencing the process become available through that enhanced understanding.

This more cautious but eventually more successful and useful way of proceeding has characterized economic analysis in the area of our concern. Take the already venerable debate about the positive or negative economic effects of customs unions. Jacob Viner, who initiated this debate thirty years ago, argued that the improvement in resource allocation due to the lowering of tariffs among the participating countries would

lead to "trade creation," whereas the discrimination against nonpartic-
ipants implicit in the arrangement would lead to "trade diversion."[7] In
evaluating a customs union from the global welfare point of view, the
benefits of trade creation therefore must be set against the harmful effects of trade diversion.

This sort of analysis refrains from making an outright prediction about
the net economic effects (the prospective benefits) of a customs union;
once again, it will be noted, this effect depends on the difference between
two magnitudes (trade creation *minus* trade diversion) and prediction is
thereby made hazardous. On the other hand, the analysis seems to lead
to a straightforward policy advice: Trade creation should be fostered and
trade diversion combated.

At this point in the argument, the political analyst may well seize upon
the economist's categories for his own purposes. Suppose he wishes to
gauge the likely political support for the customs union within the countries that are to enter it. To do so he can take over with profit the very categories of economic analysis—except that they work in a very different
fashion. As a first approximation, the political chances for forming and
maintaining a customs union will be bolstered by trade diversion and
threatened by trade creation. The larger the trade-creating effects, that
is, the greater the need to reallocate resources in the wake of tariff abolition, the greater will be the resistance to the union among various highly
concentrated and vocal producer interests of the member countries. The
gains from trade creation, on the other hand, lie in the future and are
likely to be diffused among numerous firms and among the consumers
at large. Thus trade creation is on balance a political liability. Trade diversion implies, on the contrary, that concentrated producer groups of
the member countries will be able to capture business away from their
present competitors in nonmember countries. These effects will therefore endear the customs union to the interest groups concerned and will
provide some badly needed group-support for a union.[8]

It seems likely to me that this sort of analysis could be quite useful in
understanding the dynamics of the European Community. For example,
the common agricultural policy had strong trade-diverting characteristics, but this was precisely the reason why it played a crucial role in gaining
support for the Community within some very important but occasionally
vacillating member countries whose farmers were—or were expected to
be—the beneficiaries of that policy. It is, on the contrary, the prospect of

trade creation in agriculture, that is, the prospects of a stepped-up degree of competition and consequent need to reallocate resources which is the major obstacle in the way of enlarging the Community at the present time, through the accession of Spain, Portugal, and Greece.

Here, then, is a good example of economic analysis and its distinctions being useful to political analysis, but also of the way in which the introduction of political considerations modifies the prescriptions of the economist. The straightforward policy conclusion of Viner's theory was that in the formation of a union the principal task is to maximize trade creation and to minimize trade diversion. But bringing in political considerations leads to a very different advice: in view of its political benefits, it may well be desirable to arrange for some trade diversion so as to make use of interest group support for the union in its difficult formative years. The policy problem then becomes that of keeping trade creation to politically safe limits while providing for a vitally needed minimum of trade diversion—quite a difference from the original prescription!

Spillovers and Linkages: A Parallel between Political Integration and Economic Development

Economic and political objectives are not *always* antithetical, of course. As has often been pointed out, the two effects noted by Viner look at economic union from the point of view of the allocation of given, fixed resources, and one of the principal purposes of the union is to have a positive effect not on more effective utilization and allocation of existing resources but on their growth, through economies of scale, more intensive communication, more confident entrepreneurship and the like.[9] Insofar as such dynamic effects take hold and lead to sustained economic improvement, it seems not unreasonable to think that they will strengthen the political solidity of the union so that in this case, in contrast to the previous one, positive economic (growth-promoting) and positive political (union-strengthening) effects should go hand in hand. As a result of disappointing experience in many countries over the past twenty years or so, we have, however, become much more cautious in making such inferences from economic to political performance. Moreover, not only are the interrelations between economic growth and what was fleetingly called "political development" circa 1960 far more complex and ambivalent than had been thought: Even the concept of economic growth has lost its once uncontested solidity and unambiguous meaning.

But the very difficulties we have in comprehending both economic and political change, let alone their interaction, point to the possibility of a much more modest enterprise: that of opening up communications between those who attempt to analyze these processes so as to ascertain whether certain modes of thinking about economic development can be useful to the understanding of political change and vice versa. It is admittedly a case of the blind leading or trying to lead the blind, but this metaphor is not meant here in a dispiriting vein: in interpreting its use in the Bible, one must recall that most of the time the blind are in fact better off if they hold on to each other while moving about (as they still do today in many poor regions of the world), however desperate or laughable the enterprise may look to those who can see.

When the processes of economic development and of economic-political integration are examined in this spirit, there appears a certain formal similarity between them which makes it tempting to "borrow" or "translate" from one to the other. The essence of the similarity consists in some very elementary properties and characteristics: the pace and progress of both economic development and of integration depend on whether "one thing leads to another" in the face of strong resistance from existing institutions, social and political structures, attitudes, values and so on. The virtue and appeal of Haas's analysis was precisely that with his "spillover" he had identified forces that would make for progress toward European unification through incremental steps, in spite of the obvious resistance from the powerfully entrenched interests of the national state system. Thus he wrote:

> . . . it is inconceivable that the liberalisation not only of trade, but of the conditions governing trade can go on for long without "har-monisation of general economic policies" spilling over into the fields of currency and credit, investment planning and business cycle control. . . . The spill-over may make a political community of Europe in fact even before the end of the transitional period.[10]

The leading idea here is that, once freedom of trade is irrevocably established among a group of countries, compelling pressures will arise toward uniform tax, social security, and eventually also monetary and general economic policies, presumably because otherwise the disparities and uncertainties under which national producers would have to operate, would be intolerable. It sounds like *la force des choses* and a quite reasonable prediction, but something went wrong: either the pressures were not as compelling as was thought, or some unexpected counterforces arose. In general, the latter explanation has been appealed to in accounting for the stalling of the integration process in the sixties: but was it really all the fault of Gaullism? The more fundamental reason for which the spillover lacked in dynamism was that within the framework of a continuously and rapidly growing European economy the pressures for harmonization of economic policies were not nearly as compelling as seemed a priori likely. These pressures were thought to result from the much higher degree of competition and the consequently precarious positions of many firms and even sectors within national economies that the abolition of tariff barriers would bring. But this was essentially reasoning for a more or less stationary economy in which the trade-creating effects of a customs union make for painful reallocation of resources. In an environment of all-round growth, very few existing firms were or felt threatened and therefore were not particularly interested in further integration moves that would equalize the conditions of competition. *Perhaps it was then the vigorous growth of the Western European economies in the fifties and sixties that made the spillover dynamic so much less compelling than had been thought.* This conclusion is confirmed by events of the last twelve months: the new move toward a common European currency, known as the European Monetary System, is in large part a response to the continuing inflation, unemployment, and structural readjustment problems presently facing Western Europe.

So much for the interaction between theory and practice in the field of European integration. Now that I have told the story in broadest outline, it is easy for me to translate it into at least one view about economic development—my own. Merely at the linguistic level, Haas's "spillover" sounds rather like my "(forward and backward) linkage effects" and also has something in common with my characterization of development as a "chain of disequilibria."[11]

It may therefore be of some interest to pursue this surface similarity. Just as Haas, I was looking for a compelling dynamic that would unfold in spite of manifold and entrenched resistances. For that reason I emphasized the need for stronger spurs than the placid generation and investment of capital along the lines of the then popular Harrod-Domar growth model. The strategy of unbalanced growth in general and the backward and forward linkages in particular—primarily in connection with industrialization—were seen as supplying such a more compelling and directive push.

The parallelism goes further. For Haas's spillover to function, it was necessary that there first be some initial integration move (such as a customs union). Similarly, for the backward and forward linkage dynamic to get under way, some fairly important initial import-substituting industries must first be in place. The spillover arises in part because of the initiative of the "Eurocrats," but fundamentally because of interest-group pressures for further integration moves, in the name of assuring "fair play" and of equalizing the conditions of competition. The linkage dynamic, on the other hand, was based on the idea that investments in backward- and forward-linkage industries are privileged in relation to investments that are comparatively unrelated to already ongoing activities; a basic assumption was here that development would proceed under conditions of foreign exchange shortage so that the imported inputs for the newly established industries would at some stage become highly eligible for being substituted in turn by domestic production.

As it turned out, both the spillover and the linkage dynamic were less reliable than had been thought originally. They worked nicely enough for a while; but just as the spillover dynamic failed the integration process in the mid-sixties, so there appeared at about the same time some evidence (and much talk) about a leveling off of the process of industrialization via import substitution.[12] While the label that was given this slowdown—the "exhaustion of import substitution"—was highly exaggerated, it became clear in retrospect that there was some justification for distinguishing between an "early and easy" stage of import-substituting industrialization and a more halting and difficult subsequent stage during which domestic production of basic industrial materials and of some capital goods would move into the center of the stage of the industrialization effort while the country would also become an industrial exporter of some consequence. This development became often possible only in the larger developing countries, such as Brazil and Mexico, and owed much to the new balance-of-payments pressures that arose in the seventies, largely as a result of the oil crisis and the concomitant recession in the advanced industrial countries. Once again, there is a parallel here to the current *relance* of European integration under the pressures of the special economic difficulties of the now-ending decade.

It is possible to draw some lessons from our parallel. One is that social scientists invariably seem to overestimate the strength and durability of whatever social forces and processes they uncover. Correlatively, as soon as these forces toward change meet with the first obstacles, their *total* demise is widely proclaimed when in fact there is still quite some life left in them. These first two lessons make interesting footnotes to the sociology of knowledge. Then there is a third, more basic lesson: forces that are expected to subvert quietly and a bit deviously the existing order through economic pressures rather than change it in the course of an open political confrontation tend to labor for that very reason under a specific handicap: the absence of a strong ideology under whose banners they can mobilize support when difficulties appear.

These are the kind of conjectures we might not have come upon, or might have less confidence in, if we had not—somewhat laboriously—translated the language of economic development into that of political integration.

Some Uses of Exit-Voice Reasoning

In the preceding section the autonomy of the political has been scrupulously respected. Concepts elaborated for the purpose of understanding economic development—the linkage effects—were not in any sense directly "applied" to the study of integration. They were merely shown to have a great deal in common with concepts such as the spillover that had arisen out of the study of the integration process, and, as a result, something was learned about both processes.

In this section I intend to be less respectful. I shall intrude the exit-voice model into the discussion and attempt to show that it permits a better understanding of the integration process, in connection with some specific problems.

Capital Mobility, Reform, and Integration

As was pointed out in the preceding chapter, the possibility of exit of the wealthy and of their capital—a possibility that emerged with the rise of various forms of *movable* capital—was hailed in the eighteenth century as a restraint on the caprices and on vexatious or confiscatory policies of the sovereign. The power of capitalists to react through exit (capital flight) to actual or prospective policies they disliked was thus deemed a beneficial restraint on public policy. The eighteenth-century analysts did not perceive the possibility that exit or threat of exit could be used as a veto, not only of arbitrary exactions, but also of policies that might well be in the general interest. Once this is recognized, the veto weapon no longer looks so beneficent. Moreover, the possession of this veto reduces the need for the owners of movable capital to formulate proposals and policies of their own, that is, to develop their voice. This sort of situation can of course be quite damaging to the capacity of a state to achieve a meaningful consensus about needed reforms. Quite apart from competitive considerations, it becomes difficult for any individual state to undertake a reform opposed by its capitalists.

Suppose now this situation prevails in a group of states which serve mutually as safe havens for their national capitalists: how would it change as a result of full-fledged economic and political integration?[13] It is easy to perceive two consequences. In the first place, what was formerly the export of capital is now a mere interregional movement; as a result, the owners of capital may have to subject themselves to the indignity of actually having to argue their case in public. Exit will be transformed into voice. Secondly, the possibility of significant reform being adopted in one country *alone* is now formally ruled out. But this is not really a substantial change as in the previous situation such reforms were in effect subject to being vetoed or disrupted through capital flight.

The impossibility for a single country in the group to move ahead of the others with respect to, say, some social reform or some redistributive taxation was already a fact before integration, but it was hidden from the public and the policymakers and became apparent only after the futile expenditure of large-scale proreform energies. With integration this impossibility is visible to all and energies can now be productively directed to the adoption by the group as a whole of whatever reforms are believed to be called for. Through the exit-voice logic, we have here developed a perhaps important pro-integration argument: under modern conditions of mobility of capital, the ability of capitalist states to undertake reforms is enhanced by the formation of political-economic units that are large and inclusive enough to make the blocking of reforms through large-scale capital flight impractical.

Regional Imbalances and Integration

Whether integration alleviates or aggravates regional disequilibrium and conflict *within* states has become a major performance test for any project of closer economic and political union *among* states. The reason is that these persistent disequilibria and conflicts present many states with one of their major contemporary problems. An important argument *against* integration has therefore been the suspicion that it might aggravate these problems.

The reasoning that would lead to that suspicion is now well known: market forces as well as certain public policies favoring concentration would be given freer play as a result of integration and would lead to an even greater agglomeration of economic resources in the most advanced sectors and regions of the integrating countries, at the expense of the poorer and more backward portions of each cooperating country's economy and territory. These poorer regions would be left in a backwater at best; more likely they would be further depleted and exploited by the now even more weighty center or centers. I have no doubt about the existence of such "backwash" or "polarization" effects (as Myrdal and I, respectively, called them some twenty-odd years ago) nor about the likelihood that they would be strengthened as a result of economic union of two or more countries, *in the absence of countervailing policies*. But this last assumption is both crucial for the argument and anything but justified today. For the problem of polarization has by now become widely recognized as one that must be forcefully dealt with by public policy. In Europe the worry that economic union may widen the differentials between advanced and backward regions has inspired new institutions (in particular the European Social Fund) and policies specifically designed to pour resources into the poorer regions and to accelerate their development. These European-wide institutions and policies came of course on top of national policies attempting to deal with the problem.

Awareness of the problem and the existence of institutions and policies designed to deal with it provide of course no guarantee that the regional disparities will disappear or even narrow. Unintended effects of other community policies—the common agricultural policy, in particular—have in fact gotten in the way of the policies aiming at reducing interregional differences in income. Nevertheless, in comparison to what would be likely to happen under purely laissez-faire auspices, any actual polarization effects are going to be muffled and closely monitored in present circumstances.

But this is a somewhat weak conclusion, for it only says that regional underdevelopment and the ensuing region-center conflict will not get much worse as a result of integration. It seems intuitively plausible that integration can make a positive contribution by lessening the sharp conflicts and tensions that have arisen between certain regions and the national authorities. To understand why this should be so, attention must be focused on the more crucial noneconomic aspects of the center-region or region-region conflict. That economic underdevelopment is not a primary reason for the conflict is suggested by the fact that in a fair number of cases a region has developed considerable hostility toward the center (or another region) even though it is the economically *more* developed part of the country. In such cases—as with the Flemish part of Belgium and with Catalonia and the Basque provinces of Spain—the region feels aggrieved because it is made to pay for what it considers laziness, extravagant living, and parasitism of the people in the economically backward regions which in these cases often include the capital city. As both underdevelopment and superior economic performance are invoked as grounds for complaining about the center, one comes to suspect that the economic argument is subsidiary to the principal grievance of the region which is usually to be found in more basic matters, such as a protracted history of conflict and subjection as well as linguistic, religious and cultural differences.[14] Regional conflicts of this sort have multiplied and intensified in the post-World War II period because the European national states have lost their previous status as world powers, a position that implied special opportunities for *all* the citizens of these states; more important perhaps, that status was simply awe-inspiring and deterred any idea to challenge national unity. It is in fact surprising that there has not been more disintegration in the wake of the loss of status that European states have suffered.

Looking at the matter in this perspective makes it tempting to analyze it in terms of exit and voice. In the postwar period a number of regions have become disaffected from the national state as a result of old and new grievances or because of the disappearance of certain benefits or disciplines. Normally dissatisfaction with an organization can lead to either voice or exit. As a result of centuries of domination, conflicts, and misunderstandings, the dissatisfied regions do not believe in the possibility of obtaining gains through the use of *voice*. Voice has become degraded. Hence the regions have been given more and more to uttering threats of exit. On its part, the center refuses to take such threats seriously or routinely represses them, as when they occasionally explode into terroristic acts. It looks as though we had here the worst of both worlds: voice is discounted as ineffective by one of the two parties while exit-like behavior and its threat are either ignored or suppressed by the other.

In this situation integration holds out hope for a break in the impasse. It creates a new interlocutor—the wider community in formation— which is not weighed down by the heritage of past conflicts and outrages. With integration the aggrieved region can put its case, or at least portions of its case, before a new forum. This regeneration of voice can be one of the major benefits of integration. Correspondingly, with the autonomy and prerogatives of the nation-state being deemphasized, the region will find that separation-exit from the nation-state is no longer essential; it also may strongly wish to be part of the new entity in formation. Even though the achievement of genuine supranational power by this entity may be a long way off, it can act as a concerned third party or even as an ombudsman in relation to the grievances of disaffected regions.[15]

We end up with a rather ironic conjecture: the European Community arrived a bit late in history for its widely proclaimed mission, which was to avert further wars *between* the major Western European nations; even without the Community the time for such wars was past after the two exhausting world wars of the first half of the twentieth century. Perhaps one of the Community's real missions will turn out to be the avoidance of civil wars or wars of secession *within* some of the Western European countries, as it provides the newly secession-prone regions with novel channels for voice.

Integrative and Disintegrative Crises

In addition to the somewhat specialized contributions just attempted, the exit-voice framework might be called upon to help in the analysis of the European integration process in general, its progress, difficulties, and prospects.

Expectations ought to be fairly low in this regard, for two reasons. First of all, the process of voluntary integration among sovereign states is among the least frequent political phenomena—there simply is very little historical experience that could suggest, confirm, or refute hypotheses, no matter what the conceptual framework. Take, for purposes of comparison, processes such as the breakdown of democracies and their transformation into authoritarian regimes, or the opposite political change from authoritarianism to pluralism: even though these processes are highly complex and, in the latter case, quite rare, the empirical material at hand is still comparatively much richer and the invitation to generalize and theorize correspondingly stronger.

Secondly, there is some question as to the "fit" between the exit-voice framework and the integration process. The concepts of exit and voice have been developed and have been found most useful in analyzing *fully established* organizations and their capacity to react against decline in performance. But in the case of political integration, interest centers on a different topic: on the chances of the novel and insecure supranational organizations to grow, to *become* well established and to assume new functions. If the concepts of exit and voice are still to be of service in so different a context, the meanings they had on their native ground are likely to undergo substantial modification, as will now be shown.

Suppose an organization and its members live through events strongly affecting their interests and inviting some action; the organization is not specifically mandated to deal with the problem, but it stands ready to do so if invited by the members. The alternative facing the members in this situation is not exit or voice with respect to the organization and to some action conceivably proposed by it, but whether or not to invite the organization to act or to propose action in the first place. Exit simply means here that members decide to ignore the organization and to behave as though they were independent agents: in contrast to the ordinary exit situation there is not yet any door to go through or to throw shut behind one. Voice means precisely the building of such a door: it is the attempt to involve the organization in the new problem, with the expectation that some advantage will accrue to the members from a common approach.

Suitably and substantially redefined in this fashion the notions of exit and voice can perhaps be of some help in understanding the integration (or disintegration) process. We are led, not wholly unexpectedly, to distinguish between two types of crises: the *disintegrative crisis* that leads the individual members (i.e. nation states) to go it alone and the *integrative crisis* that, on the contrary, impels members to look for some concerted action recommended "from above," that is, from the common organization that is in the process of being built and that may well be strengthened as a result of the new task it is called upon to assume.

It is interesting to speculate about the respective characteristics of these two crisis types. Here we do have some recent historical experience to draw on: the sharp jolt of the oil crisis of 1973 led to a fairly universal go-it-alone, if not *sauve-qui-peut*, reaction on the part of the individual members of the European Community, whereas the subsequent common, protracted and poorly understood problems of unemployment, inflation, and slow growth experienced by the leading European countries in the course of the seventies made them rather more interested in exploring common courses of action. Is it possible to conclude that sudden crises with a clearly identifiable cause will be disintegrative whereas more slowly developing difficulties that are poorly understood will turn out to be integrative? For the time being we can do no more than ask this question while adding our suspicion that matters are in reality quite a bit more complex. For example, it is certainly not correct to look at each crisis by itself, without regard to what happened before. The disintegrative impact of one crisis will itself exert some force on the way in which the next crisis is tackled: if it is evident that the fledgling organization can hardly survive another similarly disintegrative crisis and if there is some desire to assure its survival, the next crisis may well be integrative regardless of its precise characteristics.

As I announced earlier, the various applications of exit-voice to integration problems that have been attempted here hardly qualify as expansionist expeditions of an economist intent on annexing territory hitherto controlled by political scientists. The reason is of course that the exit-voice dichotomy itself does not exclusively dwell in the economic sphere; at times, in fact, it rather seems to fall wholly within the political. Moreover, the injection of exit-voice reasoning has not pretended to produce fundamental new solutions to some major puzzles of integration. What then is the point of the exercise? Perhaps that it sensitizes us to certain situations which can be effectively *reformulated* in terms of exit and voice. Such reformulations will not leave things exactly as they were: occasionally they will make us see the forces at work as well as possible options and outcomes in a new light. And that is about as much, I have come to think, as we can expect from social theory.

Notes

Originally prepared for a conference on economic approaches to the study of international integration, held at the European University Institute in Florence, Italy, in June 1979.

1. See Perry Anderson, *Lineages of the Absolutist State* (London: N.L.B., 1974) and Immanuel Wallerstein, *The Modern World-System* (New York: Academic Press, 1974). The same point had been made in Jean Baechler, *Les origines du capitalisme* (Paris: Gallimard, 1971), translated into English as *The Origins of Capitalism* (Oxford: Blackwell, 1975).

2. First published in 1958 by Stevens and Sons Ltd., London. Reissued with a new preface by Stanford University Press, 1968. Another influential work on the dynamics of the integration process, written at approximately the same time, but more cautious in its conclusions and predictions, is Karl W. Deutsch et al., *Political Community and the North Atlantic Area* (Princeton, N.J.: Princeton University Press, 1957). Based on an intensive reading of the historical record over a wide area and a long historical period, this book also gave an important impulse to further studies of integration.

3. Research Series No. 25, Institute of International Studies, University of California, Berkeley, 1975.

4. *Bias for Hope* (New Haven: Yale University Press, 1971), pp. 3–4.

5. See Stanley Hoffmann, "Obstinate or Obsolete? France, European Integration, and the Fate of the Nation-State," originally published in *Daedalus,* Summer 1966 and reprinted in his *Decline or Renewal? France since the 1930's* (New York: Viking, 1974), pp. 363–99.

6. *Regards sur le monde actuel* (Paris, 1931), p. 51.

7. Jacob Viner, *The Customs Union Issue* (New York: Carnegie Endowment for International Peace, 1950).

8. Even though Viner, in his book, devoted a chapter to the "Political Aspects of Customs Unions" he did not make use of the economic categories he had created for the analysis of that chapter.

9. See Tibor Scitovsky, *Economic Theory and Western European Integration* (London: Allen and Unwin, 1958) and Paul Streeten, *Economic Integration* (Leyden: Sythoff, 1964).

10. *Uniting of Europe,* p. 311.

11. Haas's *Uniting of Europe* and my *Strategy of Economic Development* were both published in 1958; while we became later very much aware of one another's writings, our two books were written independently.

12. I have discussed these matters in "The Political Economy of Import-Substituting Industrialization in Latin America" (1968), reprinted in this volume.

13. I should make it clear that I am writing in the hypothetical mood. The integration that is postulated in this section is much more far-reaching than the one presently achieved in Western Europe. The reasoning has nevertheless some relevance for possible European developments.

14. Peter Gourevitch argues that economic grievances are the ingredient in the center-periphery relationship that will exacerbate the underlying tensions, in "The Reemergence of 'Peripheral Nationalisms': Some Comparative Speculations on the Spatial Distribution of Political Leadership and Economic Growth," *Comparative Studies in Society and History* 21 (July 1979): 303–22.

15. For some suggestions along these lines on the part or on behalf of presently embattled minorities in Corsica and Northern Ireland, see *Le Monde* of August 21 and September 1, 1979.

OPINIONATED OPINIONS
AND DEMOCRACY

"Is it a good thing to have opinions?" asked Hirschman. When he posed this question in 1989, not only was it meant to chide those who worried that strong opinions were threats to democracy, but he was enjoining his fellow economists to consider the analysis of more unruly subjects than their preferred choice of more objectively valued goods. But the point was more than just to be mischievous, though that was clearly in Hirschman's sights. He was concerned with a double problem. One was the quality of democratic discourse in Europe and America. The other was the way in which economists had removed themselves from subjects that did not easily fit inside their conceptual schemata. Beginning in the mid-1980s, Hirschman was returning to Berlin, his city of birth, with greater frequency. These sojourns gave him an opportunity to reflect on the events and polarizations that had brought down the Weimar Republic and to recall the effects of degraded political discourse. He was also watching South American countries make fitful transitions to democracy. To expand the possible mixtures of democracy and capitalism, he wondered how democratic discourse might prosper by thinking of democracy with consumers and markets with citizens.

—*Jeremy Adelman*

She thought it could scarcely escape him to feel that a persuadable temper might sometimes be as much in favour of happiness as a very resolute character.

—Jane Austen, *Persuasion*

WHEN ECONOMISTS FOCUS on the quality of life, their minds turn to ingredients of human satisfaction other than the bundles of consumer goods and services that have traditionally been the main subject of economic analysis. In recent decades we have rediscovered that man does not live by bread, nor even by GNP, alone, and have realized that a number of heretofore neglected items must be incorporated into individual utility functions: examples are reasonably clean air, feelings of participation and community, and an atmosphere of security and trust within and among nations. While being nondivisible, difficult to measure, and public, such "goods" have nevertheless been thought to partake of some basic characteristics of the typical consumer good: satisfaction increases indefinitely as their availability increases, and does so at a decreasing rate. As a result, traditional and powerful economic concepts and tools, such as "maximization under constraints" and "equalization at the margin," could continue to be applied to the new goods. Under the circumstances, economists have perhaps not learned as much as they might have from the widening of their horizon that no doubt has taken place. I now wish to look at a good that, it seems to me, is not nearly as "well behaved" as those that have previously been selected for study.

The good—or ingredient of the quality of life—I shall examine is that of *having opinions*. Is it a good thing to have opinions? In his short story "The Darling," Chekhov appears to answer this question very much in the positive:

> And what was worst of all, she [Olenka] no longer had any opinions whatever. She saw the objects about her and understood what was going on, but she could not form an opinion about anything and did not know what to talk about. *And how awful it is not to have any opinions!* You see, for instance, a bottle, or the rain, or a peasant driving in his cart, but what the bottle is for, or the rain, or the peasant, and what is the meaning of it, you can't say, and could not even for a thousand rubles. When she had Kukin, or Pustovalov or, later, the veterinary surgeon, Olenka could explain it all and give her opinions about anything you like, but now there was the same emptiness in her head and in her heart as in her yard outside. She was filled with dread and bitterness. . . . (1984, p. 16; emphasis added.)

Here Chekhov seems to be saying that not to have any opinions is tantamount to not having individuality, personhood, identity, character, self. And a person who has no self can hardly have any self-respect.

Not to have opinions is thus symptomatic of a basic lack and of a desperate predicament. It is, in fact, the opposite condition that has been widely commended by social scientists, psychologists, and philosophers: to have opinions very much of one's own. Wilhelm von Humboldt went perhaps farthest in this direction when he proclaimed *individuality (Eigentümlichkeit)* and *originality (Originalität)* as "that on which all the greatness of man rests in the last instance and after which he must ceaselessly strive" (1851, p. 1). Humboldt's views strongly influenced John Stuart Mill, who cited and explicated them at length in his essay *On Liberty* (1859), in a chapter with the demonstrative title "Of Individuality, as One of the Elements of Well-Being."[1] Closer to our time, Erik Erikson stressed the struggle to achieve identity as a crucial formative life experience, and John Rawls, in his *Theory of Justice* (1971), included self-respect (presumably based on identity, character, and the holding of opinions) among the "primary goods" that a well-ordered society must supply to its citizens.

At first blush, it seems therefore that, like other aspects of the quality of life, opinions can be treated like consumer goods: the more the better, as well as, in this case, the stronger the better. Not only in social thought, but in much of Western culture has this position been endorsed, and the value of exhibiting strong opinions and of taking a principled stand celebrated, to the point where there is even some doubt whether the principle of decreasing returns applies to the good under examination. Conversely, indifference and lack of conviction have been denounced in the harshest terms, as illustrated by Dante and his scathing portrayal of the angels who would not take sides in the battle between God and the devil, and of the lukewarm in general. In a powerful passage he singled out these wretches as deprived of the "hope of death" and relegated them to the vestibule of Hell for the reason that, if they were let in, the damned would have someone to look down on (*Inferno* III, 25–50).

A few centuries later, much the same value judgment found another famous poetic expression: "The best lack all conviction, while the worst / Are full of passionate intensity." Yeats explicates here how it is that "things fall apart" (1959, p. 185). To him it is apparent that a well-ordered society requires the inverse arrangement: the best, not the worst, should be full of passionate intensity, that is, of sharply articulated and firmly held opinions.

In short, vacillation, indifference, or weakly held opinions have long met with utmost contempt, while approval and admiration have been bestowed on firmness, fullness, and articulateness of opinion.[2]

Yet matters are hardly that simple. Indeed, Chekhov's story itself intimates that to have a lot of ready-made opinions can be as ridiculous as to have no opinions is "bitter." For all his Olenka does in her happier moments is to parrot, each time with considerable conviction and aplomb, the opinions of her successive husbands and lovers. When Anthony Downs wrote his *Economic Theory of Democracy* (1956), he thought it was one of the advantages of political parties to offer citizens a full range of ready-made and firm opinions on all the issues of the day. In the meantime, however, we have come to appreciate that this time-saving feature of political parties, particularly of those with an ideological bent (those that in Germany were called *Weltanschauungsparteien*), and the ensuing "free ride" to a full set of strong opinions, actually come at a considerable cost. We express our doubts about the value of the Downs mechanism by designating those who take advantage of it as "knee-jerk liberals," or "knee-jerk conservatives." Perhaps, to paraphrase a famous Chicago theorem, there ain't no such thing as a free *ride*!

Introducing the knee-jerk concept complicates the appraisal of the benefits that flow from having opinions. Apparently it can be just as much a denial of individuality, personhood, and self—a sort of damaging "escape from freedom"—to be outfitted with a full set of strong opinions on all the issues of the day, as to suffer Olenka's "awful" condition of not having any opinions whatever. While the goods we buy in the market are unambiguously conducive to material welfare, opinions are not necessarily the key to individuality and self-respect; it all seems to depend on some further, complex specifications regarding the more or less autonomous manner in which the opinions have been formed.

Some progress can perhaps be made with our topic if it is viewed from a collective rather than from an individual angle. Thus far I have primarily inquired into the contribution to *individual* satisfaction and happiness that is made by the acquisition and possession of a wide set of strongly formulated opinions. But surely such opinions, widely diffused among the citizenry, also have important effects, positive and negative, on the character of society. An important influence on the quality of life of individual citizens could then be exerted in this indirect way. The desirability of economic progress has often been evaluated in this dual fashion. One looks not only at the impact of, say, economic growth on individual well-being, but also on its contribution to the maintenance and strengthening of a free democratic society. Ecology aside, the consensus has lately been that the social and political effects of economic growth are as beneficent as its direct effect on the individual's welfare. But such harmony between the direct and indirect, or individual and social, effects was not always taken for granted. Up to the eighteenth century, for example, political economists and philosophers frequently worried about the corrupting effect of increases in wealth on the state. In the end, the state's ruin would then affect its citizens adversely, however much they may have prospered for a time.

Old-fashioned as it may seem, this sort of reasoning may well be worth refurbishing in conjunction with the problem at hand. Recent contributions to the theory of democracy have stressed the role of deliberation in the democratic process: for a democracy to function well and to endure, it is essential, so it has been argued, that opinions *not* be fully formed *in advance* of the process of deliberation.[3] The participants in this process—both the public at large and its representatives—should maintain a degree of openness or tentativeness in their opinions and be ready to modify them, both as a result of the arguments that will be put forward by the contending parties and, more simply, in the light of new information that could be developed in the course of public debates. Without a political process that manifests at least some aspiration toward this admittedly somewhat idyllic picture, democracy loses its legitimacy and will thus be endangered.

If this view has merit, then the traditional strong emphasis of Western culture on the virtue of strong opinions turns out to be curiously wrongheaded. The suspicion arises that this emphasis is rooted in a long aristocratic tradition, and has not been suitably modified by the subsequent, still rather young democratic age. As is well known, ideological relics of this sort have considerable potential for mischief. Social scientists and psychologists who hold forth so volubly on the virtues of individuality, personality, and identity might therefore do well to explore how to combine these desiderata with such democratic qualities as intellectual openness, flexibility, and readiness to appreciate a new argument, perhaps even pleasure in embracing it.

To put the matter in the economist's language: given the basic need for identity in our culture, the forming and acquiring of opinions yields considerable utility to the individual. At the same time, if carried beyond some point, the process has dangerous side-effects—it is hazardous for the functioning and stability of the democratic order. Under present cultural values these noxious side-effects do not enter the individual calculus—they are what economists call external diseconomies. Hence there will be an *overproduction* of opinionated opinion.[4] The most straightforward way of avoiding this overproduction would be for individuals to change the value system under which they operate. Might they learn to value both having opinions and keeping an open mind, to mix the delights of winning an argument with the pleasures of being good listeners and of having Jane Austen's "persuadable temper"?

In conclusion I return to the earlier argument, which evaluated the utility of having opinions from the individual, rather than collective, point of view. There I suggested that holding many strong opinions is an ambiguous indicator of well-being: it may or may not lastingly fulfill the promise of endowing the holders with true identity and rich personality. I also showed that the possession of opinions will be the less effective in those respects the more the opinions are acquired through the wholesale embrace of an ideology, that is, the more pronounced is their knee-jerk character. Now one way of acquiring opinions in the opposite, personality-enriching manner is to give them definite shape only after they have passed through intense confrontation with other views, that is, through the process of democratic deliberation. It turns out, therefore, that the public interest in democratic decision-making converges nicely with the private interest in forming opinions in such a manner as to enhance one's self-respect.

I have moved far away from economics. In fact, I may as well admit that I have been out of order all along, for my principal motivation in writing this note was to raise a point in the theory of democracy, to reflect on an ancient theme—the micro or personality foundations of a democratic society. But the argument I have developed about opinions may yield some helpful hints for a matter of interest to economics in general, and to the quality of life in particular: the concept of tastes and of changes therein.

Clearly, the traditional concept of the consumer with exogenously given, firm, and *non-est-disputandum* tastes bears a considerable resemblance to that of the citizen with a full array of strong and fully formed opinions. It is in fact likely that the two concepts owe something to, and reinforce, each other. I have argued here that our traditional bias in favor of strong opinions ought to be modified, in part because it might be dangerous to the health of our democracy. The question may therefore be raised whether a similar change is to be recommended for the concept of given tastes. To be sure, tastes are different from opinions: to become effective in the marketplace, they do not have to go through the process of deliberation characteristic of opinions in a democracy. But as a result of newly accumulating medical, environmental, and other research findings, many entrenched tastes (for tobacco, for cholesterol-laden foods, for using the automobile rather than public transportation, and so on) are being questioned ever more frequently, in both the individual and the public interest. As with our opinions, it therefore becomes increasingly desirable also with respect to our tastes that we do not regard them as being etched in granite.

A final suggestion. Those who labor to change some specific taste, say for cigarettes, have generally mounted a head-on assault on the habit, primarily by trying to convince smokers of the baneful consequences that follow from indulging their taste for tobacco. This approach could be usefully complemented, in line with the present discussion, by an indirect strategy. As part of their education for democracy, consumers could be encouraged to look at their tastes in general in a slightly questioning mood: any single consumption habit may be easier to rein in or give up once people no longer consider their tastes as proud possessions that cannot be altered or abandoned without some grievous loss of personality, character, identity, or self.

References

Chekhov, Anton. *The Darling and Other Stories* (*The Tales of Chekhov*, vol. 1), transl. by Constance Garnett. New York: Ecco Press, 1984.

Downs, Anthony. *An Economic Theory of Democracy*. New York: Harper and Row, 1957.

Gutmann, Amy, and Thompson, Dennis. "The Place of Philosophy in Public Affairs." in Judith Lichtenberg and Henry Shue, eds., *The Public Turn in Philosophy*. Totowa: Rowman and Allanheld, 1989.

Humboldt, Wilhelm von. *Ideen zu einem Versuch, die Grenzen der Wirksamkeit des Staats zu bestimmen*, Breslau, 1851. Published in English as *The Limits of State Action*, introduction by J. W. Burrow. Cambridge: Cambridge University Press, 1969.

Mill, John Stuart. *On Liberty*. 1859.

Rawls, John. *A Theory of Justice*. Cambridge, Mass.: Harvard University Press, 1971.

Scitovsky, Tibor, *The Joyless Economy*. New York: Oxford University Press, 1976.

Trollope, Anthony. *Barchester Towers*, eds. M. Sadleir and F. Page. London: Oxford University Press, 1953.

Yeats, W. B. "The Second Coming," in *The Collected Poems*. New York: Macmillan, 1959.

Notes

Published under the title "Having Opinions—One of the Elements of Well-Being?" in *American Economic Review—Papers and Proceedings,* 19 (May 1989), 75–79. Originally written for the annual meetings of the American Economic Association, this essay was presented in a session on "The Quality of Life." Most of it was incorporated into the talk I gave at the Freie Universität of Berlin, where I was awarded an honorary degree in November 1988. On this occasion I added an autobiographical note, which is reproduced here as Chapter 7. A shortened version of the Berlin talk was published in *Dissent* (Summer 1989), 393–395. The reference to Trollope's *Barchester Towers* (n. 4) has been added here, along with Jane Austen's epigram.

1. Originally written in 1792, Humboldt's essay was published in its entirety for the first time in 1851, long after his death. An English translation appeared in 1854, just as John Stuart Mill began drafting *On Liberty.* See J. W. Burrow's introduction to Humboldt, 1969.

2. Recently I have come across a remarkable exception to this rule: the inability (on a *man's* part, moreover) to come forward with a strong opinion about a much debated issue is not only not denounced, but is implied to be outright lovable. This rare moment in the annals of Western literature occurs toward the end of Trollope's *Barchester Towers,* in the crucial scene where Eleanor Bold and Francis Arabin are finally united in love after a series of misunderstandings and quarrels that had kept them apart for hundreds of pages. The scene starts

with a rather awkward conversation about the comparative merits of "progress" and "old-fashionedness":

"I don't know about that," said Mr. Arabin, gently laughing. "That is an opinion on which very much may be said on either side. It is strange how widely the world is divided on a subject which so nearly concerns us all, and which is so close beneath our eyes. Some think that we are quickly progressing towards perfection, while others imagine that virtue is disappearing from the earth."

"And you, Mr. Arabin, what do you think?" said Eleanor. She felt somewhat surprised at the tone which his conversation was taking, and yet she was relieved at his saying something which enabled herself to speak without showing her own emotion.

"What do I think, Mrs. Bold?" and then he rumbled his money with his hands in his trowsers pockets, and looked and spoke very little like a thriving lover. "It is the bane of my life that on important subjects I acquire no fixed opinion. I think, and think, and go on thinking; and yet my thoughts are running ever in different directions" (vol 2, p. 232).

Barely two pages after this exchange, Eleanor and Francis are in each other's arms!

3. See Bernard Manin, 1987, and Amy Gutmann and Dennis Thompson, 1989.

4. A formally similar argument is made by Tibor Scitovsky, 1976. He shows how certain socially useful activities, such as careful shopping, are not engaged in by consumers because the ensuing benefits are widely diffused as external economies.

REACTIONARY RHETORIC

In 1988 the American presidential elections saw public discourse hit new lows. The Republican candidate, George H. W. Bush, charged his opponent, Michael Dukakis, with being a *l-i-b-e-r-a-l*, a "card-carrying member of the ACLU." Hirschman joined with Fritz Stern, Daniel Bell, George Soros, Ken Arrow, John Hope Franklin, Donna Shalala, Felix Rohatyn, William Styron, and others to place an ad in *The New York Times* to defend the integrity of the "L" word and of a more tolerant contest. That winter, upset by a dispiriting outcome (Dukakis was trounced), Hirschman labored to sort out what was so pernicious about the opposition's talk. He circled back to familiar themes, like the Scottish Enlightenment and unintended consequences, Marx and romanticism. He sensed he was returning to the beginning of a cycle that had begun decades earlier in his pleas for reform. To understand why reform was so fraught, he needed "better understanding [of] why reform movements arouse resistance and passionate antagonism, why they run into decreasing returns, why they are subject to (totalitarian, etc.) dérapage." By the next summer, ideas were crystallizing around the keyword "reaction."[1] He put the final touches to his ruminations and sent it to James Fallows, editor of the *Atlantic Monthly*, which published the long essay in May 1989. It charged the self-described "neo-conservatives" of being unwilling to argue directly with those who advocated reform. Instead, what they wielded were word games, a theme from *The Passions and the Interests*, to chart the arguments for capitalism in its ascent. Two centuries after the publication of Adam Smith's *Wealth of Nations*, with Latin American economies tearing down old

---

[1] Notes—Summer 1985; Notes—Summer 1986, Box 56, f. 10, AOHP.

restrictions and Communist verities trembling behind their walls, capitalism *was* triumphant. And yet its apostles were deafer than ever to the voices of those who wanted it to be a little less savage.

—*Jeremy Adelman*

IN A FAMOUS 1949 LECTURE on the "development of citizenship" in the West, the English sociologist T. H. Marshall distinguished among the civil, political, and social dimensions of citizenship and then proceeded to explain, very much in the spirit of the Whig interpretation of history, how the more enlightened human societies had tackled these three dimensions one after another, conveniently allocating about a century to each. According to his scheme, the eighteenth century witnessed the major battles for the institution of *civil* citizenship, from freedom of speech, thought, and religion to the right to evenhanded justice—in other words, for the "Rights of Man." In the course of the nineteenth century it was the *political* aspect of citizenship—that is, the right of citizens to participate in the exercise of political power—that made major strides, as the right to vote was extended to ever larger groups. Finally, the rise of the welfare state in the twentieth century extended the concept of citizenship to the *social* and *economic* sphere, by recognizing that minimum standards of education, health, economic well-being, and security are basic to the life of a civilized person as well as to the meaningful exercise of the civil and political attributes of citizenship.

When Marshall painted this magnificent canvas of staged progress, the third battle for the assertion of citizenship rights, the one being waged on social and economic terrain, seemed to be well on its way to being won, particularly in the Labour Party–ruled, social-security-conscious Britain of the immediate postwar period. A generation or so later it appears that, as Ralf Dahrendorf recently reminded us, Marshall was overoptimistic on that score and that the notion of the socioeconomic dimension of citizenship as a natural complement of the civil and political dimensions has run into considerable difficulties and stands in need of substantial rethinking.

Indeed, is it not true that not just the last but each and every one of Marshall's three progressive thrusts has been followed by ideological counterthrusts of extraordinary force? And have not these counterthrusts often led to convulsive social and political struggles, and to setbacks for progressive programs, and to much human suffering and misery? The backlash so far elicited by the welfare state may in fact be rather mild in comparison with the onslaughts and conflicts that followed upon the assertion of individual freedoms in the eighteenth century and upon the broadening of political participation in the nineteenth. Once we contemplate this protracted and perilous seesawing of action and reaction, we come to appreciate more than ever the profound wisdom of Alfred North Whitehead's well-known observation that "the major advances in civilization are processes which all but wreck the societies in which they occur." It is surely Whitehead's statement, rather than any account of smooth, unrelenting progress, that catches the deeply ambivalent essence of the story Marshall so blandly called the "development of citizenship."

There are good reasons, then, for focusing on the *reactions* to the successive forward thrusts. It is not my aim here to write yet another essay on the nature and deep roots of conservative thought. Nor am I going to embark on a broad and leisurely historical review of the successive reforms and counterreforms, theses and countertheses, since the French Revolution. Rather, I shall focus on the common or typical arguments unfailingly made by the great reactive movements of the past two centuries. My emphasis will be on the major polemical maneuvers engaged in by those who set out to debunk and roll back "progressive" policies and movements of ideas—by the forces, that is to say, of reaction. Chief among these arguments is what might be called the thesis of the perverse effect.

The thesis of the perverse effect is closely connected with the semantic origin of the term *reaction*. The couple *action* and *reaction* came into currency as a result of Newton's Third Law of Motion, which asserted that "to every Action there is always opposed an equal Reaction." Having thus been singled out for distinction in the prestigious science of mechanics, the two concepts spilled over into other realms and were widely used in the analysis of society and history in the eighteenth century. No derogatory meaning whatsoever attached at first to the term *reaction*. The remarkably durable infusion of such meaning took place during the French Revolution—specifically, after its great watershed, the events of

Thermidor. It is already noticeable in Benjamin Constant's youthful tract *Des Réactions politiques,* written in 1797 expressly to denounce what Constant perceived as a new chapter of the Revolution, in which the re-actions against the excesses of the Jacobins might themselves engender far worse excesses. This very thought may have contributed to the pe-jorative meaning that was soon attached to the term. More important, the spirit of the Enlightenment, with its belief in the forward march of history, survived the Revolution, even among its critics, notwithstand-ing the Terror and other mishaps. One could deplore the excesses of the Revolution, as Constant certainly did, and yet continue to believe both in history's fundamentally progressive design and in the Revolution's part in it. Such must have been the dominant contemporary attitude. Otherwise it would be hard to explain why those who "reacted" to the Revolution in a predominantly negative manner came to be perceived and denounced as "reactionaries."

The semantic exploration of *reaction* points straight to an important characteristic of reactionary thinking. Because of the stubbornly pro-gressive temper of the modern era, reactionaries live in a hostile world. They are up against an intellectual climate that attaches a positive value to the lofty objectives proclaimed and actively pursued by their adver-saries. Given this state of public opinion, reactionaries are not likely to launch an all-out attack on those objectives. Rather, they will endorse them, sincerely or otherwise, but then attempt to demonstrate that the actions undertaken in their name are ill conceived; indeed, they will most typically argue that these actions will produce, by way of a series of unintended consequences, the *exact contrary* of the objectives that are being pursued.

This, then, is the thesis of the perverse effect. It asserts not merely that a movement or policy will fall short of its goal or will occasion unex-pected costs or negative side effects but that *the attempt to push society in a certain direction will result in its moving in the opposite direction.* Being simple, intriguing, and devastating (if true), the argument has proved popular with generations of reactionaries as well as with the public at large. It is not, of course, the exclusive property of reactionaries, and it is most generally to be heard among groups that are out of power. In what follows I intend to look at how the argument has been wielded against attempts to expand the civil, political, and social and economic aspects of citizenship.

A Vengeful Providence?

Like many other elements of reactionary thinking, the thesis of the perverse effect was first put forward in the wake of the French Revolution. Actually, there was little need for inventive genius: As *liberté, égalité, fraternité* turned into the dictatorship of the Comité de Salut Public (and later into that of Bonaparte), the idea that certain attempts to achieve liberty are bound to lead to tyranny instead almost forced itself upon the mind. Edmund Burke predicted such an outcome as early as 1790, in his *Reflections on the Revolution in France*. There he prognosticated that "an ignoble oligarchy founded on the destruction of the crown, the church, the nobility, and the people [would] end all the deceitful dreams and visions of the equality and rights of men." He conjured up the specter of military interventions during various civil disorders and exclaimed, "Massacre, torture, hanging! These are your rights of men!"

The argument took root and was to be repeated in many forms. Perhaps the most general, if heavy-footed, formulation is that of the German Romantic political economist Adam Müller, who proclaimed, when the Revolution and its Napoleonic aftermath had run their course,

> The history of the French Revolution constitutes a proof, administered continuously over thirty years, that man, acting by himself and without religion, is unable to break any chains that oppress him without sinking in the process into still deeper slavery.

Here Burke's conjectures have been turned into a rigid historical law that could serve as an ideological prop for the Europe of the Holy Alliance.

Burke's uncanny ability to project the course of the French Revolution has been attributed to the very strength of his passionate engagement with it. But his formulation of the perverse effect may well have had an intellectual origin as well: he was steeped in the thought of the Scottish Enlightenment, which stressed the importance of the unintended effects of human action. The best-known application of this notion was the "invisible hand" doctrine of Adam Smith, with whose economic views Burke had expressed total agreement.

Smith, like Mandeville and others (such as Pascal and Vico) before him, had shown how individual actions motivated by greed—or, less insultingly, by self-interest—can have a positive social outcome in the shape of an orderly or prosperous commonwealth. Expressing these ideas with poetic pith toward the end of the century, Goethe defined his Mephisto as "a part of that force that ever wills evil, but ever brings forth good."

In this manner the intellectual terrain was well prepared for arguing that on occasion the opposite might happen. This was exactly what Burke did in contemplating the unprecedented effort of the French Revolution to reconstruct society: he switched the places of good and evil in Goethe's statement and asserted that the social outcome of the revolutionaries' striving for the public good would be evil, calamitous, and wholly contrary to the goals and hopes they were professing.

From one point of view, then, Burke's proposition looks (and may have looked to him) like a minor variation on a well-known eighteenth-century theme. From another, it was a radical ideological shift from the Enlightenment to Romanticism and from optimism about progress to pessimism. It seems possible to me that large-scale and seemingly abrupt ideological shifts often take place in this fashion. Formally they require only a slight modification of familiar patterns of thought, but the new variant has an affinity with very different beliefs and propositions and becomes *embedded* in them to form a wholly new gestalt, so that in the end the intimate connection between the old and the new is almost unrecognizable.

In the present case, the old was the slow emergence of a new kind of hope for world order. From the sixteenth century on it was widely agreed that religious precept and moral admonition could not be relied on to restrain and reshape human nature so as to guarantee social order and economic welfare. But with the rise of commerce and industry in the seventeenth and eighteenth centuries, influential voices proposed that some of the ineradicable "vices" of men, such as persistent self-seeking, could, properly channeled, produce a workable and perhaps even a progressive society. To Pascal, Vico, and Goethe, this paradoxical process suggested the intervention of a Providence that is remarkably benign, forgiving, and helpful as it transmutes evil into good. The optimism of this construction was enhanced further when the pursuit of self-interest through trade and industry lost its stigma and was accorded social prestige instead. At that point there was no longer a sharp contrast between the means and the end, or between process and outcome, and the need for the magical intervention of Divine Providence became less compelling: Adam Smith barely allowed it to survive, secularized and a bit anemic, as the invisible hand.

The French Revolution caused Divine Providence to be pressed back into active service but in a shape that was anything but benign: its task now was to foil the designs of men, whose pretensions to the building of an ideal society were to be exposed as naive and preposterous, if not criminal and blasphemous. "*Der Mensch in seinem Wahn*" (man in his delusion), that "worst of terrors," as Schiller put it in one of his best-known poems, had to be taught a salutary if severe lesson.

Joseph de Maistre in particular ascribed refined cruelty to the Divine Providence that he saw at work throughout the Revolution. In his *Considérations sur la France* (1797) he came forward with an extravagant formulation of the perverse effect as the very essence of Divine Providence.

> The efforts a people make to attain a certain objective are precisely the means employed by Providence to keep it out of reach. . . . If one wants to know the probable result of the French Revolution, one only needs to examine the points on which all factions were in agreement: all wanted the . . . destruction of universal Christianity and of the Monarchy; *from which it follows* that the final result of their efforts will be none other than the exaltation of Christianity and Monarchy.
>
> All those who have written or meditated about history have admired this secret force which mocks human intentions.

Maistre's construction of Divine Providence is no doubt exceptional in its elaborate vengefulness. But the basic feature of the perversity thesis has remained unchanged: man is held up to ridicule, by Divine Providence and by those privileged social analysts who have pierced its designs, for setting out to improve the world radically and for going radically astray. What better way to show him up as half foolish and half criminal than to prove that he is achieving the exact opposite of what he is proclaiming as his objective?

The Foolish Majority

This line of reasoning surfaces again during our next episode, the broadening of the franchise in the nineteenth century. New reasons for affirming the inevitability of a perverse outcome of that process were now put

forward by the emergent social sciences. To appreciate the climate of opinion in which these arguments arose, it is useful to recall contemporary
attitudes toward the masses and toward mass participation in politics.

European society had long been highly stratified, with the lower
classes being held in the utmost contempt by both the upper and the
middle classes. "The occupation of a hairdresser," Burke wrote, "or of a
working tallow-chandler cannot be a matter of honor to any person—to
say nothing of a number of other more servile employments. . . . the state
suffers oppression if such as they . . . are permitted to rule." He commented on the "innumerable servile, degrading, unseemly, unmanly,
and often most unwholesome and pestiferous occupations to which by
the social economy so many wretches are inevitably doomed."

Such remarks, made in an offhand manner, suggest that Burke's primary emotion toward the "lower orders" was not so much class antagonism and fear of revolt as utter contempt, a feeling of total separateness,
even outright physical revulsion, much as in caste societies. This mood
carried over into the nineteenth century and could only have been enhanced by the cityward migration of impoverished rural folk which came
with industrialization. It was compounded by fear as Burke's "wretches"
took to staging violent political outbreaks, particularly in the 1840s.
After one such episode, in 1845 in Lucerne, the young Jacob Burckhardt
wrote from Basel,

> Conditions in Switzerland—so disgusting and barbarous—have
> spoilt everything for me, and I shall expatriate myself as soon as I
> can. . . . The word freedom sounds rich and beautiful, but no one
> should talk about it who has not seen and experienced slavery under
> the loud-mouthed masses, called 'the people.' . . . I know too much
> history to expect anything from the despotism of the masses but a
> future tyranny, which will mean the end of history. . . .

It would be easy to collect additional evidence on the extent to which
the idea of mass participation in politics, even in the watered-down
form of universal suffrage, seemed aberrant and potentially disastrous
to a good part of Europe's elites. Universal suffrage was one of Flaubert's
favorite *bêtes noires,* a frequent butt of his passionate hatred of human
stupidity. The farther universal suffrage extended its sweep across Europe, the more strident became the elite voices that stood or arose in

unreconciled opposition to it. For Nietzsche, popular elections were the ultimate expression of the "herd instinct," a telling term he coined to denigrate all trends toward democratic politics. Even Ibsen, acclaimed in his time as a progressive critic of society, harshly attacked the majority and majority rule. In *An Enemy of the People* (1882) the play's hero, Dr. Stockmann, thunders,

> Who forms the majority in any country? I think we'd all have to agree that the fools are in a terrifying, overwhelming majority all over the world! But in the name of God it can't be right that the fools should rule the wise!

The undoubted advance of democratic political forms in the second half of the century occurred despite a diffuse mood of skepticism and hostility. Then, toward the century's end, this mood found a more sophisticated expression, as medical and psychological discoveries showed human behavior to be motivated by irrational forces to a much greater extent than had previously been acknowledged. Among the several political ideas that can be considered to be, in this manner, reactions to the advances of the franchise and of democracy in general, one of the more prominent and influential was articulated by Gustave Le Bon, in his best-selling *Psychologie des foules,* first published in 1895. The book also exemplified once again the attraction of reactionary thinkers to the perverse effect.

Le Bon's principal argument challenged commonsense understandings by invoking what is known to economists as the fallacy of composition. What applies to the individual, he insisted, does not necessarily hold for the group, much less for the crowd. Impressed by recent research findings on infection and hypnosis (but unaware of the simultaneously proceeding work of Freud, which would shortly show individuals themselves to be subject to all manner of unconscious drives), Le Bon drew a sharp dichotomy between the individual and the crowd: the individual was rational, perhaps sophisticated, and calculating; the crowd was irrational, easily swayed, unable to weigh pros and cons, given to unreasoning enthusiasms, and so on: "None too good at reasoning, the crowd is on the contrary much given to action."

In *fin de siècle* Europe, Le Bon's theory had obvious political implications. It saw the prospects for national and international order as quite gloomy: with the franchise spreading, Le Bon's irrational crowds were installed as important actors in an ever larger number of countries. Moreover, the book's last two chapters, "Electoral Crowds" and "Parliamentary Assemblies," supplied specific arguments against modern mass-based democracy. Here Le Bon did not argue directly against universal suffrage; rather, like Flaubert, he spoke of it as an absurd dogma that was unfortunately bound to cause a great deal of harm just as had earlier, superstitious beliefs. The perverse effect is invoked in the final, crowning argument of the book: democracy will increasingly turn into the rule of bureaucracy through the many laws and regulations passed in "the illusion that equality and liberty will be better safeguarded thereby." In support of these views Le Bon cited Herbert Spencer's book *The Man versus the State* (1884). Spencer was a contemporary scientific authority who had taken a strongly conservative turn. Spencer, too, had chosen the perverse effect as a leitmotif, particularly in the essay titled "The Sins of Legislators," where he put forward an extravagantly general formulation: "Uninstructed legislators have in past times continually increased human suffering in their endeavours to mitigate it."

Once again, then, a group of social analysts derided those who aspired to change the world for the better. And it was not enough for them to show that these naive do-gooders fell flat on their face; they sought to prove that the do-gooders' efforts actually left the world in worse shape. Moreover, they insisted that the worsening occurred along the very dimension where improvement had been intended.

"The Arch-Creator of Distress"

The thesis of the perverse effect was to achieve special prominence during the third reactionary phase, to which I now turn: the present-day assault on the social and economic policies that make up the modern welfare state.

In economics, more than in the other social and political sciences, the perverse-effect theory is closely tied to a central tenet of the discipline: the idea of a self-regulating market. To the extent that this idea is dominant, any public policy aimed at changing market outcomes, such as prices or wages, automatically becomes noxious interference with beneficent equilibrating processes. Even economists who favor some measures of income and wealth redistribution tend to regard the most obvious "populist" price- or wage-policy measures as counterproductive.

The perverse effect of specific interferences—a decree setting a maximum price for bread, or a minimum-wage law—has often been argued by tracing the supply-and-demand reactions to such measures. For example, as a result of a price ceiling for bread, flour will be diverted to other uses and some bread will be sold at black-market prices, so that the average price of bread may go up rather than down. Similarly, after a minimum wage is imposed, less labor will be hired, so that the income of workers may fall rather than rise.

There is actually nothing certain about such perverse effects. In the case of minimum-wage legislation, in particular, it is conceivable that the underlying supply-and-demand curves for labor could shift as a result and that the officially imposed increase in wages could have a positive effect on labor productivity and consequently on employment. But the mere possibility of demonstrating a perverse outcome as the first-order effect of interference makes for a powerful debating point that is bound to be brought up in any polemic.

The long public debate about social assistance to the poor provides ample illustration. Such assistance is admittedly rank interference with "market outcomes" that assign some members of society to the bottom of the income scale. The economic argument that perverse effects will ensue was first put forward during debates about the poor laws in England. The critics of these laws, from Defoe to Burke, from Malthus to Tocqueville, scoffed at the notion that the poor laws were merely a "safety net"—to use a modern term—for those who had fallen behind, through no fault of their own, in the race to earn a livelihood. Given the human "proclivity to idleness" (Mandeville's phrase), this "naive" view neglected the supply reactions, the incentives built into the arrangement: the availability of the assistance, it was argued, acted as a positive encouragement to "sloth" and "depravity," and thus *produced* poverty instead of relieving it. Here is a typical formulation of this point, by an early-nineteenth-century English essayist:

> The Poor-laws were intended to prevent mendicants; they have made mendicancy a legal profession; they were established in the spirit of a noble and sublime provision, which contained all the theory of Virtue; they have produced all the consequences of Vice. . . .

The Poor-laws, formed to relieve the distressed, have been the arch-creator of distress.

A century and a half later, in the most highly publicized attack on the welfare state in the United States, Charles Murray's *Losing Ground* (1984), one reads:

We tried to provide more for the poor and produced more poor instead. We tried to remove the barriers to escape from poverty, and inadvertently built a trap.

Except for a slight toning down of nineteenth-century coloratura, the music is exactly the same. The perverse effect would seem to work unremittingly under both early and late capitalism.

Not that the ideological scene has remained unchanged throughout these hundred and fifty years. The success of Murray's book in fact owes much to the rather fresh look of its principal point, epitomized in its title—almost any idea that has been out of view for a long time has a good chance of being mistaken for an original insight. What actually happened is that the idea went into hiding, for reasons that are of some interest to our story.

As Karl Polanyi showed memorably in *The Great Transformation* (1944), the English poor laws, especially as supplemented and reinforced by the Speenhamland Act of 1795, represented a last-ditch attempt to rein in, through public assistance, the free market for labor, and to ameliorate its effects on the poorest strata of society. By supplementing low wages, particularly in agriculture, the new scheme helped to ensure social peace and to sustain domestic food production during the age of the Napoleonic Wars.

But once the emergency was over, the scheme came under strong attack. Fueled by belief in the new political-economy "laws" of Bentham, Malthus, and Ricardo, the reaction against the Speenhamland arrangements became so powerful that in 1834 the Poor Law Amendment Act (or "New Poor Law") fashioned the workhouse into the primary instrument of social assistance. Workhouse assistance was now organized so as to do away once and for all with any conceivable perverse effect. What public assistance there was stigmatized those who used it by (in the words of a contemporary observer)

imprisoning [them] in workhouses, compelling them to wear special garb, separating them from their families, cutting them off from
communication with the poor outside, and, when they died, permitting their bodies to be disposed of for dissection.

It was not long before this new regime aroused, in turn, the most violent criticism across a wide political and social spectrum. A particularly
powerful and influential indictment was Charles Dickens's novel *Oliver
Twist*, published in 1837–1838. A strong opposition movement arose,
complete with demonstrations and riots, during the decade following
enactment, and as a result the provisions of the law were not fully applied. The experience with the New Poor Law was so searing that the
argument that had presided over its adoption—essentially, a claim that
social-welfare assistance had a perverse effect—remained discredited for
a long time.

Eventually the argument reappeared, however, though not at first in
its crude form. Rather, it would seem that to be reintroduced into polite
company, the old-fashioned perverse effect needed some new, sophisticated attire. One of the early general attacks on social-welfare policy in
this country, which had the intriguing title "Counterintuitive Behavior of
Social Systems," was published in 1971 by Jay W. Forrester, a pioneer in
the simulation of social processes with computer models. The article is a
good example of what the French call intellectual terrorism. At the outset
the reader is told that he or she has a very poor chance of understanding
how society works, since we are dealing with "complex and highly interacting systems," with social arrangements that "belong to the class called
multi-loop non-linear feedback systems" and similar arcane "system
dynamics" that "the human mind is not adapted to interpreting." Only
the highly trained computer specialist can unravel these mysteries—and
what revelations does he come up with? "At times programs cause exactly
the reverse of desired results." Joseph de Maistre's vengeful Providence
has returned in the guise of "multiloop non-linear feedback systems."

In an influential article also written in 1971, titled "The Limits of Social Policy," Nathan Glazer joined Forrester in invoking the perverse effect, proclaiming, "Our efforts to deal with distress themselves increase
distress." Glazer did not employ computer models but spelled out some
plain sociological reasons. Welfare-state policies, he argued, are meant to
deal with distress that used to be dealt with by traditional structures such

as the family, the church, and the local community. As these structures break down, the state comes in to take over their functions. In the process, the state further weakens what remains of the traditional structures. Hence the situation gets worse rather than better.

But Glazer's reasoning was too softly sociological for the harder, conservative mood that became fashionable during the 1980s. Charles Murray's formulation of the perverse effect of social-welfare policy returned to the blunt reasoning of the proponents of poor-law reform in early-nineteenth-century England. Inspired, like them, by the simplest economic verities, he argued that public assistance to the poor, as available in the United States, acts as an irresistible incentive to those working or potentially working for low wages (his famous "Harold" and "Phyllis") to flock to the welfare rolls and to stay there—to become forever "trapped" in sloth and poverty.

Does Everything Backfire?

Just as earlier I have not controverted Burke or Le Bon, it is not my purpose here to discuss the substance of the various arguments against social-welfare policy in the United States and elsewhere. What I have tried to show is that the protagonists of this reactionary episode, like those of the earlier ones, have been powerfully attracted time and again by the same form of reasoning—that is, the claim of the perverse effect. In closing, I nevertheless wish to give some quite general reasons why the perverse effect is unlikely to exist in nature to anything like the extent that is claimed.

One of the great insights of the science of society—found already in Vico and Mandeville and elaborated magisterially during the Scottish Enlightenment—is that because of imperfect foresight, human actions are apt to have unintended consequences of considerable scope. The perverse effect is a special and extreme case of the unintended consequence. Here the failure of foresight of the ordinary human actors is well-nigh total, because their actions are shown to produce precisely the opposite of the result intended; the social scientists analyzing the perverse effect, however, experience a great feeling of superiority—and revel in it. Maistre naively said as much when he exclaimed in his gruesome chapter on the prevalence of war in human history: "It is sweet to fathom the design of the Godhead in the midst of general cataclysm."

But the self-flattery of this situation should put the analysts of the perverse effect, as well as the rest of us, on guard: could they be embracing the effect for the express purpose of feeling good about themselves? In any event, are they not suffering from an attack of hubris when they portray ordinary human beings as wholly groping in the dark, while in contrast they make themselves look so remarkably perspicacious? And, finally, are they not rendering their task too easy by focusing on just one privileged and simplistic outcome of a program or a policy—the opposite of the intended one? For it can be argued that the perverse effect, which appears to be a mere variant of the concept of unintended consequences, is in one important respect its denial and even its betrayal. The concept of unintended consequences originally introduced uncertainty and open-endedness into social thought, but the exponents of the perverse effect retreat into viewing the social universe as wholly predictable by means of a rather transparent maneuver.

There is no denying, to be sure, that the perverse effect does show up here and there. By intimating that it is likely to be invoked for reasons that have little to do with its relevance, I have merely intended to raise some doubts about whether it occurs with the frequency that is claimed. Indeed, the perverse effect is by no means the only conceivable variety of unintended consequences or side effects.

In the first place, as Adam Smith and Goethe tried to teach us, there are unintended consequences and side effects of human actions that are *welcome*. But we rarely pay much attention to them, because they do not pose urgent problems to be addressed. Second, there are actions, policies, and inventions that have no unintended consequences, welcome or otherwise. These situations, similarly, tend to be neglected entirely. Finally, there are situations where secondary or side effects detract from the intended effect of some purposeful action. Here we are getting closer to the perverse case. But typically some positive benefit survives the onslaught of the negative side effect. There is, in fact, something intrinsically plausible about this type of outcome and something correspondingly implausible about the perverse effect as a frequent occurrence. This is so at least to the extent that policy-making is a repetitive, incremental activity: yesterday's experiences are continually incorporated into today's decisions, so that tendencies toward perversity stand a good chance of being detected and corrected.

I hope I will have convinced the reader that it was worthwhile to trace the thesis of the perverse effect through the debates of the past two hundred years, if only to marvel at certain constants in argument and rhetoric— just as Flaubert liked to marvel at the constant *bêtise* of his contemporaries. To see how the participants in these debates lumber predictably through their paces may even have some practical value. On the one hand, it may incline advocates of reactionary causes to plead their case with greater originality, sophistication, and restraint. And on the other hand, it may help reformers and sundry progressives: they are here given notice of the kinds of arguments and objections that are most likely to be raised against their programs.

EXIT, VOICE, AND THE STATE

Hirschman's best-known book was *Exit, Voice, and Loyalty: Responses to Decline in Firms, Organizations, and States*. The book made him one of the most renowned social scientists in the world, and for the first time Hirschman was invited to globe trot well beyond Latin America and the United States. It was this book, for instance, that opened doors to Europe, where Hirschman had begun his intellectual formation. Most of the book focused on varieties of consumer behavior; the implications for understanding the state were not clear. As Latin American citizens increasingly fell under the boot of military regimes, as the numbers of defectors from the Eastern bloc rose, Hirschman grew more aware of the ties between his earlier formulation and thinking about democracy. By the mid-1970s, with his return to Europe, memories of his past departure from Berlin in 1933 also came back. In the preface to the German translation of *Exit, Voice, and Loyalty* he directly addressed his inaugural exit for the first time—expressing his sense of guilt at having left behind so many other Jews instead of remaining loyal or exercising voice. Invited to help celebrate the five hundredth anniversary of the University of Uppsala, Hirschman turned his thoughts to how citizens' exit and voice affect state power and expanded his thinking to include a range of political possibilities, from stateless societies and small states to the ones that behave like global hegemons.

—*Jeremy Adelman*

THERE ARE TWO MAIN TYPES of activist reactions to discontent with organizations to which one belongs or with which one does business: either to *voice* one's complaints, while continuing as a member or customer, in the hope of improving matters; or to *exit* from the organization, to take one's business elsewhere. *Exit, Voice, and Loyalty*[1] was built on this dichotomy.

One of my main contentions was that economists, with their emphasis on the virtues of competition (i.e., exit), had disregarded the possible contributions of voice just as political scientists, with their interest in political participation and protest, had neglected the possible role of exit in the analysis of political behavior. The book, however, gave more attention to the former point and dealt only briefly with the political scientist's principal object of study: the state.[2] In the present paper, I shall attempt a more extensive survey. The importance of exit in relation to the state is the common theme of the diverse situations, ranging from the stateless societies of tropical Africa to the modern small welfare state, that I will explore.

Exit, Rousseau's Savage, and Stateless Societies

Does the exit-voice model have something useful to contribute to the analysis of the state? It does, in the opinion of Jean-Jacques Rousseau.

In the *Discourse on the Origin and the Foundations of Inequality among Men* he wrote:

> When the savage has had his dinner he is at peace with all of Nature and friends with everyone around him. What if a dispute arises about the meal? In that case, he will never become involved in a real fight without having first compared the difficulty of winning with *that of finding elsewhere the means of subsistence*; and since considerations of pride are of no consequence the fight is rapidly settled by the exchange of some fisticuffs: the winner eats, the loser *goes to look for better luck elsewhere (va chercher fortune)* and everything is at peace again; but with man in society things are altogether different. . . .[3]

Rousseau allowed here for a strictly limited amount of nonverbal voice— "some fisticuffs" in the unusual case in which there is a fight at all—and exit was for him the principal way in which the "savage" manifests non-conformity with other members of his group. This way of dealing with dissent has the virtue of minimizing conflict; it also is likely to keep any one group quite small. For exit to function in this beneficial manner, Rousseau's principal condition is the absence of "pride"—elsewhere he called it *amour propre* and contrasted it with the commendable *amour de soi* which is concerned with the satisfaction of basic physiological needs. The question whether the "savage" would be able to fill these needs after having exited from a group was taken up by Rousseau in his *Essay on the Origin of Languages* and, consistently enough, received a resoundingly affirmative answer.

> . . . the origin of languages is not due to the first needs of men; it would be absurd to hold that from the *cause that separates men* there should derive the instrument that unites them. Where, then, does language originate? In the moral needs, in the passions. Passions bring men closer together *while the need to stay alive obliges them to flee from each other.*[4]

Most readers of the *Essay* are of course interested in Rousseau's remarkable theory of language which is brought underway with these vigorous sentences. I choose to emphasize here his view that breaking away from a group is not necessarily a bar to survival, so that exit becomes a feasible option in case of conflict. It is well to remember that the *Essay* was originally part of the *Discourse*;[5] the two quoted passages are different aspects of the same thought. Jointly they constitute a theory of a small, stateless society in which the availability of exit has the dual function of defusing conflict and of assuring a continuous process of fission—and thereby the continuation of the condition of statelessness.

Observation of certain so-called primitive societies in recent decades has turned up a number of situations that correspond to Rousseau's model. Writing in 1944, Claude Lévi-Strauss gives the following account of political life among the Nambikuara of Central Brazil:

> No social structure is weaker and more fragile than the Nambikuara band. If the chief's authority appears too exacting, if he keeps too many women for himself, or if he does not satisfactorily solve the food problem in times of scarcity, discontent will very likely appear.

Then, individuals, or families, will separate from the group and join another band believed to be better managed. . . . Therefore, Nambikuara social structure appears continuously on the move. The bands take shape, they disorganize, they increase and they vanish. Within a few months, sometimes, their composition, number and distribution cannot be recognized.[6]

A similar pattern of social and political behavior, also from Central Brazil, is reported by Joan Bamberger about a tribe called Kayapó:

> Should traditional leadership fail to re-establish harmony after a dispute has broken out, the contestants and sometimes their supporters, which in the most dramatic instance includes the entire community, may engage in physical combat. Fighting of this kind is institutionalized among the Kayapó in the formal duel, known as *aben tak* ("hitting together"). . . . whoever loses an *aben tak*, whether it is a two-person fight or a community brawl, must leave the village. The Kayapó say that the vanquished depart because they have too much "shame" (*piaam*) to remain in the same village with those people with whom they have fought. . . .[7]

The similarity to Rousseau's fisticuffs scenario is remarkable, even though the Kayapó seem to be afflicted with more than a trace of pride and *amour propre*. The disaffected Kayapó also resemble Rousseau's savage in that they simply exit without necessarily *entering* or joining some other group that seems to them to be better managed (as is the case for the group described by Lévi-Strauss); a breakaway group is here apparently willing and able to go it alone.

On turning from America to Africa, one meets with many more illustrations of the phenomenon of fissiparous politics—known to the anthropological literature under such titles as acephalous or stateless societies, segmentary lineage systems, fission and fusion, and the like. A large part of that literature deals with what in modern politics is known as "secession" rather than as "emigration." In other words, the tendency toward fission frequently takes the form of a group detaching itself from a larger one while staying (or moving about, in the case of nomadic tribes) in the same area as before. The exit concept could, of course, be extended to cover cases of this sort. I shall, however, limit myself here to situations in which physical moving away of individuals or groups is an essential characteristic of the splitting-up process.

Frequent recourse to exit in this sense appears to be an important ingredient of statelessness in a number of African societies. Evans-Pritchard says about the Nuer that "any Nuer may leave his tribe and settle in a new tribe of which he thereby becomes a member."[8] In their Introduction to *Tribes Without Rulers*, Middleton and Tait write, "In much of Central Africa, for example, there are politically uncentralized societies in which . . . the main political structure is provided by relations between chiefs and villagers of cognatic kin, related in various ways to a headman and free to choose their village residence where they please."[9] Reporting on Bushman bands in South Africa, Lorna Marshall points out that "the possibility of choice and change of members from one band to another . . . allows for adjustment in the size of the band to the relative scarcity of food and water" and that "a new band can be formed at any time that circumstances permit and people desire to form one." Friction in human relations is one reason for such new band formation.[10]

The most elaborate description of the fission process via geographical separation is in Turnbull's account of Mbuti pygmy bands in the tropical rain forest of Central Africa. Here fissions that have little to do with lineal relationships are frequent occurrences, specially on the occasion when a camp moves.

> Sites are even chosen because they afford greater privacy between the various sections, thus minimizing any serious disputes that are in progress. Some interpersonal hostilities will persist, however, and it is these and not lineal relationships that are reflected in the final fission, when the camp divides into a number of independent camps, or sub-bands, each going its own way. If the dispute is serious, one or another sub-band may go off to another territory, and seek to join up with that band. . . .
>
> So the monthly change of camp is an opportunity not only for a diplomatic rearrangement of the layout, minimizing latent hostilities, but it is also an opportunity for improving the economic strength of the band by either adding to it or subtracting from it.[11]

By bringing together these various situations—which Rousseau hit upon by pure deduction—I hope to have demonstrated that some forms of statelessness are closely associated with the possibility and regular practice of exit. But it is by no means easy to interpret the nature of this association. The fact that my most explicit examples in America and Africa come from bands living in thinly populated tropical rain forests or savannahs suggests that the availability of at least minimally fertile, unoccupied natural resources makes exit permanently attractive and prevents the emergence of any larger political grouping with state-like authority. Such availability, however, is not a sufficient condition for statelessness: within a lord-peasant or lord-laborer context, exactly the same situation has been quite plausibly invoked by Nieboer and others as favoring the introduction of *slavery*.[12] The presence of "open resources" is no doubt important in shaping political forms; but, depending on other system determinants, it can lead either to a highly coercive system or to one that lacks any specialized and permanently constituted political authority. Moreover, these two polar opposites do not exhaust the universe of possibilities: after all, Nieboer's "open resources" are not so far from Turner's "open frontier."[13]

In any event, I do not wish to propound here an ecological theory of stateless societies. What interests me is not so much the fundamental reason for which exit takes place with such regularity as the political effects of institutionalized exit. One of these effects is the non-emergence of large, centralized societies with specialized state organs. Another is the apparent stability of the statelessness-cum-exit condition over wide areas and through time. Political arrangements that are unstable at the level of individual bands, with their constant fission and fusion, have been remarkably stable—as though frozen in this pattern of instability—when looked at from a slightly more macro point of view. One reason is that the exit pattern of conflict behavior, once set, is very difficult to change except through some outside event such as invasion or exhaustion of the "open resources." Once again, the practice of exit is self-reinforcing. Once this avoidance mechanism for dealing with disputes or venting dissatisfaction is readily available, the contribution of voice—that is of the political process—to such matters is likely to be and to remain limited.[14]

In accounting for stability, one would wish to know something about the feedback effect of exit on the organization that is being left: does the organization take notice of exits by its members and act in consequence in such a manner as to remedy its weaknesses and inefficiencies? Unfortunately, the anthropological studies I have cited do not supply much material in answer to this question. When exit occurs as a result of disputes between the two parties, it probably just produces satisfaction for the one that remains, and a "good riddance" reaction. According to some of the descriptions, however, exit results not only from the push of internal dispute, but also from the pull of "superior management" of other bands. In such a case, the bands that are losing members are more likely to react to the loss by attempting to improve their own performance. In view of the stability of these societies through time, one may perhaps infer that such a stabilizing feedback process must be at work: if exit were always cumulative, with losing bands never being able to recoup their losses, a tendency toward consolidation of the many bands into one would have asserted itself. (Another explanation why this does not occur would be that there is some sort of optimal size for bands with diseconomies of scale setting in if this size is exceeded.)

The exit behavior characteristic of the societies just reviewed, particularly when exit from one band involves entry into another, "better managed" one, is remarkably similar to what has been called "voting with one's feet." Because it resembles the working of the market where a buyer is free to switch from one seller to another, some quarters have celebrated this mechanism as far more "efficient" than the "cumbersome" political process for the redress of people's grievances or the fulfillment of their demands.[15] Unfortunately, because of differences in income and wealth, the ability to vote with one's feet is unequally distributed in modern societies. In the United States, where the problem is compounded because of race discrimination, inequality in access to exit has had some appalling consequences, such as the "ghettoization" and partial ruin of our big cities. It is possible that a more satisfactory approximation of the neo-laissez-faire economist's political dream is found in the societies of the forest people in Central Brazil and Central Africa; in historical perspective, of course, theirs has not been a perfect solution either, since they have turned out to be no match for the perhaps less efficient, but more powerful societies—exitless and endowed with a centralized political organization—that arose elsewhere.

Movable Property and Its Exit
as a Restraint on the State

The European state system of the 17th and 18th centuries is precisely that sort of society in one of its purest forms. To a considerable extent, the absolutist state arose as a result of a laborious and eventually successful fight for the formation and territorial unification of a geographical unit. Particularly on the European Continent, the state was, as Samuel Finer has remarked, "obsessed by the demon of exit," exit being taken here in the sense of territorial autonomy or secession.[16] It is ironic, then, and was so sensed by some 18th-century observers, that as soon as one form of exit had been brought under control, another raised its head because of the expansion of commerce and finance which was actively promoted by the absolutist state. With this expansion, a new form of wealth assumed increasing importance. It was named *movable* wealth, in contrast with the unmovable form—land and buildings—in which the bulk of assets had traditionally been held. Montesquieu defined it as "money, notes, bills of exchange, stocks of companies, ships, all commodities and merchandise"; he noted that this form of wealth could move about from one country to another.[17]

What was the reaction of the state and of enlightened opinion to the discovery of this new form of wealth and to the possibility of its exit? The fears and hopes aroused by the rise of movable capital in the 17th and 18th centuries offer many interesting parallels with similarly contradictory perceptions caused quite recently by the rise of the multinational corporation.[18] A comparative study cannot be undertaken here, but a brief survey of reactions to the earlier phenomenon will perhaps be suggestive.

Initially, there was a lag in the perception of the new form of wealth, and particularly of its possible importance for politics. The case of James Harrington is striking. He is justly famous for his theory relating political forms and stability to the concentration and distribution of property. Nevertheless, at a time when the major mercantilist tracts about trade and bullion were being written, his principal work, *Oceana* (1656), focused exclusively on landed property and its distribution as a determinant of politics. Criticized on this score by some of his contemporaries, he later justified his position by pointing, with an elaborate metaphor drawn from falconry, to the superior ability of "Mony" to take to flight:

> Tho Riches in general have Wings and be apt to bate; yet those in Land are the most hooded, and ty'd to the Perch, whereas those in Mony have the least hold, and are the swiftest of flight. . . . a Bank never paid an Army; or paying an Army soon became no Bank. But where a Prince or a Nobility has an Estate in Land, the Revenue whereof will defray this Charge, there their Men are planted, have Toes that are Roots, and Arms that bring forth what Fruits you please.[19]

Here was an eloquent defense of the model used by Harrington. But the very "flightiness" of money which he stressed for this purpose raised questions about favorable or unfavorable *political* consequences that were to be expected as movable property became a substantial proportion of a country's total wealth.

One century later a debate along such lines was in full swing. It was not ever fully joined: those who looked at the new phenomenon with hope or alarm, respectively, usually dealt with different varieties of movable property. For example, one of the strongest denunciations of the new form of wealth was issued by David Hume as he focused on the public debt. In one of his later "conservative" essays, he predicted that "a grievous despotism must infallibly prevail" were England to allow the public debt to expand indefinitely; he castigated the holders of the debt, the "stockholders . . . who have no connexions with the state, who can enjoy their revenue in any part of the globe in which they chuse to reside. . . ."[20]

Exit of the "stockholders," or "stockjobbers" as they were also called in a pejorative vein, is here judged as an act of disloyalty and near-betrayal, without any redeeming features. But this passage stands quite alone in Hume's writings; he had only praise for the new forms of mobile wealth generated by trade and industry—as did some of his friends and contemporaries, such as Adam Smith and Montesquieu. Actually, the latter discovered grounds for hailing the newly emerging forms of property, not in spite but *because* of their capacity for self-expatriation. This is a rather unexpected argument that is worth reviewing in some detail.

Always on the lookout for ways in which the overweening power of the sovereign could be checked, Montesquieu saw much promise in the invention and expanding use of the bill of exchange.

> ... through this means commerce could elude violence, and maintain itself everywhere; for the richest trader had only invisible wealth which could be sent everywhere without leaving any trace. . . .
>
> Since that time, the rulers have been compelled to govern with greater wisdom than they themselves might have intended; for, owing to these events, the great and sudden arbitrary actions of the sovereign (*les grands coups d'autorité*) have been proven to be ineffective and . . . only good government brings prosperity [to the prince].[21]

Thus, the fact that, with the bill of exchange, a large portion of wealth had become mobile and elusive and was capable of both hiding and expatriation is here celebrated as a restraint on the *grands coups d'autorité* of the prince and as a positive contribution to good government.[22]

The new inability of political authority to seize the citizens' wealth at will also struck others as making a fundamental difference to the way in which government was likely to be carried on; the argument was formulated in a general way (that is, not just with regard to the bill of exchange) by Sir James Steuart: As private wealth expands, it "avoids [the statesman's] grasp when he attempts to seize it. This makes his government more complex and more difficult to be carried on; *he must now avail himself of art and address* as well as of power and authority."[23]

Capital flight—the possible exit of capital (and of the capitalists)—was perceived as a salutary restraint on arbitrary government by both Montesquieu and Sir James Steuart, who put forward several far more sanguine speculations about the likely political effects of economic expansion. Although Adam Smith differed with them in these respects,[24] he went along to the extent of arguing that the mobility and elusiveness of "capital stock" make it impossible for taxation to be as "vexatious" as it might otherwise be:

> There are . . . two different circumstances which render the interest of money a much less proper subject of direct taxation than the rent of land.

First, the quantity and value of the land which any man possesses can never be a secret, and can always be ascertained with great exactness. But the whole amount of the capital stock which he possesses is almost always a secret, and can scarce ever be ascertained with tolerable exactness. . . . An inquisition into every man's private circumstances . . . would be a source of such continual and endless vexation as no people could support.

Secondly, land is a subject which cannot be removed, whereas stock easily may. The proprietor of land is necessarily a citizen of the particular country in which his estate lies. The proprietor of stock is properly a citizen of the world, and is not necessarily attached to any particular country. *He would be apt to abandon the country in which he was exposed to a vexatious inquisition, in order to be assessed to a burdensome tax, and would remove his stock to some other country where he could either carry on his business, or enjoy his fortune more at his ease.* By removing his stock he would put an end to all the industry which it had maintained in the country which he left. Stock cultivates land; stock employs labour. A tax which tended to drive away stock from any particular country, would so far tend to dry up every source of revenue, both to the sovereign and to the society. . . .

The nations, accordingly, who have attempted to tax the revenue arising from stock, instead of any severe inquisition of this kind, have been obliged to content themselves with some very loose . . . estimation.[25]

It would almost seem, then, as though everything were for the best: on the one hand, the dangerous exit in the form of secession had been more or less successfully exorcised by the power of the 17th- and 18th-century state; on the other, according to the converging testimony of Montesquieu, Sir James Steuart, and Adam Smith, that power was curbed by a new and beneficial variety of exit that surfaced as a result of economic expansion: the ability of capital and capitalists to "remove their stock" or, in modern terms, to "vote with their feet" for the best available "business climate."

It is useful to recall these early perceptions, if only to marvel at the distance by which they are separated from contemporary ones. Today the international mobility of capital is infinitely greater (within the capitalist world) than at the time of Montesquieu and Adam Smith. There are numerous varieties of such mobility: transnational corporations can move subsidiaries from one country, considered unsafe, to another; more threateningly, mobility can take the form of international banks refusing to "roll over" their loans to a country that is considered to be "out of line." Still, the principal weapon is wielded by the country's own citizens—particularly of course by the more opulent ones among them—as they engage in capital flight on a massive scale whenever they feel threatened by domestic developments.

Occasionally these various exits do occur, according to the 18th-century script, in response to the arbitrary and capricious actions of the sovereign. But a much less favorable interpretation may be in order: exit of capital often takes place in countries intending to introduce some taxation that would curb excessive privileges of the rich or some social reforms designed to distribute the fruits of economic growth more equitably. Under these conditions, capital flight and its threat are meant to parry, fight off, and perhaps veto such reforms; whatever the outcome, they are sure to make reform more costly and difficult. It looks, therefore, as though the availability of the kind of exit that was hailed by Montesquieu and Adam Smith were today a serious menace: it damages the capability of capitalism to reform itself.

Actually, this situation does not affect all countries equally. Capital flight is obviously much less of a weapon in the largest and most powerful countries where the owners of capital feel that there is no place else to go. Here it can be expected that voice will be activated by the impossibility of exit. Capitalists will make elaborate attempts to influence public opinion and public policy. An ideology in defense of capitalism will arise. At the same time, concessions are likely to be forthcoming where reforms of the system are obviously needed and are essential to the demonstration that the capitalist system can itself evolve and ameliorate the problems it creates. Purely on the basis of the differential availability of exit for capital and capitalists, one might therefore expect that the largest and most central countries of the capitalist system would be, at one and the same time, the ideological bulwarks of the system and its most active problem-solvers; the more peripheral states, on the other hand, might be in the grip of an anticapitalist ideology, and would at the same time exhibit unconscionable extremes of wealth and poverty. This "prediction," based on a most parsimonious exit-voice model, is surprisingly correct in a number of respects. The combination of an attitude of "standing up for capitalism" with attempts to remedy the system's worst evils is exemplified by both Victorian England and the United States of the 20th century; in many less developed countries, on the other hand, the absence of any strong ideological support for capitalism coexists rather oddly with extraordinary difficulties faced time and again by attempts at effective reform. Here is perhaps a key to the old puzzle why anticapitalist revolutions have consistently broken out at the periphery rather than at the center of the capitalist system.

Fortunately, the model does not explain everything. In particular, it does not deal satisfactorily with an important group of small countries. A few additional factors must therefore be introduced.

Exit as a Threat to the Small Modern State and Some Defensive Strategies

In the 18th century, as has just been noted, the potential exit of capital and of the capitalists was actively discussed in terms of its harmful or beneficial effects on the capital-losing state. This manner of looking at out-migration—so congenial to the exit-voice framework—almost disappeared in the 19th century, which witnessed human migration, mostly from Europe to America, on an unprecedented scale. Only recently have the economic and political effects of out-migration on sending (rather than receiving) states again attracted attention, primarily in conjunction with the so-called brain drain, a phenomenon that has more in common with capital flight than with mass migration.

The enormous out-migration from Europe during the 19th and early 20th centuries did not occasion much reflection about the feedback effect on the sending states and their political system because the outflow did not provoke any visible political problems or dangers. On the contrary—and this also explains why emigration, long prohibited during the mercantilist and absolutist eras, was so freely permitted—it *alleviated* a number of problems, economic as well as political. From the social and economic points of view, the outflow dampened the rapid increase in population as well as the concomitant rural-urban migration, and in spite of its massive proportions, emigration never reached the point where it was perceived to interfere with the recruitment of labor for expanding domestic industry. From the point of view of the political managers, out-migration had similar and related beneficial effects. People who chose emigration were obviously dissatisfied in some way with the country and society they were leaving. With exit available as an outlet for the disaffected, they were less likely to resort to voice: the ships carrying the migrants contained many actual or potential anarchists and socialists, reformers and revolutionaries. The inverse relationship between emigration and the socialist vote has been statistically demonstrated for Italy, in a study for the decade preceding World War I.[26] Moreover, new immigrants tend to be, at least initially, relatively unvociferous members of society; mass migration thus reduced social protest in the European-American state system as a whole and not only in the sending countries.

But the containment of social protest was not the only political effect of out-migration. Throughout the 19th century and up to World War I, the right of suffrage and other civil rights were extended in many of the very European states from which large contingents of people were departing. In other words, exit and a certain kind of voice increased hand-in-hand, even though, at the same time, exit lowered the volume of another more militant kind of voice. These two developments may be causally connected: because a number of disaffected people had departed, it became comparatively safe to open up the system to a larger number of those who stayed on. In this manner, exit-emigration may have made it possible for democratization and liberalization to proceed in several European countries prior to World War I without political stability being seriously imperiled.[27]

Besides being intrinsically interesting, these connections could contribute to the understanding of contemporary attempts at democratization. Might it be said, for example, that the large-scale emigration of Greek, Portuguese, and Spanish workers to France and Germany during the prosperous 60's and early 70's has made it easier for these countries to negotiate the difficult passage to a more democratic order than would have been the case otherwise?

In part, this topic has not received attention because the connection is rather remote and counterintuitive. That emigration of dissenters will strengthen an authoritarian regime in the short run is obvious; not content with allowing emigration, many such regimes have taken it upon themselves to deport or ban their political enemies—that is, they dealt with them in this particular manner during their more humane moments. But the likelihood that opening the gates and permitting out-migration may allow a regime to liberalize itself seems farfetched—except to those who have taken an advanced course in exit and voice.

Probably the main reason for the lack of interest in the political effects of emigration is that, as explained earlier, these effects had long been so positive. We do not investigate whatever seems to be going well no matter how poorly we understand the underlying process.

In recent years, however, emigration has not been wholly benign in its effects on the migrant-losing countries. This applies first of all to the brain drain: the size of the literature that has grown up around this topic strongly suggests that it is widely viewed as a problem. But even the 19th-century kind of emigration became a problem when it gave a repeat performance in the 20th, such as, for instance, the large-scale Irish emigration to England during the postwar period. The long decline of the Irish population, due to low birth rates and emigration, had come to a stop during the 25 years following Independence (1922), which coincided with the Depression and the Second World War. But after the war and particularly in the 50's, emigration, mostly from rural districts into urban Britain, surged once again and reached the highest levels in a century, in relation to the resident population (15 per mille per year in 1956–1961. This outflow aroused deep concern and became an important public and political issue that led to a decisive turn in economic policy. By the late 50's, the old description of emigration as a "safety valve" had been replaced by the image of a country suffering from hemophilia with "blood running out of its veins." The increasing concern that "Ireland was a dying country . . . led to calls for new economic policies, the adoption of various plans by the different political parties, the appearance of emigration as an issue in a parliamentary election for the first time, and finally the unopposed acceptance (in 1958) of a national economic plan designed to develop Ireland and prevent emigration."[28] The plan was successful in attracting foreign capital and spurring industrialization, but it is an open question to what extent the considerable drop in emigration in the 60's was due to the plan's success or to the diminished absorptive capacity of the British economy which itself became increasingly troubled during that period.

With the Irish immigrants encountering a similar environment and a familiar language in England, Irish emigration came to assume unusually large proportions and was eventually perceived as a threat to Ireland's national existence. A similar situation arose in East Germany, which in the 1950's experienced a flood of (illegal) emigration toward West Germany. Beset with concerns rather similar to those of the Irish, the government of the D.D.R. did not bother to look around for ways of making itself more attractive to its citizens: in 1961 it simply closed its frontiers more effectively than before by building the Berlin Wall.

The reactions of the two countries that felt threatened by mass emigration were thus very different, in parallel to similarly different reactions of various European countries to the sudden availability of cheap wheat from North America and Russia in the 1870's.[29] East Germany adopted a primarily defensive strategy—comparable to the imposition of higher tariffs on wheat by France and Germany in the late 19th century; Ireland, on the other hand, attempted to meet the challenge of mass exit by changing the underlying conditions that had resulted in the outflow— and this "creative response" is similar to Denmark's policies of agricultural transformation.

Both Ireland and East Germany, however, had something in common: a new perception of exit as a threat. They reacted with considerable determination, as though they were fully persuaded, in line with the thesis of the first section of this essay, that the existence of the state is incompatible with the virtually costless availability of exit and with resort of citizens to it as a routine response to dissatisfaction.

No doubt, these two countries and their experiences in the 50's were special pathological cases. But for that very reason they are of interest as they reveal potential trouble spots in the present state system. With closer communication, easy circulation of capital, and unprecedented international mobility of high-level manpower, states are today exposed to more exit pressures than ever before. Small states are particularly vulnerable to these pressures: a large country can often rather easily accommodate an inflow of capital or manpower from a small country, while as an outflow these resources may represent a critical loss for the small country.

Why is it that there have not been more Irelands and East Germanys in the last 30 years or so? In part, no doubt, because *entry* has by no means been totally unregulated.[30] But in view of the considerable freedom of movement that has prevailed for capital and people (especially for trained personnel), it is likely that many states, and particularly small ones, have hit on various devices and strategies through which they have parried excessive tendencies toward exit. I shall briefly investigate how such strategies might work.

In the case of Ireland, the remedy for exit consisted of improved economic policy and conditions; indeed, countries worrying about exit do well to satisfy the basic economic aspirations of their citizens, particularly of the more mobile among them. But fortunately, individual economic welfare is not the only criterion on the basis of which the difficult and often agonizing decision to exit from one's own country is made.

What is needed in order to avoid excessive emigration and crippling brain drain is for a society to provide its members with *some* "attractions" that will reinforce their normal reluctance to leave. Besides an adequate supply of goods available for individual consumption, such attractions can also consist of what is known to economists as "public goods"; that is, goods that any member of a society can enjoy (consume) without thereby depriving others of their enjoyment (consumption) of these goods. A country's power and prestige, for example, are a public good that may be enjoyed by all of its citizens, including the most lowly and powerless. Along these lines it has lately been pointed out that social justice may be a public good: individuals may find it enjoyable to live in a society where income distribution is comparatively egalitarian.[31] Other public goods that come to mind include a long record for not becoming involved in international conflict or for guaranteeing human rights and democratic liberties. The latter two would make a country attractive to its citizens, especially in a world where destructive warfare frequently erupts and where many governments habitually suppress criticism and mistreat their political opponents.

The availability in a country of any one of these public goods serves to hold exit at bay and to increase loyalty.[32] It is possible to visualize a state system in which, in spite of close contact and free movement of people and capital, exit would never assume threatening proportions because each country would supply its citizens with a different assortment of public goods, with emphasis on one area (or a cluster) as a special attraction for its own citizens. Different countries would then "specialize" in power, wealth, growth, equity, peacefulness, the observance of human rights, and so on. Such specialization would certainly result in a more stable situation than if performance of nations were rated only along one dimension, such as per capita GNP; in the latter case, it would become possible to establish an unambiguous rating among countries, and exits toward the best performers would mount dangerously. Achievements along the various dimensions just mentioned are not easily combined into a unique preference scale or welfare function; it is likely, however, that if a country's citizens were equipped with a modicum of loyalty to start with, they would value the particular area in which their country excels—whatever that may be—more highly than that of the others. An ethnocentric welfare function of this sort may therefore be a condition for a stable state system under modern circumstances of high potential mobility.

The foregoing "polyphonic" solution to the problem is perhaps too beautiful to be real. Among its difficulties is the obvious one that the pursuit of peace by one country may be incompatible with that of power by another. Then there is the fact that, frequently, "all good things go together": one or a very few countries may be doing best, or are perceived to do so, along several important dimensions such as power, wealth, education, and general opportunity. A related problem is that a hegemonic country may impose its own preferences and welfare function upon public opinion around the world. As a result, especially in a world with intensive communication networks, citizens of non-hegemonic countries would tend to give a higher rating to the achievements of the leading country than to those of their own.

In the face of such difficulties, do smaller countries have a second line of defense? Is there, in other words, some further highly valued public good that a smaller country can provide for its more mobile citizens so that they will still think twice before emigrating? A remark by the American sociologist Renée Fox, who has been studying Belgian society for many years, is illuminating in this regard. Explaining her long involvement with that country, she says that she originally found Belgium tempting because, among other things, she was led to believe that "a small country . . . would be simpler than a large country to comprehend in a sociological sense." But that premise turned out to be totally untrue; many years later she exclaims, "if I were now asked to formulate a sociological hypothesis about the relationship between the size of a country and the complexity of its social system, I would be tempted to suggest that there is an inverse relationship between the two; that is, the smaller the country, the more complex its social system!"[33]

In conjunction with the concern over excessive exit, this remark raises the question whether complexity could perhaps be part of a country's attraction for its citizens, as much as any positive achievement of the previously mentioned kind. For it is *understood* complexity insofar as the country's citizens are concerned; *they* know how to navigate expertly, not only in their country's language, but among its idiosyncratic ways, its conflicts and familiar frustrations.[34] When I first came to live in Colombia, explanations offered by Colombians of various to me puzzling situations would invariably start with the sentence "Es que ese es un país muy raro" ("you must realize that this is a very odd country"). Clearly, they took considerable pleasure in enlightening me about something *they* understood so well. *Understood complexity* may then be another public good a society can supply to its citizens, and that is perhaps a clue to Renée Fox's paradox about small countries being more complex than large ones. With the latter having so much going for them, the smaller countries defend themselves against excessive exit through a plentiful supply of understood complexity; and, with respect to this particular asset, there is full assurance that "you can't take it with you."

Notes

This paper was originally written for a symposium held in June 1977 at the University of Uppsala, Sweden, on the occasion of the 500-year jubilee of the foundation of the University. It is reproduced here with some changes. The author is grateful to Ulf Himmelstrand who organized the Uppsala symposium, and to Karen Blu and Clifford Geertz for discussion and critical comments.

1. Hirschman, *Exit, Voice, and Loyalty: Responses to Decline in Firms, Organizations, and States* (Cambridge: Harvard University Press 1970).

2. Primarily in connection with the issue of resignation of officials who are in disagreement with public policies see "Exit, Voice, and Loyalty: Further Reflections and a Survey of Recent Contributions," and "Exit and Voice: Some Further Distinctions," in *Essays in Trespassing: Economics to Politics and Beyond* (New York: Cambridge University Press, 1981). I have touched on emigration in relation to the state in two subsequent papers: "Exit, Voice, and Loyalty: Further Reflections and a Survey of Recent Contributions," *Social Science Information,* XIII (February 1974), 7–26, and "Political Economy: Some Uses of the Exit-Voice Approach—Discussion," *American Economic Review, Papers and Proceedings,* Vol. 66 (May 1976), 386–89. Secessionist movements are brought into the exit-voice framework by Stein Rokkan, "Dimensions of State Formation and Nation-Building: A Possible Paradigm for Research on Variations within Europe," in Charles Tilly, ed., *The Formation of National States in Western Europe* (Princeton: Princeton University Press 1975), 562–600, and

by Samuel E. Finer, "State-Building, State Boundaries and Border Control: An Essay on Certain Aspects of the First Phase of State-Building in Western Europe, Considered in the Light of the Rokkan-Hirschman Model," *Social Science Information,* XIII (August–October 1974), 79–126.

3. Rousseau, *Oeuvres complètes* (Paris: NRF, Pléiade 1966), III, 203; emphasis added.

4. See Rousseau, *Essai sur l'origine des langues . . .* , edition, introduction, and notes by Charles Porset (Bordeaux: Ducros 1970), chap. II, 43; emphasis added.

5. *Ibid.,* 11 (introduction by Porset).

6. Lévi-Strauss, "The Social and Psychological Aspects of Chieftainship in a Primitive Tribe: The Nambikuara of Northwestern Mato Grosso" (1944), reprinted in Ronald Cohen and John Middleton, eds., *Comparative Political Systems: Studies in the Politics of Pre-Industrial Societies* (Garden City, N.Y.: Natural History Press 1067), 53–54.

7. Bamberger, "*Exit* and *Voice* in Central Brazil: On the Politics of Flight in Kayapó Society," in David Maybury-Lewis, ed., *Dialectical Societies* (Cambridge: Harvard University Press, 1979).

8. Evans-Pritchard, "The Nuer of the Southern Sudan," in M. Fortes and E. E. Evans-Pritchard, eds., *African Political Systems* (London: Oxford University Press 1940), 279.

9. John Middleton and David Tait, eds., *Tribes Without Rulers: Studies in African Segmentary Systems* (London: Routledge & Kegan Paul 1958), 3. It should be noted that the book does not deal with these societies; it concentrates on those having "segmentary lineage systems," where exit resembles secession rather than emigration.

10. Marshall, "!Kung Bushman Bands" (1960), reprinted in Cohen and Middleton (fn. 6), 17, 34–35.

11. Colin M. Turnbull, *Wayward Servants: The Two Worlds of the African Pygmies* (London: Eyre & Spottiswoode 1965), 106. Turnbull attempts to explain this constant "flux and instability" of the Mbuti bands by their antagonistic relationship with the settled villagers who, as a result of this confusion, are unable to assert the lineal and territorial rights they claim over the Mbuti.

12. H. J. Nieboer, *Slavery as an Industrial System* (The Hague: Nijhoff 1900); Evsey Domar, "The Causes of Slavery or Serfdom: A Hypothesis," *Journal of Economic History,* XXX (March 1970), 18–32.

13. Nieboer and Frederick Jackson Turner were contemporaries, but were probably unaware that one was speaking of "open resources" as a factor

conducive to slavery and the other of the "open frontier" as conditioning American-style democracy.

14. This is true even for so elaborate a function as that of the "leopard-skin chief" of the Nuer in mediating disputes. See Evans-Pritchard (fn. 8), 291–95.

15. Milton Friedman, *Capitalism and Freedom* (Chicago: Chicago University Press 1962), chap. 6; Charles M. Tiebout, "A Pure Theory of Local Expenditures," *Journal of Political Economy*, Vol. 64 (October 1956), 416–24.

16. See Finer (fn. 2), 115

17. Montesquieu, *Esprit des lois*, XX, chap. 23.

18. See Hirschman, *The Passions and the Interests: Political Arguments for Capitalism before Its Triumph* (Princeton: Princeton University Press 1977), 95, and Part Two, passim.

19. See "The Prerogative of Popular Government," in James Harrington, *Oceana and Other Works*, ed. John Toland (3d ed.; London: A. Millar 1747), 243.

20. From essay, "Of Public Credit" in Hume, *Writings on Economics*, ed. E. Rotwein (Madison: University of Wisconsin Press 1970), 98–99. For a number of telling 18th-century quotes denouncing the new world of stockjobbers and finance, see Isaac Kramnick, *Bolingbroke and His Circle: The Politics of Nostalgia in the Age of Walpole* (Cambridge: Harvard University Press 1968), 47–48, 71–76, 220, 246.

21. Montesquieu (fn. 17), XXI, chap. 20.

22. Later in the century, Turgot based very similar hopes on the emigration of persons. Commenting on Richard Price's *Observations on the Importance of the American Revolution* he wrote: "The asylum which [the American people] opens to the oppressed of all nations must console the earth. The ease with which it will now be possible to take advantage of this situation, and thus to escape from the consequences of a bad government, will oblige the European Governments to be just and enlightened." (Letter to Price of March 22, 1778, in *Oeuvres*, Paris: Delance 1810, IX, 389.) Turgot here argues about the state losing citizens as though it were a firm impelled by the exit of customers to improve its performance. The actual political effects of emigration on the sending country and their considerable diversity are explored in the next section.

23. Steuart, *Inquiry into the Principles of Political Oeconomy* (1767), I, ed. A. S. Skinner (Chicago: University of Chicago Press 1966), 181; emphasis added.

24. Hirschman (fn. 18), 100–113.

25. Smith, *The Wealth of Nations,* Modern Library ed., 800; see also pp. 345 and 858 for related passages; emphasis added.

26. John S. MacDonald, "Agricultural Organization, Migration and Labour Militancy in Rural Italy," *Economic Historic Review,* 2d series, XVI (1963–1964), 61–75.

27. I have looked in vain for any speculation along such lines in the notable monographic studies on European migrations to the United States published as *Dislocation and Emigration: The Social Background of American Immigration* in D. Fleming and B. Bailyn, eds., *Perspectives in American History*, VII (Harvard University 1974). Professor Bailyn tells me that in his current work on 17th- and 18th-century emigration to North America considerable attention is being given to the social and political context of emigration in the sending country.

28. Nicholas R. Burnett, "Exit, Voice and Ireland, 1936–58," unpub. (1977), 15; also Burnett's doctoral dissertation, "Emigration and Modern Ireland" (School of Advanced International Studies, Johns Hopkins University 1976).

29. See Charles P. Kindleberger, "Group Behavior and International Trade," *Journal of Political Economy*, Vol. 59 (February 1951), 30–46; and Peter A. Gourevitch, "International Trade, Domestic Coalitions, and Liberty: The Crisis of 1873–96," *Journal of Interdisciplinary History*, VIII (Autumn 1977), 281–313.

30. See Aristide R. Zolberg, "International Migration Policies in a Changing World System," to be published in William H. McNeill and Ruth S. Adams, eds., *Human Migration* (Bloomington: Indiana University Press 1978).

31. Lester C. Thurow, "The Income Distribution as a Pure Public Good," *Quarterly Journal of Economics,* Vol. 85 (May 1971), 327–36; David Morawetz and others, "Income Distribution and Self-Rated Happiness: Some Empirical Evidence," *Economic Journal,* Vol. 87 (September 1977), 511–22.

32. See Hirschman (fn. 1), chap. 7, particularly p. 78.

33. Fox, "An American Sociologist in the Land of Belgian Medical Research," in Phillip E. Hammond, ed., *Sociologists at Work* (New York: Basic Books 1964), 349.

34. On the difference between the "native's" views of his society and the outside observer's, see Clifford Geertz, "On the Nature of Anthropological Understanding," *American Scientist*, Vol. 63 (January–February 1975), 47–53.

MORALITY AND THE
SOCIAL SCIENCES
A Durable Tension

Berkeley was the site of a major conference in the summer of 1979. Heavyweights like Jürgen Habermas, Richard Rorty, Michel de Certeau, and Charles Taylor were on hand to debate the role of morality in the social sciences. Hirschman was one of the few economists present—and he witnessed a rant-fest against the strong norms of American social science that tried to remove normative blood from human inquiry. Hirschman, however, was skeptical of the monotone. He was certainly no fan of scientistic social science, but neither did he think intellectuals should swing to the other extreme. When he was then asked to deliver the Frank E. Seidman Lecture the following year in Memphis, he brought his thoughts together. He was critical of efforts to make it all about morality *or* all about science and objectivity, of dividing the heart and the mind. This is a theme that ran through his pathbreaking book, *The Passions and the Interests*. If social science was born in the effort to break free of traditional moral reasoning, this tension could never be excised, and trying to do so deprived social scientists of opportunities to create alternative orders. While Hirschman was writing the essay, he was deeply concerned with the role that some economists were playing in authoritarian regimes in Latin America. What he sought was to identify the tension between morality and the social sciences and recognize its inescapable centrality—and in that way have social scientists think more openly about their commitments.

—Jeremy Adelman

WHAT IS THE ROLE of moral considerations and concerns in economics? More generally, what can be said about the "problem of morality in the social sciences"? In commenting on these questions— the second was the subject of a conference I attended not long ago—I shall first give some reasons why this sort of topic does not come easily to the social scientist; only later shall I show why there is today an increased concern with moral values, *even* in economics—that rock of positivist solidity. In conclusion, I shall suggest some ways of reconciling the traditional posture of the economist as a "detached scientist" with his or her role as a morally concerned person.

To deal usefully with the relationship between morality and the social sciences one must first realize that modern social science arose to a considerable extent in the process of *emancipating* itself from traditional moral teachings. Right at the onset of the modern age, Machiavelli proclaimed that he would deal with political institutions as they really exist and not with "imaginary republics and monarchies" governed in accordance with the religious precepts and moralistic pieties that have been handed down from one generation to the next by well-meaning persons. Modern political science owes a great deal to Machiavelli's shocking claim that ordinary notions of moral behavior for individuals may not be suitable as rules of conduct for states. More generally, it appeared, as a result of the wealth of insights discovered by Machiavelli, that the traditional concentration on the "ought," on the manner in which princes and statesmen ought to behave, interferes with the fuller understanding of the "is" that can be achieved when attention is closely and coldly riveted on the ways in which statecraft is in fact carried on. The need to separate political science from morality was later openly proclaimed by Montesquieu, another principal founding father of social science, when he wrote:

> It is useless to attack politics directly by showing how much its practices are in conflict with morality, reason, and justice. This sort of discourse makes everybody nod in agreement, but changes nobody.[1]

A similar move from the "ought" to the "is" was soon to be made in economics. As the actual workings of trade and markets were examined in some detail from the seventeenth century on, a number of discoveries as shocking and instructive as those of Machiavelli were made by writers on economic topics. I am not referring just to Mandeville's famous paradox about private vices leading, via the stimulation of the luxury trades, to public benefits. Quite a bit earlier, in the middle of the seventeenth century, a number of deeply religious French thinkers, the most prominent of whom was Pascal, realized that an ordered society could exist and endure without being based on love or "charity." Another principle, so they found, could do the job of making the social world go round: the principle of self-interest. This ability of doing without love came to them as an uneasy surprise and as a worrisome puzzle: a society that is not held together by love is clearly sinful—how could it then be not only workable, but so intricately and admirably constructed that Divine Providence seems to have had a hand in it?

A century later, such worries had given way to outright celebration: Adam Smith evinced no religious qualms when he bestowed praise on the Invisible Hand for enlisting self-interested behavior on behalf of social order and economic progress. Yet, the idea of morality supplying an alternative way or ordering economy and society still lurks somewhere in the background as Smith mocks it in one of the most striking formulations of his doctrine: "It is not from the *benevolence* of the butcher, the brewer, or the baker, that we expect our dinner," so he writes, "but from their regard to their own *interest*."[2] Smith fairly bubbles over here with excitement about the possibility of discarding moral discourse and exhortation, thanks to the discovery of a social mechanism that, if properly unshackled, is far less demanding of human nature and therefore infinitely more reliable. And, once again, the refusal to be satisfied with the traditional "ought" created a *space* within which scientific knowledge could unfold.

Marx remained strictly in the Machiavelli-Montesquieu-Smith tradition when, in his attempt to interpret and, above all, to change the prevailing social and political order, he consistently refused to appeal to moral argument. He scoffed at the "utopian socialists" precisely for doing so in their critique of capitalist society and for resorting to moral exhortation in putting forth their proposed remedies. In spite of the ever-present moralistic undertone of his work, Marx's proudest claim was to be the father of "*scientific* socialism." To be truly scientific, he obviously felt that he had to shun moral argument. True science does not preach, it proves and predicts: so he proves the existence of exploitation through the labor theory of value and predicts the eventual demise of capitalism through the law of the falling rate of profit. In effect Marx mixed, uncannily, these "cold" scientific propositions with "hot" moral outrage and it was perhaps this odd amalgam, with all of its inner tensions unresolved, that was (and is) responsible for the extraordinary appeal of his work in an age both addicted to science and starved of moral values.

The tension between the "warm" heart and the "cold" or, at best, "cool" head is a well-known theme in Western culture, especially since the Romantic Age. But I am speaking here not only of tension, but of an existential incompatibility between morality and moralizing, on the one hand, and analytical-scientific activity, on the other. This incompatibility is simply a fact of experience. Our analytical performance becomes automatically suspect if it is openly pressed into the service of moral conviction; and conversely, moral conviction is not dependent on analytical argument and can actually be weakened by it, just as religious belief has on balance been undermined rather than bolstered by the proofs of God and their intellectual prowess. The matter has been best expressed by the great German poet Hölderlin in a wonderfully pithy, if rather plaintive, epigram. Entitled "*Guter Rat*" (Good Advice), it dates from about 1800 and, in my free translation, reads:

If you have brains and a heart, show only one or the other,
You will not get credit for either should you show both at once.[3]

The mutual exclusiveness of moralizing and analytical understanding may be nothing but a happenstance, reflecting the particular historical conditions under which scientific progress in various domains was achieved in the West. These conditions have of course left strong marks on cultural attitudes, marks so well identified by Hölderlin.

But the hostility to morality is more than a birthmark of modern science. With regard to the social sciences in particular, there are some more specific reasons to think that antimoralist petulance will frequently recur, because of the very nature of the social scientific enterprise and discourse. Let me briefly explain.

In all sciences fundamental discovery often takes the form of paradox. This is true for some of the principal theorems of physics, such as the Copernican proposition about the earth moving around the sun rather than vice versa. But it can be argued that social science is peculiarly subject to the compulsion to produce paradox.

The reason is that we all know so much about society already without ever having taken a single social science course. We live in society; we often contribute to social, political, and economic processes as actors; and we think—often mistakenly, of course—that we know roughly what goes on not only in our own minds, but also in those of others. As a result, we have considerable intuitive, commonsense understanding of social science "problems" such as crime in the streets, corruption in high places, and even inflation, and everyone stands forever ready to come forward with his or her own "solution" or nostrum. Consequently, for social science to *enhance* our considerable, untutored knowledge of the social world it must come up with something that has not been apparent or transparent before or, better still, with something that shows how badly commonsense understanding has led us astray.[4] Important social science discoveries are therefore typically counterintuitive, shocking, and concerned with *unintended* and unexpected consequences of human action.

With the commonsense understanding of social science problems having usually a strong moral component (again much more so than in the natural sciences), the immoralist vocation of the social sciences can in good measure be attributed to this compulsion to produce shock and paradox. Just as one of social science's favorite pastimes is to affirm the hidden rationality of the seemingly irrational or the coherence of the seemingly incoherent, so does it often defend as moral, or useful, or at least innocent, social behavior that is widely considered to be reprehensible. In economics, examples of this sort of quest for the morally shocking come easily to mind. Following the early lead of Mandeville and his rehabilitation of luxury, many an economist has carved out a reputation by extolling the economic efficiency functions of such illegal or unsavory activities as smuggling, or black marketeering, or even corruption in government.

Lately this taste for the morally shocking has been particularly evident in the "imperialist" expeditions of economists into areas of social life outside the traditional domain of economics. Activities such as crime, marriage, procreation, bureaucracy, voting, and participation in public affairs in general have all been subjected to a so-called "economic approach" with the predictable result that, like the consumer or producer of the economics textbook, the actors involved, be they criminals, lovers, parents, bureaucrats, or voters, were all found to be busily "maximizing under constraints." Such people had of course long been thought to be moved and buffeted by complex passions, both noble and ignoble, such as revolt against society, love, craving for immortality, and devotion to the public interest or betrayal thereof, among many others. In comparison with this traditional image of man's noneconomic pursuits, their analysis at the hands of the imperialist economist, with the emphasis on grubby cost/benefit calculus, was bound to produce moral shock; and, once again, the analysis drew strength from having this shock value.

In a book review, my colleague Clifford Geertz recently wrote a marvelous first paragraph that is eminently applicable to the writings to which I have just been referring:

> This is a book about the "primary male-female differences in sexuality among humans," in which the following things are not discussed: guilt, wonder, loss, self-regard, death, metaphor, justice, purity, intentionality, cowardice, hope, judgment, ideology, humor, obligation, despair, trust, malice, ritual, madness, forgiveness, sublimation, pity, ecstasy, obsession, discourse, and sentimentality. It could be only one thing, and it is. Sociobiology.[5]

To most of us this sounds like a scathing indictment, but partisans of the book under review may well feel that its author deserves praise precisely for having cut through all those "surface phenomena" listed by Geertz to the *fundamental* mechanism which lays bare the very essence of whatever the book is about. In the same way, practitioners of the "economic approach" to human behavior probably take pride in their "parsimonious" theory, and whatever success they achieve is in fact largely grounded in the reductionist outrageousness of their enterprise.

One cannot help feeling, nevertheless, that this particular way of achieving notoriety and fame for the economist is running into decreasing returns. For one, the paradigm about self-interest leading to a workable and perhaps even optimal social order without any admixture of "benevolence" has now been around so long that it has become intellectually challenging to rediscover the need for morality. To affirm this need has today almost the same surprise value and air of paradox which the Smithian farewell to benevolence had in its own time. Second, and more important, it has become increasingly clear that, in a number of important areas, the economy is in fact liable to perform poorly without a minimum of "benevolence."

The resurgence and rehabilitation of benevolence got started in micro-economics. One of the conditions for the proper functioning of competitive markets is "perfect" information about the goods and services that are being bought and sold. We all know, of course, that this condition is frequently far from being met, but imperfect information might not be too damaging to the market system if it were limited and widely shared among all citizens, be they sellers or buyers. What happens, however, if, as is often the case, the knowledge of the buyers about a certain commodity is far inferior to that of the suppliers and sellers? In that case the stage is set for exploitation of the buyers by the sellers unless the latter are somehow restrained from taking advantage of their superiority. Government could be and has been entrusted with that task, with varying success: we all know by now that government will not necessarily succeed where the market fails. An ingenious solution would be for the sellers to subject themselves voluntarily to a discipline that keeps them from exploiting their superior knowledge. For example, surgeons could take on the obligation, as a condition for the exercise of their profession, never to prescribe an operation when none is needed. This is the case, pointed out some time ago by Kenneth Arrow, where adherence to a code of professional ethics can remedy one specific form of market failure. So we are back to benevolence: in a somewhat institutionalized form, it is here invoked as an input essential for the functioning of a market economy in which sellers have more information than buyers.

The fact that there is a need for ethical behavior in certain situations in which the market system and self-interest, left to their own devices, will result in undesirable outcomes does not mean, of course, that such behavior will automatically materialize. Perhaps it tends to do so when the need is particularly imperious, as it is in the case of surgeons and surgery. In any event, we worry quite a bit more about "being had" when we buy a secondhand car than when we consult a doctor about the need for an operation. Economists have recently identified a number of areas, from the market for "lemons" to day-care services and psychotherapeutic advice, where the performance of the market could be much improved by an infusion of "benevolence," sometimes in the modest form of cooperation and exchange of information between suppliers and customers.

The need for ethical norms and behavior to supplement and, on occasion, to supplant self-interest appears with great clarity and urgency in the just-noted situations of "market failure." But this need is actually always there to some degree: if only because of the time element contained in most transactions, economic efficiency and enterprise are premised on the existence of trust between contracting parties, and this trust must be autonomous, that is, it must not be tied narrowly to self-interest. To quote a recent, sweeping statement of this point: "Elemental personal values of honesty, truthfulness, trust, restraint and obligation are all necessary inputs to an efficient (as well as pleasant) contractual society. . . ."[6] If all these needed personal values are added up, the amounts of benevolence and morality required for the functioning of the market turn out to be quite impressive!

So much for microeconomics. But the really giant, if unacknowledged, strides in the rehabilitation of morality as an essential "input" into a functioning economy have taken place in the macro area, as a result of the contemporary experience with, and concern over, inflation. In spite of all the noise caused by certain technical debates (demand-pull vs. cost-push, monetarist vs. Keynesian or post-Keynesian views), there is in fact wide agreement—because it is so self-evident—that the understanding *and* control of contemporary inflation require probing deeply into the social and political underlay of the economy. For example, suppose it is correct that increasing public expenditures must be blamed for the inflation, then the question surely is: Why is the modern state subject to ever increasing pressures for dispensing an ever more comprehensive set of public services to newly assertive interest groups? Similarly, if it is true that wage and price restraint could do much to hold back inflation, then why is it that such restraint is so difficult to come by? A British sociologist has written, in answer to such questions, that "conflict between social groups and strata has become more intense and also to some extent more equally matched, with these two tendencies interacting in a mutually reinforcing way."[7] Here is a well articulated expression of the widespread view that inflation reflects increasing combativeness or, in colorful British parlance, "bloody-mindedness" on the part of various social groups that have heretofore been viewed in our textbooks as "cooperating" in the generation and distribution of the social product. The result of this sort of sociological analysis of inflation is then to plead for a "new social contract" which would hopefully result in inhibiting and reducing "bloody-mindedness" all around.[8]

The observation that is in order at this point will already have occurred to the reader: this nasty attribute, "bloody-mindedness," which it is so important to restrain, is nothing but the obverse of benevolence which it is therefore essential to foster. Hence, getting on top of our major current macroeconomic problem turns out to require the generation and diffusion of benevolence among various social groups! So it definitely would seem time for economists to renounce the amoral stance affected, at least in the *Wealth of Nations*, by the illustrious founder of our science: for the solution of both micro- and macroeconomic problems, the pursuit of pure self-interest on the part of each individual member of society is clearly inadequate.

So far so good. But have we gotten very far? We have learned that we should not scoff at benevolence and at moral values in general. We can also appreciate that Malthus had a point when, in endorsing the Smithian rule according to which everyone should be left free to pursue his self-interest, he systematically added the reservation "while he adheres to the rules of justice."[9]

But this sort of addition of a qualifying, moralizing afterthought is not really much of a contribution. Granted the important place of moral thought and values for economics, how should we map out the new terrain and become aware of all the insights we have missed because of our previous exclusive concentration on self-interest? One way to proceed is to attempt a head-on attack. The opposite of self-interest is interest in others, action on behalf of others. So the obvious way of making amends for their previous disregard of moral values and "generous impulses" is for economists to study altruism. A number of works on this topic have indeed appeared in recent years.[10] They are instructive and useful but suffer perhaps from the attempt to make up for lost time in too much of a hurry.

In my opinion, the damage wrought by the "economic approach," based on the traditional self-interest model, is not just the neglect of altruistic behavior. It extends to wide areas of traditional analysis and is due to far too simplistic a model of human behavior *in general*. What is needed is for economists to incorporate into their analysis, whenever that is pertinent, such basic traits and emotions as the desire for power and for sacrifice, the fear of boredom, pleasure in both commitment and unpredictability, the search for meaning and community, and so on. Clearly this is a task that cannot be accomplished once and for all by a research project on the injection of moral values into economics. Any attempt of this kind is likely to yield disappointing results and would thus invite an extension to economics of the French saying, "With beautiful sentiments one makes bad literature."

An effective integration of moral argument into economic analysis can be expected to proceed rather painstakingly, on a case-to-case basis, because the relevant moral consideration or neglected aspect of human nature will vary considerably from topic to topic. The task requires a conjunction of talents that is difficult to come by: first, familiarity with the technical apparatus of economics; and second, openness to the heretofore neglected moral dimensions whose introduction modifies traditional results.

A fine example of such a conjunction—and also of its difficulty—is Robert Solow's recent presidential address to the American Economic Association on the topic of labor markets and unemployment. In explaining why the labor market is not smoothly self-clearing, he stressed the fact that workers pay a great deal of attention to "principles of appropriate behavior whose source is not entirely individualistic," such as the reluctance of those who are out of work to undercut those who hold jobs. "Wouldn't you be surprised," so he asked, "if you learned that someone of roughly your status in the profession, but teaching in a less desirable department, had written to your department chairman offering to teach your courses for less money?"[11] Here is an important recognition of how certain moral-social norms profoundly affect the working of a most important market: they make it less perfect from the point of view of self-clearing, but certainly *more* perfect from almost any other conceivable point of view!

I now turn to the difficulty of coming up with such an observation. Note that its vehicle was Solow's presidential address. Is there perhaps a tendency in our profession to wait until one has reached the pinnacle before coming forward with such, after all, only mildly moralistic and heretical views? Now I am quite sure (at least in the case of Solow) that it is not pusillanimity and the desire for advancement that are responsible for such *late* blooming of moral emphasis; rather, the explanation lies in that mutual exclusiveness of heart and head, of moralizing and analytical understanding, on which I dwelt at the beginning of this essay. When one has been groomed as a "scientist" it just takes a great deal of wrestling with oneself before one will admit that moral considerations of human solidarity can effectively interfere with those hieratic, impersonal forces of supply and demand.

There is a notable instance here of what Veblen called a "trained incapacity." It is so strong, in fact, that we will often not avow to ourselves the moral source of our scientific thought processes and discoveries. As a result, quite a few of us are *unconscious* moralists in our professional work. I have a personal story to illustrate this point, and here is how I told it in the special preface I wrote for reasons that will be apparent—for the German edition—of *Exit, Voice, and Loyalty*:

> As is related in my book, its intellectual origin lies in an observation I made some years ago in Nigeria. But quite a while after the book had been published in the United States, it dawned on me that my absorption with its theme may have deeper roots. A large part of the book centers on the concern that exit of the potentially most powerful carriers of voice prevents the more forceful stand against decline that might otherwise be possible. This situation is not altogether unrelated to the fate of the Jews who were still in Germany after 1939. Most of the young and vigorous ones, like myself, got out in the early years after Hitler took over, leaving a gravely weakened community behind. Of course, the possibilities of any effective voice were zero in the circumstances of those years no matter who left and who stayed. Nevertheless, the real fountainhead of the book may well lie in some carefully repressed guilt feelings that, even though absurd from the point of view of any rational calculus, are simply there.[12]

At this point, a further afterthought suggests itself: it was probably fortunate that I was *not* aware of those deeper moral stirrings when I wrote the book; otherwise the presentation of my argument might have been less general, less balanced as between the respective merits of exit and voice, and less scientifically persuasive. My excursion into autobiography thus points to an odd conclusion: One, perhaps peculiarly effective way for social scientists to bring moral concerns into their work is to do so unconsciously! This bit of advice is actually not quite as unhelpful as it sounds. For the reasons given, it seems to me impractical and possibly even counterproductive to issue guidelines to social scientists on how to incorporate morality into their scientific pursuits and how to be on guard against immoral "side effects" of their work. Morality is not something like pollution abatement that can be secured by slightly modifying the design of a policy proposal. Rather, it belongs into the center of our work; and it can get there only if the social scientists are morally alive and make themselves vulnerable to moral concerns—then they will produce morally significant works, consciously or otherwise.

I have a further, more ambitious, and probably utopian thought. Once one has gone through the historical account and associated reasoning of this essay, once we have become fully aware of our intellectual tradition with its deep split between head and heart and its not always beneficial consequences, the first step toward overcoming that tradition and toward healing that split has already been taken. Down the road, it is then possible to visualize a kind of social science that would be very different from the one most of us have been practicing: a moral-social science where moral considerations are not repressed or kept apart, but are systematically commingled with analytic argument, without guilt feelings over any lack of integration; where the transition from preaching to proving and back again is performed frequently and with ease; and where moral considerations need no longer be smuggled in surreptitiously, nor expressed unconsciously, but are displayed openly and disarmingly. Such would be, in part, my dream for a "social science for our grandchildren."

Notes

Originally presented as a lecture on September 25, 1980 when the author received the Frank E. Seidman Distinguished Award in Political Economy in Memphis, Tennessee, and published as an occasional "Acceptance Paper" by the P. K. Seidman Foundation at Memphis in October 1980.

1. *Oeuvres complètes,* ed. Roger Caillois (Paris: Pléiade, NRF, 1949), Vol. 1, p. 112.

2. *Wealth of Nations,* Modern Library Edition (New York, 1937), p. 14.

3. "Hast Du Verstand und ein Herz, so zeige nur eines von beiden, Beides verdammen sie Dir, zeigest Du beides zugleich."

Hölderlin's distinction between *Verstand* (reason) and *Herz* (heart) reflects the rehabilitation of the passions in the eighteenth century that led to the "heart" standing for the many generous moral feelings, impulses, and benefi- cent passions man was now credited with while reason was becoming down- graded; at an earlier time, the contrast, not between the heart and the head, but between the passions and reason, or the passions and the interests, carried a very different value connotation. I have dealt with these matters in *The Passions and the Interests,* pp. 27–8, 43–4, and 63–6.

4. See Gilles Gaston Granger, "L'explication dans les sciences sociales," *Social Science Information* 10 (1971), p. 38.

5. Review of Donald Symons, *The Evolution of Human Sexuality* (New York: Oxford University Press, 1979) in *The New York Review of Books,* January 24, 1980, p. 3.

6. Fred Hirsch, "The Ideological Underlay of Inflation," in Fred Hirsch and John H. Goldthorpe, eds.. *The Political Economy of Inflation* (Cambridge, Mass.: Harvard University Press, 1978), p. 274.

7. John H. Goldthorpe, "The Current Inflation: Toward a Sociological Ac- count," in *The Political Economy of Inflation,* p. 196.

8. An alternative solution is to fight fire with fire and to apply what might be called "countervailing bloody-mindedness." The recently much-discussed idea of making it expensive for management to increase wages through a special tax levied on payroll increases beyond a certain norm has the avowed purpose of "stiffening the back" of management as it faces militant labor. The monetarist injunctions can also be regarded as a proposal to counter the bloody-mindedness of various social groups by that of the Central Bank (something that in a number of countries turns out to require strong-arm regimes as well as *real* bloodletting). See also "The Social and Political Matrix of Inflation: Elaborations on the Latin American Experience," *Essays in Tres- passing: Economics to Politics and Beyond* (New York: Cambridge University Press, 1979), for a more extended examination of the sociological aspects of inflation.

9. *Principles of Political Economy* (London: John Murray, 1820), pp. 3 and 518. This qualifying clause was brought to my attention by Alexander Field; see his paper "Malthus, Method, and Macroeconomics," unpublished, May 1980. As Field points out, in the numerous expositions of the principle with which *The Wealth of Nations* is studded, Adam Smith added the similar phrase, "as long as he does not violate the laws of justice," only once. See Modern Library edition, p. 651.

10. For example, Kenneth E. Boulding, *The Economy of Love and Fear: A Preface to Grant Economics* (Belmont, Cal.: Wadsworth, 1973); Edmund S. Phelps, ed., *Altruism, Morality and Economic Theory* (New York: Russell Sage Foundation, 1975); David Collard, *Altruism and Economy: A Study in Non-Selfish Economics* (Oxford: Robertson, 1978).

11. Robert M. Solow, "On Theories of Unemployment," *American Economic Review,* 70 (March 1980), pp. 3, 4.

12. Original English text of preface to German edition in Albert O. Hirschman, *Abwanderung und Widerspruch* (Tübingen: J.C.B. Mohr, 1974), p. vii.

SOCIAL CONFLICTS AS PILLARS OF DEMOCRATIC MARKET SOCIETY

The year 1989 was annus mirabilis for Hirschman. The Berlin Wall came down, thus reuniting the city in which he was born, and Hirschman returned with greater and greater frequency. The same year also saw elections in Chile, after many years of dictatorship; Hirschman traveled to Santiago to celebrate the inauguration of Patricio Aywlin. Meanwhile, in the United States a chorus of "communitarians" was arguing that democracy was thinning out because societies were losing their community spirit. Having just toppled right-wing nationalists in South America and Communist collectivism in East Germany, new democracies were beginning to grapple with the challenges of pluralism. Hirschman urged intellectuals not to fall prey to calls for a renewed or new sense of "community spirit." Instead, he extolled the virtues of bargaining, tension, and conflict as means to experiment and compromise—without leading to false consensus or conformity. Whereas much social theory saw conflict and instability as debilitating, Hirschman spotlighted its necessary strengths; it offered pathways to new ways of organizing societies and living democratically. Politics, for Hirschman, was an art; like Machiavelli he believed that one's loyalties came from a political life and did not precede it. Two countries contending with unsavory pasts, Germany and Chile, might tutor other democracies with their open embrace of social contention as a basic value.

—*Jeremy Adelman*

THE QUESTION "how much community spirit (*Gemeinsinn*) Does Liberal Society Require?" made me go back to a well-known tale of Tolstoy with a similar sounding title, namely, "How Much Land Does a Man Require?" This is the story, you may remember, of a peasant called Pakhom who becomes obsessed by the passion for acquiring more and more land. Giving in to temptation he subjects himself at one point to an excessive exertion that is supposed to bring him riches but actually leads to physical exhaustion and death. At this stage, of course, Pakhom needs only the small area of land where his body is being put to rest—"three Russian ells." Even though these words, coming at the very end of the story, look like the answer Tolstoy gives to the question he asks in the title, he obviously did not mean to say that this is all the land that peasants truly require. His real point is that this is the amount of land we may well end up with if we fall prey to the accumulating passion.

From *Gemeinschaftsschwärmerei* to *Verfassungspatriotismus*

Here there may be a lesson for the question before us: How much community spirit does a society require? As was the case for Pakhom and his passion for land, so there may be danger for a group of people to become fascinated with the idea of, or with the passion or *Schwärmerei* (enthusiasm) for, community spirit. Recent German history provides the most emphatic warning in this regard. During the Weimar period there was much complaint in Germany about the lack of certain characteristics a community was then supposed to exhibit: a sense of direction and mission, a feeling of togetherness and warmth—a community spirit, in short. The rise of the Nazi movement owed much to its promise to provide all of these alleged "needs" in abundance by creating a newly compact *Volksgemeinschaft*. The catastrophe that followed gave a long-lasting bad name to the very terms of community and community spirit, in the Federal Republic at any rate. From 1945 on, all the patriotism that Germans were supposed to have was to be based on the consciousness—with perhaps, little by little, a bit of pride—that their country was now firmly built on a liberal constitution guaranteeing basic human and civil rights—hence the term *Verfassungspatriotismus*, or patriotism grounded on the Constitution. Originally suggested by Dolf Sternberger and later endorsed by Jürgen Habermas, this concept became popular: it conveyed

346

a new and minimalist kind of patriotism, far removed from earlier varieties. It was as though Pakhom, the peasant of Tolstoy's tale, had come back to life, had learned from his misadventures, and had decided to settle from now on for a radically down-scaled plot of land.

The "Communitarian Critique of Liberalism" in the United States and Its Reception in Germany

The events of 1989–90 then led to some new reflections as reunification gave rise to serious economic, cultural, and moral problems. The existence of these problems and particularly their unexpected persistence were often attributed to some deficiency in common spirit or purpose. Arguing along such lines was facilitated at this point by the close contact between German and American intellectual circles. The need for greater community spirit could be argued by borrowing from the debate that had developed in the United States in the 1970s and 1980s, largely in reaction to John Rawls's *Theory of Justice* (1970), and became known as the "communitarian critique of liberalism."[1] Significantly, earlier German contributions to the debate were hardly mentioned. That contribution starts, of course, with the classic monograph *Gemeinschaft und Gesellschaft* by Ferdinand Tönnies, who, as early as 1887, had engagingly portrayed— and, to be sure, vastly overdrawn—the contrast between "atomistic" society and "cohesive" community. That book certainly contributed to an intellectual climate marked by a widespread yearning for *Gemeinschaft* (and corresponding scorn for "mere" *Gesellschaft*). Nevertheless, there were countercurrents, such as the subtle, if rather opaque, critique of the Gemeinschaft creed in Helmuth Plessner's *Grenzen der Gemeinschaft* (Limits of Community).[2] But in recent German volumes devoted to the discussion around community spirit—now called pointedly *Kommunitarismus* rather than *Gemeinsinn*, *Gemeinschaftslehre*, or some such German term—there is hardly any mention of Tönnies or Plessner; instead, one learns a great deal about the thoughts of Michael Sandel, Alasdair MacIntyre, Robert Bellah, Charles Taylor, and Michael Walzer.[3] Obviously, it was found attractive to revive the discussion around the need for greater community and community spirit—to "launder" the concept, as it were—by importing the contemporary debate that had just run its course in the United States.

This does not mean that the American communitarians made a triumphant entry into Germany. In the new circumstances a feeling did arise that Verfassungspatriotismus was no longer quite enough, that it was too minimal a conception of the ties and mutual obligations that were now required among the citizens of the suddenly reunited country. Hence there was much interest in the American communitarian voices. But at the same time and for the solid historical reasons already noted, the resistance against having the reunited Germany propped up by some Bellah-style "civil religion" remained considerable.

Some time ago, while reflecting on the impact of the views on economic development I put forward in the 1950s, I proposed a distinction between two effects of new ideas. The first, direct, and obvious effect—often the only one to be considered—is the "persuasion effect": the new theory is adopted more or less widely by the people who already are working in the field. The second effect of a new theory is that the field itself "comes alive with discussion and controversy and [thereby] attracts some of the more intelligent, energetic, and dedicated members of a generation."[4] This I called the "recruitment effect" and then pointed out that, as the result of this effect, the influence of new ideas is far more unpredictable than would be the case if only the persuasion effect were taken into account: new thinkers may be drawn into the discussion but may end up generating ideas that are quite different from those that originally "seduced" them into the field. It is conceivable for the recruitment effect to swamp the persuasion effect.

Something of this sort appears to have happened in Germany. A recent collective volume assembling in German translation some of the major American articles of the communitarian debate carries an introduction by Axel Honneth that is rather critical of the communitarian position.[5] Another collective volume with comments by German authors on the American debate contains far more critical than favorable articles on the communitarians.[6] Finally, it is in the logic of the recruitment effect that a discussion, which was stimulated by some new position, should lead to ideas that represent an original alternative to that position. This happened for one participant in the debate: Helmut Dubiel, of the Frankfurt Institut für Sozialforschung, put forward a *new minimalist* position on the need for community spirit, which seems to me of considerable interest. Let me present and discuss it.

The Gauchet-Dubiel Thesis:
Conflict as the Builder of Community

Dubiel radically repudiates the possibility as well as desirability for modern societies of building up any kind of consensus on the "good life" based on commonly accepted substantive ethical values or standards. But he accepts and affirms the need for a degree of social integration that goes beyond Verfassungspatriotismus, that is, the universal acceptance of the constitutional norms. This integration of modern societies is to result quite simply, unbeknownst to its citizens, from their experience of passing through and somehow managing or tending (*hegen*) a variety of *conflicts.*[7] Generally, conflicts have, of course, been viewed as dangerous, corrosive, and potentially destructive of social order and therefore precisely in need of being contained and resolved by some standby reserve supply of community spirit. But Dubiel argues that social conflicts produce themselves the valuable ties that hold modern democratic societies together and provide them with the strength and cohesion they need.

Dubiel is fully aware that he proposes a paradox and readily acknowledges his indebtedness to contemporary French theorists of democracy, primarily Marcel Gauchet who put forward similar ideas in the late 1970s and early 1980s. In a remarkable article, ostensibly written as a comment on Tocqueville, Gauchet undertook to show how conflict is an "essential factor of socialization" in democracies and how it is an "eminently efficient producer of integration and cohesion." He too is aware of the paradox he is thus putting forward, for he speaks of the process as the "democratic miracle."[8] The miracle happens as, in a democracy, human beings and social groups go through all the motions of out-and-out confrontation and end up building in this odd manner a cohesive democratic order.

Permit me one side remark here. Social scientists, such as Dubiel and Gauchet, who analyze the democratic process in this manner are obviously quite proud of having come upon what is (and probably must remain) largely hidden from the participants. In watching these authors with a great deal of admiration, I can perhaps be forgiven if I in turn call attention to a matter *they* have apparently overlooked: their paradoxical and miraculous process has much in common with Adam Smith's invisible hand, where the individual, pursuing "only his own gain," also achieves a positive overall outcome that is "no part of his intention."[9]

Gauchet wrote his article at a time when many French intellectuals, shaken by Solzhenitsyn's account of the Gulag, broke definitively with various neo-Marxist doctrines that had long been influential in postwar France. Gauchet's sophisticated argument became an important stage in the itinerary of a generation that was ready to reappreciate the attractions of democracy. The class conflicts that Marxists had long considered as constituting the "contradictions" that would lead to the breakup or breakdown of capitalism were suddenly declared to act as true pillars of society!

Some ten years later, the same point provided a way out of the quite different ideological problems being faced in Germany after reunification: with Verfassungspatriotismus no longer considered adequate and given the continuing distaste for proposing some synthetic "community spirit" as a prerequisite for national coherence, Dubiel welcomed the thought that such a spirit was already being adequately produced through the process of "tending" the various domestic conflicts that arise naturally in the course of events.

Social Thought about the Contribution of Conflict to Cohesion

The idea that conflict can play a constructive role in social relationships has a long history. An early and spectacular contribution comes from Heraclitus with his fragment "war is the father of everything."[10] It is continued by Machiavelli and his chapter in the *Discourses* entitled "How the Disunion between the Plebs and the Senate Made [the Roman] Republic Free and Powerful."[11] Yet the dangers posed and the damage caused by conflict and crisis have been most of the time so obvious and overwhelming that the major effort of social thought has gone into the search for order, peace, harmony, and equilibrium, that is, for the *absence* of feared, abhorred conflict. Thus, at any given period, the idea that conflict, or some degree of conflict, can play a constructive role in social relations strikes the persons who happen to think of it as a nonconformist, paradoxical, and wholly original insight. As a result, they typically *do not bother to look for forerunners* and the thought is *reinvented* with considerable regularity.

Gauchet and Dubiel confirm this proposition. They do not even mention the numerous kindred social scientists, who in *our* century have written extensively about the positive function of conflict. The earliest and most famous among them is Georg Simmel, whose *Soziologie,* published in 1908, contains a long chapter on *Streit,* which is better translated by "conflict" than by the literal "quarrel."[12] Simmel's contribution was rapidly forgotten and to some extent buried by the overwhelmingly destructive impact of the conflicts through which the world passed during the period 1914–1945. But Simmel's ideas on conflict were reawakened by an English translation that appeared in the United States in 1955 and by Lewis Coser's *The Functions of Social Conflict* (1956), which was presented as an extended commentary on key paragraphs taken from Simmel. In his important book, *Class and Class Conflict in Industrial Society* (1957), Ralf Dahrendorf largely endorsed Coser's propositions on the positive functions of conflict. At about the same time, the South African anthropologist Max Gluckman published *Custom and Conflict in Africa* (1955) in which he dwelt on the essential role played by conflict in ritual. My own books of that period, *The Strategy of Economic Development* (1958) and *Journeys Toward Progress* (1963), emphasized the positive role of imbalance in economic development and of crisis in the achievement of social and economic reform in Latin America. At about that time, Michel Crozier published his influential *The Bureaucratic Phenomenon* (1963), which also assigned to crisis a key role in the promotion of progressive change in organizations.

Even closer to the spirit of Dubiel are the writings of some political scientists who were rejecting, also in the 1960s, the notion that democracy can be successfully instituted in a country only if some "preconditions," such as the existence of a consensus about democratic values, are properly fulfilled (or if some "obstacles" are lifted). This idea may have arisen as a transfer to politics of the concept of institutional and cultural "prerequisites" (or of "obstacles") to economic development that was then fairly popular among students of that problem. Here the concepts of prerequisite or "obstacle" were sharply criticized by Alexander Gerschenkron and myself as an evasion of the needed praxis of economic development.[13] The political version of the "prerequisite" idea was in turn rejected by a political scientist in terms strikingly similar to those used today by Dubiel when he doubts the need for some prior community spirit:

It is often thought that for [politics] to function, there must be already in existence some shared idea of a 'common good', some 'consensus' or *consensus juris*. But this common good is itself the process of practical reconciliation of the interests of the various . . . aggregates, or groups which compose a state; it is not some external and intangible spiritual adhesive . . . These are misleading and pretentious explanations of how a community holds together. . . . *Diverse groups hold together because they practice politics—not because they agree about 'fundamentals'*, or some such concept too vague, too personal, or too divine ever to do the job of politics for it. The moral consensus of a free state is not something mysteriously prior to or above politics: it is the activity (the civilizing activity) of politics itself. (p. 24, my emphasis)

This passage comes from the well-known book *In Defence of Politics* (1962) by the English political scientist Bernard Crick. It was approvingly cited and applied to the problems faced by countries searching for democratic development by Dankwart Rustow in an article that has remained a standard reference in the political science literature on developing countries.[14] Rustow strongly argued that democracy has generally come into existence not because people wanted this form of government or because they had achieved a wide consensus on "basic values" but because various groups had been at each other's throat for a long time and finally came to recognize their mutual inability to gain dominance and the need for some accommodation.

Conflict as Glue and as Solvent

The literature on the positive effects of conflict and crisis turns out to be quite rich. But I must criticize it, including my own contributions, in one respect. It tends to be so conscious of staging a perilous attack on orthodoxy that it often limits itself to accomplishing that daring feat and does not proceed to a careful examination of the conditions under which the paradox of conflict and crisis actually generating progress does or does not hold.

Clearly, Dubiel does not affirm that *any* kind of social conflict will produce the sort of useful residue that will make for integration. The very verb *hegen* (to tend) he uses in conjunction with conflict evokes the sort of controlled promotion of natural growth that is practiced in botanical gardens or nurseries and also implies that there are types of conflict that are neither behaved nor can be managed so properly.

Is it possible to distinguish between two varieties of social conflict, those that leave behind a positive residue of integration and those that tear society apart? An attempt to make such a distinction was made at one point by Soviet analysts who, in the 1950s, could not help noticing that their own society and economy was passing through considerable difficulties as industrial expansion was being pushed forward by successive five-year plans. With bottlenecks, excess capacities, and other problems appearing at various points, in spite of the smooth expansion path obviously intended by the planners, the Soviet analysts hit on a marvelous semantic invention meant to put their minds to rest. First of all, they followed the Marxist convention according to which any more or less conspicuous and recurring difficulties experienced in an economic regime are automatically categorized as "contradictions" of that regime. The Marxist scheme then suggested to them a basic distinction: the contradictions that are experienced in capitalist countries and that can only be resolved by revolution are bound to be far more serious than those occurring in countries where capitalism has already been overthrown and where revolution is therefore pointless and inconceivable. Given these certainties, the contradictions experienced by the capitalist countries were labeled, logically enough, "antagonistic," whereas those affecting the socialist world were declared to be of the far milder "nonantagonistic" variety.[15] It turned out, of course, that the societies said to be afflicted by antagonistic contradictions have weathered them fairly well and have outlived those regimes that were allegedly experiencing just nonantagonistic ones! (Here, one is reminded of a passage in Koestler's *Darkness at Noon* where the prisoner in a Soviet jail who is an old-time partisan of the Tzar has a far better prospect of survival than the novel's hero, an Old Bolshevik, who has been recently arrested on account of "deviations from the party line.")

The story lends itself to pouring heavy, if rather cheap, irony on the communist ideologues, but a serious conclusion can be drawn from it: in order to decide whether the difficulties or conflicts a society faces are destructive and lethal, or whether we can "manage" and "tend" them, we seem to need the *wisdom of hindsight*—to want to make this determination firmly in advance would be to commit instead the *folly of foresight* (the folly of pretending to foresight).

So there arises a problem with Gauchet-Dubiel's attractive idea that conflicts will provide society with the "social capital" (to use Robert Putnam's term) it needs to be kept together.[16] What if, in addition to producing this capital or social "glue," conflict also acts as a solvent which dissolves social ties or as dynamite which blows them apart? To view conflict in this apprehensive way is, after all, closer to the conventional wisdom, which should not be entirely discounted. The problem can also be formulated as follows: how does Gauchet-Dubiel's idea relate to Whitehead's penetrating observation that "the major advances in civilization are processes which all but wreck the societies in which they occur"?

Could Whitehead and Gauchet-Dubiel both be right? This interpretation becomes possible if we view Whitehead's somewhat delphic phrase in an optimistic light: his "all but" qualification could be taken to point to a world where narrow escapes from threatening disaster are somehow always happening:—conflicts *almost* wreck societies but never quite do so and therefore actually strengthen them because of the salutary experience of passing through crisis and struggle; in the end, crisis is likely to strengthen societies *the more* the greater the crisis. This is close to Hölderlin's beautiful lines: *Wo aber Gefahr ist, wächst/Das Rettende auch* (But where there is danger/Salvation also grows) and to Nietzsche's kindred, if more brutal, maxim *Was mich nicht umbringt, macht mich stärker* (That which does not destroy me makes me stronger).

Unfortunately, this century has definitively taught us that we cannot rely on narrow escapes any more than on miracles. Despite the beauty of Holderlin's lines, there simply is no providential proportionality between the dangers caused by conflict and the chances of overcoming them. Hence there is no alternative to an independent evaluation of these dangers and chances, hopefully to be undertaken in a less doctrinaire spirit than the one that presided over the distinction between antagonistic and nonantagonistic contradictions.

Conflicts Typical of Pluralist Market Society . . . and the Others

To make some progress with this task, it is necessary to step down from the exalted level of generality of Hölderlin, Nietzsche, and Whitehead. The question whether conflicts act predominantly as glue or as solvent cannot be decided in general; it must be brought down to earth through a closer look at the interaction between a specific kind of society and its typical conflicts.

When Gauchet and Dubiel affirmed that conflicts enhance social cohesion, they did refer specifically to the democratic market societies of the West. But the systemic reasons for this happy outcome were rather left in the dark. In the following, I hope to make the argument more persuasive by drawing on the political economy of pluralist market society; in the end, I shall also point to situations where the interaction between conflict and social system is likely to be more complex and less auspicious.

In my book *The Passions and the Interests,* I wrote about the favorable political effects that eighteenth-century observers like Montesquieu and Sir James Steuart expected to arise from the expansion of market society: they were greater control of the "passions" in general and more predictability of the actions of the sovereign and restraints on *grands coups d'autorité* in particular, thanks to increased stability and *douceur* in the management of human affairs. After presenting these hopes and expectations, which had been largely forgotten, I was obliged to point out, on the basis of the evidence accumulated in the course of the two subsequent centuries: those eighteenth-century visions were engaging, ingenious, and . . . wrong.

Can we do better today in visualizing the interaction between economics and politics? We can try. Perhaps we should pin our hopes not so much on the *douceur* invoked by Montesquieu but on a seemingly negative factor, the frequency and ubiquity of *conflict*!

Conflict is indeed a characteristic of pluralist market society that has come to the fore with remarkable persistence. It is the natural counterpart of technical progress and of the ensuing creation of new wealth, for which market society is rightly famous. Conflicts arise from newly emerging inequalities and sectoral or regional declines—the counterpart precisely of various dynamic developments elsewhere in the economy. In societies with freedom of speech and association, concerns about those matters tend to mobilize both those who are immediately affected as well as citizens who are sensitive to more or less widely shared feelings about social justice. Hence there arise demands for corrective action and reform, demands that are based *both on self-interest and on genuine concern for the public good,* or, to use a distinction due to Jon Elster, on *both bargaining and arguing.*[17] The secret of the vitality of pluralist market society and of its ability to renew itself may lie in this conjunction and in the successive eruption of problems and crises. The society thus produces a *steady diet of conflicts* that need to be addressed and that the society learns to manage. Correspondingly, the basic reason for the deterioration and loss of vitality of the Communist-dominated societies may be in the success these societies had in suppressing overt social conflict.

As long as the Communist systems were in approximate working order it could never be suggested that the strength of market society may lie in its propensity and vulnerability to conflict: the Communists proclaimed that the conflicts were signs of the imminent or eventual collapse of capitalism, and the partisans of market society were too defensive about the system to dwell on a characteristic that is normally viewed as damaging.

Significantly, one type of conflict escaped from this defensive stance prevailing in the West: the famous "cross-cutting cleavages" that result from the many affiliations that citizens normally entertain not only to a social class but to race, gender, religion, and so forth.[18] During the Cold War, a great deal was made by Western social science of these conflicts, for it was plausible that the presence of multiple affiliations would *reduce* the intensity of conflict that would be characteristic of a society where people are arrayed along a single axis, such as the capital-labor dimension privileged by the Marxists.

But cross-cutting cleavages are just one type of conflict resulting from the multiplicity and ubiquity of conflict prevailing in democratic market societies. By singling out and celebrating this variety, Western social scientists implicitly accepted the notion that conflict is normally destructive and kept themselves from fully appreciating the extent and characteristics of conflict in their societies.

For one thing, with pluralist market society spawning a never-ending series of social conflicts in fairly rapid succession, it differs from other types of socio-political arrangements in one important respect: it cannot pretend to establish any permanent order and harmony; all it can aspire to accomplish is to "muddle through" from one conflict to the next.[19] The muddling-through mode of problem solving is facilitated not only by the quantity and variety of conflicts likely to erupt in market society but also by their quality. Many conflicts of market society are over the distribution of the social product among different classes, sectors, or regions. Highly varied though they are, they tend to be divisible conflicts over more or less, in contrast to conflicts of the either-or or nondivisible category that are characteristic of societies split along rival ethnic, linguistic, or religious lines.[20] Nondivisible conflicts have recently also become more prominent in the older democracies and particularly in the United States, as a result of the importance assumed by such issues as abortion and multiculturalism.

The distinction between the two categories is not always clear-cut as nondivisible issues have ordinarily some components that are negotiable. Conversely, conflicts that look as though they were over more or less often have a nondivisible component or source. In Latin America, for example, striking workers have often proclaimed that they are fighting not just for higher wages but primarily for *respeto* (respect), which they felt was being withheld from them by the upper classes with their distinct racial or ethnic background. In Europe, some historians have similarly seen the chasm between the upper and lower classes in the nineteenth century as going back to residual ethnic hatreds between the Saxons and their Norman conquerors in England, between Gauls and Franks in France, or between Slavs and Teutons in much of Germany.[21] It is nevertheless useful to abstract from these complications for the moment and to contrast the two types of conflict—the more or less and the either-or—as though they could be found in "pure" form.

As is well known, conflicts of the more-or-less type are intrinsically easier to settle than conflicts of the either-or variety: even when the parties are initially far apart they can theoretically "split the difference" or "meet halfway" ("half a loaf is better than none") whereas these kinds of compromise solutions are often less available when the sections making up a society and coming into conflict are divided by matters of religion, language, race, or gender. In the light of this distinction, it is today difficult to understand how Marxism was so long so successful in presenting social conflict, impressively dressed up as *Klassenkampf* or "class struggle," as the principal, ultimate, and most irreconcilable type of conflict of modern society, when it is in fact the conflict that lends itself most readily to the arts of compromise.

The distinction between more-or-less and either-or types of conflicts reinforces the previous point about the prevalence of the muddling-through mode of conflict solving in market societies. Take first the either-or type of conflict. Ways have, of course, been found to overcome it, either through the outright elimination of one contending group or through a "toleration" agreement to "live and let live." These are very different "solutions," but in both cases the impression tends to arise that the problem has been solved *once and for all*. Often, this turns out to be an illusion, of course, but the idea of the existence of, or of the possible return to, some "just," "good," or "well-ordered" society from which conflict has been banished remains intact. The difference with the more-or-less conflict typical of market society is considerable: whatever compromise is reached in the distribution of the social product between various classes, sectors, and regions, it is here clear to all concerned that agreements are temporary, are tied to the particular circumstances in which they were made, and can be reopened at the next opportunity.

To summarize, the conflicts typical of pluralist market society have the following characteristics:

1. They occur with considerable frequency and take on a great variety of shapes.
2. They are predominantly of the divisible type and therefore lend themselves to compromise and to the art of bargaining.
3. As a result of these two features, the compromises reached never give rise to the idea or illusion that they represent definitive solutions.

A society that has substantial practice over a prolonged period in dealing with conflicts of this type is indeed likely to have the positive experience described by Gauchet-Dubiel. All the support that such a society needs is that which derives from its cumulative experience of muddling through its numerous conflicts: these conflicts are or become its pillars. The period that corresponds most closely to this pattern is probably the "glorious" thirty-year period of all-round vigorous growth in Western market societies that followed the conclusion of the Second World War.

Unfortunately, there *are* other types of conflicts around, and our problem today seems to be that this category is everywhere on the increase, from abortion to fights over ethnicity and fundamentalism. When Benjamin Constant was faced with the restless Napoleon, he cried out, full of nostalgia, *"Que Dieu nous rende nos rois fainéants!"* (May God give us back our do-nothing kings!). Similarly today, as we experience the surge or resurgence of conflicts around nondivisible issues, we feel like exclaiming, "May God give us back the class struggle!"

This reflection actually helps to push the discussion forward by calling attention to matters of timing and sequencing. The "class struggle" or the "social question" may have loomed so formidable in the nineteenth century, in part because of the residual ethnic cleavages mentioned earlier, but even more because those conflicts were seen as being similar to the wars of religion that were in fresh historical memory. This historically conditioned misdiagnosis probably contributed to the conviction that the conflict between capital and labor required radical solutions: either Socialism-Communism, which would eliminate one of the two sides to the conflict, or Corporatism-Fascism, which would make sure that the two sides are permanently yoked together. Only after World War II did it become generally accepted that the social conflicts typical of the industrialized countries were amenable to gradual mitigation and ever shifting compromise.

But just as this experience had been assimilated, very different types of conflict appear to be reemerging. Having behind us a lengthy experience of dealing with negotiable conflicts we are now liable to experience the optical illusion opposite to the one that prevailed in the nineteenth century: we cannot quite bring ourselves to believe that the participants feel as strongly as they do about the issues involved. Extremely serious mistakes can once again be committed in consequence: two examples that come to mind are the underestimate of mutual hatreds existing in Yugoslavia after the breakup of that country and the underestimate of economic and cultural distances between East and West Germany after forty years of separation.

But the long practice in bargaining and in searching for compromise solutions that is characteristic of the more recent experience with conflict management in the West should not have only negative consequences for our ability to "tend" the new conflicts. However formidable and irreconcilable they may look at first sight, they could, for example, have negotiable parts or aspects that will be easier to tease out when they are approached with a spirit that is well trained in the art of bargaining and experimentation.

Two final remarks. I said before that the discussion about the constructive or destructive effects of conflicts must be "brought down to earth" by focusing on different types of conflict that arise characteristically in whatever specific society is being investigated. The concept of muddling through and the distinction between divisible and nondivisible conflicts were meant to serve this purpose. But these notions are meant only as a first approximation to "earth" and should not be seen as a definitive or unique key or paradigm. After all, we should learn something from the sad fate of the earlier attempt at discriminating between "constructive" and "destructive" conflicts, the one that relied on the distinction between antagonistic and nonantagonistic contradictions! I suspect, for example, that the category of either-or or nondivisible conflicts is essentially a convenient label for a vast array of new and unfamiliar problems having quite different degrees of manageability. These conflicts can only be properly mapped out as we experience them.

Second, I must briefly return to our main theme, the need for community spirit. I have agreed in part with Dubiel's new minimalism—the community spirit that is normally needed in a democratic market society tends to be spontaneously generated through the experience of tending the conflicts that are typical of that society. But what about the "atypical" conflicts and problems that seem to be on the increase today? Does community spirit truly come into its own here? I have my doubts. To invoke the need for community spirit in these situations is essentially an admission that concrete ways of dealing with the respective problems have not yet been discovered—community spirit is called upon as some deus ex machina. What is actually required to make progress with the novel problems that a society encounters on its road is political entrepreneurship, imagination, patience here, impatience there, and other varieties of *virtù* and *fortuna*—I cannot see much point (and do see some danger) in lumping all of this together by an appeal to Geimeinsinn.

Notes

1. This is the title of an article by Michael Walzer, in *Political Theory* 18 (February 1990): 6–23, which strikes me as an incisive critique of the critique.

2. Bonn: Friedrich Cohen, 1924. Wolf Lepenies underlines the current interest of this book in *Folgen einer unerhörten Begebenheit* (Berlin: Siedler, 1992), 67–70. A useful summary and comment on Plessner's book are in Joachim Fischer, "Plessner und die politische Philosophie der zwanziger Jahre," in Volker Gerhardt et al., eds., *Politisches Denken, Jahrbuch 1992* (Stuttgart: J. B. Metzler, 1993), 53–76.

3. See, for example, Christel Zahlmann, ed., *Kommunitarismus in der Diskussion* (Berlin: Rotbuch, 1992); and Axel Honneth, ed., *Kommunitarismus: Eine Debatte über die moralischen Grundlagen moderner Gesellschaften* (Frankfurt: Campus, 1993).

4. Albert O. Hirschman, "A Dissenter's Confession: *The Strategy of Economic Development* Revisited" in Hirschman, *Rival Views of Market Society and Other Recent Essays* (1986 and Cambridge: Harvard University Press, 1992), 34.

5. Honneth (n. 2), 7–17.

6. Zahlmann (n. 2); see, in particular, article by Wolfgang Fach.

7. Helmut Dubiel, "Konsens oder Konflikt" (manuscript, 1991); "Das ethische Minimum," *Süddeutsche Zeitung*, March 27–28,1993; and "Zivilreligion in der Massendemokratie" *Soziale Welt*, 41 Heft 2 (1990): 125–43.

8. Marcel Gauchet, "Tocqueville, l'Amérique et nous," *Libre*, Nr. 7 (1980): 116–17. This and related articles by Gauchet and other French authors are brought together in German translation in Ulrich Rödel, ed., *Autonome Gesellschaft und Libertäre Demokratie* (Frankfurt: Suhrkamp, 1990).

9. Adam Smith, *Wealth of Nations* (New York: Modern Library, 1937), 423.

10. Writing over two hundred years before Heracleitus, Hesiod made a distinction between two kinds of strife: one that "fosters evil, war, and battle, being cruel" and another that is "far kinder to men. . . . [It] stirs up even the shiftless to toil . . . and neighbor vies with neighbor as he hurries after wealth. This strife is wholesome for man" *(Works and Days,* 11–26). With this distinction, which he makes at the outset of his poem, Hesiod corrected his own previous statement in *Theogony* (225) where he characterizes *Eris* (strife) as purely destructive: "Toil . . . and Famine . . . Sorrows, Battles, Murders, Quarrels, Lying Words, Disputes, Lawlessness and Ruin . . .". I owe this remarkable point in intellectual history to André Laks.

11. Chapter 4 of Book 1.

12. As noted by Kurt H. Wolff who translated Simmel's text into English. See Georg Simmel, *Conflict and the Web of Group-Affiliations*, translated and with an introduction by K. H. Wolff (Glencoe, IL: Free Press, 1955), 11.

13. Alexander Gerschenkron, "Reflections on the Concept of 'Prerequisites' of Modern Industrialization," in *Economic Backwardness in Historical Perspective* (Cambridge, MA: Harvard University Press, 1962), 31–51; Albert O. Hirschman, "Obstacles to Development: A Classification and a Quasi-Vanishing Act," in Hirschman, *A Bias for Hope: Essays on Development and Latin America* (New Haven, CT: Yale University Press, 1971), 312–27.

14. "Transitions to Democracy: Toward a Dynamic Model," *Comparative Politics* 2 (April 1970): 337–64.

15. V. Kozlovskii, *Antagonisticheskie i neantagonisticheskie protivorechiia* [Antagonistic and nonantagonistic contradictions] (Moscow: Moskovskii Rabochii, 1954). These concepts probably go back to Stalin's *Economic Problems of Socialism in the USSR* (Moscow: Foreign Languages Publishing House, 1952), 24–27, where Stalin speaks of "essential" and "nonessential distinctions" between town and country, between mental and physical labor, and so on, with only the "nonessential" ones still to be found in the Soviet Union. Later, the distinction between "antagonistic" and "nonantagonistic contradictions" was given considerable prominence by Mao Tse-Tung, in a speech he made in 1957. See "On the Correct Handling of Contradictions among the People," in *Selected Readings from the Works of Mao Tse-Tung* (Peking: Foreign Languages Press, 1967), 350–87, in particular 351 and 359. For some of the above references, I am grateful to Björn Wittrock, Bo Gustafsson, and Luca Meldolesi.

16. Robert D. Putnam, *Making Democracy Work: Civic Traditions in Modern Italy* (Princeton, NJ: Princeton University Press, 1993), 167–85.

17. Available so far only in Italian: *Argomentare e negoziare* (Milan: Anabasi, 1993).

18. See, e.g., Seymour Martin Lipset, *Political Man* (New York: Anchor, 1963), 76–79 and passim.

19. See C. E. Lindblom's classic article, "The Science of Muddling Through," *Public Administration Review* 19 (1959): 79–88.

20. An early discussion of this difference is in W. Arthur Lewis, *Politics in West Africa* (Toronto: Oxford University Press, 1965), chap. 3. The most important contributions to the discussion around it are to be found in the writings of Arend Lijphart, Kenneth McRae, Val Lorwin, and David D. Laitin.

21. This is an important theme of a course Michel Foucault gave in 1976 at the Collège de France. Notes taken at this course have been published so far only in an Italian translation, *Difendere la Societá: dalla guerra delle razze al razzismo di stato,* edited and translated by Mauro Bertani and Alessandro Fontana (Florence: GEF, 1990). See also Rudy Leonelli, "Gli eruditi delle battaglie: Note su Foucault e Marx," *Altre Ragioni* 2 (1993): 139–50, for comments on these Foucault lectures and specific references to the historical literature on which Foucault based his assertion. My sincere thanks to Giovanna Procacci for this information.

Afterword

Emma Rothschild and Amartya Sen

ALBERT HIRSCHMAN had an exceptional capacity, as these essays make so clear, to understand the shifting worlds in which he lived. His work will endure for two dissimilar reasons. One is his "world-view": a skeptical optimism, in Fernando Henrique Cardoso's description, endlessly unconvinced by universal prescriptions, simple accounts of individual lives, and general laws of the social world, and endlessly open to possibilities for change. The other is a series of ideas, including explanatory arguments, that are themselves simple enough: exit and voice, or passions and interests, or obstacles and development.[1] This contrast between the observation of complicated lives and the simplicity of explanation was at the heart of Hirschman's thought. His own insight, as early as *The Strategy of Economic Development*, was that tension and indecision were themselves conducive to economic development, and that "difficulties, conflict, and anxiety" should be understood as something more than uniquely "pathogenic agents."[2] A generation later, in the final essay in this volume, he concluded that society was likely to derive its strength from the cumulative experience of "its numerous divisible conflicts: these conflicts are or become its pillars."[3] "You know what? Daddy has no world-view!" Hirschman described himself as exclaiming to his sister, in Berlin in 1928, and his own worldview was a view of the world without uniform or universal explanations.[4] The

---

[1] Fernando Henrique Cardoso, "Albert Hirschman, um otimista cético," *Folha de S. Paulo*, March 24, 2013.

[2] Albert O. Hirschman, *The Strategy of Economic Development* (New Haven, Conn., 1958), pp. 25, 125, 132, 209.

[3] Albert O. Hirschman, "How much Community Spirit (*Gemeinsinn*) does Liberal Democracy Require?" (Institute for Advanced Study, Princeton, N.J., 1993).

[4] Albert O. Hirschman, *A Propensity to Self-Subversion* (Cambridge, Mass., 1995), pp. 111–12.

conflict between complexity and simplicity was particularly apparent in Hirschman's changing relationship to political economy. Even in his earliest writings, Hirschman was preoccupied with the place of economic life, or "purely 'economic man,'" within a larger universe of political and moral existence: "true it is that ever since Max Weber economists have had some doubts about the meaningfulness of the term economic when applied to ends and not to means."[5] He was resistant, in the 1950s, to the widespread view of "less developed countries" as simple societies, susceptible of universal economic prescriptions: "'these countries were not all that complicated.'"[6] He was sceptical, too, of views of "the economy" as an entity, a "to-be-deferred-to" automaton.[7] His later critique of the "economic approach"—a "would-be conquering discipline," whose "onward sweep" had "revealed some of its intrinsic weaknesses"—was directed, most sharply, against what he described as the "simpleminded" view of the self-interested, isolated individual. It was a perspective, in Hirschman's account, that eschewed any investigation of the "complex psychological and cultural processes" that lay behind "observed market processes," and that was inadequate, in turn, to explain even "such fundamental economic processes as consumption and production."[8]

Hirschman's own cultural turn—his "reaction [to authoritarianism in Latin America]," he wrote in 1979, "was to withdraw into history, and more specifically into the history of ideas"—was a return to what he described as an earlier, more open, and less ascetic economic thought.[9] The limits of the economic, the political, and the psychological were easily traversed, in early modern European thought, and political economy was one inquiry among many, in a collective enterprise of understanding market societies. Montesquieu and Sir James Steuart, in Hirschman's evocation, were figures from a lost world of ideas, ever conscious of

---

[5] Albert O. Hirschman, *National Power and the Structure of Foreign Trade* (Berkeley, Calif., 1945), pp. 3, 78.

[6] "The Rise and Decline of Development Economics," see above, p. 69.

[7] "Authoritarianism in Latin America," in Albert O. Hirschman, *Essays in Trespassing* (Cambridge, 1981), p. 102.

[8] "Against Parsimony: Three Easy Ways of Complicating Some Categories of Economic Discourse," see above, p. 249.

[9] "Authoritarianism in Latin America," in Hirschman, *Essays in Trespassing*, p. 99.

the "incredible complexity of human nature."[10] It was only with the rise of laissez-faire political economy, following the publication in 1776 of Adam Smith's *Inquiry into the Nature and Causes of the Wealth of Nations* Hirschman suggested, that theorists took the eventual "reductionist step" of confounding the passions and the interests, with a consequent "narrowing of the field of inquiry" of social thought.[11]

But Hirschman, too, was enticed by the simplicity of understanding and explanation. His essay "Against Parsimony" ends with a description of foundations: "two basic human endowments and two basic tensions that are part of the human condition." His "piccole idee" were small insights into very large conditions, and they can be depicted in formal terms (very often, as it happens, in the form of a 2 × 2 matrix).[12] Hirschman thought like an economist, even as he became a compelling critic of economic policy and economic postulates. There was an enduring affinity, in his writing, to the way of thinking of the classical political economists, as described by another of his longstanding sources, G. W. F. Hegel: "the interesting spectacle (as in Smith, Say, and Ricardo) of thought working upon the endless mass of details which confront it at the outset and extracting therefrom the simple principles of the thing."[13]

There is very little sense, in Hirschman's writing, of complexity or involution as a condition that is creditable in itself. He was an inspiring critic of successive varieties of economic thought, but his ideas cannot be mapped in any straightforward way on to a dichotomy of the "orthodox" versus the "heterodox," the "rational" versus the "fully empirical," or the "thin" versus the "thickly descriptive." He aspired to both, and he embraced the conflict between them.

Hirschman's writing is similarly difficult to map onto the dichotomy of state planning versus market fundamentalism. As he wrote in "A Dissenter's Confession," he went to Colombia in 1952 "as economic and

---

[10] "Against Parsimony," p. 261.

[11] Albert O. Hirschman, *The Passions and the Interests* (Princeton, N.J., 1977), pp. 109, 112.

[12] "Against Parsimony," p. 262; and see, for example, *Essays in Trespassing*, p. 3, and "Rival Views of Market Society, above, p. 253.

[13] G. W. F. Hegel, *Hegel's Philosophy of Right* (1821), trans. T. M. Knox (Oxford, 1967), pp. 126–27.

financial adviser to the newly established National Planning Council" that had been set up on the initiative of the World Bank. But he had a "healthy respect (based on watching the misadventures of the French economy) for the efficiency of the price system." When the Bank "attempted to condition its lending on countries' establishing some form of overall economic planning," he wrote, "I almost lost my advisory job in Colombia because I refused to push hard in this direction." A generation later, he was a brilliant critic of the "free-market credo as a universal remedy" and of the lectures to which Latin American economic policy makers were subjected, "on the virtues of free markets, privatization, and private foreign investment, and on the perils of state guidance and intervention as well as excessive taxation, not to mention planning."[14]

Hirschman was a devastating critic, even, of the universal prescription of finding an optimal union of the state and the market. This was the prescription of minimal (or what might now be called "smart") government, which he described in 1971 (not without irony) as "the 'asymptotic' conception of the state's role": "government action in the economic field is thus conceived as a corrective and complement of private action. . . . all the areas in which the market tends to fail will be ferreted out, and the best possible mix of market and nonmarket decision making will be approached and permanently established."[15] But he rejected, in his Eva Colorni Memorial Lecture of 1990, the "bitter and mean-spirited" prediction of conservative critics of social programs, that all reforms will fail.[16]

In *The Passions and the Interests*, Hirschman identified motivations that standard economics tended to ignore, which undermined the easy defense of the adequacy of a market-based world. Market accounting left out many of the most significant human relationships—important for personal well-being and also for social initiatives and innovations. Hirschman provided deep insights into the importance of these human relations and also showed how they can undermine many of the standard

---

[14] "A Dissenter's Confession," in Albert O. Hirschman, *Rival Views of Market Society and Other Recent Essays*, pp. 6–7; Albert O. Hirschman, "The Political Economy of Latin American Development," *Latin American Research Review* 22, no. 3 (1987): 31.

[15] Albert Hirschman, *A Bias for Hope: Essays on Development and Latin America* (New Haven, Conn., 1971), p. 23.

[16] Albert O. Hirschman, "Two Hundred Years of Reactionary Rhetoric: The Futility Thesis," in *Living as Equals*, ed. Paul Barker (Oxford, 1996), p. 83.

arguments of conventional economics about what markets can single-handedly achieve and how. That is surely a compelling argument against market fundamentalism (to be placed next to Paul Samuelson's analysis of "public goods" and Kenneth Arrow's exposition of informational asymmetry). But Hirschman also showed how the market mechanism can achieve positive things that the market fundamentalists miss out altogether. He went back to Montesquieu's praise of the market's ability to make use of the benign and constructive role of self-centred interests in subduing evil passions. As he wrote in *The Passions and the Interests*, though *passions* may prompt people to be "wicked," "they have nevertheless an *interest* in not being so." In his account, this classic, but quite neglected argument blossomed into an alternative way of looking at the market economy—not in terms of economic efficiency, but in terms of taking people away from violent passions in pursuit of nationalism, religious intolerance, communal tensions, or racial hostilities.

Hirschman's enduring commitment, in all these intellectual and public journeys, was to question the oppression of imposing universal and uniform prescriptions on individuals whose lives and experiences were always diverse. It was a form of oppression to see individuals in "less developed countries" as different, simpler beings. It was oppressive to see all individuals as "self-interested, isolated" and without any inclination toward self-evaluation.[17] It was oppressive to deny the anxieties and conflicts that were so much a part of human experience, and foolish, in turn, to preclude the possibility of a world in which conflicts and differences are divisible and susceptible of unviolent solutions. Hirschman's own journeys, as the biography by Jeremy Adelman, *Worldly Philosopher*, shows so convincingly, were formed by his work in resisting oppression, and rescuing the oppressed, in Nazi-dominated Europe in the 1930s and 1940s. The public and private journeys were connected, in this sense; they were the rejection of a world in which some individuals were different, lesser, and less than fully human. Hirschman did very unusual and very daring things in his political activities; and he did the same in his intellectual life as well.

---

[17] "Against Parsimony," pp. 248, 262.

Acknowledgments

PERMISSION to reprint the previously published essays in this volume is gratefully acknowledged.

"Political Economics and Possibilism"
Albert O. Hirschman, *Bias for Hope: Essays on Development and Latin America* (1971). New Haven: Yale University Press. Reprinted with permission of Katia Salomon and the estate of Albert O. Hirschman.

"Underdevelopment, Obstacles to the Perception of Change, and Leadership"
Albert O. Hirschman, "Underdevelopment, Obstacles to the Perception of Change, and Leadership." *Daedalus*, Summer 1968, 97:3, pp. 925–937. © 1968 by the American Academy of Arts and Sciences.

"The Rise and Decline of Development Economics"
Albert O. Hirschman, "The Rise and Decline of Development Economics," in *Essays in Trespassing*, pp. 266–284. Cambridge: Cambridge University Press. Copyright © 1981 Cambridge University Press.

"The Changing Tolerance for Income Inequality in the Course of Economic Development"
Albert O. Hirschman, "The Changing Tolerance for Income Inequality in the Course of Economic Development: With a Mathematical Appendix." *Quarterly Journal of Economics*, November 1973, 87(4), pp. 544–565. Reprinted by permission of Oxford University Press.

"The Political Economy of Import Substitution Industrialization in Latin America"
Albert O. Hirschman, "The Political Economy of Import-Substituting Industrialization in Latin America." *Quarterly Journal of Economics*, February 1968, 82(1), pp. 2–32. Reprinted by permission of Oxford University Press.

"The Search for Paradigms as a Hindrance to Understanding"
Albert O. Hirschman, "The Search for Paradigms as a Hindrance to Under-
standing." *World Politics*, April 1970, 22(3), pp. 329–343. Copyright ©1987.
Trustees of Princeton University. Reprinted with permission of Cambridge
University Press.

"A Generalized Linkage Approach to Development, with Special Refer-
ences to Staples"
Albert O. Hirschman, "A Generalized Linkage Approach to Development, with
Special References to Staples," in *Essays in Trespassing*, pp. 59–96. Cambridge:
Cambridge University Press. Copyright © 1981 Cambridge University Press.

"The Concept of Interest: from Euphemism to Tautology"
"The Concept of Interest," from *Rival Views of Market Society* by Albert O.
Hirschman, © 1986 by Albert O. Hirschman. Used by permission of Viking
Penguin, a division of Penguin Group (USA) Inc.

"Rival Views of Market Society"
"Rival Views of Market Society," from *Rival Views of Market Society* by Albert
O. Hirschman, © 1986 by Albert O. Hirschman. Used by permission of
Viking Penguin, a division of Penguin Group (USA) Inc.

"Against Parsimony: Three Easy Ways of Complicating Some Categories
of Economic Discourse"
"Against Parsimony: Three Easy Ways of Complicating Some Categories
of Economic Discourse" from *Rival Views of Market Society* by Albert O.
Hirschman, © 1986 by Albert O. Hirschman. Used by permission of Viking
Penguin, a division of Penguin Group (USA) Inc.

"Three Uses of Political Economy in Analyzing European Integration"
Albert O. Hirschman, "Three Uses of Political Economy in Analyzing European
Integration," in *Essays in Trespassing*, pp. 294–306. Cambridge: Cambridge
University Press. Copyright © 1981 Cambridge University Press.

"Opinionated Opinions and Democracy"
Albert O. Hirschman, "Opinionated Opinions and Democracy," which was first
published as "Having Opinions—One of the Elements of Well-Being?" in *American Economic Review—Papers and Proceedings*, 19 (May 1989), pp. 75–79.

"Reactionary Rhetoric"

"Two Hundred Years of Reactionary Rhetoric," reprinted by permission of the
publisher from The Rhetoric of Reaction: Perversity, Futility, Jeopardy by Albert O. Hirschman, pp. 1–10, Cambridge, MA: The Belknap Press of Harvard
University Press, Copyright © 1991 by the President and Fellows of Harvard
College.

"Exit, Voice, and the State"

Albert O. Hirschman, "Exit, Voice, and the Fate of the German Democratic Republic: An Essay in Conceptual History." World Politics, January 1993, 45(2),
pp. 173–202. Copyright © 1993. Trustees of Princeton University. Reprinted
with permission of Cambridge University Press.

"Morality and the Social Sciences: A Durable Tension"

Albert O. Hirschman, "Morality and the Social Sciences: A Durable Tension,"
in Essays in Trespassing, pp. 59–97. Cambridge: Cambridge University Press.
Copyright © 1981 Cambridge University Press.

"Social Conflict as Pillars of Democratic Market Societies"

Albert O. Hirschman, "Social Conflicts as Pillars of Democratic Market
Society." Political Theory, 22(2), pp. 203–218, copyright © 1994 by Albert O.
Hirschman. Reprinted by Permission of SAGE Publications.

Index

abilities, 259–61

activities, instrumental vs. noninstrumental, 252–58

Adelman, Jeremy, 367

Africa, stateless societies in, 312–14

agrarian development, 28–29

agrarian reform, 38, 44

agriculture, and spatial mobility, 170–73

aid. *See* foreign aid

Althusser, Louis, 151–52

altruism, 210, 339–40

American exceptionalism, 238

Anderson, Charles W., 47n4, 235

Arendt, Hannah, xii, xv

Argentina: class alienation in, 85; industrialization in, 124; power generation in, 183–84; social change in, 35

Arrow, Kenneth, 258, 337, 367

artisan activities, 161

Atlantic Monthly (magazine), 293

attribution theory, 99n24

Austen, Jane, 284, 289

Aywlin, Patricio, 345

backward linkages, 58; defined, 160; determinants of, 118–25; in import-substituting industrialization, 115–17; inside vs. outside, 169–70; promotion of, 121–24; resistance to, 118–23; technology and, 124–25, 166. *See also* forward linkages

backwardness: analytical approaches to, 147–49; benefits of, 47n3; and industrialization process, 109–10; signs of, 37–38

backwash effect, 63, 277

balanced growth: criticisms of, viii, xvi, 49; development economics and, 55; Lewis and, 49

balance of payments, industrialization and, 59, 106–7, 121

Baldwin, Robert, 158–59, 191n24

Bamberger, Joan, 312

bananas, 167

banking linkage, 189n10

Baran, Paul, 158, 235

basic needs, 68

Becker, Gary, 251, 252

behavioral economics, 248

Bell, Daniel, 222

Bellah, Robert, 347, 348

Bentham, Jeremy, 304

Bergson, Henri, 234

big push, 58

Bismarck, Otto von, 198

blessings in disguise, 10, 23–24

Bobbio, Norberto, xiv

Bolingbroke, Henry St. John, Viscount, 221

Bolivia, 35, 38

bottleneck industries, 117–18

Bourdieu, Pierre, 195

bourgeoisie: capitalism and, 16, 223, 231–36; and industrialization, 129; values of, 203, 223

brain drain, 321, 323, 325

Brazil, 35; coffee production in, 111, 163, 168, 172, 183–84; development in, 78–79; income distribution in, 68; industrialization in, 110–11, 120, 124; power generation in, 183–84; social change in, 41; sugarcane production in, 183–84; tribal politics in, 311–12

Breton, Andre, xv

Britain, 294, 323. *See also* England

British Parliament, 149

brutalization, human response to, 25–26

Burckhardt, Jacob, 300

bureaucracy, 302

Burke, Edmund, 202, 205, 206, 297–98, 300, 303

buses, 39

Bush, George H. W., 293

Bushman bands, 313

business-cycle theory, 50

import-substituting industrialization
(*continued*)
  patterns in, 112–13; initial phase of,
  107–14; late vs. late late, 108–11; motive
  forces behind, 105–7; tightly-staged character of, 108–9
import-swallowing industrialization, 106
income distribution, 68, 158–59
income inequalities: cultural cleavages and,
  11; desirability, 78; psychology of, 76–80,
  82–83, 86–89; tolerance for, in economic
  development, 75–96; tunnel effect and,
  76–80, 82–87
income redistribution, 10, 135n17
India, development in, 53, 105
indifference curves, 3, 4
individuality, 286, 287
Indonesia, 171; sugarcane production in,
  183; tree crops in, 183
industrialization: changes accompanying, 38;
  criticisms of, 64–65, 106–7; geographical
  factors in, 124; import-substituting, 14,
  17, 102–33, 105, 182; in Latin America,
  103–5; political implications of, 113.
  See also late industrialization; late late
  industrialization
inequality. *See* income inequalities
inflation, 59, 338
information, in markets, 337
infrastructure, 174
Innis, Harold, 161, 183
inside linkage, 169–73
instrumental activities, 252–58
integration, political. *See* political integration
intellectual terrorism, 305
interdisciplinary approach, viii–ix
interest, 195–211; attacks on concept of,
  204–6, 227; attitudes toward, 196; in
  contemporary usage, 196, 209–10; in early
  modern period, 198; economic emphasis
  of, 198–99, 208–9; euphemistic uses of,
  196, 197, 199, 209; expansion and dilution
  of concept of, 208; financial sense of, 196;
  and individual behavior, 198–201; and
  the Invisible Hand, 203–4; meanings of,
  195–96; political benefits of, 201–4; restraints accompanying, 198, 200; statecraft
  and, 197–201. *See also* self-interest
internal colonialism, 83

international investment, 8
investment, fiscal linkages and, 164
Invisible Hand, 199, 203–4, 297–98, 333,
  349–50
Ireland, 323–25
irrationality, 209, 234
irrigation, 174–75
Italy: class alienation in, 85; industrialization
  in, 109–10; Risorgimento in, 234

Japan, 110
J-curve hypothesis, 82
Jesus, 32n9
Johnson, Harry, 251
Judeo-Christian tradition, 33n25

Kayapó, 312
Kelman, Steven, 252
Keynes, John Maynard, xiii, 54, 207, 208
Keynesianism, 54–56, 59, 207, 224
Kierkegaard, Søren, 152
Koestler, Arthur, 353
Kommunitarismus (community spirit), 347
Kubitschek, Juscelino, 114, 120
Kuhn, Thomas, 156, 157

Labour Party, 294
Labrousse, Ernest, 98n16
language, Hirschman's knowledge of, ix
La Rochefoucauld, François de, 86
late industrialization: late late vs., 109–11;
  political implications of, 8–11; in underdeveloped countries, 57–59
late late industrialization: characteristics of,
  108–9; entrepreneurship in, 111–12; and
  exports, 125–32; late vs., 109–11
Latin America, xi, xv–xvi; agrarian reform
  in, 38; capitalism in, 235; Hirschman and,
  365–66; ideologies in, 42; import-substituting industrialization in, 102–33; industrialization in, 9, 63, 103–5; pessimism
  in, xvii, 35, 111, 145–47; policymaking
  in, 114, 116; scholars and intellectuals of,
  144–46; theories about, 144–46
law, functions of, 252
leadership: charismatic, 44–46, 143; function
  of, 46; and perception of change, 43–46;
  skilled, 44–46, 143
leading sectors, 159